Mission, Colonialism and Liberation:

The Lutheran Church in Namibia 1840-1966

Carl-J Hellberg

NEW NAMIBIA BOOKS

Verbum

New Namibia Books (Pty) Ltd.
PO Box 21601, Windhoek, Namibia

© Carl-J Hellberg, 1997

All rights reserved. No part of this publication may be reproduced, stored in a retrieval system, or transmitted in any form or by any means, electronic, mechanical, photocopying, recording or otherwise, without the prior permission of the publishers.

Edited by Karin Fischer-Buder

Printed by The Natal Witness in South Africa

ISBN 99916-31-59-3
ISBN 91-526-25354 European edition
ISSN 0585-5373 Studia Missionalia Upsaliensia Series No. LXIII

Dedication

I dedicate this book to Namibia and its President, His Excellency Dr Sam Nujoma. I wish to express my respect and deep gratitude to President Nujoma for his unfailing friendship since we first met in 1966.

Västerås, 18 September 1996
Carl-J Hellberg

Contents

List of Abbreviations	viii
Preface	ix
Introduction	1
Historiographical aspects of Namibia's precolonial history	1
Ethnography	2
Literature attempting to justify colonial occupation	3
Origin of the name 'Namibia'	6
Geography	7
The people of Namibia	9

Part I: Namibia before German Colonization: Socio-political and Economic Changes   18

1	Namibia's first, precolonial contacts with the Europeans	21
2	The Oorlam-Namas invade Nama and Herero territory	28
3	Pioneering missionary work in the interests of Christian Western civilization	39
4	Relations between the Rhenish Mission and the Oorlam-Namas and Hereros	46
	The Mission as a resource for the Oorlam-Namas	46
	The Rhenish missionaries' first encounter with Jonker Afrikaner	49
	The position of missionaries and European traders during the 1860s	52
	Growing European influence	55
5	The Rhenish Mission and demands for overseas protection	61
	Requests for British protection	61
	Successes of the Rhenish Mission in Namibia – and the beginnings of Finnish missionary work among the Ovambos	68

Part II: Church and Mission under German Colonial Domination, 1885-1915   74

6 The Rhenish Mission and German colonialism, 1884-1904   77
    German colonial policy and the Berlin Congress, 1884-1885   77
    The beginnings of German colonialism in Namibia, 1882-1885   81
    The Rhenish Mission – and the Deutsche Kolonialgesellschaft für Südwestafrika, 1885-1889   87
    The Rhenish Mission under Curt von François, 1889-1894   93
    Growing tensions between the Rhenish Mission and the colonial authorities under Leutwein, 1894-1904   98

7 The Rhenish Mission during the Namibian wars, 1904-1907   109
    The war breaks out   109
    The Rhenish Mission during the war   117
    Haussleiter – and his criticism of the peace terms   120

8 German colonization and Mission, 1907-1914   128
    Colonial policy after 1907   128
    Missionary work, 1907-1915   131

Part III: Church and Mission under South African Rule, 1915-1966   142

9 Namibia during World War I and the first years of South African occupation, 1914-1920   146
    The war up to the German capitulation   146
    Military administration and the conditions of missionary work between 1915 and 1920   148

10 Namibia as a League of Nations mandate, 1920-1939   160
    Negotiations begin on the mandated territories   160
    The German-speaking minority in Namibia under mandatory administration   162
    South Africa's racial policy in Namibia, 1920-1939   168
    Christian and syncretistic movements against racialism   171
    – Garveyanism   171
    – Uprisings inspired by Garveyanism   174

– The Bondelswarts uprising, May 1922	177
– The Rehoboth rebellion, 1925	182
– Samuel Maharero's burial, 1923, and its consequences for the Rhenish Mission	185

11 Mission under South African racial policy, 1920-1939   193

The Union's racialist legislation in the mandated territory of Namibia	193
Divided loyalties for the Rhenish Mission	196
The Finnish Missionary Society starts a Folkchurch	207
Other Missions: the Roman Catholics and the Anglicans	214

Part IV: Church and Mission, and the National Movement of Liberation   219

12 International and local commitment to the liberation struggle in co-operation with the United Nations after 1945   222

13 The Rhenish Mission and growing nationalism among its parishes   238

The Nama parishes	238
The Hereros and the Oruuano Church	244
New trends within the Mission	258

14 The formation of the Ovambo Church and the liberation movement in Ovamboland, 1939-1966   268

Conclusion	282
Bibliography	291
Index	311

List of Abbreviations

AMEC	African Methodist Episcopal Church
ANC	African National Congress
CA	Church Archives
CCLF	Council of Churches on Lutheran Foundation
CWM	Commission on World Mission
ELCRN	Evangelical Lutheran Church in the Republic of Namibia
IMC	International Missionary Council
LMS	London Missionary Society
LWF	Lutheran World Federation
NA	National Archives of Namibia
NP	National Party
OPO	Ovambo People's Organization
SWANC	South West African National Congress
SWANU	South West Africa National Union
SWAPO	South West Africa People's Organization
UN	United Nations
UNIA	Universal Negro Improvement Association
WCC	World Council of Churches

Preface

My previous books and articles on Namibia have mainly dealt with the important period of the liberation struggle, 1966-1979. During those years the Lutheran churches in Namibia, both as individual organizations and as members of the Council of Churches in Namibia, started to give their support more openly than before to the South West African Peoples' Organization (SWAPO) as the leading Namibian liberation movement. I refer to my books, *Namibia* (1973, published by Verbum in Swedish), and *A Voice of the Voiceless* (1979, Verbum), and to my article titled 'Namibia – Recent Developments' (which appeared in the quarterly publication of the World Council of Churches' [WCC's] Programme to Combat Racism, 1978, Geneva).

At the time of the liberation struggle I was facing insurmountable difficulties researching in Namibia. I had paid several visits to the country since February 1966, but after 1974 I was no longer granted a visa by the South African authorities to visit either the Republic of South Africa or Namibia. As one of the directors of the Lutheran World Federation (LWF) in Geneva, Switzerland, I was apparently considered a threat to the kind of 'law and order' which the South African government tried to impose on the oppressed people of Namibia. Consequently I could no longer carry out research work in the archives and libraries in the country.

This changed in 1989. In the latter part of that year, I was permitted to return to Namibia as the only Swede among the observers in the Church Information and Monitoring Service prior to the country's first free elections. Since then I have returned to Namibia in 1992, 1993 and 1994 for research on this study.

It has not been my ambition to produce an academic dissertation – although I have attempted to deal with my subject in an objective, factual way.

In the course of my research I found that various population groups in Namibia started their fight for human rights and freedom from oppression from the very beginning of European colonization. In this struggle the Christian ideology was an important source of inspiration.

Christianity was brought to Namibia both by the Oorlam-Nama commando groups from the Cape Colony who invaded the southern and central parts of the country from the 1820s, and by German and Finnish Lutheran missionaries. Despite the evident intention of the European missions to strengthen European imperialism by their concepts of a 'Christian Western civilization', and despite the mistrust this periodically created between the missionaries (the Rhenish missionaries in particular) and the indigenous members of their congregations, who felt a strong urge for freedom, Christian ideology played an important role from the start. There were several precedents to the courageous stand later taken by the Lutheran Church in the liberation struggle of the 1960s and 1970s.

My study of the Church's role in the liberation of Namibia is portrayed within a framework of secular, historical events that took place during the colonial occupation. Within this framework I have presented different aspects of European imperialism, for instance the oppressive policies of the colonial powers, aimed at exploiting the natural resources of the country as well as its people; or the efforts of the white immigrants to break down tribal identity and force the indigenous people into becoming 'cheap labour' for the enrichment of the colonizers.

Much of my research was done in the National Archives and in the Church Archives in Windhoek. Though the literature on Namibia is rather limited, the Bibliography presents it as extensively as possible.

This research was supported by a number of organizations, institutions, and private persons. I owe all of them my thanks. If I may mention some of them,

- the late Brigitte Lau, Chief Archivist of the National Archives, Windhoek, and the staff in the head office, in Windhoek, of the Evangelical Lutheran Church in the Republic of Namibia, for their assistance in helping me find research material;

- the Lund Mission Society, Sweden, for a 1992 travel grant to Namibia;

Preface xi

- the Swedish National Committee of the Lutheran World Federation, Lutherhjälpen, and the Church of Sweden Mission for a grant towards translating the manuscript into English;

- the publishing houses New Namibia Books, Windhoek, and Verbum, Stockholm, for accepting to publish this book in a unique Namibian-Swedish copublication venture;

- the Royal Swedish Embassy, Windhoek, and Ambassador Sten Rylander in particular, for their unfailing trust in my research, and for encouragement and support both during my visits to Namibia and during the writing of this manuscript in Sweden;

- the Diocesan Library in Västerås and its staff for sparing no efforts to meet my requests for books from libraries, literally from all over the world;

- the diocese of Västerås and its bishop, Dr Claes Bertil Ytterberg, for showing interest in the project and for their generosity;

- the late Professor Per Frostin, Lund, who in 1991 inspired me to take up this research work;

- Professor Carl Fredrik Hallencreutz, Uppsala, and Vice-Chancellor Peter Katjavivi of the University of Namibia, Windhoek, for valuable discussions and advice;

- my daughter Katarina Hellberg and my son Johan Hellberg, who spent the warmest summer months Sweden has experienced since the 1750s to work on the translation into English, in July-August 1994;

- and finally, my wife Gisela who went to Namibia with me in 1992 and shares with me a deep love and respect for the Namibian people.

Introduction

Historiographical aspects of Namibia's precolonial history

It is true that Namibia's recent history was shaped by European colonialism and European trade interests. White settlers, with their various blends of Christianity and Christian missions, brought about enormous changes in indigenous socio-political organization and economy. Later, the various political groups committed to the cause of independence imposed their changes in reaction to the oppressive measures taken by the colonial powers to keep the colonized people 'in line', in order to safeguard their own interests.

However, though all these factors have played a significant role in shaping Namibian society today, the roots of present-day Namibia can be traced back to *precolonial* history. With very few exceptions, little or no effort has been made to date to provide any realistic account of precolonial Namibian history. Most of the hundreds of books, studies, and theses on Namibia produced in the past characteristically avoided the period of history prior to 1884, which marks the beginning of German colonialism. This would create the – erroneous – impression that the history of Namibia began when Germans stepped ashore at Lüderitz. Most of the literature in other words does not credit the indigenous peoples of Namibia with any history of their own. Indeed, native Namibians are mostly referred to as some kind of exotic species of strictly ethnographic interest. And even a cursory glance at contemporary literature dealing with Namibia would indicate that one of the most readily adopted Western attitudes with respect to non-Western cultures is still largely operative when it comes to the precolonial roots of contemporary Namibian history – namely that 'history always begins with the European colonizers'.

In fact, the year of 1884 did not radically change life for the majority of people living in Namibia. There was no radical transformation of the prevailing state of things with the official onset of German colonialism: the region's multifaceted social fabric, composed of a number of autonomous societies, was in a process of continuous change, and 1884 was just one minor event within that process.

The main event shaping the course of history was in fact the arrival of the Oorlam-Nama people from the south, and the increased presence of traders from the Cape Colony – both of which happened quite independently of the German colonial annexation. These non-European events therefore played their part in shaping Namibian history, long before the German flag was hoisted.

In view of the erroneous impression referred to above, and the dearth of information available on the country's early history, it is essential at this point to provide a brief outline and evaluation of a selection of precolonial literature on Namibia. This can be divided into two main categories: *Ethnography*, and *Literature Attempting to Justify Colonial Occupation*.

Ethnography

Most of the literature covering 19th-century Namibia interprets local phenomena from a strictly colonialist viewpoint. With the notable exception of some useful genealogies of chieftains, and some praise poems dedicated to powerful groups of families, what this literature has to offer in terms of historical value does not amount to much. If anything, it pays vivid testimony to the existence, once, of a rich oral tradition which, had it not been mostly lost, would have been of inestimable worth for any research on precolonial history.

Some of the studies in this category were produced by missionaries between 1870 and 1930. Unfortunately, the reliability of this literature as a historical source is questionable owing to the authors' deplorable tendency to give their evidence an authoritative interpretation, and to constantly call attention to their colonial outlook. They do not credit the tribal communities with any development of their own or any change, and present Namibian society of the time as though it were 'undisturbed' and 'static'. This might also be said of the missionary and scholar Heinrich Vedder's extensive studies on tribal history and ethnography. The most blatant shortcoming in Vedder's scholarly contribution to this field of study is perhaps that it fails to account for the complete breakdown of traditional tribal boundaries which took place in central and southern Namibia during the 19th century. At the beginning of the German colonial period, there were hardly any tribes left in that part of Namibia – at least not in the traditional sense of the word, meaning closed entities leading quiet existences undisturbed by any changes from within or without. In fact, all the traditional patterns of social and political life were rapidly disintegrating and regrouping into a complex network of new alliances as a result of the invasion of the Oorlam-Namas.

These newcomers from the Cape Colony were a powerful and well-organized force, a fact which enabled them to dominate the entire politico-economic scene of southern and central Namibia from the 1820s onwards. They were able to tip the balance of power in their favour in the Nama-Damara region and among the Hereros in the decades preceding German colonial annexation.

These crucial shifts in the currents of local history have been largely neglected by European observers who viewed them as minor manifestations of petty rivalry and intertribal warfare. For this reason, the early writers tended to miss important points of local history and their work is riddled with misunderstandings.

Literature attempting to justify colonial occupation

The overriding aim of authors in this category is to plead for the manifold blessings of European colonialism. Their line of argument makes a case for the 'civilizing influence' of the colonial authorities upon the tribes, by allegedly putting a stop to prevailing intertribal warfare and violence, once and for all. According to their argument, the decades preceding the arrival of the German colonizers should be seen as a period of incessant and cruel war between the Hereros and the Namas. Examples of this kind of writing, by colonial officers, explorers, and missionaries, abound.[1] The emphasis on tribal warfare on the one hand, and the civilizing influence of 'European Christian civilization' on the other, provided the writers with a shared frame of reference; it also provided the European individuals operating in the field at the time, be they missionaries, traders, colonial officials, or entire groups of settlers, from the Cape or from Germany, with a convenient excuse to exploit the country and its peoples. Vedder's study, *South West Africa in Early Times*,[2] though fascinating and imaginative, must be cited among this category of colonial accounts of Namibian history.

In Vedder's opinion, cultural and racial differences were the main source of all tribal conflicts in the decades preceding German colonialism. Without the arrival of the German colonizers, he argues, these tribes would have destroyed themselves as a result of their hostilities. His attempt at writing a precolonial history of Namibia is based on a fabrication of his own making, namely his evocation of two periods which might be called 'Namaland against Hereroland' (the 1840s), and 'Hereroland against Namaland' (the 1860s). Furthermore, he introduced the notion of a 'Herero war of liberation', a war supposedly waged against the invading Oorlam-Namas. In this manner he sought to justify the political and military actions of the Rhenish missionaries and their supporters, most of whom were influential traders. The interference of the Europeans was thus presented as a show of benevolence, initiated solely to support the oppressed and suffering Hereros.

The main weakness of Vedder's account is undoubtedly his defence of the German colonial annexation. The colonizers are presented as 'last-minute saviours' who both initiated and maintained a durable *Pax Germana*, thereby preventing the rule of pagan 'warlords'.[3] In view of the above, we may be justified in claiming that Vedder's historical writings on Namibia distort the events he describes. As an explanation, however, one might point out that he was, after all, neither a historian nor a missionary in the true sense of the word; he was above all a German nationalist.

At the time of the German annexation there was no real 'war of liberation' as described by Vedder – nor were there any tribal units, in the traditional sense, in clear-cut opposition against each other. What did exist were a number of alliances between groups, based *not* on tribal affiliation, but on mutual economic and political interests. Vedder's post-World War I writings, including those which he wrote during the rise of the Nazi movement in Germany, provide ample evidence of his strong nationalist leanings. It is painfully obvious from these writings that he fell prey to pre-World War II German propaganda, which proclaimed that the German Reich should, under the leadership of Hitler, be allowed to reclaim its former colonial empire. His historical vision is therefore clouded by a blend of racist assumptions and an equally sordid glorification of German colonialism, which, it must be remembered, formed the bulk of Nazi

German policy.[4] In summary, the important events in the precolonial history of Namibia actually had little to do with any of those supposed tribal divisions and forays which Vedder refers to in his work. This factor prompts us to reconsider both the military and the diplomatic roles of the Rhenish missionaries, who seem to have also seen their real role as partners dedicated to the cause of promoting precolonial European economic – and political – interests.

Thus the major historiographic problem related to any serious study devoted to the precolonial history of Namibia comes into focus. It plainly becomes a matter of having to overcome the notion, advocated by Vedder and corroborated by other writers, that European missionaries and traders upon their arrival to the country actually encountered an indigenous population of Namibia living in traditional tribal areas well separated from each other – an indigenous population who, on the other hand, were allegedly in the midst of tribal warfare, thus compelling the Europeans to take sides and finally call upon the intervention of a colonial power to establish a state of law and order. What *actually* happened was quite different: missionaries and traders joined forces in the promotion of their own shared interests, which happened to conflict with the interests of the most influential Oorlam-Nama group of the time, the Afrikaner family. This European co-operation culminated in the peace conference of 1870, which was both initiated and supervised by the missionaries and which further consolidated the power of all Europeans residing in the country.

The 1870 conference also triggered a gradual decline in the dominance of the missionaries, as their position was taken over by the traders and Cape government agents, and later by German colonial officials.

What we have dealt with so far strictly pertains to the history of southern and central Namibia. The historical developments in northern Namibia looked entirely different, as we shall see. The Oshiwambo-speaking people of the north never came under direct colonial rule of the Germans. The inhabitants of this region maintained a number of well-established tribal kingdoms with little contact with the outside world. Though officially, the German colony extended up to the Kunene River (Namibia's present-day border with Angola), there was no effective administration in northern Namibia, and no German policing north of Fort Namutoni. In July 1915, German colonial rule in Namibia came to an end and it was not until February 1917 that the Ovambo people were to be directly affected by a white colonial power.

Origin of the name 'Namibia'

The country's present name is of recent date and alludes to the Namib Desert which stretches along the Atlantic coast. The name first gained currency through the national liberation movement SWAPO, who began using it in the early 1970s. It can be seen as the concrete expression of a popular wish to give the country, whose independence was being fought for so desperately, a name to further define its identity. In this study, despite its relatively recent origin we will make use of the name 'Namibia'.

Until the first encounter with German colonialism, the country north of the Orange River was called 'Great Namaqualand' in reference to the great plains north of the Orange River where the Namas, or 'Namaqua people', lived. These inhabitants of the plains were related to the Khoisan, or Namas, who had settled south of the Orange in the northern Cape in an area named *Minor* Namaqualand because it was small in comparison with Great Namaqualand to the north of the river.

When the Berlin Congress held in 1884-1885[5] divided the African continent into colonies, they were given geographical denominations, rather than proper names, to define the geographical areas involved. Thus, Africa was divided into east (where the Germans and British claimed territories for their own) and west (which went to the French). Namibia, a German colony on the continent's south-western coast, was referred to as 'German South-West Africa', and it was known as such for many years.

The colonial subdivision was not immediately followed by colonial administration. We must envision the process of colonial subdivision as one of future administrators drawing lines across the map of Africa with a ruler. They did not take immediate occupation. In practice, it was only viable to administer those areas that were easily accessible and had some exploitative interest. Even after colonization began in Namibia, this meant that the southern and central parts of the country were administered, but not the country's north. Southern and central Namibia had well-established trade routes with the Cape Colony. This promised lucrative business for hunters and traders of ivory and ostrich feathers. European traders, prospectors, and big game hunters had returned with reports that the country had riches to offer. However, although northern Namibia formed part of the German colony, the inhabitants of this region were never subjected to colonial administration during the German period. No surveyors or fortune hunters had returned from the north to whet the Germans' appetite and so, the Ovambo people who lived in this part of the colony could continue to pursue their traditional tribal way of life in harmony. The Ovambos' trade was with the people – Ovambos and closely related tribes – of southern Angola.

It must also be mentioned that German missionaries attached to the Rhenish Mission were among the European pioneers of Great Namaqualand. It was not until the South African military administration that Namibia can in any real sense be referred to as the country defined by its present borders. In fact, it was the South African military administration which practically incorporated northern Namibia into its central administration from its base in Windhoek after 1917.

In the present study it is therefore of crucial importance to distinguish between the separate developments that have taken place in the northern parts of Namibia, and those that took place in southern and central Namibia.

Geography

With a surface area of 823 169 km^2, Namibia is a vast yet sparsely populated country whose population is approximately 1,5 million. The central region, which includes the capital, Windhoek, and many other towns, is caught between two deserts. This strip of land fringed in the west by the Namib Desert and in the east by the Kalahari Desert supports commercial farming. During the precolonial period much of the country's population inhabited the high plateau between the Namib and the Kalahari, and lived by breeding cattle.

The Namib occupies a belt along the Atlantic coast, which prevented any significant trade between the coast and the country's interior until the late 19th century. No harbours have been established along the coast, with the exception of Walvis Bay and Lüderitz, isolated along the otherwise uninhabitable and sandy coastline.

Just north of Walvis Bay lies Swakopmund, which was chosen by the Germans as a harbour town but which, after several attempts at establishing a port had failed, went through periods of greater and lesser activity as a trading centre, holiday resort and, much later, town supporting the mining community at nearby Rössing uranium mine. The coastline north of Swakopmund is known as the 'Skeleton Coast', and not without reason, for the level beaches when whipped by desert winds or exposed to the stormy waves of the Atlantic have turned into a graveyard for many a ship and its crew. In fact, a number of rusted ships' hulls still lie buried in the sand as mute testimony to the countless seafarers who fell victim to this treacherous coast.

To the east, the sands of the Kalahari Desert loom large; the frontier between Namibia and Botswana (then known as 'Bechuanaland') was first established in an agreement between Germany and England made in 1896. It hardly presented any obstacle to those nomadic groups of Bushmen[6] whose way of life seems remarkably well adapted to a rough existence in what is perhaps one of the most inhospitable desert areas of the world.

To the south, the Orange River forms the border with the Republic of South Africa, its incredible valleys diversifying what could otherwise be described as an arid, sterile land. One might be tempted to refer to the river as a natural border – but not even a river such as this can prevent trade between two neighbouring settlements or migration across it.

The rivers in the country's north, the Kunene and Kavango, certainly never divided the people living on either side of them – people who belonged to the same tribes or were closely related. Namibia's northern border was at first informally defined by Germany and Portugal in 1896; it was more clearly defined in an agreement made between Portugal and the South Africans in 1917.

The north of Namibia is the most densely populated part of the country and is home to approximately half of Namibia's total population. It is fertile and better suited for cultivation and cattle breeding. Its rivers contain a wealth of fish.

The rest of Namibia, however, is semi-arid. The country's central high plateau, which supports the second largest concentration of the population, lies between 1 500 and 2 400 metres above sea level, and has irregular rainfalls. In fact, overall the country's annual rainfall can be estimated at 100 mm in the south and 510 mm in the north. In some years, the rains fail to come at all. Small wonder, then, that much of Namibia's history was shaped by periods of severe drought and consequent privation, causing tribes to wage battles over the few water sources and the grazing lands to ensure the survival of their cattle. During the precolonial period, Namibia's people led a nomadic existence following their herds of cattle in search of grazing. There were no borders demarcating any territory belonging to any specific group inhabiting the high plateau. The tribes who depended for survival on access to the water and the grazing grounds were not restricted by any geographical or political boundaries, although they had demarcated spheres of interest.

This traditional nomadic way of life was disturbed by the colonizers. An extensive mining industry began to establish itself, based on the country's enormous mineral wealth of copper, tin, zinc, silver and lead. These natural resources were increasingly exploited from the early German colonial period onwards, with the help of labourers recruited more or less by force from Namibia's formerly nomadic tribes. In 1908, lucrative discoveries of diamonds were made along the region's south coast.

Another major change introduced to the region by the German colonizers was white settlers taking possession of land, thus taking away a considerable amount of grazing used traditionally by the people of Namibia.

More and more, the country's tribal populations were cramped into restricted reservations which considerably worsened their chances of survival as they provided far from sufficient grazing for their cattle. For the vast majority, the only two options presenting themselves were to either seek employment on the white man's big farms, or to go and find work in the mines and factories.

The people of Namibia

The following survey of the ethnic groups living in Namibia during the precolonial period is brief for reasons of space and does not attempt to be all-inclusive. Before the colonization, the country was inhabited by groups of people living within various systems of tribal government. Each tribe had a distinct political, social and religious pattern of life. However, by the end of the precolonial period, immediately preceding the German colonial occupation, these more or less closed social systems based on a sense of tribal community soon found themselves caught up into a process of disintegration. The fundamental changes in what had been a stable traditional social structure were largely due to invasions from the south – invasions initiated by groups of warriors from various backgrounds, the Oorlam-Namas, who successfully decomposed the traditionally structured tribal way of life of the Namas, Hereros and the Damaras by relying on their military and economic superiority on the one hand, and on their close relations with the strongly European society of the Cape Colony on the other. Only the Ovambos and Kavangos in the north, the Bushmen (who were hunted by the Oorlams and sold as slaves in the Cape), and the inhabitants of Kaokoland were little affected by the new order initiated by the Oorlam-Nama people.

1   The word '**Bushman**' is worth looking into in this context. It was originally a European name for the people 'living in the bushes'. In the language of the Hereros, these people are called *ovokuruvehi*, meaning *the oldest of the earth* or *the original people*, and hence, *the most venerable*. This ethnic group consists of two related groups – the San people and the Khoikhoi. Because of their characteristic, even remarkable, way of life, these people have often been treated as ethnic curiosities. Among their most notable characteristics we might mention their ability to survive under exceedingly difficult conditions in a desert climate with no victuals other than herbs and insects, and game hunted by means of bow and poisoned arrow. Accessibility to water (which they seem capable of 'smelling' their way to underneath the desert sands before sucking it up to the surface through straw pipes) determines their constant wandering. Physically they are well adapted to a way of life where the hardships of a severe desert climate must be battled – for instance, by their ability to store food inside the body.

Although they live in nuclear or extended families the Bushmen are notable in their lack of an overriding tribal structure. It is not until recently that attempts were made by authorities as well as the Church, to urge the Bushmen to abandon their nomadic way of life. In Botswana, some have managed to maintain their own traditional and customary way of life in the harsh Kalahari Desert. However, trapped between two lifestyles (their traditional nomadic life as hunter-gatherers, a settled life on the outskirts of modern Namibian society with no land, and no marketable skills to call their own), many of them have succumbed to a life of misery, alcoholism and despair. It should be mentioned that the San people became something of a favourite of the advocates of the South African apartheid ideology who fondly referred to them as a living illustration of a 'carefree African people'. This did not prevent the South African military from frequently enlisting them as scouts during the war of liberation preceding the independence of Namibia in 1990. Being nomadic hunter-gatherers, the San were not patriotic. They did not 'belong' to any country. For this reason, they felt no emotional ties which would implicate them in the Namibians' struggle for freedom. By contrast, close and cordial relationships were often kindled between them and their South African military superiors. Even after the demobilization preceding Namibia's first free elections in 1989, there were several camps of enlisted Bushmen among the soldiers led by South African military forces.

2   The northern regions of the country bordering Angola are inhabited by approximately half of the country's total population. The largest group of the country's population are the **Ovambo** people. As is so often the case in Africa, the history of these people has not been recorded in writing. An oral tradition richly steeped in ancient myths and a wealth of fables still exists to make up for this lack of written sources. Some of this oral material has recently been transcribed. Furthermore, tribal languages and many surviving customs considerably facilitate the task of piecing together a tentative history of the Ovambos.

Africa's history is characterized by migration. According to tradition, the Ovambo tribes originally came from the north-eastern parts of Africa. After what may have amounted to centuries of nomadic wanderings further and further south they settled in the fertile territories around the Kunene and Kavango rivers. Here, they made a living on cultivation but also kept cattle and fished the rivers. As settled communities, they had little contact with the nomadic people of the south. As we have mentioned, their contacts were mostly restricted to closely related ethnic groups to the north.

The Ovambo people form seven groups of tribes originally contending with each other for supremacy. General Smuts, who visited northern Namibia during World War I, made a rather unflattering comment on the Ovambos, referring to them as a people 'riddled with witchcraft and engaged in tribal forays in which there was no security for man or beast'.[7]

Today still, the Ovambo people live in clans and extended families in accordance with tradition. Every family has its homestead, an enclosure of thorny bushes, inside of which there are several huts, each with a specific purpose. Some house members of the family, others are designed for food storage, or for keeping small stock. During the night the cattle are kept inside the enclosure of thorny bushes, or fence, of the homestead.

The Ovambo people have traces of a so-called 'matriarchal' pattern of government, which means, among other things, that in any given family the elder brother of the mother, and not the father, makes all decisions pertaining to inheritance and other concerns of mutual interest to the family. Three of the seven groups hold a hereditary chieftain mandate as well as a council of elders. The remaining four tribal groups are by tradition each led by a council of elders.

Overpopulation and a severe cattle plague in 1897 drove the Ovambo people southwards to seek employment as miners and labourers on the white settlers' farms as well as on railway and road construction sites. By the late 1970s, approximately 50 000 Ovambo labourers were employed in labour camps dotted about the country, and worked for the benefit of colonial economic interests. This so-called 'contract labour system' separated the men from their families for long periods of time and gave rise to severe social problems.

3   The **Kavango** people live east of the Ovambo region. The Kavango population is about one-tenth the size of the Ovambo population. The Kavango people, who live in clan villages, are divided into five tribal groups. Their tribal organization, like the Ovambos', has some matriarchal traits, according to which each child belongs to the clan of his or her *mother*, not father. The Kavangos' way of life as well as their main sources of nutrition are basically the same as the Ovambos'. The Kavango people are ruled by tribal chieftains who hold their mandates through a system of heredity. It is in this context that the tribe's matriarchal aspect is made plain. In fact, the chieftain's mandate can theoretically be held by members of either sex. (In practice, very few women have ever held the position of chieftain.) Along with the chieftain, the village has a council of elders constituted by members elected by the extended family, or clan, as a whole.

4   East of the region of the Kavango people lies the Caprivi, home of the **Caprivians**. However, the panhandle was not part of the original colonial territory of German South-West Africa.

5   The origin of the **Bergdamaras**, or **Damara people**, is to this day unknown. Vedder claims that the Damaras were an aboriginal people who lived in Namibia before they were driven back by the stronger and numerically superior Namas and Hereros. The Nama leader Jonker Afrikaner held a similar theory, according to Peter Katjavivi[8] – namely that this people had lived in the country for a very long period and that they could therefore be considered as having made up Namibia's original population. As they were unable to assert themselves against stronger peoples, they lost their independence and became something akin to a

slave people. As such, they also lost possession of their own language. As a defeated and enslaved people, they lacked any social or political structure.⁹

Other minor groups which can only be mentioned in passing here are the **Kaokolanders**, a group of Hereros living a strict traditional life in the north-west, and the **Batswana** of south-east Namibia bordering Botswana.

6 The **Herero people** can be divided into two communities, the Hereros and the Mbanderus, both of whom were nomadic herders. According to one traditional account, they originally came from 'the land of the sources' which may have referred to the territories around Lake Tanganyika in what is now Tanzania. From there they would have emigrated southwards until they reached Kaokoland in north-western Namibia. They were unable to push their way further west, having reached the arid fringes of the Namib Desert. Instead, they turned south-east, always in search of new grazing grounds. Their cattle not only determined their migrations but also the fabric of their entire social, religious and, indeed, political way of life.

The Herero language, combined with the political and social structure of this people, as well as their religious world-view, suggest kinship to an East African pastoral people – people who are in fact vitally connected to East African history, namely the Bahima (also known as the Bahinda or Batutsi) from Uganda and Rwanda/Burundi. These people ensured their livelihood by raising cattle around which they ordered their lives, so much so that the success and failure of a war largely depended on the total number of cattle lost or won in battle by either side. The herds were considered as the common property of the tribe and as such were divided into three parts. One-third was considered sacred and kept for sacrificial purposes, another third belonged to the entire tribe, and the last third was kept at the disposition of individual families. In his account of ancient Namibian history, Vedder writes that for Hereros to sell cattle 'was regarded as a sin against the forefathers, from whom they had been received as an inheritance'.¹⁰

If the herds of cattle were considered sacred, then this was also true of their grazing grounds. In fact, the land which provided good grazing could not be owned by anyone individually but was considered common property. Consequently, it could neither be sold nor forfeited. Selling or forfeiting land was considered a criminal offence as it would damage the very foundations of the herds' wellbeing so intimately connected with the welfare, and indeed the existence, of the tribe itself. As Vedder puts it, 'The grazing grounds [were] the common property of the tribe. No individual could acquire land, nor could the chief ... alienate any ground without the consent of all the men of the tribe.'[11]

Traditionally, no paramount chieftain reigned over the Herero people. The highest distinction was conferred upon the member of the tribe who cared for the highest number of cattle and who was thereby accorded a leading position. It was not until the battles of the late 19th century that a political system largely influenced by the Europeans came into being, transferring the entire burden of leadership of the tribe on a paramount chieftain.

The Herero people's social structure was built around an extended family community. The leading group was by definition the family with the largest number of cattle. This social structure was perpetuated in the political as well as in the religious system of the people. Just as with the Bahima in, for example, Buganda, the sacred fire was considered a vital element of Herero tribal life. The leader of a group was responsible for keeping it alive. It was accordingly only extinguished at the death of this leader, to be lit again with the succession of the new leader, always using a particular type of stick for this purpose, in accordance with a strict ritual procedure. Thus, the leader (the chieftain, and later, the paramount chieftain) held the double function of political and religious leadership. This meant that he was regarded as both the political leader and the priest of the tribe. If the sacred fire was extinguished for reasons other than his death, this had dire consequences: 'its extinction meant the ruin of the family'.[12]

Thus, the Herero people followed their cattle, and their search for grazing determined the rhythm of their lives. In fact, the history of these people is characterized by perpetual mobility. They stayed in one area for as long as they had access to water and grazing. It would be practically impossible to give an accurate estimate of when each such migration took place.

In his biography of the Herero chieftain Samuel Maharero, Pool takes this point into consideration:

According to the narratives of two Herero centenarians Vingava and Kukuri, recorded by Rev. Irle, their grandparents and parents had lived and died in the Kaokoveld. This means that the Hereros must have already lived there early in the 18th century. Irle went on to claim that the Hereros were living in the vicinity of Okahandja by 1792. If this was so, they must have reached this area very shortly before then, because in 1850/1851, the explorer Sir Francis Galton still claimed that 70 years earlier, i.e. about 1780, there were no Hereros living in what was later to become Hereroland. According to him they were still in the Kaokoveld.[13]

To summarize, then, Pool observes that access to water and grazing grounds were vital factors which determined where in Namibia the Herero people decided to settle: '... political factors such as quarrels amongst tribal leaders had very little influence on where the Hereros established themselves'.[14]

Around the mid-19th century the Hereros and Mbanderus were settled in or near the following places (the names of their chieftains are given in parentheses):

Okahandja (Maharero);
Omaruru (Manasse);
Otjimbingwe (Zacharias);
Waterberg (Kambazembi); and the area east of the White Nossob River (Tjetjo), where a strong group of Mbanderus also lived, first under the leadership of Kahimemua and later under Nikodemus.

This division into various groups resulted in internal struggles for the best grazing grounds, for the prestige of a Herero leader was, as we have mentioned, based on the number of cattle he owned – the size of his group by comparison was relatively unimportant. The search and ensuing struggles for grazing became an issue leading to clashes between the Hereros and the Namas; and the situation was exacerbated by the fact that a debilitating drought in 1829 forced the Hereros to seek grazing further south where they clashed with groups of Namas who on the same quest were migrating northwards.

7   An attempt, finally, at tracing the **Nama** people and accounting for their origins must depend entirely upon oral tradition. The Namas were originally herders related to the Khoisan people who populated the Cape region well before the arrival of the Dutch in 1652. They were given the name of 'Hottentot' because of the clicking elements of their speech. The

meaning of the Dutch name can be roughly translated as those who stammer'.

According to traditional sources, the Nama people, too, came from areas around the great lakes of East Africa. From there, tradition has it, they were pushed back by the Bahima tribe from the north and forced southward. After following the coastline along the Indian Ocean for many years they finally reached the southern tip of South Africa. Some settled in what is now the Cape Province; after 1652, they came into contact with Dutch colonizers and there was a degree of intermarriage between the Namas and the Dutch. Others made their way further north along the west coast and divided up into at least ten distinct groupings of Namas, each with its own leader, north of the Orange River, in southern Namibia. Like the Hereros, the Namas in Namibia at first had no centralized authority. The ten groupings, with their settlement areas, are given below.

The Red people, the leading Nama group before the arrival of the Oorlam-Namas from the Cape Colony, close to Hoachanas;
the Feldschuhträger (or, as they became known, Veldskoendraers), east of present-day Keetmanshoop;
the Groot-dode, on the upper Fish River;
the Fransman, at Gochas;
the Bondelswarts, in the extreme south around Warmbad;
the Tseibschen group, related to the Red people of the south, and living with them;
the Bethanie-Namas, in Bethanie;
the Topnaars, on the coast near present-day Walvis Bay;
the Riemvasmakers in Kaokoveld; and
the Swartboois, in Rehoboth.

Like the Hereros, the Namas lived on cattle breeding. They knew no individual ownership, since the cattle were considered as the common property of the tribe. However, in other respects they are said to have differed from the other indigenous Namibian peoples. For one, they are short in stature. Also, they were considered to be of a 'very enterprising disposition',[15] to quote Vedder, or 'the most gifted of all the South West African people'.[16] In terms of shaping the country's precolonial and colonial history, they were to play a major role, as the following chapters will explain.

Notes

1 For example, *see* Irle, J. 1906; also, Brincker, H. 1857; Olpp, J. 1884; and Schultze, EA. 1932.
2 Vedder, H. 1966.
3 For further reading on this kind of argument, see Von Rohden, L. 1888; also see Loth, H. 1963,10, note 9.
4 Lau, B. 1981.
5 And signed in 1885.
6 Often referred to as 'San', these people are discussed in greater detail on pp 10-11 of the Introduction.
7 Lejeune, A. 1971, 202.
8 Katjavivi, P. 1988a, 2.
9 Vedder, H, op.cit., 47-48.
10 Ibid.
11 Ibid., 48.
12 Ibid., 48 ff.
13 Pool, G. 1991, 6.
14 Ibid., 7.
15 Vedder, H, op. cit., 53.
16 Ibid.

PART I: Namibia before German Colonization: Socio-political and Economic Changes

During the early 19th century, traders, big game hunters, explorers and missionaries made their way into southern Namibia from the Cape. Their numbers were, however, small in comparison with other emigrations taking place at the time because of political developments in and around Cape Town. The British administration at the Cape, which was established when England took over the reign of power during the Napoleonic Wars and, officially, after the Peace Treaty of Vienna, was seen as a threat by the Dutch population who lived there. These Dutch citizens, or 'Boers', as they later became known, began moving northwards in search of new territories and out of reach of the English. Here, they ran into the Khoisans, or Namas, who had settled in the areas south of the Orange River. The contact between the Boers and the Khoisan people gave rise to a people of mixed origin: the so-called 'Oorlam-Namas' who in turn migrated north, away from the oppression they experienced at the hands of the Boers.

In their northward migration the Oorlam-Namas who were strongly influenced by the Boers' culture, language, and way of and outlook on life, crossed the Orange River. To the people living north of the river they soon became known as conquerors or raiders who for their own benefit seized as much cattle as they could come across.

The German colonization of Namibia was therefore preceded by a period of non-European colonial influence as the Oorlam-Namas invaded from the northern Cape. These newcomers brought about a fundamental transformation in the traditional way of life of the country's original inhabitants.

At the same time as these Oorlam-Namas arrived, Europeans increasingly began moving towards the southern and central parts of Namibia in the hope of discovering minerals and of hunting big game for ivory and other spoils. The relationship between the Europeans and the Oorlam-Namas changed progressively from co-operation of a kind to open hostility; between the Europeans and the tribal communities of the region there existed at first a kind of laissez faire which later was to turn to conflict.

The relationship between the Oorlam-Namas and the traditional tribal communities, who were drawn into a transformation process due to the newcomers' superiority both in terms of military strength and economy, fluctuated between uneasy co-existence and dependence. In many respects what relations amounted to was a certain degree of assimilation which progressively disintegrated traditional tribal patterns and loyalties. However, there was no desperate struggle for freedom against invading aliens who posed a threat to the original tribes' existence. Rather, there seems to have been a series of clashes based on divergent economic and military interests between the invading Europeans and the on the one hand, and the Europeans and the original tribes, whose tribal way of life was disintegrating, on the other.

In their attempts to defend their own interests in the face of these new economic, political and social impulses, the indigenous people of the region were given the option of either adapting to the newcomers or seeking protection through a number of treaties and alliances. This was largely also true of those Europeans who had settled down to make a living in Namibia. They constituted a minority of the total population but nevertheless were militarily superior, added to which they were able to rely on necessary reinforcements through the contacts they maintained *with the Cape. However, this did not exclude them from enforced participation in the constant shifts in innumerable treaties and alliances with the Oorlam-Namas, the Hereros, and the Nama people who were already long established in the country.*

This situation at length became untenable, both for the interested parties of European trade and for the missionaries attached to the Rhenish Mission, who needed to move about freely in the performance of their duties. This right of mobility, they claimed, should be guaranteed by a European colonial power which would be able to grant them the security and protection necessary to guarantee their continued existence in this part of southern Africa.

It was this incentive which made the traders and missionaries first seek contact with the British before getting in touch with German colonial interest groups with a petition for protection, whether in the form of swift military action or of permanent colonial occupation. The missionaries and merchants who appealed to the Germans for help can consequently be seen as having finally brought about German colonialism in Namibia. The situation deteriorated after the early 1860s, and matters eventually became so desperate that enforced participation in warlike entanglements between the Oorlam-Namas and the Hereros seemed inevitable. To the Europeans, participating in these wars would not mean taking sides with one of the two contending parties, but rather, safeguarding their own interests.

1 Namibia's first, precolonial contacts with the Europeans

The word 'Namib' means 'shield' in the language of the Hereros, and the Namib Desert does indeed serve as a shield, providing the interior with effective protection from the Atlantic coast. European seafarers sailed down the west coast of Africa to find a trade route across the seas which

During the 19th century, the Oorlam-Namas and first missionaries established themselves in Namibia.

would lead the way to an elusive Orient harbouring immense riches. For these extensive journeys, sheltered harbours were necessary to provision the ships and ensure easy access to fresh water.

The coastline of the Namib Desert did not exactly encourage plunder. However, we know that at least two Portuguese seafarers reached the coast of Namibia. In 1485, Diego Caô reached land north of Walvis Bay where he erected a cross of stone, which later gave the place its name: Cape Cross. The following year saw the arrival of the next Portuguese explorer by the name of Bartolomeu Dias. This man entered Angra Pequena (present-day Lüderitz Bay), where he noticed a group of blacks watch him reach land from a respectful distance.

Both of these landings were but brief episodes of little or no significance for the history of .

The Portuguese were soon joined by others who sought a sea route to the Far East. In 1652, a Dutchman by the name of Jan van Riebeeck landed at the Cape of Good Hope and started a base for Dutch ships *en route* to the Dutch holdings of East India. The land and climate at the Cape were well suited for European settlement and the Dutch kept a watchful eye on any potential competition along the Atlantic coast of Africa. Between 1670 and 1677, they launched expeditions northwards from the Cape along the coast to explore what might serve as potential harbour sites. These expeditions did not lead to any further action, however, for the level sands, as well as the desert stretching along the coast, were found to be sufficient protection against the possible onslaught of competing nations. So even in this respect did the Namib Desert serve as a shield.

A century was yet to pass before any Europeans from the Cape showed any burgeoning interest for what lay north of the Orange River. This time the main incentive did not lie in finding fertile land to cultivate or to provide grazing for cattle. The Europeans' main interest this time was in laying their hands on minerals and ivory. Around 1760, a Dutch elephant hunter by the name of Jakob Coetze reached what is now known as Keetmanshoop. He noticed that many of the Africans he met up with wore copperware as decoration, and also that their spear and arrowheads were made of copper. He found out that copper had long been provided from an area much further north, and reported this on his return to the Cape. In the following year, a man by the name of Hendrik Hop led an expedition into the inner regions of Namibia, attempting to discover the exact location of this vein of copper. He returned empty-handed, however.

Not only had he failed to find the copper but the interior was too inhospitable to deserve any further interest.

Yet the rumours that there were copper and even gold deposits north of the Orange River persisted. Vedder relates the story of a Swedish adventurer, Hans Johan Wiker, which may, to some extent, have fuelled rumours of a source of wealth lying dormant in the northern regions of the country. According to Wiker, the Ovambos in the far north knew how to mine and smelt copper and had a wealth of mineral deposits in their land. Wiker lacked the resources to gain any personal advantage from this information, but his reports certainly continued to keep popular interest alive for the large unexplored regions north of the Orange River.

The increase of European interest worried the Dutch at the Cape, especially the growing interest of the British to increase their hold on the seven seas. During the 1790s, the Cape Colony of the Dutch was increasingly drawn into the mire of major political events in Europe. When during the French Revolution, French forces conquered his country, the king of Holland, William of Orange, was forced to flee to England in 1795. Holland now became a republic, in conformity with the pattern imposed by the revolution. Since the Dutch navy was also seized by the French, Holland lost its ability to defend its overseas territories. The English navy promptly took possession of the Cape Colony.

England's right to take over this vital point of support on the southern tip of Africa was confirmed at the international peace conference held in Vienna after the fall of Napoleon.

The British administration of the Cape Colony introduced several major changes for the Boers who had settled at the Cape: for one, England was opposed to slavery,[1] which in 1833 led to a decision made by parliament effectively prohibiting any slavery in the British dominions overseas. The British policy to abolish slavery was viewed by the Boers as an unjust interference with their rights and a threat to their economy. The overall economic structure of Boer society was built on slavery. British 'interference' therefore affected not only their pride, and independence, but also their economic wellbeing. This caused many Boers in 1834 to leave the British-held territory of the Cape, and embark upon the Boer migration known today as 'the Great Trek'.

The majority of the trekker Boers settled in what was later to become the Boer Republics and still later, after the Boer Wars, Transvaal and the Orange Free State. Some, however, trekked northwards of the Orange

River into what is now southern and central Namibia. In spite of their small numbers, this group constituted a factor of great importance for the future course of events shaping Namibia, especially in view of the fact that they never lost touch with their former connections in the Cape Colony. This opened up a vital connection for trade and commerce for the Boers and other Europeans, and a link between Namibia and the Cape.

A second consequence of the new, English, administration at the Cape was the fact that England began to use Angra Pequena and Walvis Bay as anchorage for its merchant ships. It would take some time before Walvis Bay would become part of the British Cape Colony; however, it soon became an important anchoring site and a supply port for the country's interior, and an export harbour for the copper which was discovered in the areas around this site and further inland, in Otavi and at Tsumeb.

Thirdly, England's annexation of the Cape Colony and its clash with the Boers gave rise to a series of migrations affecting not only the Boers but the indigenous peoples as well, and reaching from the Orange River to central Namibia. The main reason for this series of migrations, which took place over approximately 120 years, was the economic and political change at the Cape in the late 18th century. Life under British rule became increasingly difficult for the Boers because of the liberal attitude of the British towards the indigenous population, and the Brits' policy of prohibiting slavery. Life in the Cape consequently altered drastically. From being an administrative centre catering to the needs of Boer farmers who came to sell their products, it progressively turned into a centre for merchants and craftsmen. Groups of Boers resettled on plots of land further and further away from Cape Town and its British administration. In practice this meant taking hold of land belonging to the Khoisan/Nama people, an increasing number of whom presently became enslaved by the Boers. The tribal pattern of these peoples was consequently dissolved. Thus, a new group of so-called 'frontier raiders', Oorlam-Namas mounted on horseback – or in Brigitte Lau's words, a 'force of commando groups' – came into being.[2] These autonomous commando groups spoke the language of the Cape – Cape Dutch, later to develop into Afrikaans – fluently; they were also in possession of firearms, which were either bought or stolen. Their cohesion was based on a common wish to shed their status as slaves or underpaid labourers of the Boers, and live by their own laws as independent commando forces living off their own cattle –

in other words, to shape a new life for themselves in freedom.

Most of the members of these commando forces were of mixed origin; and most of them were nominally Christians. They moved northwards in ever larger groupings to seek shelter on the far side of the Orange River, either to escape from the retaliation of Boers after a successful raiding operation, or to seek out isolated Boer farms to sack.

It is important to note that this invasion further and further into Namibia was not conducted by united tribal groups in search of grazing for their cattle – rather, it was effectuated by well-armed, mounted gangs of people from highly diverse backgrounds, many of whom were slaves on the run who had long since lost any ties to traditional tribal life of any kind. 'Oorlam' is, according to Lau,[3] a Malay word for an experienced person who has lived in the country for an extended period of time. The denomination of 'Oorlam-Nama' therefore does not refer to a specific tribe but rather is a collective name given to commando forces made up of people from highly diverse ethnic backgrounds. (Later, the Oorlams were to mix with largely Nama people, hence the double name.) As mentioned earlier, these people often belonged to slave families who had been cut off from their tribal connections or from their land, and who were consequently uprooted from their original, tribal way of life – belated victims of the Boers' seizure of their land.

One leader of such a commando force was the progenitor of an Oorlam-Nama group which was to play a crucial part in the precolonial history of Namibia and for some decades after the arrival, in the 1840s, of the first missionaries and merchants. Jager Afrikaner was of mixed origin. Tradition has it that after murdering the Boer farmer in whose employ he was, Afrikaner took possession of the latter's cattle. He then established himself as the leader of a commando group which first settled in Blydeuerwacht (later called Hoole's Fountain), on the southern bank of the Orange River. In his way of life, Jager Afrikaner was no different from any other commando leader. According to Vedder, he gathered around him 'all the rogues he could find, and well armed with guns and horses ... he was the terror of both banks of the river'.[4] In spite of this he allowed himself and his family to be baptized in 1815 by a German missionary, Johann Leonhard Ebner, who was attached to the London Missionary Society. To thus become Christian, and further to hold a predilection for keeping a clergyman among themselves in the group, was a practice which the Oorlam-Namas had taken over from the Boers. The latter usually had a priest stay in their midst to act as a spiritual leader for the benefit of isolated farmers.

This pattern repeated itself through Jager Afrikaner's son, Jonker Afrikaner, who shortly after his father's death in 1823 took over the leadership of his group. He led his people across the Orange River and moved further and further north. He dwelt for a time in Warmbad in southern Namibia, where he came into contact with a Wesleyan missionary station. Keen to attach a missionary or clergyman to his group, he made the Methodist missionaries promise that one of them would join him as soon as he had found a place in which to settle permanently.

Jonker Afrikaner settled down close to present-day Windhoek in 1838. Instead of waiting for a missionary to arrive from Warmbad, he contacted a missionary he had met during his wanderings, Johann Heinrich Schmelen, who was attached to the London Missionary Society, and asked him to find a missionary for his people. This led to the arrival, in 1842, of the Rhenish Mission in Namibia.

Notes

1 One such influential opponent to slavery was a missionary from the London Missionary Society, the Scotsman John Philip (1774-1851) who had been based in Cape Town since 1818.
2 Lau, B. 1987, 20.
3 Ibid., 1, 19.
4 Vedder, H. 1966, 122. *Note:* All quotes in Swedish, Finnish and German translated into English by the author.

2 The Oorlam-Namas invade Nama and Herero territory

There are precious few printed sources on, and even less substance to be drawn from the oral tradition about, the events leading to the disintegration of the traditional organization of the Nama tribes and the arrival of the Oorlam-Namas who established themselves as the new predominant group.[1]

The first phase of contact between the Oorlam-Namas and the Namas seems to have been characterized by a curiosity on the Nama side; mostly, it was a question of trading relations and only occasionally did some

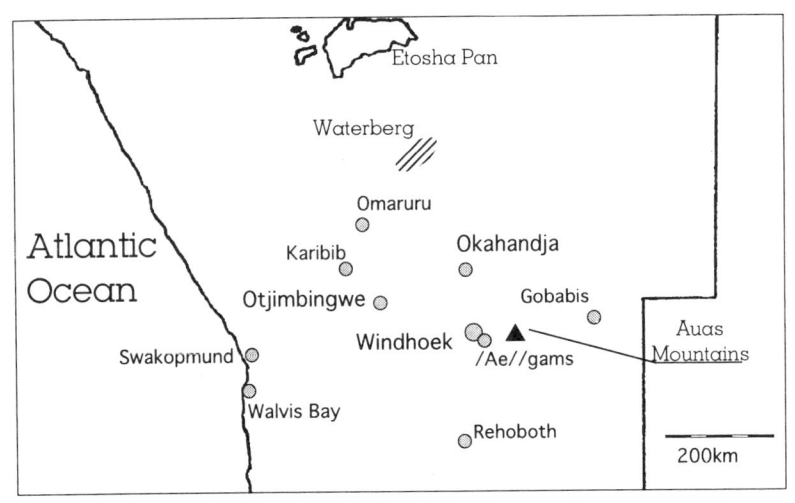

Central Namibia. The region where the Oorlam-Namas came into contact and clashed with the Herero people.

skirmishes take place. It became more and more evident as time went on, however, that the Namas, although far more numerous, were militarily inferior to the Oorlam-Namas: they only owned a few guns and horses. Having large herds of cattle, they were also less mobile than the newcomers. Increasingly the invaders took over water holes and pastures, and raided the Namas' herds. They were increasingly seen as the hostile conquerors. Occasionally some senior Nama leaders tried to maintain their freedom by establishing alliances with the powerful Oorlam-Nama commando leaders, but in general the Namas north of the Orange River began living in fear of the commando groups. As more Oorlam-Namas migrated into the country, violent conflict erupted frequently; and as Namas and Oorlam-Namas became engaged in full-scale military confrontations it became more and more dangerous for Europeans to live in the country. This can be exemplified by what happened to some of the missionaries from the Cape Colony who for some years had served among the Namas. In 1811, the Nama mission station of the London Missionary Society at Warmbad was razed to the ground by the Oorlam-Namas in order to prevent Nama chiefs from gaining access to guns and ammunition via a missionary. In 1819, Missionary Schmelen, who had accompanied the Oorlam-Namas in their crossing of the Orange River and who had established his station at Bethanie, began to serve Nama outposts and settlements in the vicinity. The Oorlam-Nama leaders in Bethanie, angered by this, forced him to leave his work. Schmelen gave his refusal to furnish 'his' people with more gunpowder as the main reason for his expulsion.[2] After 1822, when Schmelen left the station, the settlement of Bethanie disintegrated as the struggle over cattle, pastures and water holes between the Namas and the growing number of Oorlam-Namas flared and continued until 1830.

Schmelen's expulsion was not an isolated occurrence. In the same year that he was expelled from Bethanie, Missionary John Archbell of the Wesleyan Missionary Society was expelled from a nearby mission station for similar reasons. The only missionary left in Namaland after these expulsions was murdered in August 1824, when he proceeded with his work in spite of the warnings he had received from Oorlam-Nama leaders.[3] After this, all missionary work in Namaland stopped until 1834.

By about 1830, Jonker Afrikaner had established himself as the sovereign over much of southern and central Namibia. In 1836, the explorer Captain James Alexander from Cape Town referred to Afrikaner as 'the great chief of this part of the country'.[4] The development leading up to this is of great importance in understanding the position of the Europeans, including the missionaries, in this part of Namibia until the 1870s. During his wanderings northwards, Jonker Afrikaner had come into contact with groups of Hereros who fled the drought of the late 1820s.

In their search for water and grazing they had migrated south of the territories traditionally belonging to them. On their way, they had found no difficulty in defeating the Nama groups whose grazing they invaded.

One group especially affected by the Herero invasion were the so-called 'Red people' who had settled near Hoachanas. At the time, this group was led by a woman, Games, widow of the group's chieftain, who had assumed temporary leadership until her son would be of age to become the chieftain. Finding herself in a tight spot, Games felt compelled to seek the help of Jonker Afrikaner against the Hereros. Afrikaner did not hesitate to come to her assistance. With the help of his group of well-armed, mounted Oorlam-Namas, he routed the invading Hereros after three encounters: at Keetmanshoop, Gibeon and finally in the Auas Mountains near Windhoek. Soon afterwards, Jonker Afrikaner settled down with his people around the water spots at /Ae//gams located near present-day Klein Windhoek. This site was of great strategic advantage, situated on a hill from where any raiding Herero parties, or other enemies, could be spotted at a distance.

At the request of the Namas in Hoachanas, Jonker Afrikaner had already established his rule in the border area between Namaland and Hereroland by the late 1820s. By again defeating the Hereros, Afrikaner now clearly demonstrated his superiority. Some major Nama chiefs formed alliances with him. The deal in such alliances was for the Afrikaner Oorlam-Namas to protect the Nama chiefs, and make it possible for the Namas to move further north, into areas formerly held by the Hereros. Thus, by defeating the Hereros in response to the requests of the Nama leaders, Jonker Afrikaner became the recognized leader of the people and territories in the entire area. This was confirmed in an agreement between Jonker Afrikaner and Chief Oasib of Hoachanas in 1858. Jonker was further declared the overlord of Hereroland, and found himself in a position to incorporate whole groups of Hereros and their vast herds of cattle into a network of dependants and followers.[5]

However, before we go into the relations between the Oorlam-Namas and the Hereros, we should mention the changes that were taking place in the Nama society as a direct result of the Namas' contacts with the Oorlam-Namas. By the 1840s, records show a Namaland totally changed from that described by the early European observers. All political and social relations had been transformed. The Namas were assimilating with the Oorlam-Namas' social system. New patterns of social organization were emerging, based on the commando institution and on commodity exchange with the Cape. The nomadic lifestyle of the Namas began to change as people clustered around certain leading Nama and Oorlam-Nama families. These families claimed territories for their own use and built their own headquarters. The notion of private property became established. With this new kind of socio-political life in place, laws were introduced to regulate and maintain the political power divisions and social hierarchy. This was based on private ownership, mostly of guns and cattle.

For the first time, therefore, there was competition for resources and ownership. The Nama people had largely moved away from traditional tribal, kinship-governed relations of reciprocity and hereditary wealth. Instead, the new economic and socio-political system, which had its roots in the Cape society, manifested itself also in the European notion of Christianity as the dominant ethic of these new communities. This is demonstrated by the fact that there was a drive to give the missionaries an influential role. However, the movements of the missionaries and other Europeans were tightly controlled, especially as far as travels into Hereroland or the north-western hunting grounds were concerned.

Trade with the Cape became the focus of attention – but a trade controlled by the local communities, and without any domination by foreigners. Under Jonker Afrikaner, /Ae//gams near Windhoek, his headquarters, became a flourishing commercial centre.

By 1844, Jonker Afrikaner had built two major roads – one west to Walvis Bay, the other leading southwards through the Auas Mountains – thus connecting central Namibia with the sea and with the Cape.

In summary, it can be said that the socio-historical distinctions between the original Nama groups and the incoming Oorlam-Namas vanished more and more with the emergence of a new socio-political and economic pattern. This was neither tribal (as the Namas had been) nor was it quite a continuation of the life of the raiders (which the invading Oorlam-Namas had led just north of the Orange River). A new society developed, increasingly depending on its trade links with the Cape, and jealously guarding its independence against the small but growing number of European traders and missionaries.

The merger of the Namas and Oorlam-Namas into a new, self-styled community resulted in a kind of colonial power within southern and central Namibia. To ensure its continued existence, it had to control and dominate both the Europeans and the Hereros; and at the same time it had to struggle against disintegrating forces from within - a built-in weakness caused by different interest groups who competed with each other for domination. Efforts to overcome this weakness were manifested in a never-ending series of alliances between the various groups of this emerging new community. This fact became decisive in later dealings with the Hereros.

In the 1820s, the Hereros, in their quest for grazing and water, had pushed beyond the limits of their traditional tribal territories. As we have mentioned, this led to conflict with the Namas and final confrontation with Jonker Afrikaner. It eventually widened Afrikaner's sphere of interest: after the battle in the Auas Mountains, he was able to set up his headquarters at /Ae//gams, which not only lay inside the tribal territory of the Hereros, but was a traditional Herero place of worship. From here, Afrikaner could extend his influence into areas that were central to the lives of the Hereros, as well as into the grazing and water spots so vital for the survival of the Hereros' cattle.

The only option now left to the two main groups of Hereros, under the command of the chieftains Kahitjene and Tjamuaha, who had ventured southwards and run into the Namas, was to make peace. And so, on 24 December 1842, peace was concluded between Jonker Afrikaner, leader of the Oorlam-Namas in alliance with the Namas, and the two Herero groups. This did not mean that the two Herero leaders were deposed. The peace settlement was in actual fact an alliance similar to that formed between the Oorlam-Namas and the different Nama groups.

At the time of the signing of this treaty the first three Rhenish missionaries in the country, Carl Hugo Hahn, Hans Heinrich Kleinschmidt, and Hans Christian Knudsen, had just reached Jonker Afrikaner's headquarters. They had come in response to Afrikaner's request to Missionary Schmelen, and intended to work both at Afrikaner's headquarters and further north in Herero territory. The three were not aware of the actual significance of the peace treaty, a fact made plain by Hahn's diary notes made on Christmas Eve, 1842, in which he wrote: 'Never before have I experienced such a glorious Christmas. What has just occurred is the best Christmas gift we could ever receive.'[6]

The underlying message of this entry is: the way is paved for missionary intervention in the principal region of Jonker Afrikaner and from there, into the territory of the Herero people. This, according to

Hahn, was mainly a consequence of a peace which extended Jonker Afrikaner's leadership into Herero territory. In actual fact, the peace treaty formulated an agreement which recognized the continued leadership of both the Herero chieftains over their groups, albeit in exchange for their granted commitment to support Afrikaner in his further raiding expeditions against still hostile Nama groups and other Herero tribes. This support for Jonker Afrikaner would in turn be rewarded by a share in the loot as well as access to horses and firearms.

To be on the safe side, however, Afrikaner ruled that the two Herero chiefs with their people were to be based close to his camp. He needed to be able to control them and place them in a position of dependence where they would serve his interests; his method was identical to the tactics which he used to absorb the Nama groups. However, his alliance with the Hereros did not grant any protection to Kahitjene or Tjamuaha whenever their own cattle herds were plundered by Nama groups. In 1844, for instance, the leader of the Red people, Oasib, attacked Kahitjene's tribe and seized his cattle, conspicuously unimpeded by any interference from Jonker Afrikaner.

In the relationships he maintained with his many different allies, Jonker Afrikaner can be described as a pragmatic politician who either gave or withheld assistance depending on what would best serve his own immediate interests. In this case, Oasib was a tried and trusted ally. Jonker Afrikaner could not, therefore, find any reason to object to his enriching himself at the expense of a Herero leader whose loyalty might still be questionable.

This event prompted Kahitjene to take his people and his cattle herds farther out of Jonker Afrikaner's reach and settle down at Okahandja, in central Herero territory. Not that Jonker Afrikaner objected much: Okahandja was not very far from his own headquarters, and so he would be able to keep a watchful eye on Kahitjene. Added to which, he could use this move to his own advantage, as it provided him with ample opportunity to extend his influence to other groups of Hereros based at Okahandja.

Thanks to his alliance with the diverse tribes of southern and central Namibia, Jonker Afrikaner was also able to check the movements of European merchants and missionaries more effectively. To him, all these Europeans represented potential competition to his own ambitions. On the other hand, he could use them as channels of information on the financial scene of Cape Town. In addition to this, they could provide him with weapons and any other items he might wish in order to maintain his position of dominance.

Afrikaner's wish to keep an eye on the Europeans was one important reason for refusing Missionary Hahn's request to spread missionary activity any farther into Herero territory. It was only later that he found out that Kahitjene had made land available to the Rhenish Mission for the establishment of a missionary station in Okahandja. Immediately he sent a retributive expedition, on 23 August 1850, which was ordered to raze the place. His men spared no effort in murdering men, women and even children, and drove away great numbers of the Hereros' cattle. Many Hereros lost all their livestock and sought refuge in Kaokoland, which had in fact once been their home, and where some of their tribal kinsmen still lived. This movement towards safety grew to a veritable exodus once Jonker Afrikaner himself decided to settle in Okahandja in 1854 where he helped himself to the cattle of the Hereros.

Jonker Afrikaner's military, financial and strategical superiority had far-reaching consequences for the entire Herero population. For one, the Hereros based near /Ae//gams and at Okahandja had found that their traditional way of life, which mainly gravitated around cattle raising, was seriously threatened. Afrikaner's strategy was based on his wish first to force the Herero people to assume the economic and socio-political lifestyle of the Oorlam-Namas, and then to impel them to live under the Oorlam-Namas' leadership. Many Hereros had in fact adapted to this new system of values, while others, who through the loss of their cattle found themselves uprooted from their traditional tribal way of life, had chosen to join the steadily increasing throngs of European traders who had managed to gain a firm foothold in the country, despite Afrikaner's efforts to gain overall control.[7] Both cases delineated above – submitting to the Oorlam-Namas' rule or joining the Europeans – equally threatened to dissolve traditional Herero community life. Those Hereros who joined the exodus to Kaokoland would best be able to maintain their traditional sense of community around their herds of cattle where life was led obeying the dictates of traditional leadership.[8]

The Oorlam-Nama chief therefore practised a form of indirect rule over all those groups of Namas and Hereros whom he defeated or allied himself with. In spite of Jonker Afrikaner's attempts to assert his superiority, however, tensions mounted due to rivalry among these groups. Also, a number of treaties were signed among them to counter their dependence on Afrikaner and his group – a fact which in many ways weakened his position of superiority. Furthermore, these inner tensions caused many fissures in the fabric of his south-central Namibian empire, indirectly paving the way for European colonialism.

This is not the place to give in detail all the particulars of the disintegration of the Oorlam-Namas' dominance. A few points, however, must be clarified in order to provide some background information which might shed some light on the course of subsequent developments:

1   The group of Oorlam-Namas led by Jonker Afrikaner were never given full endorsement by Afrikaner's peers leading other Oorlam-Nama groups. This was true of the Bondelswarts group, among others, who had settled near the south-north trade route from the Cape Colony, where it crossed the Orange River. In their own contacts with Cape Town, they never let themselves be controlled by Jonker Afrikaner, who restricted the movement of the European traders in this regard. The Bondelswarts cemented their treaties with the traders, and also with other Oorlam-Nama and Nama groups. From their settlement area on the trade route, they were in a position to stop and, on several occasions, rob Jonker Afrikaner's cattle caravans going south and transportation treks carrying goods back north.

2   There was growing dissatisfaction with Jonker Afrikaner among those defeated groups of Namas whom he forced into treaties of alliance or of vassalage. Often, Afrikaner demanded cattle as payment for the so-called 'protection' he provided. Whenever someone refused to pay their dues he would use martial means to persuade them. In an attempt to shake off the yoke, many of the Nama leaders strove to revive their ancestral way of life based on tribal community life.

One such leader was Oasib, who had once turned to Jonker Afrikaner for protection against the ravages of the Herero people and who later in fact prompted Kahitjene's move to Okahandja. In the late 1850s, Oasib became the leader of a group of Nama tribes who, inspired by their own conception of tribal community life, attempted to forge an alliance of Namas to fight against the Oorlam-Namas led by Jonker.

The same was true of Tjamuaha, leader of the group of Hereros who had remained close to Afrikaner's headquarters after the peace treaty of December 1842. Tjamuaha used his alliance with Jonker Afrikaner to provide his warriors with arms and adequate training. In 1860, Jonker Afrikaner took his men up north to steal cattle from the Ovambos, and

Tjamuaha seized this opportunity to make his way to Kaokoland, organize the Hereros there and incite them to revolt against Afrikaner and his people by appealing to their feelings of tribal community.

Already in 1858, at a meeting of leaders representing Oorlam-Nama and Nama tribes based at Hoachanas, Jonker Afrikaner saw himself compelled to agree to a number of concessions and compromises. Every group represented at this meeting asserted their right to enter into alliances and treaties of their own without always having to yield to Afrikaner's will.

3   Jonker Afrikaner's attempts to gain a monopoly over all the trade within his area of interest demanded an increasing export of cattle to the Cape. To control his area of interest and gain monopoly over trade meant constantly having to obtain more horses and more rifles. All of this became increasingly costly. It was not long before Afrikaner was financially dependent on European traders to grant him credit. His constant looting of other people's cattle eventually led to a situation where cattle was more difficult to come by. With this shortage in exchange commodity, the only way out for Afrikaner was to plead for greater and greater credit from the European merchants. With him at their mercy, the merchants raised their prices and exploited their power to withhold those goods which Afrikaner demanded and so badly needed to maintain his position of dominance.

In the long run this meant that merchants were able to establish their own market monopoly. In other words, every trump card was now in their hands as they were fully able, by withholding their deliveries of goods as well as their credit, to undermine Jonker Afrikaner's position of power.

4   Jonker Afrikaner's dominance over central and southern Namibia had in fact indirectly opened up the country for infiltration by Europeans of diverse categories – explorers, big game hunters, merchants, missionaries, to name but a few, most of whom were based at the Cape. Thus this part of Namibia gradually grew into a sphere of interest for those Europeans. And Jonker Afrikaner had in fact facilitated this process by building roads from the Orange River to the north and from the coast to the innermost regions of the country. Here lay great riches soon to be discovered and soon to prompt further European interest.

Thus paradoxically, the invading Oorlam-Namas with their determination to create a monopoly in this part of Namibia laid the foundations for

European colonialism and mission. As Lau states, 'due to [the] specific history and nature of the [Oorlam-Nama] commando groups, forms of European colonial domination were introduced into Namaland long before official annexation and conquest'.[9] Southern and central Namibia thus became available to yet another influx of foreign people – this time in the form of European colonialism.

Notes

1. *See* Dedering, T. 1989, 2.
2. In a letter to the board of his Mission, dated 26 September 1822, Schmelen gives a detailed account of the situation he describes as a 'civil war'. LMS Archives, Cape Town.
3. Broadbent, S. 1857.
4. Alexander, J. 1838, 151.
5. Lau, B. 1984a, 467 and 519.
6. Ibid., 96.
7. Charles John Andersson, explorer and successful businessman, is an example of a European trader who managed to gain a firm foothold in the country despite Jonker Afrikaner's efforts to gain control.
8. For more background information, see Lau, B. 1987, 105 ff.
9. Ibid., 106.

3 Pioneering missionary work in the interests of Christian Western civilization

The new era of missionary activity in Namibia in the 19th century was supported by the prevailing European cultural optimism and belief in evolution aligning Darwinistic theories of biological evolution with so-called 'Christian' beliefs, at the expense of the so-called 'weaker species'. This attitude, characteristic of its time, expressed itself in the many voyages of discovery, combined with missionary operations, that were launched in this period. David Livingstone's idea of missionary work is an example of this. For him, missionary work had an important cultural purpose. Its justification lay in its capacity to leaven the alleged 'primitiveness' of African society with Christian Western culture. Missionary zeal, trade and colonial dominance together formed 'the impact of the civilized and Christian society'.[1] This belief in the superiority of all things European was based on an innate racial ideology which was soon to have frightening consequences, especially in southern Africa.

In an investigation dealing with racialism in Nazi Germany, Müller-Hill[2] sees the phenomenon of Nazism as the final outcome of the development of an ideology based on notions of European superiority, which pervaded the German pioneering colonial era in Africa. Colonization was thus inspired by an ethnic, cultural and 'Christian' imperialism which denigrated the human dignity of the African people, who supposedly were an 'inferior race'. It was an important task for spokesmen of this Christian Western civilization to see to the cultural and religious development of these people and also, to deny them the right to claim any equality with the so-called 'white race'.

This sort of denigration of the 'non-whites' can be illustrated by a statement made in 1913 by a man who was said to be an expert on colonial matters in German South West Africa. Concerning the ethnic group known as Basters based in Rehoboth, he gave the colonial authorities the following piece of advice: 'We should provide them with the minimum of protection which they require for service as a race, inferior to ourselves, and we should do this only as long as they are useful to us. After this free competition should prevail and, in my opinion, this will lead to their decline and destruction.'[3]

The 19th century, then, saw a fervent revival of Christian mission, though tainted by racialism, and a determination of making the entire world turn to Christ. The missionaries working towards this aim must be seen within the context of their own time; consequently, they were strongly influenced by the commonly held view of Christian Western civilization as the pinnacle of human cultural development – quite apart, of course, from the question of private faith and a strong sense of calling. Christianity being the religion of Europe was thought of as the divine revelation and as the power of salvation which on its own could change 'heathens' into fully 'human' beings.

This missionary revival led to the foundation of a number of new missionary societies. Many of these were non-confessional and, to begin with, contented themselves with placing their own missioners at the service of already established missions.[4]

As has been said, however, an equally large number of secular motives lay behind the fervour of this newly kindled missionary revival. One of these was the growing nationalist fervour, coupled with the wish to benefit the interests of the fatherland through its colonial and mercantile operations abroad. This meant that many of the recently founded missionary societies were directly supported by colonial circles. In Germany, several missionary societies were even directly founded by parties with colonial interests. One of these was the Evangelische Missionsgesellschaft für Deutsch-Ostafrika (sometimes known as 'Berlin III'), which was founded in 1886 by the leader of a German colonial enterprise based in East Africa, Carl Peters.[5]

The questions of 'Germanism' and German mission were among the main topics debated at the first major missionary congress held in Berlin in 1886. German missions were encouraged to take an active part in the 'realization of a national, colonial programme'. Furthermore, they were discouraged from 'restrict[ing] missionary activities to mission work'; instead, they should 'help to establish German culture and German thought in the colonies'.[6]

Against this background it is important to account for the missionary theology practised by the leader of the Rhenish Mission during the Mission's first decades in Namibia, Friedrich Fabri (1824-1891). Fabri who became inspector of the Rhenish Mission in Wuppertal-Barmen in 1857 can undeniably be described as a man in tune with his time. Fabri's missionary theology made a profound impact on the Rhenish Mission's activities in Namibia until well into the 20th century.

Mission and colonialism were, according to Fabri, but two sides of the same coin. In his basic theological assumptions he was anti-confessional, harbouring strong theosophical sentiments – in other words, a belief in the innate capacity of a human being under divine guidance to develop his or her divine origins with all that this entails in the way of gaining new powers to achieve perfectibility.

Fabri was appointed leader of what was soon to become one of Germany's leading missions. For him, it was important that the Rhenish Mission avail itself of the prevailingly Christian cultural optimism of the time. Thus, he can be seen as representing contemporary missionary thought, which sought to achieve intimate co-operation between mission and colonialism. According to Fabri, there must be constant interaction between Christianity and culture,[7] and Christianity was by definition the vessel of the highest form of genuine culture.[8]

It is important to take note of the particular brand of Fabri's optimism upon which he laid the foundations of his faith in the Church as the highest cultural principle. This was later to shape Fabri's views on colonialism. To him, just as mission was the precondition for colonialism, so a well-ordered state of affairs run by a strong colonial power was also the necessary prerequisite for missionary work as a whole.

In tune with this concept of colonialism among non-Christian people, Fabri believed that the Mission, as the bearer of the Gospel, could even become an evangelizing factor back home, in the mother country: 'Colonialism is of missionary interest to the entire world – including its Christian as well as its non-Christian parts – as a counter-balance to the increasing growth of materialism.'[9]

Fabri resigned as inspector of the Rhenish Mission in 1884, at the onset of German colonialism in Namibia. He had by then left his stamp on the Rhenish Mission with its favourable views on and active support of German colonialism. From now on, he devoted his life to questions of colonial and political interest as a member of the presidium of the German Colonial Association.

With Fabri, we encounter at least three principles which influenced the pioneering work of the Rhenish Mission based in Namibia.[10]

1   Mission and colonialism were to him two aspects of a 'historically determined duty to be assumed by Germany and its national, humanitarian and cultural vocation'.[11]

2   The internal affairs of contemporary Germany demanded intimate collaboration between the missionary and colonial efforts abroad. Economic factors inside Germany had become a major driving force for German colonialism, causing a considerable number of Germans to emigrate to the colonies Germany held abroad. Fabri placed great emphasis on the successful preservation of the Germanism of these emigrants – in other words, that they preserve their cultural identity as Germans. An indispensable element of this German cultural heritage was German Christianity. Only as bearers of their heritage in its totality – including, in other words, their Christian cultural heritage – could the representatives of what Fabri refers to as the 'Germanic race' develop their capacity to conduct a just form of colonialism. Germanism, then, in its definition of 'German cultural heritage', was believed by nature to own a 'colonialist capability'.[12] Besides being a necessary political development, colonization was, to Fabri, a matter of 'establishing a prudent, and largely unpolitical, emigration policy'.[13]

3   Co-operation between mission and colonialism was also claimed to carry a vital humanitarian/cultural aspect. Colonialism, according to Fabri, meant 'a moral duty ... to develop the colonial people to higher culture through education and extensive self-administration'.[14] Mission, along with the Gospel, brought about potential elevation of the entire human race in concert with colonialism.

Fabri provides us with an interesting and vivid example of contemporary ideology with its peculiar blend of evolutionary theory, coupled with cultural-Christian optimism. The co-operation between mission and colonialism should be viewed from this angle as well. The very conception of such co-operation was taken for granted as it was very much in tune with the then prevalent ideas stemming from major currents of thought within theological and missionary theory on the one hand, and humanist ideology then firmly entrenched under the banner of cultural optimism on the other. Christian religion and European politics were seen at the time as together making up a unity, the overriding aim of which was 'world salvation' achieved through the triad of mission, trade, and colonialism.

To these three items, a fourth might be added, namely the nationalistic impetus, or the concept of 'Germanism'. Similar ideas were presented concerning German missionary work in East Africa by, among others, the inspector of mission attached to the 'Berlin III' Mission, Walter Trittelvitz. In a speech he gave at a missionary conference in Herrnhut, Germany, in 1906, he claimed: 'The political and cultural conquest walks hand in hand with the missionary conquest.'[15]

It will be recalled that Fabri's attitude towards the Christian mission as the mediator of a superior Christian Western civilization implied a denigration of African culture, religion and traditional way of life. Mission was a matter of civilizing what was crudely generalized as a 'primitive' people. They were *primitive* because they had not been Christened; their so-called 'primitivism' was also seen to consist of a lack of 'morality', culture, and anything of historical value. In other words, the people who were to be civilized were generally thought of as living in a spiritual vacuum. The task of the Mission was therefore not limited to offering the 'heathens' a faith that would lead them to salvation but extended to bringing them up into an entirely different cultural pattern which would radically transform their way of life. Until they were thus civilized to accept the dictates of 'Christian' moral, religious and legal values they were regarded as 'inferior' and were expected to submit to their 'teachers': their missionaries and 'overlords', and all other European colonial representatives as well.

It was important for these teachers and 'overlords' from Europe to acquire a good command of the languages and customs of the people they dealt with. Not that they were motivated by the desire to acquire a deeper understanding of the Africans' culture! Such desire would imply a positive evaluation of their way of life, traditions, and value system. Rather, it was seen as a necessary step in eliminating expressions of primitivism and replacing them with 'Christian, Western' values.

As representatives of the superior civilization, the Europeans were not placed under any obligation to show respect, and it was of no consequence what the primitive people thought of their actions.

Generally speaking, this already was the attitude of most missionaries and other Europeans in their dealings with the people of Namibia during the precolonial period. No-one in these circles was concerned with the fact that Namibia was just then undergoing radical socio-political changes as a result of the Oorlam-Namas' invasion. An interesting question is how these representatives of Europe were seen by the leaders of the Oorlam-Namas, and how this paved the way for the ensuing major conflict which made the Rhenish Mission one of the pioneers of the German colonial empire. We shall look at this question in the following chapters.

Notes

1. Hellberg, C-J. 1965, 46 ff.
2. Müller-Hill, B. 1988.
3. Ibid., 3; see also Fischer, E. 1971.
4. The Gossner Mission and the Rhenish Mission Society were examples of such missionary societies in Germany. Their blend of revivalism caused them to give their support even to low church Anglican Missions such as the non-confessional evangelical London Missionary Society.
5. Hellberg, C-J, op. cit., 52 ff.
6. Ibid., 92, note 11.
7. For more on Fabri's theology, see Schmidt, WR. 1965.
8. Fabri missed one important point, however: on the one hand, the Church cannot grow without transforming its surroundings and thus influencing history – on the other, historical development constitutes a major influence on the growth and formation of the Church itself.
9. Schmidt, WR, op. cit., 76 ff.
10. Ibid.
11. Ibid.
12. Ibid.
13. Ibid.
14. Ibid.
15. Hellberg, C-J, op. cit., 100.

4 Relations between the Rhenish Mission and the Oorlam-Namas and Hereros

The Mission as a resource for the Oorlam-Namas

The majority of the Oorlam-Nama leaders were Christian and keen to attach a missionary to each of their groups. He would be the spiritual leader responsible for leading worship and for religious instruction. There was thus great interest to support regular Christian activity. But there were other reasons, besides religious, which prompted the Oorlam-Namas to desire the presence of a missionary among them. This later also applied to those groups of Namas whom the Oorlam-Namas dominated or influenced in various ways.

In her investigation of this period of Namibian history, Lau makes the following observation concerning the Oorlam-Nama relationship with the missionaries: 'Oorlams tried to safeguard and cement their supply and trade lines with the Cape by inviting European missionaries to come and stay with them. Alternatively ... they took the missionaries along with them when they left the Cape. By the 1830s, Nama chiefs, too, were recorded as building up supplies of guns and ammunition, and as trying to achieve this by accepting a missionary.'[1]

On the whole, having a missionary in their midst was of vital importance for the new way of life which had been introduced by the Oorlam-Namas and which influenced, and even transformed, the Nama society. The Nama chiefs needed to maintain and strengthen their contacts with the Cape in order to obtain valuable information in connection with their own trading activities. In this transformation process from a traditional tribal social organization to the new political and social system of the Oorlam-Namas, the missionaries, as European representatives, were assigned a significant role which was not limited to spiritual leadership.

Thus, in the new, recently established settlements which grew out of the new social organization initiated by the Oorlam-Namas, and consisted of fortifications used both as administrative centres and for storage of goods and cattle, the joint presence of a missionary and a parish church became something of a prerequisite. Where no missionary could be found who could be attached to the settlement, the leader would attend to the regular conducting of worship himself. According to Carl Hugo Hahn, Jonker Afrikaner was one such leader who often preached with 'prophetic ardour' to his own supporters, but also to those groups of Hereros whom he deprived of their cattle.[2]

A missionary who became attached to a group of Oorlam-Namas was required to subordinate himself entirely to the leader of the group – so much so that he would not be allowed to move about freely or take any initiative of his own. In all things, the leader's permission had to be obtained. In the same vein, the church buildings erected near the headquarters of the group had to serve, when the occasion arose, as a form of defensive works whose church bell would be used as an effective alarm system.

The most important aspect of this relationship between the Oorlam-Namas and Namas and the missionaries was the fact that the missionaries were seen primarily as contact persons with the Cape. Then there was the added attraction that many European visitors came to see them. Merchants from the Cape, for example, used missionary stations as central offices from where they supervised their activities. Furthermore, the missionaries themselves as Europeans required various goods which could only be acquired through Cape Town. Requisitions of this kind coming from the missionaries often included goods which were of use to the Oorlam-Namas, but which the Cape would not willingly deliver to 'the native population'. Missionaries would sign requisitions for weapons, ammunition and horses, all of which were needed by the Oorlam-Namas for their raiding expeditions to obtain cattle as trading goods. This special function of the missionaries naturally caused the leaders of the Oorlam-Namas to keep these religious men under scrupulous control.[3]

The missionaries also supplied valuable news about events in the Cape Colony or any other part of the outside world. Most of this concerned information of relevance to trade, such as prices and supplies of goods.

Despite the above control which the missionaries were exposed to on a daily basis, they were able to exert extensive influence over the development of the Oorlam-Namas' domestic judiciary systems along with their ethical value systems. One good example of how a missionary drafted legislation both civil and criminal within a settlement is provided by Missionary Hans Christian Knudsen of the Rhenish Mission who worked amongst the Bondelswarts in Bethanie in southern Namibia. The preamble to this code of laws which he instituted and which took effect on 1 January 1847[4] was formulated thus: 'The Word of God shall be the law by which all shall be judged.'

It was usually at the discretion of the chieftain or leader to decide what, in every particular case, was in line with God's law. Murderers would be sentenced to death, and it was the duty of the leader to see to it that this death sentence was duly carried out. Reference was made to Genesis 9:6, which reads, 'He who spills human blood, will see his own blood by man be spilt, for God shaped man into his own image.'[5]

Polygamy was forbidden, and unchastity was punished with 40 lashes of the rod. The law further formulated details pertaining to criminal or civil proceedings.

In the long run, the Namibian leaders were unable to control the missionaries' activities or infringe on their freedom of movement, nor could they always count on the missionaries' compliance to act as obedient resource persons. The missionaries' close contacts with the Cape and the internal cohesion between European traders and the missionaries undermined such external control over the long term. Consequently the Oorlam-Namas began to view the Europeans as a threat and rival against whom action should be taken. Tension grew in the their relations with the missionaries, giving rise to a number of conflicts. In some cases missionaries were driven away in spite of the fact that the groups to which they were attached, along with their leaders, were Christians. Thus in 1811, Jager Afrikaner destroyed a mission station in Warmbad. In 1822, Missionary Schmelen was forced to leave Bethanie; and Missionary Knudsen, who re-opened the station in 1842, was forced to leave in 1850.

The same missionaries who had been so urgently summoned to the settlements as resource persons were increasingly seen as troublesome representatives of a powerful group of Europeans beginning to gain a considerable amount of influence in this part of the country. This explains the odd reception the pioneer missionaries of the Rhenish Mission were given when they arrived at Jonker Afrikaner's headquarters at /Ae//Gams in December 1842.

The Rhenish missionaries' first encounter with Jonker Afrikaner

The Rhenish Mission's three missionaries, Hans Kleinschmidt (1812-1864), Carl Hugo Hahn (1818-1895), and a Norwegian attached to the Mission, Hans Christian Knudsen (1816-1854), arrived at Jonker Afrikaner's camp at /Ae//Gams in December 1842, in response to Missionary Schmelen's mediation of a request for missionaries from the Rhenish Mission. On their journey from Cape Town the three of them spent some time with the Wesleyan missionaries in Warmbad. Their Warmbad hosts were perplexed by their explicit intention to start a mission at /Ae//Gams, an initiative sanctioned, as they claimed, by Jonker Afrikaner himself. The Wesleyans interpreted this as an attempt to compete with them, which in turn confused this group of inexperienced missionaries freshly arrived from the Rhenish Mission. They had set out for Namibia's interior in good faith, in response to an 'expressed invitation from the local tribal leader'.

The three stayed at Warmbad during July of 1842. It was not until February 1843 that Pastor Cook wrote the following letter in a report made on behalf of the Wesleyans based in Warmbad, in which he asserted that the Rhenish Mission 'was disregarding all that had been said of our labour there and other efforts with the Cape District Meeting and the Home Committee to supply a missionary to Jonker'.[6]

The newly arrived missionaries had not heard the last of it, of course. They were at first well received by Jonker Afrikaner who did not further inquire into their background. They arrived just in time for the pact made between Afrikaner and the Herero chieftains Tjamuaha and Kahitjene, on Christmas Eve in 1842. The notes found in Hahn's diary relating the event plainly express how he experienced it as a God-given opportunity for them to reach out to the African chieftains of those tribes whom they in the service of their Mission had been sent to evangelize.[7]

As peace had now been made between the chieftains, Hahn eagerly requested Jonker Afrikaner's permission to extend his missionary activity to the Herero people north of /Ae//Gams. Much to his disappointment and astonishment, Afrikaner refused to grant him this permission. Hahn wrote in his diary: 'Jonker openly declared that he had no intention of giving us any support for this, nor would he leave any interpreters at our disposal should we wish to go; further, that there were people among the Hereros of this region who would murder us and that the English authorities of Cape Town would then hold him responsible.'[8]

Hahn was particularly surprised by the reference to the British government. What influence could it possibly exert upon a 'tribal' chieftain in one of Namibia's innermost regions? There are many such instances pointing to the fact that Hahn was unaware of Jonker Afrikaner's actual position as a leader of a commando group with no tribal affiliation. Hahn took Jonker Afrikaner for a genuine African tribal chieftain.

Now Jonker Afrikaner was not interested in giving 'his' missionaries access to the Hereros whom he wished to exploit for his own purposes. Nor did he wish to let the missionaries out of sight. Furthermore, if anything happened to them this would draw unwelcome attention from Cape Town whose authorities would then be provided with an excuse to cause damage to his trade connections with the south. In other words, his ambitious plans would be seriously thwarted.

What Jonker Afrikaner wished above all to safeguard was the right to gain advantages and wealth, and control the Hereros, with no outside interference. He and his people who originated from the Cape Colony had been 'taught ... how to use firearms and how to be a Christian by the Dutch settlements at the Cape'; they were 'gunned and civilized Hottentots, more ready for war than [for] peace, and had asserted over their country cousins, the still cow-riding Namas, a complete supremacy'.[9] Soon, if things went according to plan, he would extend that supremacy to the Hereros.

Hahn and his colleagues were soon to see in what manner Jonker Afrikaner planned to curtail their freedom of movement by not allowing them to visit other tribes, 'particularly the Hereros as he wished to obviate the possibility of potential enemies being supplied with firearms'.[10] Hahn and Kleinschmidt stayed on with Jonker Afrikaner at /Ae//Gams from December 1842 to October 1844. Knudsen moved to the south.

Jonker Afrikaner's was a settlement consisting of nearly 2 000 people, half of whom lived in the densely populated, fortified area which had a stone church with room for 600 people. Afrikaner had raised this church himself and regularly conducted services there long before the arrival of the Rhenish missionaries.

Hahn and Kleinschmidt raised their mission station at /Ae//Gams with the support of Jonker Afrikaner.[11] Conditions all seemed in favour of successful missionary work to be conducted from this focal centre.

However, in conducting their missionary work the Rhenish missionaries applied strict rules against what they felt were degenerate heathen elements in the people's way of life. They vehemently opposed drunkenness, traditional dancing, nudity, and lack of discipline, among other things. Soon their interference 'in normal tribal customs produced a feeling of antagonism towards them ... and robbed their teachings of all influence'.[12] Jonker Afrikaner grew increasingly weary of the missionaries' demands for what they called morally upright and chaste living. At the beginning of August 1844, without informing Hahn, Afrikaner wrote a letter to the Wesleyans in South Africa, asking them to send missionaries to /Ae// Gams. Within weeks, two Wesleyan missionaries arrived at his stronghold. Their arrival created open conflict with the Rhenish missioners, which prompted Jonker Afrikaner to intervene by declaring his preference for the newly arrived missionaries.

One interesting document on missionary history expresses in plain terms Jonker Afrikaner's reaction to the competition between the missionaries, and the confusion it gave rise to, as well as reiterating his demands to exert control over 'his missionaries'. He writes,

> I give this as proof that I, Jonker Afrikaner, Chief of the Afrikaner tribe and all belonging thereto, have invited the missionaries of the Wesleyan Missionary Society to become my missionaries because the missionaries of that society laboured with me previous to the London (Rhenish) [sic] Mission Society; and further the letter serves to show that I received the Rev. Mr. Kleinschmidt with the understanding that he belonged to the same [Wesleyan Missionary] Society as Messrs. Cook and Tindall. As soon as I discovered that this was not so and that there existed strife about my place, between the missionaries, I sent a letter to the Wesleyan missionaries to call them and now that they have come I receive them as missionaries of my place and for my people.[13]

Hence, the Rhenish missionaries were compelled to abandon their missionary work at /Ae//Gams in October 1844. Though they remained stationed at /Ae//Gams, Kleinschmidt joining Knudsen shifted his activities southward, whereas Hahn was granted permission by Jonker Afrikaner to preach the Gospel among the Hereros living in Otjikango and Otjimbingwe. The Hereros in this area were to grow in numbers after

1850, when many left Okahandja after Jonker Afrikaner's forays in this region. Many became absorbed into a non-tribal socio-political pattern of life, gravitating around European merchants and missionaries. These were the so-called '*ovatjimbos*' – 'people struggling for their livelihood, without cattle and without supportive kin network, victimised by their patron'.[14]

By allowing the missionaries to practise not far from his headquarters, Afrikaner hoped to continue controlling them; however, he forbade them to seek contact with any other Hereros. He was 'determined to prevent the establishment of any relations between European missionaries and Herero chiefs independent of his control'.[15]

The position of missionaries and European traders during the 1860s

Vedder's very influential description of this background has largely become accepted as the received version of subsequent events.[16] According to Vedder, Tjamuaha kept up an appearance of complicity in maintaining his alliance with Jonker Afrikaner after 1842; in reality, he wanted to strengthen his own position in order to enlarge his cattle herds, arm his people, as well as train them to fight, and wait for his opportunity to rally them into a war of independence against the oppressor Jonker Afrikaner. Vedder relates how Tjamuaha went to Kaokoland in 1860 as a freedom fighter to rally the routed groups of Hereros while Afrikaner was in Ovamboland[17] on a raiding expedition. Both Tjamuaha and Jonker Afrikaner died before any decisive confrontation could take place between them. After Tjamuaha's death, his second son, Maharero, succeeded him as chief of the Hereros in Okahandja. Vedder writes that he was elected paramount chieftain of all Hereros, in accordance with existing tribal laws. Vedder further relates how with great cunning Maharero later managed to sneak away from a position dangerously close to Jonker Afrikaner's son, Christian, in Okahandja, and take his cattle and armed troops to Otjimbingwe, which besides being the central outpost of the Rhenish Mission also served as headquarters for European merchants under the leadership of Charles John Andersson.

These Europeans now made common cause with Maharero and helped inflict a series of defeats on Afrikaner and his people. Out of gratitude for his assistance and as a token of acknowledgement for his skill as a general, the Hereros later elected Andersson as their 'king' with practically unrestricted endowments of power and authority. Andersson died shortly afterwards, however; and the missionaries managed to negotiate peace between Maharero and the Afrikaner group in 1870.

The whole point of Vedder's account was to present the various European groups in Otjimbingwe as unselfish allies in 'the Hereros' war of independence'. This line of argument is maintained right up to the period of German colonialism. In other words, Vedder casts the European merchants and missionaries attached to his own mission in roles of selfless collaborators devoted to the liberation of an African people so that peace could be sealed between the African tribes, and law and order prevail in the country.

However (again according to Vedder), this laudable aim was thwarted by Maherero's weakness and what Vedder termed his 'moral degradation', because of which, a new, dangerous tyrant was able to rise. His name was Hendrik Witbooi, and he became a threat to Europeans and Hereros alike. At this juncture there was no alternative left for the Europeans in Namibia but to turn to England and Germany for protection. They appealed to the colonial powers to create durable peace in Namibia.

There is a strongly apologetic tone to this part of Vedder's rendition of historical events – virtually amounting to a justification of the missionaries' and other Europeans' active participation in the struggles that took place in the 1860s. Only when no other solution presented itself, says Vedder, were they compelled to turn to the European colonial powers. And thus began German colonization, in 1884.

Against this background, it is crucial to reanalyse politics and the actual events taking place in Namibia from the late 1850s. What was emerging were a number of power constellations fighting for power and influence in the country as a whole.

1   What did the situation at the end of the 1850s and the beginning of the 1860s look like to Jonker Afrikaner, with his pretensions to power? Since the 1830s, Afrikaner had carved out a territorially unrestricted empire. He had made skilful use of his military superiority to build up a new economic and socio-political system which undermined the traditional family and tribal loyalties from within, by effectively assuming power over those populations he managed to overrun. In his political practice Jonker Afrikaner did not take traditional ethnic boundaries into consideration. His position of power was based on his military strength

alone, by means of which he strove to control all indigenous groups of this part of the country, and also the growing number of Europeans.

In this process the Hereros did not constitute as great a threat to Jonker Afrikaner's pretensions to power as did the Nama groups from whom he expected absolute obedience. The Namas' resistance was prompted not so much by the desire to return to their nomadic way of life as by an attempt to break Afrikaner's monopoly of trade and other profits made from the economic and socio-political system.

In her work on Jonker Afrikaner, Lau draws attention to the ambiguity of Afrikaner's relations to other indigenous groups, irrespective of tribal origin: 'Jonker Afrikaner possessed political insight won by a long history of struggle against the servile role imposed by Dutch and British colonialism [in the Cape Colony]'.[18] When he presently attempted to create a future for his people outside the immediate influence of the European colonial powers he himself behaved exactly as the Boers had done when they prompted him and his people to cross the Orange River: he 'imposed similar slavish roles on the natives beyond the colonial borders'. His motto was 'Africa to the Africans, but Namaland and Hereroland to us'.[19]

The steadily growing opposition to his colonial dominance weakened Afrikaner's position from the 1850s onwards. His supremacy was increasingly questioned. As we have mentioned, cattle thieving had become increasingly difficult and yet Afrikaner needed cattle to strengthen his position of power. This then became a decisive factor prompting him to carry out his last major expedition to the north, to Ovambo territory, in 1860.

2   What we have covered so far leads us to investigate the second powerful unit contending for power and influence during the political contest of this period. Despite their dependence on Jonker Afrikaner, the traditional Nama groups were far from weak.

The Namas can be divided into two categories: one group had been entirely subjugated by Jonker Afrikaner; the other refused to subordinate themselves to him. The members of the first group were among Jonker Afrikaner's troops and were entirely dependent on his protection to ensure their existence. The members of the second group, which steadily increased in force, built up their own economic and military strength. Not only did they themselves steal cattle, both from each other and from the Hereros, but they even pushed into the territory of the Ovambos in northern Namibia. To strengthen their position they stayed in close contact with the Rhenish mission stations where they were able to establish connections with European traders.

3   The abovementioned development compelled missionaries and the European traders who were attached to the mission stations to establish their own forces within the new, burgeoning power constellations. In the long run, the Europeans could not allow themselves to be controlled by Jonker Afrikaner. They withdrew from his immediate sphere of influence and formed their own bands and armies, often in close connection with Nama groups who were opposed to Afrikaner.

4   Yet another unit in this political power contest were the Herero people whose position had weakened after the peace of 1842 which placed large groups of Hereros under the vassalage of Jonker Afrikaner. Afrikaner seemed to make a point of systematically depriving the Hereros of their cattle herds – the very foundations of their existence. After 1850, many Hereros became *ovatjimbos*. Impoverished and rootless, they sought to carve out an existence for themselves outside of traditional Herero community. Many found refuge with Europeans who provided them with diverse forms of employment. Later, some became miners or were enlisted as soldiers in the steadily growing private armies owned by Europeans. Others at Okahandja tended Jonker Afrikaner's cattle, which he had in fact stolen from them or their kinsmen. Thus they became cattle herders tending cattle which had originally belonged to them.

Yet other groups of Hereros had fled with the remainder of their herds to Kaokoland. We may therefore be justified in claiming that by the late 1850s, the Hereros were weakened and hardly in a position to fight a war of independence against Jonker Afrikaner.

So the decisive political tensions which unleashed the struggles of the 1860s were not so much between the Afrikaner group and the Hereros, but between the Afrikaners and the Rhenish missionaries and European traders, with their increasing military resources.

Growing European influence

The most prominent figure among the Europeans was the Swede Charles John Andersson, a big game hunter and explorer. In 1850-1852, Andersson and Francis Galton had explored north-western Namibia up to the Kunene River and Lake Ngomi in present-day Angola. On returning, Andersson settled in Otjimbingwe, where he set himself up as a merchant in collaboration with the Rhenish Mission in 1860.[20] In that year he acquired the Walvis Bay Mining Company, a copper mine with administrative buildings and storage facilities attached to the Rhenish mission station. His trading activities were heavily dependent on the cattle herds of the Namas and the Hereros who lived within the interest area of Jonker Afrikaner. To protect his own cattle caravans, Andersson relied on his well-armed group of soldiers, many of whom were *ovatjimbos*.

Andersson's activities greatly disturbed Jonker Afrikaner, who claimed in vain that Otjimbingwe lay inside his territory, thus trying to prohibit Andersson from establishing himself there. When a severe cattle plague broke out in 1860, Afrikaner forbade any cattle caravans to use the roads he had built, allegedly in order to prevent the spread of the disease. At that time, Jonker Afrikaner was in the Ovambos' territory on his cattle-thieving expedition. The huge cattle herds he seized in this region soon fell victim to the plague.

Andersson ignored Afrikaner's prohibition and sent a caravan of 1400 head of cattle south to the Cape. The caravan was attacked by Afrikaner's allies, but Andersson's armed forces gained the upper hand and the caravan was permitted to continue on its way. This incident increased the tension between Andersson and the Oorlam-Namas. Andersson reinforced the military garrison at Otjimbingwe.

It was soon after this incident that Jonker Afrikaner and Tjamuaha died. Maharero succeeded his father as chief of the Hereros in Okahandja. Vedder's interpretation of this event, which was that Maharero was appointed paramount chieftain of all Hereros at this early stage, is erroneous, however.[21] Maharero and his group of Hereros saw Andersson as their only means of protection from the Afrikaner group which was now being led by Jonker Afrikaner's son, Christian. Maharero therefore moved with his people and the cattle (which they were tending for the new Oorlam-Nama leader, Christian Afrikaner, but which, it will be remembered, had been misappropriated from the Herero people by the Afrikaner group) to Otjimbingwe where Andersson was based. In response to this, and to the fact that during a skirmish Andersson had killed a relative of his, Christian Afrikaner gathered an army of about 500 men to attack Otjimbingwe on 15 June 1863. Maharero and his people did not take part in this battle during which Christian fell and his troops fled southward pursued by Andersson.

This was, however, no decisive defeat, as Christian Afrikaner's brother, Jan Jonker Afrikaner, took over the leadership of the Afrikaner group. In March 1864, Andersson's troops captured /Ae//Gams but the war raged on in the form of guerrilla attacks on Andersson's trading caravans.

This war changed the position for the Europeans in Otjimbingwe. For Andersson, it became vital to be able to mobilize a large enough number of troops to defeat Jan Jonker Afrikaner once and for all: and Maharero's Hereros who had just arrived in Otjimbingwe were potential recruits for a larger military force.

Maharero and his people did not rate highly in the opinion of either Andersson or the leader of the Rhenish Mission in Otjimbingwe. In May 1864, Missionary Hahn made the following notes in his diary: 'The Herero[s] can be kept in order only by fear.'[22] In fact, he, Hahn, was unable to find 'a single Herero worth trusting'. He therefore advised Andersson to 'have a small army, a few hundred men, quite dependent on you, who would keep them [the Hereros] in order and obedience'.[23]

These comments, together with other, similar, remarks, do not suggest any sympathy for the Hereros, and least of all do they imply any desire on the part of the Europeans to help the Hereros in a war of independence. The wars in which the Europeans became involved were in fact waged only to safeguard their own private interests. For Andersson, it was a matter of protecting his trading business; the interests of the Rhenish Mission lay in routing the Oorlam-Namas led by the Afrikaner family, besides wanting to extend its influence over the Hereros and break the deadlock that missionary work among this people had reached.[24]

Hahn's great plan for how missionary work among the Hereros could be carried out first appeared to him in 1863 during home leave in his mother country. He hoped to be able to build up a missionary colony with an agricultural school and trading activities attached to it, which would support the actual missionary work. A vital precondition for the fruition of such a project was that the Afrikaner group's influence over the Herero people be broken. Hahn counted on the support of Andersson in concretizing these plans. In his correspondence to the latter,[25] he assured Andersson of the full support of the missionaries in the war waged against Jan Jonker Afrikaner.

It was now imperative for Andersson to forge an alliance between himself and Maharero's people to ensure himself of reinforcements in the event of war. Andersson managed to persuade the Hereros to elect Maharero as their paramount chieftain. For him, it was vital to bring about a 'collective symbol', which would serve the twofold aim of uniting all the Herero groups under one leader, and of relying on them to follow directives. In order to further strengthen his position among the Hereros, Andersson managed, with the help of Hahn, to induce chieftains and council members to elect him, Andersson himself, as the 'regent and supreme commander' of the Hereros, for life or for 'as long as he himself wished to assume this office'.[26] We may therefore say that a Swede assumed the denomination of 'king' – 'King Andersson', lord over all the Hereros, with Maharero as his vassal. This fact alone would suffice to show how untenable were Vedder's, and other historians', speculations about an Otjimbingwe-based European alliance with the Hereros who were engaged in a war of independence of their own.

As the leader of an army, the bulk of which consisted of well-paid, loyal mercenaries, Andersson tried as soon as the opportunity arose to wage a decisive battle against Afrikaner. However, he was wounded in battle, and now became increasingly pessimistic about the future, especially in view of the cost involved in maintaining an army and in continuous fighting. During the latter part of 1864 he sold his Otjimbingwe properties to the Rhenish Mission and set off for what was to be his last hunting and exploration journey. Andersson died in present-day Angola on the border with Ovamboland in 1867.

The war went on without him, kept alive by the determination of the Rhenish missionaries along with the leadership of Maharero. In the long run it became a war of attrition for all parties involved, never reaching a conclusion. In mid-1870, peace negotiations were initiated between Jan Jonker Afrikaner and Maharero, with Missionary Hahn acting as mediator. The most difficult point in these negotiations concerned the dominion of /Ae//Gams, a place of great religious significance for the Hereros, and a spot of decisive strategic importance for the Afrikaner family. A compromise was finally reached, giving the Afrikaners a 'right of disposal' provided they recognized the Hereros' *de facto* right of ownership. Peace was thus made on 23 September 1870 in Okahandja, to which Maharero had returned in 1868.

The main consequence of this war was a consolidation of European influence and power which undermined the Afrikaner family's position of dominance for good. Despite the Afrikaners' defeat, merchants and missionaries alike were acutely aware of their own precarious position as a minority. In the long run they would need both the protection and the support of an outside European power to guarantee their continued stay in the country. This was further demonstrated by an incident which occurred in 1867, which prompted all the Europeans to gather and jointly demand protection from the British colonial authorities in the Cape.

We will return to this incident in the following chapter. However, it is important to realize that the entire sequence of events of the 1860s related above indirectly paved the way for German colonization. The Europeans, already firmly established in Namibia, had strengthened their hold on southern and central Namibia and now needed the protection of an outside colonial power to further their interests.

Notes

1 Lau, B. 1987, 78 and 87 ff.
2 Lau, B. 1984a, 95 and 102.
3 Ibid., 78-79.
4 Baumann, J. 1985.
5 The missionaries were in general not opposed to capital punishment; however, this kind of punishment was alien to the tradition and laws of both the Oorlam-Namas and the Namas. See Lau, B, 1987, 76 ff.
6 Lau, B, 1984a.
7 Goldblatt, I. 1971, 15.
8 Lau, B, op. cit. Annotations December 1942 - January 1943.
9 Ibid., 98.
10 Mossolow, N. (year of publication unknown), 136.
11 Goldblatt, I, op. cit., 15-17.
12 Lau, B, op. cit., 85; see also Moritz, E. 1916.
13 Goldblatt, I, op. cit., 15-17.
14 Lau, B. 1987, 109.
15 Ibid., 110.
16 Vedder, H. 1966; see also ibid.
17 Lau, B, op. cit., 121.
18 The home of the Ovambo people, which is today subdivided into Omusati, Oshana, Ohanguena, and Oshikoto, has been known under different names, such as 'Amboland', 'Ovamboland', and 'Ovambo'. Since it was referred to as 'Ovamboland' during most of the period under discussion, it will be referred to as 'Ovamboland' throughout. See *Map* on p 69.
19 Lau, B, op. cit., 121.
20 Ibid.
21 Andersson, CJ. 1989.
22 Vedder, H. 1929, 8.
23 Andersson, CJ, op. cit., 199.
24 Ibid.
25 The first group of Hereros, a group of eight, were baptized as late as 1859.
26 Andersson, CJ, op. cit., 200.
27 Goldblatt, I, op. cit., 33; also, Metzkes, J. 1959.

5 The Rhenish Mission and demands for overseas protection

Requests for British protection

One of Andersson's closest collaborators, an Englishman from the Cape Colony, was killed in 1867 when a group of Oorlam-Namas led by Jan Jonker Afrikaner ambushed a trading caravan on its way to Walvis Bay. This was reported to the authorities in Cape Town as 'murder' of a British citizen. Through its representative at Cape Town, the Rhenish Mission requested British protection for all Europeans living in Namibia.

Up to this point the British had shown no interest whatever in granting protection to Europeans – British or other – living in Namibia. Through its colonial administration in Cape Town, England had shown a measure of interest in Namibia by using Walvis Bay as anchorage for its trading ships. However, the Brits did not respond to the solicitations for protection in 1867, even though a British citizen had been killed.

The restlessness among the Europeans living in Namibia grew in May 1868 when Hahn received a letter from Jan Jonker Afrikaner, in which the latter urged all Europeans to leave the country as soon as possible, as he intended to kill Maharero and his people and level all the Herero settlements to the ground. In June 1868, eighty-seven European missionaries and traders gathered in Otjimbingwe. They took a decision to send a general appeal to the British governor in Cape Town, Sir Philip Woodhouse, demanding British protection. Even Maharero and his members of council (who were about to move back to Okahandja) were among the signatories. Not only did the appeal ask for help, but it also demanded, in Vedder's words, 'how a stop could be put to these outrages'.[1]

Cape Town's reaction was nothing more than a halfhearted attempt at a power demonstration by a British warship which dropped anchor at Walvis Bay, raised the Union Jack, and sent out a dispatch of men who were to seize 'the murderers'. After that, 'the commander said a few plain words to the effect that everyone who laid hands on the life and property of Europeans would be hanged in the future'.[2] Then the British warship returned to Cape Town.

At about the same time, however, the Board of the Rhenish Mission in Germany turned to the Prussian government with a request for protection of German missionaries based in Namibia. The Mission's inspector Friedrich Fabri managed to obtain an audience with William I, but was disappointed at the outcome. The Prussian king merely expressed his interest in the matter in fairly general terms.

Fabri had hoped at least to inspire the idea of a German annexation of Namibia as a colony.[3] However, in those days in Berlin, other more pressing matters took priority. No-one was particularly keen on becoming involved in some conflict-ridden African territory. Fabri was advised to turn to the British authorities in London. He duly got in touch with the Minister of Foreign Affairs in London, and used the opportunity to express his disappointment in the unsuccessful British mission to Walvis Bay in June 1868. He added that 'the dispatch of the warship had only made the position of the Europeans more precarious, because any farther action had not followed the demonstration'.[4]

Failing to receive an answer from London, Fabri again turned to the Prussian government, requesting that the government should 'most graciously communicate the accompanying representation and request for intervention and protection of the lives and property of the German missionaries in Namaland and Hereroland to the Foreign Office in London, and give it wholehearted support'.[5]

What followed was a tossing back and forth of applications demanding protection, in a circuit involving Berlin, London, and Cape Town. Still, the demands did not yield immediate results. The Europeans based in Namibia did, however, manage to attract a certain degree of attention from Berlin and London. The two centres became increasingly aware of the state of affairs in this part of Africa which had until then failed to attract their interest. It was, however, Cape Town, with its British colonial administration and its status as the centre for all trade and import facilities, and not Berlin or London, which still acted as the key locality for all foreign contacts in southern and central Namibia.

In 1872, two years after the peace treaty between Afrikaner and Maharero, the Herero chieftain sent a message from Okahandja to the British governor of Cape Town, Sir Henry Berkley, demanding protection against Jan Jonker Afrikaner. Interestingly enough, Jan Jonker Afrikaner soon afterwards turned to the same governor, demanding protection for himself against the Hereros. None of these attempts to make contact produced any immediate results; the English had no interest in entering Namibia with armed forces.

One reason for the Hereros and the Oorlam-Namas to take up contact with the British administration at the Cape was that they were becoming increasingly worried about the Boer immigrations from the Cape Colony, some of which had reached as far as the Kunene River in Ovamboland. A statement made by Maharero, quoted at length by Pool, suggests that Maharero feared that 'the admission of any other nation, more especially for [sic] one who we have been led to believe has always looked upon the black tribes with scorn and indignation and who both recognised and practised Slavery [would cause a] fearful and sanguinary War throughout the country'.[6] What worried Maharero most, however, was that the Boers, who also owned cattle, would intrude upon his own people's grazing.

Amongst the British from Cape Town operative in Namibia in those days was an explorer and merchant by the name of William Coates Palgrave. This man appeared to Maharero as a person who could provide the help and support he needed to deal with the two major problems afflicting him: Jan Jonker Afrikaner, and the threat of increasing immigration of Boers. In a letter addressed in 1876 to the British governor of Cape Town, Maharero demanded that Palgrave be recognized as a leader in the land of the Hereros. Maharero suggested that Palgrave be given supreme authority on all issues concerning the non-Hereros living in the area, so that he could curtail both the Oorlam-Namas' and the Boers' potential influence.

The Herero chief wrote, 'We want to live at peace with each other, and with our neighbours, and we want to have our country kept for us.'[7] Maharero offered to cover all of Palgrave's costs with cattle; he also promised a plot of land as remuneration for Palgrave's favour – land which did not belong to him, however, but to the Ovambo people in the north.

As far as Palgrave was concerned, it served his interests as a merchant to maintain good relations with Maharero – in fact, he even expected this would give his business activities a boost. He arranged, among other things, for an invitation to be issued by the governor, requesting the company of Maharero's sons, William and Samuel, as his guests in Cape Town for four months at the beginning of 1879.

In 1878, England annexed Walvis Bay and environs. This worried the Rhenish missionaries who saw the step as a threat to the Mission's own trade interests. The Rhenish Mission sensed that there was a connection between the annexation and Palgrave's increasing influence among the Hereros. In a letter dated 12 November 1879 and addressed to the German consul in Cape Town, Missionary Carl Gotthilf Büttner described the effect of the annexation on the Mission's trading activities.[8] The traders attached to the Mission owned warehouses in Walvis Bay for storing ivory and ostrich feathers used as payment for their goods. They, too, feared that the annexation might harm their interests.

In her work *Namibia in Jonker Afrikaner's Time*, Lau informs us of the Rhenish Mission's attempts to 'establish a formal trade connection between Namaland and Germany in 1845 to improve prices and bypass profit-hungry Cape traders'.[9] The importance of ostrich feathers and ivory as trade commodities had increased ever since Jonker Afrikaner's death, when hunting ceased to be monopolized by the Namas and the Oorlam-Namas. In a report to the Board of the Mission in Germany in May 1868, Hahn observed how these goods yielded 'a good profit ... for the Mission Society'.[10] He mentioned that Walvis Bay's annexation by the Cape Colony inhibited the Germans from putting the area to fruitful use for their own purposes. However, Büttner related that yet more Englishmen had begun to conduct operations in the inner regions of the country via Walvis Bay, which involved the shooting of so many elephants and ostriches that the traders now had to use *cattle* as currency for their goods instead. The cattle could not be shipped via Walvis Bay but had to be driven in caravans all the way to the Cape Colony, at great expense to the owners. Büttner further observed that Palgrave was beginning to behave like some kind of governor in all matters pertaining to the Europeans in the country, and that more often than not he acted on behalf of British interests. He, Büttner, therefore urged the German consul to use the appropriate channels and contacts in Berlin to persuade Germany to seal an agreement with the country's 'uncivilized peoples' in support of German interests. Finally, he suggested that the Germans in Namibia should be granted juridical supremacy in the country, something which could be done only if Germany claimed this part of Africa as its colonial area of interest.[11]

Büttner's letter to the German consul was followed by a letter from Friedrich Fabri, dated 30 April 1880, which he sent to the vice-chancellor in Berlin,[12] and in which he reminded Berlin of the Mission's earlier solicitations of help from Germany. He pointed out that it had also sought the assistance of the British governor to safeguard German interests. In so doing, he had not asked for a British annexation of Namibia, but had merely demanded protection. In response, Fabri received a telegram from the German consul in Cape Town requesting him to forward a request to the government in Berlin for immediate German intervention on behalf of German interests. If it was true that, as Fabri had warned, the government in London planned to give up Namibia, Berlin should immediately send word to London for extended British protection. Should London decide to reject such a request, then Germany should at least consider measures to ensure the safety of its own citizens living in Namibia. Bismarck's own commentary in response to Fabri's letter, dated 13 May 1880, stated that he did not have much confidence in Mr Fabri and his plans,[13] and furthermore that he, Bismarck, did not intend to give serious consideration to Fabri's proposal and plans.

It was not long before Fabri once again turned to the German authorities, in a letter dated 3 June 1880.[14] In this missive he reported that Palgrave had entered into treaties with local chieftains, which signified the recognition of British supremacy among the chieftains concerned. According to Fabri, the missionaries were irresolute about what course to take in the face of this and were asking their Board in Wuppertal-Barmen for advice and instructions. They had by now come to cultivate the notion that they could hardly expect any protection from their own national government. They had consequently decided that British protection was better than none at all, and had for this reason pledged their support to Palgrave, even to the extent of acting as interpreters during his negotiations with the local chieftains.

Ensuing events, however, Fabri continued, pointed to a certain lack of substance in the British treaties' guaranties of peace, security and protection. England, it seemed, was too weak to be able to inspire any respect, added to which, general opinion among missionaries and the local chieftains led them to sense irresolution within British official circles concerning continued British intervention in this part of Africa. For this reason the missionaries demanded, through the agency of Fabri, that German intervention be effectuated in order to prevent a new 'racial war' from breaking out between the Herero people and the Oorlam-Namas. In an insertion, Fabri proposed that Germany through its diplomatic connections could inform the British authorities of the gravity of the situation. He added that it would do no harm for a German warship to hoist the German flag outside Walvis Bay. The commander of this ship should be authorized to negotiate with the German missionaries about the situation in the country and investigate the possibilities of establishing a German harbour along the coast north of Walvis Bay. Fabri was aware, he added, of official Germany's lukewarm interest in colonies during this period. He was therefore appealing to the government's national responsibility to warrant the protection of German citizens in a danger spot of the world. He mixed in these patriotic motives with overt references to trade interests. Fabri concluded by pointing out how mission and trade worked together in this area towards strengthening the foundations of Christian Western civilization.

In Namibia in the meantime, confusion grew after 1870 as fighting continued between the Hereros and Jonker Afrikaner. In search of grazing, the Hereros moved south once again. And soon their cattle was seen grazing near Windhoek, which, according to the peace treaty, was the principal locality of Jan Jonker Afrikaner. Renewed hostilities broke out between the Hereros and Afrikaner. Many cattle were slaughtered, including animals from Maharero's herd of sacred oxen, which were only supposed to be slaughtered on the occasion of a chieftain's death. The first act of this drama ended with the Oorlam-Namas' flight to Jan Jonker Afrikaner, whilst the Hereros fled to Maharero in Okahandja, on 23 August 1880.

When Maharero heard what had happened to the sacred oxen he ordered that all Namas and Oorlam-Namas found within Herero territory be killed in retribution. This led to bloodshed at Okahandja on the night of 23 and 24 August, exactly 30 years after Jonker Afrikaner's massacre of Kahitjene's people in 1850, and on the very same site. In response to the 1880 incident in Okahandja the Namas, Oorlam-Namas and Basters formed a united front against the Herero people.

Jan Jonker Afrikaner was yet again to play a crucial part here. In September, October and December of 1880, he carried out several swift attacks on the Hereros' cattle herds. Maharero's eldest son, William, fell in battle during one of these – a hard blow for the ageing Maharero.

In his struggle against this united front, Maharero increasingly sought support from the Rhenish Mission, thereby indirectly paving the way for German colonialism. Pool comments, 'Maharero being completely ignorant of the workings of international politics, did not realise that his country was on the verge of a German onslaught.'[15]

Meanwhile, Palgrave's influence had weakened substantially as a result of the renewed fighting. Soon after the events of August 1880, he was summoned back to Cape Town 'in pursuance of the policy of the Government approved by Parliament that no further steps should be taken in the direction of the annexation'.[16] There was no desire to enter 'intertribal disputes which have resulted in bloodshed and war'.[17]

To summarize, European interests represented by traders and the Rhenish missionaries in a fundamental way led to the ensuing development leading up to German colonialism. The Rhenish Mission which at first had participated in presenting a request for British protection from Cape Town, was not keen on this alternative, as British influence via Cape Town would be experienced as a possible threat to the Mission's own trade interests, especially since the British had incorporated Walvis Bay as a part of their colony in the Cape. Through the agency of the Missionary Board in Germany, and especially through the Mission's inspector Friedrich Fabri with his contacts in colonial circles, the missionaries in Namibia attempted once again to arouse interest in German colonial intervention in Namibia.

The European interests in Namibia which had gradually established themselves during the time of Jonker Afrikaner in the early 1860s were by now divided: merchants with a British background sought contact with the British colonial administration of the Cape Colony, while the German missionaries wanted German colonialism. The colonial political power games in Europe and in other parts of southern Africa finally contributed to turning Namibia into a German colony in 1884. Before we look at this development, however, we must briefly examine the results of the Rhenish Mission's activities in southern and central Namibia, and the first contacts made between the Ovambo people and European mission.

Successes of the Rhenish Mission in Namibia – and the beginnings of Finnish missionary work among the Ovambos

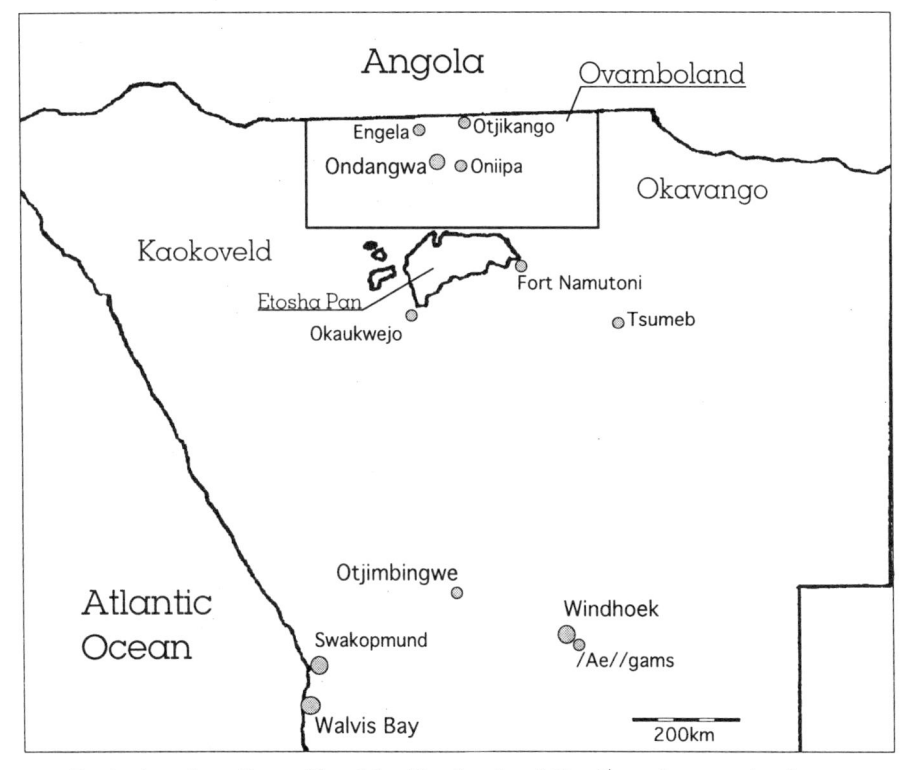

Central and northern Namibia. The lands of the Ovambo peoples lay north of the great white pan of Etosha. The Germans built Fort Namutoni east of the pan as their initial attempt to establish control over the north of the country.

When the first Rhenish missionaries arrived in Namibia, they entered what might be termed prepared grounds, coming as they did in response to the Oorlam-Namas' invitation. The first missionaries to have paved the way for missionary activity in Namibia were either from the London Missionary Society, or South African Methodists. These two Missions left Namibia at the onset of the 1850s, however, thus transferring their responsibilities to the Rhenish Mission. By the mid-1840s, this Mission had established several mission stations attached to a number of Oorlam-Nama and Nama groups.

We have already seen to what extent the freedom of the Rhenish Mission was restricted. To the Oorlam-Namas, it was a matter of principle that all European activities in southern and central Namibia should be kept under their control, and the Rhenish Mission was no exception. This gave rise to a series of conflicts. Enforced control in turn prompted the Mission to align itself all the more with European traders, who in turn wanted to break the Oorlam-Namas' monopoly of, or attempts to monopolize, domestic commerce. The Rhenish Mission, through its alliance with the European traders, contributed to the military effort of local Europeans against the Afrikaner group after 1862, with Charles John Andersson as the leading figure.

One positive outcome for the Mission of its contact with the Oorlam-Namas was the fact that it could quickly establish itself in the southern and central parts of the country. In several places the Oorlam-Namas had established a number of Christian parishes long before the arrival of the missionaries, some of which counted more than a hundred members. In spite of restricted freedom, therefore, the contact with the Oorlam-Namas also introduced many favourable conditions for increasing missionary activity.

Conditions for missionary work among the Hereros were very different, however. It will be recalled that Missionary Hahn, following the peace of 1842, asked for Jonker Afrikaner's help to expand the Mission to the Herero people, and was refused. Jonker Afrikaner was not interested in permitting European activity of any kind among the Hereros because it might challenge his control of the Hereros. He was unable to accept the prospect of European mission which might lead to increased European settlement in the traditional tribal area of the Hereros, and hence outside of his control. When Chief Kahitjene, in spite of Afrikaner's prohibition, granted the Rhenish Mission permission to establish a mission station at Okahandja, the Oorlam-Nama leader sent a punitive expedition, in 1850, against that Herero chief and his people.

The Rhenish Mission was, however, granted permission to work among Hereros who were dispossessed of their land, and uprooted from their tribal connections. Thus Otjimbingwe became the centre of missionary work among the Herero people. After 1860, Otjimbingwe also became the centre for Charles John Andersson's business activities.

The Rhenish Mission's attempts to evangelize among detribalized Hereros can hardly be called successful. By 1859, only eight Hereros had been baptized, and a tenacious resistance to the Christian faith prevailed. These discouraging results prompted Hahn, the leader of this working unit based among the Hereros, to investigate the possibilities of finding another field for his missionary work. He was interested in possibly beginning missionary work in northern Namibia among the Ovambo people. Even here Jonker Afrikaner attempted to prevent the Rhenish Mission's plans to expand its field of endeavour.[18] Much to the Oorlam-Nama leader's chagrin, however, Hahn set off to lead an expedition of inquiry to southern Ovamboland in 1857.

One reason for Jonker Afrikaner's reaction was that he had just at this time begun to negotiate a treaty with the Ovambo chieftain in Ondangwa, Chief Shikenga. Jonker Afrikaner would supply the chieftain with horses, weapons and ammunition in exchange for cattle and ivory which Afrikaner needed for his trade activities with Cape Town. Now that he hoped to expand his own area of interest into Ovamboland, Afrikaner did not need any Europeans around to interfere.[19]

Despite Afrikaner's resistance, however, Hahn set off to Ondangwa together with a missionary colleague. They arrived on 24 July 1857 but shortly after their arrival became involved in a heavy conflict with the local chieftain over etiquette and were forced to return empty-handed, accompanied by an armed escort, all the way back to Otjimbingwe.

Ovamboland was until 1851 largely unknown to the outside world. The entire area was an outpost of a Portuguese colonial area with its centre in Luanda, in present-day Angola. Contact between the Ovambo people and the Portuguese on the Atlantic coast was at best sporadic. The Ovambo chieftains obtained products such as weapons and ammunition from the Portuguese in exchange for slaves and ivory.

The first European contact with central Ovamboland was established in 1851 by the explorers Galton and Andersson who sought out the chieftain in Ondangwa to ask for free passage through the country as far up as the Kunene River. Their visit though brief was significant in establishing the Ovambos' future relations with southern and central Namibia. It was Andersson who in 1857 encouraged Hahn to undertake his expedition of inquiry when the latter was based in. It is said that

Andersson's suggestion for this journey of exploration was 'hailed enthusiastically'.[20] The missionaries in Otjimbingwe were by this time discouraged by the difficulties involved with missionary work among the Hereros. In fact, minutes taken at a missionary conference during which Hahn's journey to the Ovambos was discussed express the general opinion that 'the Mission among the Herero[s] has come to an end, and it cannot form a foundation for any efforts amongst the tribes who live in the north'.[21]

It was after Hahn's fruitless trip to the Ovambos that plans for trade mission, agricultural education and training in handicrafts began to be made. The Mission was later to introduce agricultural and crafts training as part of its missionary work among the Hereros. Although this form of 'protomission' began in 1863, it hardly amounted to anything much until after 1870, when peace was sealed between the Hereros and the Afrikaner group under Jan Jonker Afrikaner. Maharero had by then settled back in Okahandja. With him as the 'paramount chieftain' based at Okahandja, the Rhenish Mission was able to finally build its principal station for work among the Hereros at the heart of the Herero people's traditional tribal area.

An important consequence of the Rhenish Mission's initial contacts with the Ovambo people – despite Hahn's failure – was that it opened the way for the Finnish Missionary Society to establish itself among the Ovambos from 1870 onwards. The Finnish Missionary Society was founded in 1859 but was as yet without any mission field of its own. Instead, it sent its missionaries to assist other evangelical Missions, including the Rhenish Mission in South Africa.

After Hahn's failed attempts to gain a foothold for his mission among the Ovambos, he still maintained connections with one of Shikenga's rivals. The latter was later to visit the Rhenish Mission in Otjimbingwe and even sent his son to the Mission for his formal education.[22] This contact paved the way for a renewed attempt to obtain permission from the Mission's headquarters in Germany to conduct missionary work in Ovamboland – however, Wuppertal-Barmen did not consider their staff facilities or their resources sufficient to expand their missionary operations. But the Rhenish Mission did contact the Finnish Missionary Society, suggesting that it seize this opportunity to gain its own missionary territory while maintaining close contacts with, as well as benefiting from a certain degree of support from, the Rhenish Mission.

The Finnish Missionary thus began its activities in Ovamboland in 1870. Thirteen years were to pass before this Mission could conduct its first baptism of six people, in 1883.

Notes

1 Vedder, H. 1966, 357; also, Metzkes, J. 1959, 60.
2 Vedder, H, op. cit., 358.
3 Metzkes, J, op. cit., 60.
4 Vedder, H, op. cit., 358.
5 Ibid.
6 Pool, G. 1991, 45.
7 Ibid.
8 Büttner, CG. 1885, 15.
9 Lau, B. 1987, 87.
10 Lau, B. 1984a.
11 'Reichskolonialamt, Akten betr. des Hererolandes', vol. I, file No. 2098, 24 ff; National Archives, Windhoek.
12 Ibid.
13 Ibid.
14 Ibid.
15 Pool, G, op. cit., 56.
16 Ibid.
17 Ibid.
18 Lau, B. 1987, 136-137.
19 Williams, F-N. 1991, 143.
20 Lau, B. 1984a, entry of 10 March 1856; see also Vedder, H, op. cit., 307-308.
21 Williams, F-N, op. cit., 119.
22 Ibid., 144.

PART II: Church and Mission under German Colonial Domination, 1885-1915

The Rhenish Mission's national connection with the German empire, which was founded in 1871, became a driving force which contributed to the colonization of Namibia. Many German citizens were based in Namibia in the service of the German Mission. So when Germany began to talk expansionism in 1871 it was natural that these citizens be viewed as representatives of German nationalism. The Rhenish Mission had contributed to stimulating German interest, both in Namibia and Germany, in this part of Africa. Businesses and factories in Germany began clamouring for Namibia's natural resources and minerals, rumours of which had filtered through to them via the missionaries' accounts. They claimed that here was a territory which would welcome German emigrants as colonizers. The presence inside Namibia of missionaries belonging to the mother country, who, what is more, possessed first-hand knowledge of local geography, would greatly facilitate German annexation.

The Rhenish Mission was therefore seen as an important asset for German colonial projects in this part of Africa. All the necessary conditions for a profitable colonial enterprise had been met.

Germany's first steps towards colonizing the country were in the form of 'indirect imperialism'. This meant transferring the responsibility of colonizing to German trade companies through granting them the protection of the German government.

The relationship between the Rhenish Mission and the German colonizers went through a series of different stages:

1   First, the Mission helped seal treaties between African leaders and German trade companies acting 'in the service of the emperor'. During this stage, the Mission gained an increasing amount of influence.

2   From the 1890s, when German central government authorities were obliged to take over increasing responsibility of colonial administration, the colonial authorities, both locally and in Berlin, demanded that missionaries when conducting their duties among the indigenous population should also contribute to the betterment of German colonial interests. This led to increasing opposition from the missionaries. They did, however, take care to avoid head-on conflict in this issue. As Germans, they felt they had the right to openly criticize colonial measures which could potentially harm the local population. Yet at the same time they were anxious not to jeopardize their own good relations with the authorities, and never allowed themselves to forget their own national affiliation. On the whole, the African population were inclined to feel that 'their' missionaries were on their side, and this in turn stimulated the growth of parishes.

3   Later, the war of 1904-1907 caused the existing tension between the Mission and the colonial authorities to increase in intensity. The Mission was vividly opposed both to the ruthless warfare conducted against the so-called 'rebellious tribes', and to the severe treatment of the vanquished. After the war, the Mission could, however, do nothing to prevent the colonizers' policy of breaking down, once and for all, any form of tribal community. From now on, the duties of the Mission were further curtailed by the colonial racialist politics which cut off the missionaries from any normal daily contacts with the indigenous population. The missionaries now appeared increasingly in the light of defenders of African interests.

In the parishes, tribal community was to some extent preserved, along with the tribal language and the chance for all to exercise their own tribal *influence through active participation in parish management affairs. This provided a guarantee of sorts, which ensured the preservation of a sense of community in the face of the colonial power's systematic attempts to eradicate the very notion of such a community.*

4 *German South West Africa as a colony, established for the benefit of German economic and political interests, never, administratively speaking, reached northern Namibia which was inhabited by the Ovambo and Kavango people. The influence of the German administration was basically limited to the so-called 'police zone' in the southern and central parts of the country. Here, German police were in charge, defending the interests of German colonizers. In principle this meant that the African population were bereft of their legal rights.*

In the north, the Finnish Missionary Society carried out its own work in direct contact with the African population, without much disturbance and without having to take heed of any officially enforced racialist policy. The foundations were thus laid during the German colonial period for a close and trustful co-operation between the Finnish Mission and the indigenous peoples of the north. This in turn was to lead to the foundation of a popular Folkchurch in this part of Namibia – a fact which largely contributed to nurturing the close co-operation between the independence movement and the Church throughout the country during the last stages of the struggle for Namibia's independence in 1990.

6 The Rhenish Mission and German colonialism, 1884-1904

German colonial policy and the Berlin Congress, 1884-1885

In his work, *Det Tyska Kejsarriket 1871-1918*,[1] the historian Hans Ulrich Wehler lists a number of motives underlying German colonial policy.

The duration of Germany's overseas colonial conquests was no longer than two years: from 1884 to 1886. Before this, there had been no official interest on the part of the German government to found any overseas colonies of its own.

According to Wehler, there were a number of internal political motives which prompted Germany, then under Chancellor Otto von Bismarck, to engage itself in the European race for colonies on other continents. Following the victory over France in 1871, the foundation of the German empire gave rise to a strong German national sentiment. With Austria and France defeated, Bismarck realized his plans for a unified German empire and was now free to conduct his own brand of politics within this framework.

Wehler describes Bismarck as extremely conservative in his outlook, suspicious of any contemporary trends which might threaten the type of feudalism he envisaged as the fundamental pillar of a powerful German empire. The entire social fabric was hierarchically determined, with the emperor as the empire's foremost representative, and a willing and obedient lower class providing the broad base of the society. The middle class consisted of a conservative group of landowners and bureaucrats, most of whom belonged to the traditional nobility or had recently been endowed with nobility as a token of imperial recognition. In addition to this, there was the military class which grew in importance as defenders of the imperial state. Anything which could disturb this well-established scheme of things was experienced as a threat.

At the same time, Bismarck could not overlook the fact that times, in the world as well as in German society, were changing. Growing industrialization contributed to create new living conditions for the German people. The old agrarian society gradually gave way to new classes of industrial leaders and labourers. Commerce and industry demanded not only a greater part in politics but also increased freedom to develop in response to increasing competition from within and outside Germany. The country was trapped inside a narrow frame of a feudalistic social organization, which was limiting industrial development. The steady growth of the working classes meant that an increasingly large percentage of the population migrated to the city, uprooted from their traditional agrarian way of life.

This social phenomenon, of people forced to live in an increasingly crowded urban environment where individual workers were exploited by their employers, gave rise to new and increasingly complex social problems. The labouring masses represented a fertile breeding ground for the seeds of socialism which spread through the political ideology of Marx and Engels, demanding social equality and justice for society in general, and the proletarian working class in particular.

In the eyes of Bismarck, socialism was more of a threatening spectre. Through a repressive legislation he tried to limit the extent to which it might influence German politics. However, since even he realized that times were changing, he granted liberal concessions to industrialists and businessmen, to avoid having to grant them direct access to any position which would bring along any degree of self-determination. To appease the working classes, Bismarck brought about legislation for a social programme which was fairly progressive for its times. This was in order to both meet the living needs of this social group, and also prevent socialism from gaining a foothold and threatening political power.

Germany's economy, like that of the rest of Europe between 1870 and the 1880s, went through continuous and severe fluctuations between prosperity and depression. In conservative circles there was fear that Europe might again be plunged into revolution, as happened in the 1840s, and this was indeed a threat if the increasing discontent of the poor could not be soothed – among other things, through measures involving foreign policy. Bismarck was a master at deferring domestic problems by redirecting attention to purported foreign political danger zones. To instil in the people the feeling that the entire nation is in danger is usually an effective means of bridging internal antagonism, and of kindling a sentiment of national community.

Germany was hit by a recession in 1882-1884, and it was in 1882 that the Deutscher Kolonialverein[2] was founded and placed under the leadership of Fürst Hermann zu Hohenlohe-Langenburg. The latter was of the opinion that the procurement of colonies could act as a safety valve for domestic policy's 'overheated steam boiler'.[3]

German colonialism on other continents would stimulate patriotism and national unity, as well as divert attention from domestic problems. This was extremely important, since parliamentary elections were coming up in 1884. Bismarck seemed in agreement with this view. In 1884-1886, Germany extended its colonial empire by colonies in Togo, Cameroon, German South West Africa and German East Africa on the African continent, as well as additional possessions held in the Pacific. The method applied was of the kind known as 'informal imperialism', which meant that private companies would receive an imperial warrant to annex colonies in the name of the German emperor. These individual companies, however, were left to their own devices, that is, without any intervention from the government, to manage all affairs pertaining to administration, defence, and development of these colonies. This soon proved too difficult for them.

This fact, along with what general opinion deemed to be the necessity for Germany to start asserting its position in the international race for colonies, soon drove Bismarck to follow a plan of action which moved increasingly along the lines of direct, formal imperialism. National colonies were now placed under the charge of the central government in Berlin through the formal establishment of a colonial division in the Foreign Office.

This background provides us with the historical reasons for Bismarck to convene an international colonial congress held in Berlin in 1884-1885. He wished to distract from any criticism levelled at his domestic policy by focusing on foreign politics. Perhaps he even hoped, by so doing, to tone down the demands of certain financial groups for greater influence in domestic policy by meeting their increasing demands to establish a German colonial empire.

The Berlin Congress was of course chaired by Bismarck himself. In all, 14 European nations attended, and the USA acted as an observer. As far as Africa was concerned, the congress only dealt with the coastline and the coastal areas along the major rivers, as important waterways. However, the underlying aim was to acquire land upstream in collusion with the participant nations. A General Act established the conditions under which African colonies could be procured. This Act of 26 February 1885 contained 38 articles serving as recommendations for all countries taking part in the congress. It was only through strict adherence to these articles that any individual act of colonization would receive international recognition.

Germany had strong motives for this colonial enterprise. One of these has already been discussed, namely that the attainment of colonies would allow for some of the pressure which was due to social problems at home, to be taken off the shoulders of the central government. The overriding aim was to distract from all the internal problems by redirecting the nation's attention to the colonies.

A factor of major importance – one which has borne dire consequences well into our own times – was the spread of a particular social brand of Darwinism which in turn led to pan-Germanism. The main tenets of this line of thought were that Darwin's theories of natural selection, which were generally applied to individuals, families, and species belonging to the plant and animal kingdoms, were now uncritically applied to the concepts of 'nation' and 'race'. It was suggested that through the said natural selection, the strongest nation, and the 'most highly developed' race, should by definition have priorities and rights over weaker nations and 'less developed' races. This theory came to be applied both to the working classes at home – the 'underdeveloped' categories within every individual nation – and to the colonial populations. The attempts of both workers and colonial subjects to fight for freedom and their rights were seen, by adherents to this theory, as unwarranted attempts at revolting against the 'strong', who by definition possessed all rights.

In the light of this *Weltanschauung* it was natural to view rapid economic growth, along with successful colonization, as evidence of the strength of a nation, and consequently of its people's special, natural qualification to subjugate and lead other peoples. From here, the step to racism in its purest sense was given. As Wehler puts it: 'Without a shade of doubt it [pan-Germanism] provided an essential ingredient among all those other poisonous elements which together composed that particular ideological blend that later gave rise to Nazism'.[4]

The key word of the Berlin Congress became 'effective occupation', which, in practice, meant 'the establishment of authority in the regions occupied ... on the coasts of the African continent, sufficient to protect existing rights, and ... freedom of trade and of transit under the conditions agreed upon'.[5] It has often been pointed out that the principal objective of the Berlin Congress was to reach a peaceful partitioning of Africa, thereby avoiding any future hostilities between the colonial powers.

The most interesting article in the concluding document of the congress is, for our purposes, Article 6, which concerned the work of the Mission and the question of religious freedom:

> Christian missionaries ... shall likewise be the object of special protection. Freedom of conscience and religious toleration are expressively guaranteed to the natives, no less than to subjects and to foreigners. The free and public exercise of all forms of Divine worship, and the right to build edifices for religious purposes, and to organise Missions belonging to all creeds, shall not be limited or fettered in any way whatsoever.[6]

It is interesting to note here that the term 'natives' was used conjointly with 'subjects'. Both the 'natives' and the 'subjects' were to be granted equal rights as far as religious freedom was concerned.

It is also interesting to note that though the congress delegates acted as the official representatives of their countries, they lacked any personal knowledge whatsoever of the colonial interest areas which were being discussed. For the partitioning of Africa, the points of the compass were used as geographical indications. Hence, negotiations were about what was to become German *South West* Africa, British and German *East* Africa, and so on. People and tribes were lumped together into European colonies delimited by straight frontier lines, literally drawn on the map with a ruler, with no consideration for any prevailing social conditions.

The beginnings of German colonialism in Namibia, 1882-1885

For reasons discussed, when German business enterprises began to manifest an interest in this country, Chancellor Von Bismarck was obliged to pay attention to their demands. He granted them permission to colonize in the name of the emperor, and under the protection of the German flag, provided they sent no bills to the German government!

In November 1882, a merchant by the name of Adolf Lüderitz demanded imperial permission to seal treaties, with the support of the German government, with local chieftains in an unspecified area south of Walvis Bay. To begin with, his plans aroused no enthusiasm in Berlin, which caused Lüderitz to protest through the German press. One of the articles, interestingly enough, was written by the inspector of the Rhenish Mission, Friedrich Fabri. Here was a Mission official writing in support of a colonizer!

Lüderitz was a tobacconist, and sought land on which to cultivate the leaf. This at least was the official reason he gave for his colonial interest. He did in fact have other reasons, too. A German harbour independent of Walvis Bay would, so he reasoned, open up ample opportunities for him to conduct a lucrative business of trading firearms with the indigenous populations, without any possible interference from the English. In his formal application to the German government he sought the protection of the German flag; he also drew attention to the fact that a German harbour might help stimulate the sale of German products. He further expressed his hopes of discovering rich mineral deposits.

As I have mentioned, to begin with, Lüderitz did not meet up with much encouragement from the German government. In carefully worded terms, he was requested to first investigate local conditions. This especially meant prying any possible reactions out of the English.[7] Bismarck did not wish to antagonize the English at the time. The free trade system of England also represented, according to him, Walvis Bay as a reasonable starting point for German business.

So Lüderitz sent an expedition of inquiry to Namibia. After casting anchor at Cape Town on 6 January 1883, the officer of his ship *Tilly*, Heinrich Vogelsang, sought out, among others, the German pastor of the town. The latter, who was familiar with the local conditions, advised Vogelsang to make his way to Angra Pequena, where he arrived at the beginning of April 1883.

At about the same time, Bismarck got in touch with the British authorities in London, in an attempt to effectuate a British agreement guaranteeing protection for German citizens living in Namibia. At this stage, Bismarck did not envisage any German colonization of what seemed a British area of interest. It must have come as a surprise to him when he was informed of Vogelsang's action in Angra Pequena. With the assistance of the Rhenish missionary Bam, who was based at Angra

Pequena, Vogelsang had sealed a treaty with the local chieftain, Josef Frederick in Bethanie, according to which, Lüderitz was assured of the protection of the entire bay, including some territory inland, in exchange for payment of £100 sterling and 200 rifles.[8] After the signing of this treaty, the German flag was hoisted as a token of German annexation and sovereignty. The entire operation occurred without any official authorization.

Bismarck's reaction to this rash action was: 'Sovereignty over this country now lies either with the Negro prince [sic] concerned, or with Lüderitz, but not with the Reich.'[9] Lüderitz was given a warning against such unauthorized interference, and was urged to avoid any action in the future which would endanger Anglo-German relations.

However, not long after this word of warning, a company in Cape Town voiced their protest, making reference to their own right of property over the area concerned, in accordance with a treaty of 1863, which had been sealed with the local chieftain's father. In response, Vogelsang quickly signed a new treaty with Josef Frederick (again with the help of Missionary Bam acting as interpreter and assistant), in which he procured a piece of land for the Lüderitz firm, situated on the 26th degree of latitude, and extending 150 kilometres inland.

This new treaty was sealed on 25 August 1883. In an insertion, Josef Frederick declared that the treaty sealed with the firm in Cape Town in 1863 only covered the right to exploit mineral resources in the area. The firm in question had not paid the sum agreed upon, which meant that the treaty could no longer be seen as a valid document. (Of course, neither Vogelsang nor Bam defined what they meant when using the measurement of 'miles'. In this part of the world distances were calculated using English miles!)

The German colonization of Namibia had thus begun – though as yet without any official recognition from the authorities in Berlin. German press reported enthusiastically about Lüderitz' colonization among the 'Hottentots'. And whatever his real feelings might have been on the issue, Bismarck did not overtly disapprove of this action. After all, German financial interests were at stake, a fact which he could not afford to overlook.

A series of diplomatic dealings between England and Germany were now initiated concerning the future of Namibia as a European colony. Bismarck, skilful political schemer that he was, managed to outmanoeuvre

England where Angra Pequena was concerned. And so it was that in March 1884 – exactly a year before the signing of the Berlin Congress – Lüderitz received an official exhortation from the German government, urging him to ensure German ownership of the entire Namibian coastline up to the Portuguese territory of Angola. Bismarck also instructed the German consul in Cape Town to support and protect Lüderitz in his doings. The commander of a German gunboat, *Nautilus*, which was sent by the Berlin government to observe the reactions which Lüderitz' actions aroused locally, reported that Cape Town officially refused to recognize the new German territorial gains.

Undoubtedly, the colonial authorities in Cape Town had good reason to worry about the extent to which Lüderitz' territorial gains spread out, both along the coastal area, and further into the interior of the country. In a report to London, they urged that England should immediately declare its sovereignty over the entire coastal territory. On 4 June 1884, Bismarck in response wrote a note to London in which he contested England's right of dominion over any Namibian territory other than that already laid claim to by the British – namely, Walvis Bay and a surrounding area of minor importance. Bismarck's note caused an outrage in London. So the German chancellor intended to establish a German colony in southern and central Namibia!

It was now vital for the Germans to ensure German supremacy over as large an area of the country as possible. This occurred through a series of treaties with local chieftains, especially in areas inhabited by Namas. The missionaries of the Rhenish Mission took an active part in all these negotiations, acting as interpreters, and as influential auxiliaries, when it came to having to persuade the chieftains. The German consul in Cape Town also took part, either in person, or through a representative. This added some judicial weight to the process.

Sometimes treaties were sealed where previous treaties for mining rights existed between a Cape Town-based company and a local chieftain. Then the previous treaties were effectively cancelled. Mostly the official reason for cancelling past treaties was that mining had still not taken off, or that it had proved entirely unsuccessful. A new treaty was then quickly signed, which contained very favourable terms for Lüderitz – and even here, incidentally, the missionaries willingly assisted.[10] For example, a treaty was signed with Jan Jonker Afrikaner on 21 August 1885, according to which the latter cancelled an agreement made earlier with a mining company in Cape Town, granting them the rights to conduct work within the Afrikaner people's territory. In a new, special treaty drawn up on the same day, Jan Jonker Afrikaner re-established his people's borders, and entrusted Lüderitz with the right to conduct mining operations, and also to dispose of any minerals in the Afrikaners' territory.

The Rhenish Mission had by now dissuaded Maharero from maintaining contact with Palgrave and establishing links with the colonial authorities in Cape Town. After the bloodshed of 1880, Maharero found himself confronted with a united front of Namas, Basters, and Oorlam-Nama groups determined to crush the Hereros and deprive them of their cattle and their grazing.

At about this time, a new Oorlam-Nama leader entered the scene of events, namely Hendrik Witbooi, who constituted yet another menace to the Herero people. Following the advice of the Rhenish missionaries, Maharero prepared himself to enter into negotiations with German colonizers to provide protection for himself and his people.

One step in these preparations involved the demarcation of frontier lines defining the interest area of the Hereros, and to ensure that these were drawn as generously as possible. They were formally established in a declaration signed by Maharero on 19 September 1884. With the help of missionaries, he even translated the treaty into German.

The total area delimited by these frontier lines stretched as far as Kaokoland in the north, to the Atlantic coast in the west (including the stretch of land from the Swakop to the Omaruru river mouth), and as far as Rehoboth in the south. Pool states that 'Maharero undoubtedly had political motives in publishing this proclamation. The fact that he had it translated into German and laid claim to areas which were obviously outside his sphere of influence, showed that he wished to increase his negotiating power as far as the Germans were concerned.'[11]

Soon afterwards, Maharero received a missive from Vogelsang, dated 26 November 1884, in which the latter urged him to enter into an agreement with the Germans.[12]

Meanwhile Palgrave, pressured into action by developments, himself hurried into entering protection agreements with Maharero. When Bismarck found out about this in Berlin, he intervened by means of an address, sent to the authorities in London, in which he declared that Palgrave's treaty was unacceptable, as it laid claims to what was already a German colonial area. In London nobody had ever shown much interest in Namibia, but Bismarck's letter of protest was received with great concern. After debating the question in the House of Commons, the British cancelled contact with, and recognition of, Palgrave as an official person. As has been mentioned, Palgrave was summoned back to Cape Town and thus his political influence in Namibia ended.

Lüderitz in the meantime, having failed to secure any financial support for his commitments in Namibia from the German government, soon found himself in a tight financial spot. In the autumn of 1884, he tried to start a syndicate of German businessmen in Africa. In this he was hoping to rely on the help of Friedrich Fabri, who not only had contacts with a wide circle of businessmen and politicians, but had also begun to conduct business in Namibia himself, supported by a German firm which specialized in mining operations.

Despite this useful contact, Lüderitz failed in his efforts to widen the financial basis of his commitments in Namibia and consequently threatened to sell his share of rights in Namibia to some likely British buyers in the Cape. This caused a great deal of concern in German colonial circles, where it was believed that transactions of such kind might have serious consequences for questions relating to Germany's domestic policy. Lüderitz was granted support to found a German Colonial Association for German South West Africa, whose goal it was to raise capital of 1.2 million Marks to be used for the exploitation of fruitful investments in Namibia. This organization bought Lüderitz free from his commitments and took over the responsibility for the various treaties with the local leaders.

All this took place during the first half of 1885, during the colonial congress in Berlin. Consequently it was for political, financial, domestic, and, of course, foreign policy reasons that Bismarck actively engaged the German nation in the colonization of Namibia. In August 1885, England finally agreed to recognize German colonial pretensions to what was now increasingly being referred to as 'German South West Africa'. The German government had begun to play an active part in the sealing of treaties with local chieftains, and had given an official sign of recognition by sending naval units to the territory to ensure the protection of German interests, and by giving the permission to hoist the German flag. A German state representative, charged with safeguarding German interests, was sent to the colony to be based there permanently. It now remained for German colonizers to revise treaties so as to favour official German policy, and to see to it that new treaties would be sealed with peoples as yet untouched by German colonization. The Rhenish Mission, both locally and from its headquarters in Germany, played a decisive role in these early initiatives to turn Namibia into a German colony. The Mission welcomed German colonization as it promised itself ample support from the government for its work in Namibia. Perhaps the presence of the German colonial government would even result in a major breakthrough for missionary work among the Hereros.

The Rhenish Mission – and the Deutsche Kolonialgesellschaft für Südwestafrika, 1885-1889

The Deutsche Kolonialgesellschaft für Südwestafrika, founded by Lüderitz on 15 April 1885, received an imperial warrant to carry out and administer the German colonization of Namibia. An official representative of the German government was dispatched to the colony. On 23 April 1885, the lawyer and magistrate Heinrich Ernst Göring[13] entered the duties of this office bearing the title of Commissioner of the Reich.[14] He was to have two officials as his assistants.

Göring's close connections with the Rhenish Mission were made conspicuous by his choice of headquarters alone. He settled down in Otjimbingwe, in a house which the Mission provided.

In their negotiations with tribal chieftains, the newly arrived agents acting on behalf of the German government needed the help of their countrymen the missionaries, who were both familiar with the country and mastered one or several of its languages. Following the recommendation of the Board of the Rhenish Mission in Germany, the former Rhenish missionary Büttner was employed in the colonial service for a while. He left his parish in Germany, to return to Namibia 'in the service of the emperor', to work for the German colonial administration. In this new position he was supported by his former missionary colleagues.[15]

Despite the missionaries' continued assistance through this stage of colonization, and despite the trust the missionaries had engendered in many of the indigenous population, the colonizers met with resistance from the locals.

Of all the Oorlam-Nama leaders, none was more aggressively

outspoken against German colonization than Hendrik Witbooi. Striving to prevent the threat that it represented, he sought alliance with his principal adversary, the Herero chieftain Maharero.

Hendrik Witbooi resembled Jonker Afrikaner in more ways than one, especially in view of his aggressive claims of inspired leadership. He was the leader of a group of Oorlam-Namas who had settled in Gibeon, central Namibia, in 1863. As was customary among his people, he had attached a missionary from the Rhenish Mission to his group. Another trait that Witbooi shared with Jonker Afrikaner was that he was a political and religious visionary with a near-revivalist messianic consciousness concerning the future of his people under his own leadership. He claimed that God had appeared to him in a vision, exhorting him to lead his people to power and glory.

Witbooi is believed to have been born in 1834; he was baptized in 1868 by Missionary Johannes Olpp who was attached to the Gibeon group. When the Afrikaner group under Jonker Afrikaner weakened in their influence, Witbooi began to make claims to the status of leadership among the Oorlam-Namas.

Witbooi was deeply suspicious of the Germans and the Hereros. He rejected any form of foreign dominion, and especially German colonization. He also insisted on his independence in his relations with the Rhenish Mission. He forbade the missionaries to pursue politics of any kind, urging them instead to devote themselves entirely to religious concerns. The Church that he had raised for his people in Gibeon was, as he himself claimed, his own, and the Mission should not have any part in it. The Mission and the colonial authorities were soon to regard him as a dangerous rebel and a factious leader.

In a report addressed to the colonial authorities in December 1885,[16] Büttner demanded that Hendrik Witbooi be 'eliminated' as he constituted a major threat to all German interests in the country. A similar address by the Board of the Rhenish Mission, dated November 1890,[17] and sent to the authorities in Berlin, emphasized how vitally important it was to have Witbooi 'crushed' as soon as possible. It was he, they claimed, who was the driving force behind the endless 'tribal wars'. He was considered all the more dangerous because he had succeeded in 'shroud[ing] himself with a spiritual nimbus'. It lay in the best interests of all concerned 'that the German government intervene and make him pay the price for his deeds'.[18]

In June 1884, Hendrik Witbooi and Maharero met in Aub, near Windhoek. After some minor skirmishes between them, the chieftains sealed a peace treaty there. Maharero recognized Hendrik Witbooi as a chieftain possessing the right to seal treaties without first procuring the permission of his people in Gibeon. On condition that he guaranteed a durable peace for the Hereros, Witbooi was now given permission by Maharero to lead his Oorlam-Namas through the Hereros' territory 'when it is time [to] seek a new dwelling place. As my people originated from various quarters, I wish that each and every one of them can settle down wherever they choose.'[19]

After signing this treaty, Witbooi returned to Gibeon where he stayed until mid-July 1885. It was around this time that Büttner arrived as a representative of the colonial administration and tried to persuade the Witbooi group to enter into negotiations for a protective treaty with Germany. Hendrik Witbooi's suspicions were roused immediately. On the strength of his alliance with Maharero and the fruitful contacts he had forged with the Baster group in Rehoboth, he felt strong enough to reject Büttner's offer. He declared contemptuously that if ever he should desire protection, he would turn to the English authorities in the Cape Colony rather than turn to these new strangers who had only recently emerged in the country.

Büttner was worried about Hendrik Witbooi's attempts to establish a united front with other tribes against German colonization. It was Göring who turned to the Rhenish Mission for help. Since the missionaries were familiar with all the intertribal rivalries, they would help him implement a policy of divide and rule. The Rhenish Mission more than willingly offered its support especially since this would mean countering the 'doctrine monger' Hendrik Witbooi, who was 'deeply embedded in a Christian ideology of his own making, nurturing his privately held conviction ... that God had selected him to act as a Messiah to forge durable peace among mutually hostile parties, and thereby to make territorial gains for himself by seizing new territories in the north'.[20]

The first step towards countering Witbooi was to dissolve the treaty between him and Maharero. However, even Maharero found cause to worry about the German colonial infiltration of his territory. He therefore sought to renew his contacts with Palgrave in Cape Town, who had promised to support him to the extent of procuring grazing for him in the south all the way up to Rehoboth. The fact that Büttner had just entered into a treaty of alliance with the Baster group in Rehoboth gave Maharero even greater cause to worry; besides, there were constant rumours that Hendrik Witbooi was approaching with his armed forces towards Okahandja.

This was the chance Büttner had waited for. He would exploit Maharero's tight position by making him an offer of a treaty which would guarantee the Hereros 'protection against Witbooi by the German government'.[21]

Maharero, however, seemed to trust Hendrik Witbooi more, with whom he had signed a peace treaty in 1884. He left Okahandja to meet Witbooi halfway. They met in Osana in 1885 where they tried to find a common means of fighting the threat of foreign domination. While the two leaders sat in negotiations, a quarrel broke out between their men concerning a watering place for the cattle herds which both groups had brought along with them. This broke up the negotiations, and fierce fighting ensued. Many warriors fell in battle, including two of Hendrik Witbooi's sons. Witbooi himself was forced to flee southwards.

Not long before this senseless bloodbath, Göring and Büttner, in collaboration with Missionary Viehe of the Rhenish Mission, had managed to negotiate a protection treaty with Maharero's rival Herero chieftain, Manasse. In terms of this treaty, the Germans were offering protection and the promise to help Manasse become independent of Maharero.

Maharero was now faced with the threat of German support of a rival among his own people. This eventually caused him to give in, and accept the terms of the alliance with the Germans. It is interesting to note how the treaty was formulated as an agreement made between two sovereigns on an equal footing. The treaty itself was written in German and began with the following pompous preamble:

> His Majesty the German Emperor, King of Prussia, ..., William I in the name of the German Reich, on the one hand, and Maharero Katjamuaha, Paramount Chieftain of the Hereros in Damaraland, on his own behalf and on that of his legitimate heirs, wish to conclude a protection and friendship treaty ...[22]

The treaty was signed on 21 October 1885 in Okahandja in the residence of Missionary Diehl, who was among the signatories on the German side. Maharero was thereby made into a tribal leader *under* the official German colonial administration – although the treaty addresses him as the paramount chieftain and as the emperor's equal.

After the signing of this treaty, it became a matter of increasing urgency for the Germans to form an alliance with Hendrik Witbooi. Büttner therefore made another visit to Gibeon but returned emptyhanded. Even Göring paid a visit to Witbooi in December 1885 but with equally negative results. In the meanwhile, Hendrik Witbooi harnessed himself to take retributory action against Maharero. He attacked Maharero in April 1886, but suffered another defeat. He made his escape to the Gamsberg mountain plateau west of Rehoboth, from where he launched swift guerrilla attacks against the Herero people.

Göring now saw it as his main task to make a durable peace in the country, and thereby to bring about favourable conditions for lucrative German colonization and immigration. But peace was impossible for as long as Hendrik Witbooi remained unchallenged. In April 1887, Witbooi attacked Otjimbingwe where Göring and his administration were based. Maharero and his people, who seemed to constantly oscillate between Otjimbingwe and Okahandja, had recently moved their base here, too. Just before attacking, Hendrik Witbooi, trying to reinforce his position, had signed a treaty with Jan Jonker Afrikaner. The two of them, by joining forces, were able to defeat Maharero. His defeat made it plain to Maharero just how unreliable the German treaty's written promises to provide protection against the Oorlam-Namas were. His defeat also made it into the German press where Göring was given scathing reviews for his alleged passivity and lack of true leadership ability.

The situation was becoming increasingly difficult, both for the Mission and for the colonial power. Göring left for Germany in June 1887, to report on the situation in the country. On his return to Namibia in October 1888, he was met with the news that Maharero had revoked his treaty with the Germans and instead, had renewed his contacts with the British authorities in Cape Town. In the meantime, Hendrik Witbooi prepared himself for renewed fighting, by making purchases of arms in Cape Town against payment made in cattle (part of which he had seized from the Herero people).

Thus the future of German colonization in Namibia was looking bleak, especially since Göring did not have any military at his disposal. (It should be mentioned in this context that Göring had demanded that German military be stationed in Namibia. He had turned for assistance to the Deutsche Kolonialgesellschaft, but as they were practically insolvent at the time they were in no position to comply with his wishes.[23]) In the German parliament, a steadily growing number of voices were heard opting for Germany's unconditional departure from Namibia. Bismarck was compelled to use his full influence to prevent this decision from being made official.

At this juncture, Missionary Brincker in Otjimbingwe took the initiative of writing a letter to Bismarck on behalf of all the German missionaries based in Namibia. He demanded that Germany send an army of at least 400 soldiers to Namibia without delay. His letter dated 13 March 1889 painted a dark picture of what Brincker envisaged as Maharero's inherent unreliability, saying, 'Kamaherero is a Negro chieftain who receives favours from whosoever pays him the most – even if it should be a Turk – and who enters upon treaties, agreeing on paper to that which he would on the following day impertinently deny. To seal treaties with Kamaherero is tantamount to forging agreements with a mere child.'[24] Brincker argued that it was:

... a matter of applying the language of force in defence of what is right. The country seems to be rich in gold deposits ... added to which the land in a moral sense belongs to our native country, since the Rhenish Mission already has invested thousands of Marks in it; here, you will also find the graves which have been dug for your own fallen missionaries. If any gain is to be made out of this colony, a European power must be based in this country with a military force counting at least 400 men, with two artillery units to ensure immediate retribution for any likely form of arrogance and insolence.[25]

He ended his delivery with a patriotic appeal: 'Most gracious Chancellor of the Reich! This cry for mercy comes from the undersigned on behalf of my colleagues as we have heard rumours that Germany plans to relinquish Damaraland, and that Lewis[26] has already begun to take steps as a result of this.'[27]

It may be that Brincker's letter prompted the German government to intervene more actively in Namibia. On 24 June 1889, a small German troop of 20 men landed in Walvis Bay under the command of a Lieutenant Curt von François. To avoid attracting the attention of the British at

Walvis Bay, this minor force arrived under the guise of a scientific expedition. A military presence had thus been dispatched to Namibia acting on the orders of the German government.

The landing of the troops in Walvis Bay was a first step towards consolidating Namibia's status as a colony under the direct rule of the emperor. Namibia had thus become a German crown colony – and the Rhenish Mission had taken active part in this process of colonization.

In the meantime, Hendrik Witbooi, in alliance with Jan Jonker Afrikaner, carried on his guerrilla warfare against the Herero people from his camp in Hoornkrantz. Jan Jonker Afrikaner fell during one of these attacks, on 10 August 1889; and his group now joined forces with Hendrik Witbooi.

The Rhenish Mission under Curt von François, 1889-1894

When Missionary Brincker appealed to the German chancellor for military intervention and the German government dispatched its first troops to Namibia, this was a major step away from practising 'indirect imperialism', through the Deutsche Kolonialgesellschaft, to 'direct imperialism' with direct government involvement. The Rhenish Mission's hopes to bring about a 'stable and authoritative' administration for the country seemed thus to have been realized.

Curt von François, who was to succeed Göring, raised military bases at strategically important locations – as the *Landeshauptmann*, Von François was endowed with the highest responsibility for both civilian and military administration. He undertook to produce a detailed map of all those areas in southern and central Namibia which might be of particular interest for the purposes of German colonization. The German colonists who, during his lifetime, began immigrating into the colony, were given large grants of land. At the same time, Germany began to systematically exploit the mineral deposits of the country. Von François and Göring marked the 'new era' by moving their headquarters from Otjimbingwe to Windhoek, which was the obvious choice for the capital of the colony since it was conveniently situated in central Namibia, at the intersection of the road network which Jonker Afrikaner had built.

Von François' first duty, according to the instructions he received from his superiors in Berlin, was to ensure peace in the colony by seeing to it that the contending parties be severed. One way of achieving this was to stop the continuous import of firearms to the indigenous population. Most importantly, Hendrik Witbooi must be prevented from having further access to firearms.

Before long, more reinforcements arrived from Germany. A military post was established at Tsaobis, near Otjimbingwe. The presence of German military enabled Göring to resume his attempts to seal a new protection treaty with Maharero. The presence of German military influenced Maharero's decision of 20 May 1890 to withdraw his cancellation of his earlier agreement involving imperial protection. In this context he even relinquished his nominal sovereignty over Windhoek, which now became a German military station. On the same day that the renewal of the formerly cancelled treaty with Maharero was signed, Göring wrote another letter to Hendrik Witbooi in which he threatened the latter with severe reprisals unless he made peace with the Herero people and withdrew to Gibeon.[28]

Witbooi was not to be so easily impressed, however. In his answer of 29 May 1890, he dismissed Göring's arrogated right to 'give him orders'. As the emperor ruled over Germany, so he, Witbooi, was the legitimate ruler of his own people. As such he was not in any position to either accept advice or tolerate any commands with impending threats. Witbooi nevertheless felt 'great concern over Maharero's treachery' involving the latter's 'surrender of his position as independent sovereign over his own people to subordinate himself to these alien authorities from Germany'. In a letter to Maharero dated 30 May 1889, he begged Maharero to cease his contacts with the German power. The text of this missive was formulated much in the manner of a declaration of independence emphasizing every people's right to self-determination. Maharero should, he said, rather than bend to the will of foreign powers, assert and preserve as he would his own life his position as 'an independent Capitaine over whom no-one is entitled to command'.[29]

When he saw that his ultimatum failed to have any impact, Göring made several other attempts to reduce Hendrik Witbooi to submission. He tried, with military assistance, to cut off all deliveries of firearms from Cape Town, as well as generally isolate Witbooi by sealing a number of separate treaties with other Oorlam-Nama and Nama groups. Furthermore, he fortified Windhoek, which had become the official colonial capital of Namibia on 18 October 1890.

Göring returned to Germany for good at the end of 1890, leaving Curt von François solely responsible for the colony's affairs.

Maharero died on 7 October 1890. Choosing a successor proved a complicated matter. The specific problem lay in the order of succession. The eldest son of Tjamuaha, Kavikuma, had died before his own father. He had had two sons, Hirarapi and Maharero. Hirarapi, the legitimate heir, was considered a weakling and consequently the younger brother, Maharero, had become the chief. Hirarapi had died in 1863, but his eldest son, Nikodemus, lived and should, by virtue of the direct line, have succeeded Maharero in 1890. However, another contestant was Maharero's son, Samuel. Nikodemus maintained his right to the office of chieftain as he – Tjamuaha's oldest great-grandson – was the rightful heir.

Maharero's position as *paramount* chieftain was, as mentioned in Chapter 4, not traditional but had been arranged by Charles John Andersson, with the support of the Rhenish Mission, and was retained after Maharero's death.

The election took place in Okahandja which had once again become the principal locality of the Herero people. The Rhenish Mission, too, had made Okahandja its principal base for conducting its work among the Hereros. The new mission station in Okahandja was built much like a fortified military camp and separated by a river bed from the Hereros' part of the settlement but still close enough to enable convenient surveillance of everything going on at the court of the 'paramount' chieftain.

As a step towards its attempts to strengthen its position among the Herero people, the Rhenish Mission had prevailed upon Maharero to let his own sons be raised under the care and supervision of the missionaries. At the time of Maharero's death Samuel Maharero, who had been named doyen of the congregation, owned a building which was a direct extension of the mission station. This close contact meant that he was the Rhenish Mission's faithful follower and thus naturally the colonial authorities' first choice of a candidate in the election of a new chieftain. In addition to this, the fact that Nikodemus did not live in Okahandja would make the task of controlling the latter as the Hereros' new paramount chieftain far more difficult. This factor determined the result of the election in spite of the blatant fact that Samuel, as a Christian, would be unable to perform the traditional religious functions of a Herero chieftain. These were therefore assigned to an elder relative.[30]

Samuel never fully enjoyed the trust of his people, however. In his position as paramount chieftain he was, just as his father had been before him, entirely dependent on the support of the Rhenish Mission and the colonial authorities. On the death of Maharero, Hendrik Witbooi had seized the opportunity to offer Samuel a peace treaty and thereby provide a united front against foreign rule in Namibia. However, Samuel's position was too weak to enable him to seal a peace with the principal adversary of the colonial power.

Meanwhile Curt von François, as the administrative leader of the colony, sought to provide land for the increasing immigration of German colonists. To ensure this, he planned 'to confine the natives [sic] to reserves and have the rest of their land as crown land'.[31] Bismarck's successor to the post of chancellor of the Reich in 1890, Leo von Caprivi, handed over Windhoek as 'a gift' to the colonists to be used, along with the surrounding grazing, as a suitable settlement area. In Germany, as well as in the colony itself, white immigration was encouraged in various ways: demobilized German soldiers, for instance, were offered generous terms for remaining in the country as settlers after completing their military service.

Hendrik Witbooi still proved to be the greatest obstacle to the realization of the colonial authorities' projects. Von François maintained a nearly continuous correspondence with Witbooi, and the two of them met to conduct personal deliberations. But Hendrik Witbooi did not allow himself to be won over.[32] In his correspondence with Curt von François, he gave free rein to a vivid rendering of what he perceived as the vision of his people's and, by extension, the whole of Africa's freedom: 'Africa belongs to us! Both through the hue of our skin and in our way of life do we belong together, and this Africa is in its entirety our own country. The fact that we possess a variety of chieftainships and diverse territories does not imply any secondary division of Africa and does not sever our solidarity.' The emperor of Germany, he said, had no business in Africa whatsoever![33]

Hendrik Witbooi nevertheless found himself increasingly isolated in his struggle against German colonial rule. The presence of the German military and its control of the trade routes from Windhoek made it all the more difficult for him to obtain firearms. The colonial power's close co-operation with the Rhenish Mission fuelled his negative attitude towards this Mission. In his increasingly isolated struggle against foreign rule, he turned to the English colonial authorities in Cape Town in August 1892, with a demand for their assistance. He pointed out that 'at a big conference' (meaning the Berlin Congress of 1884-1885), England had granted the Germans permission to rule over his country. These Germans were now oppressing his people and depriving them of their legitimate possessions. Furthermore, they were enforcing laws alien to the country and its people, and preventing free trade. All this, according to Witbooi, was contrary to the terms agreed on at the 'big conference'. Therefore, he urged England to act through the governor in Cape Town to ensure the departure of the Germans from Namibia, and to see to it that England take over the custody of the country.[34] 'You were the first to come here,' he concluded. 'We knew you – you never came to steal our country. You conducted trade with us – and did not deprive us of our freedom.'

It is not clear just how Hendrik Witbooi would have defined his use of the term 'country'. He was, after all, the leader of just one group of Oorlam-Namas. It was in this capacity that he wished to gain unlimited access to firearms. Through acquiring great military power he hoped to be able to seal alliances with other indigenous leaders, irrespective of tribal origin, to acquire, just as Jonker Afrikaner had done in his day, a leading position in the country. His letter implied that he would attempt to break the Germans' control of trade with the Cape Colony. (In this respect, too, he resembled Jonker Afrikaner, who had viewed the free trade routes to Cape Town for the use of his people as a guarantee for maintaining a dominant position in Namibia.)

Much to his disappointment, Hendrik Witbooi never received an answer from Cape Town. However, to his opponent Curt von François it became increasingly plain that Witbooi must be defeated through effective military intervention – but the forces Von François held at his disposal were hardly sufficient for this. They were far too small for 'anything except self-defence against the Witboois, who were armed with modern rifles and were led by Hendrik Witbooi – a man of immense skill and experience'.[35] Hendrik Witbooi's war tactics using swift, unexpected attacks conducted by small groups were in any case something the Germans found difficult to counter effectively.

During an ambush in June 1893, Hendrik Witbooi managed to massacre a German transport caravan from Swakopmund to Windhoek in the vicinity of the colonial capital. The Germans suffered great casualties of men and equipment, and Hendrik Witbooi gained hold of a great booty including firearms.

Curt von François had proved demonstrably incapable of defeating Hendrik Witbooi, a fact which caused immense irritation in Berlin. Von François, it seemed, lacked diplomatic and military skill, and his position both in the colony, and in the eyes of the authorities in Germany, diminished.

Growing tensions between the Rhenish Mission and the colonial authorities under Leutwein, 1894-1904

In a parliamentary pronouncement made in Berlin on 1 March 1893, the chancellor of the Reich declared that Germany had no intention of leaving the colony of German South West Africa in spite of all the difficulties and problems experienced there. Namibia belonged to Germany in accordance with the terms of an international agreement and could not simply be 'exchanged' for German interests in other parts of the world. The wars in the colony were seen as necessary military measures taken in order to put an end to this 'rebellion' against an internationally recognized German authority under a lawful German government. It was the German military's task to crush all insurrections and thereby create peaceful conditions in which German affairs and colonists might thrive. Hendrik Witbooi and his people were declared 'insurrectionists' against German supremacy.

The new governor, Theodor Leutwein, received an imperial warrant to reign over all who lived in the colony as subjects of the emperor – a blanket term covering both the indigenous population and the white colonists.[36] This position of authority was not unlike that enjoyed by emperors and kings of medieval times, who held the power of electing, as well as of deposing their vassals, crushing every rebellion and punishing all the rebels.

The present representative of the emperor in Namibia was the governor. His task involved the creation of a strong government over all who lived in the colony, including all the missionaries, and the other Europeans. Indigenous leaders, according to this system, held the function of subordinate colonial officials whose duty it was to carry out the colonial authorities' decisions.

Traditionally, there were no geographical borders between the territories of the various indigenous tribes. It was access to grazing and water which had always determined the tribal areas and tribal movement. Leutwein, however, immediately began defining frontiers between the settlements of the different tribes and groups, and even tried to introduce measures to control the size of their cattle herds. Land which was left 'unused' after this partitioning of the land was declared as crown land, which meant it was at the disposal of the German colonists. Through measures such as these the indigenous people's traditional social, cultural and religious way of life was gradually undermined.

Any kind of resistance against the colonial power was viewed as an uprising and was cut down by force. Military defeat was followed with a juridical penal procedure. In future it would no longer be possible to enter upon any specific peace treaties, or treaties involving protection for that matter. The German colonial government became the sole guarantor of peace and protection and thus cancelled the necessity for treaties of any kind whatsoever.

Governor Leutwein's administration bore consequences for the European population as well, who lived in the colony under conditions dictated by the colonial power and were obliged to follow its laws and decrees to the point. In this respect there was, in the eyes of the governor, little difference between the colonists and the indigenous population – all were subjects of the emperor. The governor held supreme authority in all matters influencing the course of their daily lives – such as the distribution of land, business activities along with credit facilities, the colonists' conditions of life and even their means of subsistence. This soon gave rise to sharp criticism. The colonists were of the opinion that Leutwein was too indulgent when it came to the indigenous population. Individual chieftains were allowed to keep their own armed forces – albeit under the condition that they would be at the call of the governor himself whenever he deemed it necessary. When Leutwein subsequently arranged for a form of compulsory colonial military service among the colonists, the latter demanded a right of participation in decision making over matters pertaining to the colonial administration – especially with respect to the indigenous population.

Even the missionaries were subject to the governor's law. Soon enough, the governor even claimed the right to exercise control over their preaching and their teaching! The Rhenish Mission protested against this, and in an attempt to assert their freedom and integrity the missionaries began to voice complaints to the governor concerning the manner in which both colonists and persons of authority were treating the indigenous population. This soon became a source of irritation for

Leutwein. As a governor he alone had the right to decide what was best for the entire population of the colony, and he would not tolerate any meddling, let alone any contestation of his directives.

Though limited, the military resources Leutwein held at his disposal ensured his position of power. Through efforts combining swift military operations with skilful diplomatic moves, he attempted to gain control of the country. It was largely a matter of balancing the interests of all the different groups in the country against each other.

This method was applied especially to the Hereros who were divided over the contending interests between Samuel Maharero and his rival, Nikodemus, the leader of a group of Hereros in Gobabis.[37] Eventually, through a demonstration of military power combined with a bit of diplomacy, Leutwein persuaded Nikodemus to recognize Samuel Maharero's position as paramount chieftain. Next, he prevailed upon Maharero to grant Nikodemus the dignity of a subordinate chieftain controlling a territory whose borderlines were later to be defined.

Leutwein was aware of the fact that Samuel Maharero's position was weak and also, that he was only chief of Hereroland in name. There was, he knew, no chance of bringing about any semblance of order among the Herero people until Nikodemus could be prevailed upon to give up his pretensions to be the Hereros' paramount chieftain. Leutwein's plan involved, with Samuel's help, to 'gradually set the scene for Nikodemus' downfall'.[38] The realization of this plan was in turn to bear consequences for Leutwein's relations with the Rhenish Mission.

Another major source of irritation for the German colonial power was Hendrik Witbooi. Like Von François, Leutwein maintained a regular correspondence with him. The idea was to induce Witbooi, by hook or by crook, to become more tractable. But Leutwein was just as unsuccessful at this as his predecessor had been. Hendrik Witbooi had meanwhile entrenched himself into his fortified camp in the Naukluft, which made his position all the more secure.

At the end of April 1894, Leutwein's patience came to an end. In a sharply worded ultimatum, he demanded that Witbooi capitulate unconditionally. Either Witbooi should subordinate himself to the emperor, or expose himself and his people to a war of extermination. Military reinforcements enabled Leutwein to launch an attack soon thereafter, and inflict a decisive defeat on Hendrik Witbooi.

Leutwein demonstrated considerable restraint in his subsequent treatment of Hendrik Witbooi. For example, he made an exception to his own rule of not allowing any treaties of protection to be sealed with 'insurgents', and signed an agreement with Witbooi on 15 September 1894, the terms of which granted Witbooi the right to remain the leader of his people. Furthermore, the Oorlam-Nama leader was granted permission to surround himself with an armed force provided he did not leave the Gibeon region in the future. In an addendum to the treaty dated 16 November 1895, Hendrik Witbooi agreed to put his armed forces at the disposal of the governor whenever the latter should demand this.

The Rhenish missionaries were present as interpreters and witnesses when Witbooi signed the treaty, which added to his humiliation. He had been defeated and his future now lay in the hands of the same colonial power which he had fought against for so long. During a visit to the German missionary in Keetmanshoop at Christmas in 1894, Witbooi said: 'There are understanding men among the Germans, who can make allowances for our character as Namas and treat us accordingly; but there are also ruthless men who can only give orders, and they frighten me. They will take their revenge on us, and will seduce our women, despising us.'[39]

Hendrik Witbooi was no longer a problem for the colonial power. Leutwein could therefore concentrate his efforts on administrative matters involving the distribution of suitable areas of land to the colonists. This was done through a series of treaties with Samuel Maharero; yet the latter did not possess any right, according to tribal law, to dispose of the grazing of his own people. The delimitation of land, by Samuel Maharero and Leutwein, particularly afflicted the Hereros under the leadership of Nikodemus, who rose in revolt. Nikodemus received help from another Herero chieftain by the name of Kahimemua. Together they attacked a German force who just managed to escape.[40] This incident led to Leutwein's final confrontation with Samuel Maharero's rival, Nikodemus.

It was Missionary Viehe in Gobabis who tried to intervene on behalf of Nikodemus, defending the latter against Leutwein. Viehe maintained that Nikodemus could hardly be held entirely responsible for the uprising. But the fact was that the relationship between Viehe and Leutwein was rather strained. Leutwein had tried to persuade Viehe to use his influence to induce the Hereros to obedience. Furthermore, Leutwein had requested Viehe's assistance when it came to controlling the size of the Hereros' cattle herds. Viehe had refused to do this. During a confrontation between

Leutwein and Viehe in April 1896, Leutwein expressed his personal views of 'insurgents': 'If a Negro has done wrong, forceful action is of more use than too much mildness.'[41]

With the support of Samuel Maharero, German military defeated Kahimemua on 6 May 1896. After Kahimemua was taken prisoner, Nikodemus surrendered without any further resistance. Both chieftains were tried before a German court of law and condemned to death. They were executed on 12 June 1896 in Okahandja. Samuel Maharero took part in the trial himself as a judge, and voted in favour of a death penalty.

The settlement with Nikodemus solved Leutwein's problem as concerns the two rival Herero groups. His intervention had demonstrated the might of the colonial power, as well as its readiness to translate that power into action. But if Leutwein now believed himself rid of all insubordination, he was mistaken. Instead, he was seen as a ruthless tyrant against whom the Hereros should defend themselves. The colonial power had through a foreign procedure of justice condemned two of their chieftains to death, and had even executed them in public! For a people whose very sense of identity and demands for freedom were founded on 'a desire for political self-determination, closely associated with the personalities of the chiefs',[42] this was an outrage and a deep humiliation.

The fate of Nikodemus constituted a major turning point in German colonial history in Namibia. It was no longer possible for anyone to question the Germans' willingness to resort to violence. More reinforcements came from Germany, and Leutwein raised many fortifications throughout the country. The presence of German military in all parts of the country, even in the most remote locations, became a constant reminder of the presence of the foreign power and its ability to intervene swiftly at the slightest sign of renewed uprisings.

Leutwein seemed not only to want to enforce obedience and respect for his rule, but also to cultivate a growing confidence in German administration. At the same time, he strove to encourage more immigration, in order to make the colony a 'profitable affair' for the Germans. This faced him with the task of weighing complicated matters against each other: more specifically, he was faced with the delicate task of having to 'gradually and peacefully bring about the very changes sought by the settlers, but at the same time to leave the natives [sic] with the impression that firmness in the exercise of authority could go hand in hand with fairness and justice'.[43]

Where does all this leave the missionaries? At first they had welcomed Leutwein and offered him their undivided support. He seemed able to create the necessary conditions for the peace and order which they so badly needed for their own activities. It was soon made plain, however, that the growing immigration of Germans was beginning to complicate relations between whites and blacks in the country. Statistically, the immigrants did not form a large group. In 1894, there were a total of 1 343 Europeans in Namibia, including the German troops. But by 1896, their number had risen to 2 025, by 1898 to 2 400, and by 1900 to 3 383. The largest concentration of troops in 1896 were found in Windhoek, with an estimate of 600 soldiers.

Despite their growing numbers, all colonists were granted huge shares of land, and a privileged position as Europeans. There were several instances of forced resettlement of indigenous people to make way for the immigrants. There was therefore an increasing sense of alienation between the colonizers and the indigenous population. This was true especially of the urban centres which had begun to grow. In Windhoek, for example, 'there was no real contact with the Africans, who lived in prison camps and in other mass billets away from the centre of the town'.[44]

This caused serious problems for the work of the Rhenish Mission among the Hereros in Okahandja. Here, the work of the Mission had progressed well, so that after 1868, several schools and small clinics had been built. The Mission had also been able to establish, largely through its close contacts with Samuel Maharero and other leaders among this people, outside stations, containing village schools and even a form of ambulatory medical care. This extensive activity demanded regular visits from missionaries who were often forced to remain at an outside station for a considerable period of time. The missionaries became increasingly resentful about belonging to the same group of foreigners and colonizers who were taking over the Hereros' best grazing and most fertile land. The Hereros had to helplessly witness this event, as the intruders upon their traditional areas were under the protection of the police and the colonial military.

Added to the missionaries' frustration that their countrymen were placing them under the obligation of establishing parishes everywhere, and of holding special church services in German for the colonizers, even 'church services did little to bring the races together. The Hereros went to church on Sunday and afterwards the missionary would hold service in his own house for the Europeans.'[45]

One missionary based in Windhoek founded the first German parish in this city, on 20 January in 1895. The size of this parish grew rapidly, from 575 members in 1903 to 778 in 1904.

But the missionaries outside Windhoek were also obliged to combine their missionary activities with parish duties amongst their fellow Germans. This further widened the gap between the missionaries and the indigenous population. The increasing alienation between the different groups led to the sinister growth of racism, which in turn influenced the attitude of the missionaries. Leutwein's efforts to gain the confidence of the indigenous people in the interests of keeping peace was not viewed mildly by the white population. An address sent to the colonial authorities in Berlin dated 21 July 1900 bears vivid witness to this burgeoning racism. The letter was drafted in connection with a debate held in German parliament on the issue of caning as a form of punishment in the colonies, and read:

> From time immemorial our natives have been used to laziness, brutality and stupidity. The dirtier they are the more they feel at ease. Any white men who have lived among natives find it almost impossible to regard them as human beings at all in any European sense. They need centuries of training as human beings; with endless patience, strictness and justice.[46]

The letter also condemned Leutwein for his passivity regarding the indigenous population, demanding that he adopt a 'tougher military policy and – if necessary – [fight] a preventive war'.[47]

In 1896-1897, as tension between blacks and whites was mounting, the colony was hit by a devastating cattle plague. Approximately 50-80 per cent of all cattle were estimated to have died – in some areas, the death rate was as high as 90 per cent. The Hereros suffered the greatest loss. Deprived of their cattle, many of them were forced to take up employment on white men's farms, under extremely harsh working conditions. Famine and destitution forced many Hereros to seek help from the Mission. The reasons for this were also religious in kind: cattle formed part of the Hereros' religious life – without cattle, the people's fundamental sense of security wavered – and they therefore sought for other religious values. This quest gave rise to a mass movement to Christianity.

Another reason why they sought out the Rhenish missionaries was that many preferred working for the missionaries than for white farmers. The missionaries, however, maintained that the main reason was a religious crisis occasioned by the loss of cattle: 'They [the missionaries] spoke of the shattering effect on the Hereros of the loss of their oxen, their real idols ... . There were ... signs of a general movement towards conversion, which the missionaries saw as a blessing in disguise.'[48]

The consequences of the cattle plague were aggravated by the methods used by white businessmen to exploit the indigenous population, who were often forced to use what was left of their land and cattle as a means of payment for food and other necessities. In this, Samuel Maharero set a bad example. His increasing dependence on alcohol made him mortgage his people's grazing, and even steal cattle from his tribesmen, to get hold of liquor. The Rhenish Mission attempted to make him change his ways, but in vain. In 1900 the Rhenish Mission described him as follows: 'Unfortunately he is of weak character. He easily gives in; he is increasingly dependent on alcohol and he is pulling many of his people down with him by setting a bad example.'[49]

Leutwein attempted to stop white businessmen from forcing the Hereros to sign away more and more of their land in payment of goods, but 'local politics [were] heading,' as Missionary Viehe explained, 'towards getting all the better land into the hands of the whites'.[50]

In a letter to the authorities in Berlin of 2 February 1901, the Rhenish Mission suggested that a reserve be made for the Herero people so as to protect them from the white businessmen's methods of exploitation. Leutwein questioned the missionaries' motives, calling in question their alleged lack of self-interest. He was of the opinion that they wished to protect their spheres of influence by means of the reserve system and thus ensure that their development plans were put into practice.[51]

Notwithstanding his protests, Leutwein was ordered by the authorities in Berlin to suggest which areas could be put aside for reserves. In June 1902, the colonial authorities in Berlin decided to appoint a commission to inquire into the issue of the giving of goods on credit to indigenous people. The commission's recommendation that the use of tribal land be forbidden as a private means of payment, and that a time limit be put on the collection of debts, made the businessmen all the more unscrupulous in their methods to collect their payment. The Rhenish Mission which, following instructions from Berlin, also formed part of the commission, had proposed that the reserves be as large as possible; the white colonists of course wanted to give the Hereros restricted areas and, what is more, areas of land deemed unsuitable for immigrants.

Samuel Maharero supported the Rhenish missionaries' proposal, but made no secret of the fact that his motive was to get hold of as much land as possible so as to continue his private transactions with the white businessmen. This and the fact that he had already mortgaged and sold a fair chunk of Herero property on his own account, made him subject to increasingly harsh criticism from his own people who were suffering extreme hardship as a consequence of the cattle plague. There was also a growing discontent, among the Hereros, with Leutwein's administration and his half-hearted attempts to protect them against the businessmen's methods, as well as with his support of the colonists.

Other Herero leaders confronted Samuel Maharero and demanded that he as the paramount chieftain lead his people in a war of liberation. Without land, the Hereros could not keep cattle, and without cattle, their lives were in danger. They saw their future as a life of slavery under foreign rulers. It was better under these circumstances to fight for their freedom in a war. Samuel Maharero was given the choice either to lead his people in such a war of independence, or to lose his position as a chieftain. He chose war.

At this time, approximately eight per cent of the Herero people were members of Rhenish congregations. Among the Namas and the Oorlam-Namas, the percentage of people who had joined the Mission was considerably higher. After a period of more than 60 years' activity, the Rhenish Mission had fully established itself as the one and only Christian Mission in central and southern Namibia. At the outbreak of the war, there were about 9 000 baptized members in the Rhenish parishes. Admittedly, many of its members had turned to the Mission as a last resort, but nevertheless the Rhenish missionaries enjoyed a position of trust among the indigenous peoples of Namibia. The war which broke out in 1904 was to be a period of trial for the Rhenish Mission in its relations both with the colonial power and the indigenous population.

Notes

1. Wehler, HU. 1991, 199-202.
2. German Colonial Society.
3. Wehler, HU, op. cit., 228.
4. Wehler, HU. 1976, 260.
5. Groves, CP. 1958, 9.
6. Ibid., 10 ff.
7. Wehler, HU, op. cit., 265.
8. Ibid., 268.
9. Ibid., 269.
10. Photostatic copies of such treaties are included as appendices in Baumann, J. 1985. They were concluded with the Trading Company of Lüderitz and the chiefs in the presence of German consular authorities from Cape Town. Missionaries served as interpreters and as such, were among the signatories.
11. Pool, G. 1991, 61.
12. Lüderitz, CA. 1945, 97 ff.
13. Heinrich Ernst Göring was the father of Hermann Wilhelm Göring, field marshal in Nazi Germany.
14. Wehler, HU, op. cit., 286.
15. In his final report to the colonial authorities in Berlin, Büttner acknowledged this support. 'I cannot conclude this report without expressing my gratitude for all the assistance given me by the staff of the Rhenish Mission. ... They supported me in my efforts to add 7 000 square miles to the Protectorate.' See 'Reichskolonialamt, Akten betr. der Expedition des Pfarrers Dr Büttner', vol. II, file 1469, December 1885; Church Archives, Windhoek.
16. Büttner, CG, in: ibid.
17. See 'Reichskolonialamt, Akten betr. der Kämpfe zwischen den Nama und Herero', vol. III, file 2130, 17 November 1890; Church Archives, Windhoek.
18. Ibid.
19. Witbooi, H. 1982, 37.
20. Loth, H. 1963, 102.
21. Ibid., 109-110.
22. See above note (10). A copy of the treaty appears in Baumann, J, op. cit.
23. Wehler, HU, op. cit., 289-290.
24. Metzkes, J. 1959, 110 and 116.
25. Ibid.
26. A representative of the British colonial power in Cape Town whom Maharero had contacted for support.

108 Mission and German Colonialism

27 Metzkes, J, op. cit., 110 and 116.
28 The letter took the form of an ultimatum, and stated, 'make peace if you wish to maintain your land and your people'. See Witbooi, H, op. cit., 85.
29 Ibid., 89 ff.
30 Pool, G, op. cit., 72 ff.
31 Goldblatt, I. 1971, 113.
32 Witbooi, H, op. cit., 126 ff.
33 Ibid.
34 Ibid., 141.
35 Bley, H. 1971, 4.
36 When Von François left, the title *Landeshauptmann* was replaced with the title of 'governor'. See Bley, H. 1968, 18 ff.
37 Ibid., 35; see also Pool, G, op. cit., 102 ff.
38 Pool, G, op. cit., 127.
39 Ibid., 93-94; see also Bley, H. 1961, 61 and 63.
40 Ibid.
41 Pool, G, op. cit., 144 ff.
42 Bley, H, op. cit., 60.
43 Goldblatt, I, op. cit., 130.
44 Mossolow, N. (year of publication unknown), 160 and 167.
45 Bley, H, op. cit., 92.
46 Ibid., 97.
47 Bley, H, op. cit., 93. It would be 'preventive' in the sense that it would forestall a surprise attack by the blacks.
48 Bley, H, op. cit., 127.
49 I.1.1-7: 1900; Church Archives, Windhoek.
50 Pool, G, op. cit., 175.
51 I.1.1-7: Minutes of the Missionary Conference of 1900; Church Archives, Windhoek.

7 The Rhenish Mission during the Namibian wars, 1904-1907

The war breaks out

Neither the colonial authorities nor the Mission suspected the Herero people of preparing themselves for a war against the German colonizers. It was not unusual for large groups of people to come to Samuel Maharero's headquarters in Okahandja. Herero leaders often gathered there for discussions, counsels, or to hold religious ceremonies. When the missionaries enquired why so many of the Hereros were assembled at Okahandja at the end of 1903, they were told that they had come for religious ceremonies being held there as a consequence of the cattle plague. Not even the fact that the men were armed attracted much attention. The indigenous people kept armed men at the disposal of the colonial authorities when so required; this formed part of the treaties made by the colonial power with these various groups.

The war was well planned. Samuel Maharero had come to know a great deal about German colonial organization and the German military situation, owing to the good contacts he had established as a paramount chieftain, and to his being recognized as such by the authorities. His decision to lead his people in the war had been taken after a great deal of hesitation, and much pressure from them. He was well aware that the enemy was strong. He hoped therefore that other tribes would join in an alliance against the foreign power just after the outbreak of the war. The cause of the war concerned not only the Hereros, but all of the peoples of Namibia. Maharero counted Hendrik Witbooi as an ally of great import, a very able and experienced military leader, well known to the Hereros through past encounters in armed conflict. And even though Witbooi had been vanquished by the Germans, and was prohibited, in terms of the treaty with Leutwein, from leaving his area around Gibeon, he was permitted to keep his own armed forces for the use of the colonialists.

Another important group whom Samuel Maharero was very anxious to win over to his side were the Basters, who had settled in Rehoboth in 1864 and whose leader was Hermanus van Wyk, also referred to as 'Captain'. Through a treaty with the Germans in 1885, the Basters had been granted self-government within the limits of the group, provided they kept a well-trained company of soldiers at the disposal of the Germans. This well-equipped company of trained soldiers would be of great help in the war Maharero was planning.

A third important ally were the Ovambo people in the north. It has already been mentioned how that isolated part of the German colony had been prepared for evangelical mission through Andersson's contacts with the Rhenish Mission. There had in the past been a tradition of mercantile connections between the Ovambos and the Hereros.[1] This primarily involved trading cattle. After the cattle plague of 1896-1897, the Ovambos' access to cattle was reduced, and so they were facing starvation. The German colonialists had given a certain amount of help to remedy the famine in the far north of their colony, and had attempted to utilize the situation to get a so-called 'treaty of protection' out of a number of Ovambo chieftains. They had also erected a fort in Namutoni, near the Etosha Pan in southern Ovamboland, in 1897. (The Rhenish missionaries, in co-operation with the Finnish Missionary Society, had established two mission stations in Ovamboland by the early 1870s. The Finnish missionaries had demanded protection from the German colonial power, as they felt threatened by the internal strife going on between rival Ovambo groups.) But while the Ovambo chieftains had rejected the Germans' attempt to conclude treaties with them, they had maintained their contact with the Hereros.

It was the Ovambos' negative attitude towards the Germans, and their friendly though superficial relations with the Hereros, which led Samuel Maharero to believe he could win them over as allies in the war. Negotiations and contacts were opened with great secrecy before the outbreak of the war.

In January 1904, the Hereros made a surprise attack on German military and German colonists in several different places in the colony. By attacking several places at the same time, they placed the German colonial power in a dangerous position. There were hardly enough German military resources in Namibia to defend the Germans in the event of a major uprising. When the war broke out in 1904, 770 soldiers were stationed in the country, of whom 280 were assigned to police duty. Furthermore, the governor being the highest military commander, was able to mobilize roughly 1 000 ex-soldiers who had settled in the colony after completing their military service. The Germans also had access to the military assistance of the Basters, and the Oorlam-Namas under Hendrik Witbooi, in accordance with the treaties concluded between these groups and themselves, as well as from those Boers who were established in the colony ever since 1902, the end of the Second Boer War.

Against these colonial forces Samuel Maharero was able to mobilize 7 000-8 000 relatively well-armed Herero warriors. He gave explicit orders to attack German military and German colonizers, and to spare women and children. All other parties, including the missionaries, were to be left alone.[2] The German forces were based in garrisons, the largest of which was at Windhoek, while minor units were also stationed in Omaruru, Outjo, and Okahandja to the north of Windhoek, and Keetmanshoop south of the capital.

At the end of 1903, Leutwein, along with a major force of his German military staff, was forced to cut down a major uprising among the Bondelswarts, an Oorlam-Nama group in southern Namibia. Samuel Maharero took advantage of this. On 11 January 1904, the Hereros struck at several places at once. A few days later, Maharero sent a letter to the leader of the Basters in Rehoboth, Hermanus van Wyk, and also sent word to Hendrik Witbooi, urging them to join the battle on his side. The war, he said, would determine the future of the entire population of the colony. He therefore urged them to strike at once. It was a matter of winning or perishing: 'Rise up, and let the whole of Africa fight against the Germans; let them rather finish us off and let them live alone in our country.'[3]

But the letter never reached Hendrik Witbooi. Maharero had sent both letters to Van Wyk so that he might forward the one addressed to Hendrik Witbooi. Instead, Van Wyk delivered both letters to the Germans, who thus found out that this was not a mere uprising of the Hereros but that a major war could soon be underway.

Samuel Maharero also sent a message to the people of Ovamboland, likewise urging them to join in the struggle against the Germans. This message was discussed at a gathering in Ondangwa on 23 January 1904, in the presence of the Finnish missionaries. The missionaries advised the Ovambos not to let themselves be drawn into the war. One of the chieftains, Nehale, rallied his people to storm Fort Namutoni near Etosha, but this was of little consequence to the outcome of the war.

The Herero people waged war through swift attacks carried out by minor groups, targeting isolated farms and settlements, as well as many German patrols who were as yet ignorant of the outbreak of the war. Panic soon broke out among the colonists, and many Germans lost their lives. Others sought refuge in German garrisons and at the mission stations.

Leutwein immediately informed the authorities in Berlin about the outbreak of the war, demanding reinforcements. These were sent and by June 1904, he had twice as many troops as before; Maharero, on the other hand, found it increasingly difficult to gather his forces. The effect of surprise had waned, and all his attempts at forging alliances had failed.

The Herero warriors were not prepared for a lengthy war. Maharero withdrew to the Waterberg, where he and his forces, which had shrunk to a mere 5 000 men, waited for the opportunity to conduct a decisive onslaught.

One of the leaders of the Bondelswarts uprising which took place during the months preceding the war of the Hereros was Jakob Morenga. On the eve of the peace treaty with Leutwein, he and his group escaped across the Orange River into the northern Cape Colony. In June 1904, when he heard of the new outbreak of war north of Windhoek he returned across the river and kept up the war effort in the form of guerrilla warfare using swift surprise attacks upon German military bases and settlements in the south of the country. Hence, Leutwein's successor, General Von Trotha would be forced to fight the war on two fronts.

Authorities in Berlin, alarmed at the grave military situation, took immediate measures to cut down the 'insurgent tribes'. One such measure was the appointment of an experienced commander to conduct this war, who would be endowed with extraordinary powers of authority, issued by the government. The choice fell on Lothar von Trotha, a veteran of the French-German war of 1870-1871, the Boxers' Revolution in China, and the fight against the Wahehe uprising of German East Africa in 1896.

Von Trotha was a typical colonial military officer who saw every uprising as the attempt of primitive heathens to destroy Christian Western civilization. He was given responsibility for all military operations in Namibia. In this position he was not subordinated to Leutwein as the governor of the colony. In accordance with his appointment issued by the emperor on 16 May 1904, he was directly responsible to the emperor, and was only liable to take orders from the general staff in Berlin.[4]

Leutwein did not receive Von Trotha with great enthusiasm. Before the arrival of Von Trotha he had attempted to combine military operations with negotiations to persuade Samuel Maharero to make peace, but had failed. Now he was given orders from Berlin that he should not interfere with any of the military concerns, and that he should least of all try to reach a compromise with the 'insurgents'. Von Trotha openly criticized Leutwein's attempts at leading a war which he characterized as 'the aimless running around of a lot of rats with their tails entangled in the vicinity of Okahandja'.[5]

The decisive battle against the Herero people was fought near Waterberg, and began on 11 August 1904. Von Trotha's troops were well equipped, having both machine guns and light artillery at their disposal. Maharero had little to hold against this – he had a mere 2 500 rifles, most of which were pitifully outdated – added to which he was inhibited by the fact that he had women, children and cattle with him in his fortified camp in Waterberg.

Von Trotha's plan was to surround Maharero's camp and fight a battle of extermination.

Waterberg is a semi-circular, steep mountain plateau which is exceedingly difficult to storm. Here, Von Trotha hoped to press the Herero troops into a tight corner where he could cut them down. There was, however, unbeknownst to him, an escape route eastwards, which led into the arid Omaheke region. Large numbers of Hereros, including women and children, and their cattle now fled by this trail, led by Maharero.

When he discovered their escape route, Von Trotha ordered that those who fled should be pursued, and killed ruthlessly. He also ordered mounted patrols to anticipate the route taken by the fleeing Hereros and contaminate all the sources of water along the escape route. He hoped that the entire multitude of these fleeing people should either perish in the harsh desert climate, or be killed by German troops.

It was in this context that Von Trotha issued his notorious proclamation of extermination, to every member of the Herero tribe, which read, translated:

I, the great General of the German soldiers, send this letter to the Herero nation. The Hereros are no longer German subjects. They have murdered and robbed, they have cut off the ears and the noses and privy parts of wounded soldiers and they are now too cowardly to fight .... The Herero nation must now leave the country. If the people do it not I will compel them with the big tube [artillery]. Within the German frontier, with or without rifle, with or without cattle [all the Hereros] will be shot. I will not take over any more women and children; I will either drive them back to your people or have them fired on.

These are my words to the nation of the Hereros.

The great General of the Mighty Emperor, Von Trotha[6]

The proclamation also contained the promise of a reward for those who would help bring Samuel Maharero or any of his captains into captivity.

Von Trotha wrote his proclamation on 2 October 1904, and sent it, through prisoners he had freed, to the Hereros who had fled to the Omaheke region.

It is a less well-known fact that on the same day Von Trotha issued a general order to all his troops, instructing them how his proclamation should be interpreted. He stressed that all Herero men should be killed, and that none should be taken prisoner. However, the war should, as he put it, by no means 'degenerate into cruelties inflicted upon women and children'. As a final twist to his declaration to the soldiers, he pointed out that the troops must 'strive to maintain the good reputation enjoyed by German soldiers'![7]

In a report sent to the general staff and the colonial division in Berlin, Von Trotha stated his motives for issuing his proclamation of extermination:

> Making terms with the Hereros is impossible, seeing that their chiefs have nearly all fled or through their misdeeds during the rebellion have rendered themselves so liable that the German government could not deal with them. I regard the acceptance of a more or less voluntary surrender as a possible means of building up the old tribal organisation again, and as such it would be a great political mistake.[8]

Thus Von Trotha argued that the Herero people must be exterminated.

In a special report of 4 October 1904, issued to his closest superior, the head of the general staff in Berlin, Von Trotha rejected Leutwein's wishes to initiate negotiations for peace with the Herero 'nation': 'I am of the opinion that this nation must be exterminated.' He added, 'The Negro is unlikely to bend to a treaty of any kind except under the dictates of pure violence.'[9] The head of the general staff, a certain General Von Schlieffen, sided with Von Trotha in this issue. Against the criticism which had begun to be levelled at Von Trotha's methods, Von Schlieffen pointed out that he believed cohabitation between whites and blacks to be impossible. What remained was to enslave the blacks.

The outcome of the Herero war was in effect conclusively settled at the battle of Waterberg, even though the killing of Hereros persisted, taking on the proportions of a near genocide.

In October 1904, Hendrik Witbooi and his soldiers sided with Jakob Morenga. It was to prove harder for the Germans to defeat these well-trained Oorlam-Nama groups than to master the Herero troops. Morenga applied a form of guerrilla war which made it difficult for Von Trotha to fight a decisive battle, although his troops now exceeded 15 000 men.

In spite of his advanced age, Witbooi took part in the battles himself. On 25 October 1905, he was fatally wounded. Morenga carried on the war, along with other Nama leaders such as Morris and Cornelius of Bethanie.[10]

It is interesting that Hendrik Witbooi, ever since the arrival of Von Trotha to the colony, had openly demonstrated a kind of disappointment over the fact that Leutwein was now no longer the solely appointed German leader. Without Leutwein, he is said to have lacked a 'feeling of security'.[11] The minute Witbooi joined the war effort, all the Nama soldiers fighting on the side of the Germans were imprisoned, and sent in chains as prisoners to German colonies held in Togo and Cameroon. The Germans put a price of 20 000 Marks on the head of Jakob Morenga.

The war itself now increasingly changed into a series of brief skirmishes, involving swift attacks and withdrawals. When the fighting appeared to peter out gradually, on 31 March 1907, the German emperor proclaimed that the war was over. The proclamation was made too soon, however. Morenga had escaped across the border into Bechuanaland (present-day Botswana). After some time he returned, only to resume the war. At the end of September 1907, he was forced flee once again – this time to the Cape Colony. He was pursued and shot by the Cape police in collaboration with a German officer, whom the German authorities had attached to the police, with the consent of the Cape government.[12] This enemy of the German colonial power who had fought with great success and courage, was therefore ironically killed by the English police.

In the end, 20 000 German soldiers had been engaged in the colony during the war. Captured Hereros were put on trial in accord with Von Trotha's severe regulations. An unknown number of prisoners of war were sentenced to death, and executed in public hangings which attracted crowds of German colonist onlookers.

More and more, the Rhenish Mission was seen as seeking to thwart the colonists' interests, and it was declared that the Mission was 'a constant security risk for the white population, [with its] undigested and muddled ideas of equality and human dignity'.[13]

For the colonists, only blacks capable of work were of any value. Therefore, it was decided to kill 'unproductive elements'. When the Mission protested, it was claimed that 'it is absolutely no business of the Mission what legal and political status the natives have; that is the exclusive concern of the secular power'.[14]

Word of Von Trotha's ruthless methods echoed through the German press and parliament. Criticism against Von Trotha became so violent and politically dangerous that the emperor was forced to retract the former's proclamation of extermination. His order of revocation of the Von Trotha proclamation declared 'that the emperor ... would exercise clemency towards those Hereros who gave themselves up voluntarily'.[15] In spite of this, there remained plenty of room for continued cruelties to be carried out against the Herero people.

An interesting detail in the imperial order of revocation was the fact that Von Trotha was ordered to accept the Rhenish Mission's offer to help the captured Hereros. Von Trotha, however, having previously rejected the Mission's attempt to create better conditions for the prisoners of war, was not that easily made to relent. Even after the emperor's order of revocation in December 1904, he used such cruel methods against the captured that he was called home, in November 1905. On his arrival back home, he was subjected to severe criticism in the Berlin parliament.

It is of interest to note that he was defended in parliament by Von Bülow, chancellor of the Reich since 1900, who had originally been against his nomination to the position of command in the colony. Von Bülow declared that Von Trotha 'had given proof of great humanity' during his period of service in Namibia!'[16] And Von Trotha continued to defend his activity during the war, claiming that 'mildness on my part would only [have] be[en] interpreted as weakness by the other side. They had to perish in the Sandveld or try to cross the Bechuanaland border.'[17] In a statement made on 23 June 1906, he maintained that the whole war really was a racial war: 'It is and remains a racial conflict, which all nations of this earth who wish to take up the economic black legacy are interested in. To apply the ploughshare before the end of the war is futile.'[18] When it came to European culture and the Europeans' future in Africa, no obstacle was allowed to stand in the way.

The Rhenish Mission during the war

When the war broke out in 1904, the colonizers accused the Rhenish Mission of having been aware of the Hereros' war plans in advance, and not having given warning to the authorities. They expressed doubt of the German Mission's loyalty to the homeland. Their criticism found its way into the German press, where it was maintained that the Mission had added fuel to the discontent of the indigenous population, and spread socialist ideas among them about rights and liberty. Germany's *Koloniale Zeitung*, an extension of the radically conservative *Kolonialbund*, 'demanded in a petition to the chancellor of the Reich that the state should control and regulate all missionary activity conducted in the colony'.[19] Henceforth, it was considered imperative to place the Mission under the obligation of reporting everything they knew about the indigenous population's plans and designs against the colonial power. A German living in a German colony should never allow him or herself to be neutral, as neutrality was tantamount to betrayal of the native country and the emperor.

This wave of opinion against the Rhenish Mission spread to the highest quarters when on 9 May 1904, the chancellor of the Reich, Von Bülow, questioned the loyalty of the Mission in the German parliament. According to Von Bülow, the Mission had not sided with its countrymen during the war.

It is against this background that the letter addressed to all the parishioners among the Herero people must be viewed. Remarkably enough, it was sent on the same day that the German chancellor attacked the Rhenish Mission in German parliament; and it defended the Mission against the accusations of disloyalty against fellow-Germans which were being levelled at it. This letter was addressed to all baptized Hereros, and not, therefore, to the Herero people as a whole.

As further background to the composition of this letter it must be remembered that the Herero warriors had in their early surprise attacks, conducted long before Von Trotha had begun to carry out his merciless onslaught, killed a number of civilians, among them women and children, in spite of Samuel Maharero's orders to the contrary. It also happened that German colonizers seeking protection at the mission stations were dragged out and killed in front of the missionaries who stood by, powerless.

To some extent, this sheds new light on the letter which has often been taken for evidence of the Rhenish Mission's unflinching support of Von Trotha's war of extermination. In view of the Germans' sentiments of the time, it is not surprising that the Board of the Rhenish Mission was eager to spare no efforts in answering the accusations of treachery against German colonial rule and German colonizers, which were being levelled at the Mission. In a separate missive to the chancellor of the Reich the Mission declared: 'The evangelical missionaries will always relate to the authorities and the native country in accordance with the clear directions given in the Holy Scriptures, with specific reference to Romans 13: 1-7.'[20]

The pastoral letter itself read:

Dearly beloved in Christ Jesus,

It is not easy for us to attach such a title to this letter. Our love for you has suffered a rude shock on account of the terrible rebellion in which so many of you took part and on account of the awful bloodshed, as well as the many atrocities associated with the rebellion for which you also share at least co-responsibility, even if we still hope that only a few of you were directly involved in these atrocities and murderous deeds. But our Saviour's love never ceases. It pursues the lost sinners to save them and make them holy. The father continues to love even the prodigal son who left his father's house and has trampled upon his father's will, just as he is prepared to forgive the same as soon as the son returns penitently to the father and says, 'Father, I have sinned against Heaven and before you and am henceforth no longer worthy to be called your son.' It is in this spirit that we continue to refer to you as dearly beloved in Christ Jesus.

We dare not conceal from you that you have made us very unhappy and have caused us great sorrow. Our hearts bleed when we think of you, as the heart of the father bled when the prodigal son turned his back to him. You too have set upon a path which will inevitably lead you to misfortune, and you will perish miserably unless you soon recognize your error and repent. You have raised the sword against the Government which God has placed over you without considering that it is written: 'Whoever takes the sword, shall also perish by the sword.'[21]

In its self-defence addressed to the chancellor, the Board of the Mission in Germany later went even further, to express its conviction that 'the inflexibly proud and disobedient Herero people' had deserved that long overdue lesson to force them into greater humility and obedience. And referring to Morenga's and Witbooi's insurrection in October 1904, it was quick to point out that the war clearly was not caused by any social evils originating in the colonial administration, but was entirely due to the Namas' refusal to subordinate themselves to 'their white rulers'.[22]

Haussleiter, the inspector of the Mission, said that to suppress the insurrection had 'not merely [been] a political, but also a moral duty'.[23] The Rhenish Mission was, he said, of the opinion that Witbooi had been influenced by a prophetic figure originating from an Ethiopian movement in the Cape Colony, with a message of liberation of the whole of Africa from the yoke of foreign rule. According to Leutwein too, he said, the principal cause of Witbooi's 'treachery' was his religious fanaticism 'called forth by the prophet from the Cape Colony, who saw himself as a representative of the Ethiopian Church'.[24]

Von Bülow interpreted these statements as evidence of the Mission's loyal support of the war effort as a means to regain peace and order in the colony.[25]

After the battle at Waterberg, the missionaries persisted in their contacts with the 'insurgents', urging them to lay down their weapons. Missionaries would often follow the movements of German troops in their pursuit of fleeing Herero soldiers, and prevail upon the Hereros to 'surrender'. The Board of the Mission in Wuppertal-Barmen expressed its appreciation of the commitment demonstrated by the missionaries, and its opinion 'that they would, in the pursuit of this policy, grant the homeland a great favour'.[26]

Though meeting its patriotic obligations of assuring the German authorities of its loyalty in the war, the Rhenish Mission intervened when it came to protecting those Hereros who were held captive in the vast prison camps at Swakopmund. In various ways, the missionaries there attempted to mitigate the treatment of the prisoners, for instance by making direct applications to Von Trotha who had decided that the prisoners should work for the whites, including the Herero men who had voluntarily given themselves up. (The others who had fled and who been caught, had been mercilessly killed.)

As we have mentioned, Von Trotha had been given orders to accept the Rhenish Mission's offer of providing assistance to captive Herero men, women and children who were in camps at Swakopmund. In a letter to the German authorities dated 18 February 1905, Von Trotha declared that it was his duty to obey orders: he would therefore heed the missioners' advice and assistance. On a more personal note he added, 'I do admire the Rhenish Mission for its courage in undertaking the responsibility of conducting missionary work among the Herero people just as it has done before – a responsibility before God, before the German people, and before themselves.'[27] It is difficult to determine just how sincere Von Trotha was in his 'admiration'. He did continue to deprive the Hereros of their cattle, and to force them, men and women alike, to work for the colonizers for no remuneration other than their daily intake of food.

Haussleiter – and his criticism of the peace terms

According to a series of consecutive imperial decrees enacted in 1905 for the Herero people, and in 1907 for the Oorlam-Namas, these people had as 'insurgents' forfeited all their rights of ownership of any cattle or territory, as well as of self-determination. Their right of existence in the colony was solely based on providing labour for whites; their property was taken from them, and through a number of regulations, their lives were regulated in minute detail.

These imperial decrees ordained, among other things, that no more than ten families belonging to the same tribe or group were to live at one and the same place. Traditional, religious or social gatherings were declared illegal, and strict measures were taken to ensure that these prohibitions were observed.

The same regulations were soon applied to *all* indigenous people living in the police zone, that is, in southern and central Namibia. Every African, including children from the age of seven, had to be registered, and was provided with a number, inscribed on a tin plate fastened on the arm. Anyone found without their plate, or without written permission from their employer, or found outside their allotted territory, was outlawed and as such, considered a free target for every colonizer. Any such person would be captured and forced into slave labour. Manhunts launched to catch such 'outlaws' were carried out with manifest cynicism and disregard of human dignity. Those who attempted to escape were either gunned down or chased into the desert, where they were sure to perish.

One of the 'experts' on German colonial policy of this time, Paul Rohrbach, gave the following definition of the task of the colonial power when it came to black people. It was desirable, he wrote, to 'deprive [the black Namibian] of his national sense of belonging and indigenous particularity in order to mould him and the other blacks into a single, coloured working class'.[28]

It is estimated that soon after the war, 90 per cent of all black Namibians in the police zone were forced into the service of white colonizers. A mere 200 Nama and Herero men were exempted from holding a labour pass.

The terms of peace for the defeated, transforming them into serfs under German colonial rule, were severely criticized by the missionary inspector Gottlob Haussleiter, the leader of the Rhenish Mission. At a colonial congress held in Berlin in 1906 and attended by representatives of the government and the Mission, and other parties interested in German colonial politics, points of view put forward led Haussleiter to write a series of articles in the *Allgemeine Missionszeitschrift*, in which he gave the background to the war, and the consequences of the peace treaties – not only for the vanquished, but for the future of the colony. His articles are important because they give a better picture of the Rhenish Mission's role in this devastating war and in postwar developments.[29]

Haussleiter asserted that the indigenous population were vital for the postwar reconstruction of the colony, a fact which had not been taken into consideration during the colonial congress. He stated further that if it was true that the indigenous population were South West Africa's greatest resource, and if the German government's aim was the preservation of the colony, then it was important to pardon what had come to pass. The survivors of the carnage would need all the hope they could get for the near future. It was therefore important both in word and in action to recognize these people, and to inspire in them a sense of value. Primarily, he said, it was a matter of regaining their confidence, and of giving them the means to right themselves.

Haussleiter continued that the colonial authorities had given ample proof of their admirable efficiency when it came to 'crushing the rebellion'. The impression this sort of action sometimes created, however, was that the old order of truth was lost. Ultimately, every war must be a war fought in the service of peace.

It did not fall to the Mission, he said, to question the punishment of murderers and instigators of rebellion; but for a large number of the indigenous population, a series of extenuating circumstances could be stated. Due to its close contact with the indigenous population, the Mission was well aware of how many Christians had been forced to take part in the war, and considering the fact that the war had been started by the Hereros of whom, approximately, eight per cent were Christians, it would seem that the work of the Mission had been in vain. Quite the contrary, however. Numerous examples could be cited of Christians who, risking their own lives, had saved European women and children. Governor Leutwein himself had admitted this on 9 May 1904 in a telegram to the Board of the Rhenish Mission. As he had put it, 'Justice demands that we recognize that white women have been saved through the assistance of black Christians.' Haussleiter added, 'The pitiable state of tribes of people in despair makes it necessary for us to attend to their future. They have lost everything in the war .... They no longer have any freedom, their pride has been crushed. The survivors are for the most part sick and without strength. They have been punished enough.' They ought to be shown mercy – an opinion which seemed to have been forgotten.

When the alternative of exercising leniency in the treatment of the defeated tribes was discussed at the 1906 conference, a representative of the colonial power had discussed the danger of 'destroying the nest but preserving the egg of the future'. However, Haussleiter argued that the continued existence of the Herero people was at risk owing to the great privation which especially Herero women had suffered during their escape. Family life was no longer possible. Presently, these people, so thoroughly defeated in the battle at Waterberg, had to be allowed to regain hope. Taking away all hope from a people, and thus turning their lives into hell, could easily transform them into devils as a consequence.

Despite all claims to the contrary, the Mission was positive in its attitude towards continued immigration to the colony. The immigrants, however, had to be of the kind with a sense of responsibility towards the indigenous population. Only in this way could the black Namibians regain their confidence in the German colonial power.

In all this, the Mission had an important task to fulfil. The colony held rich deposits of diamonds and other precious minerals. However, for 60 years, the Mission had given the colony the most precious of all things in life – namely, that which gives eternal value to one and all: Christian faith.

South West Africa was to become a German colony (after previously having been a protectorate). According to Haussleiter, this placed the German government, the colonizers, and the indigenous people under the obligation to lend a hand to start anew. For the indigenous population this meant working with the Mission. All talk of extermination had to cease immediately. The African was a fellow human being – carried by fear and hope, hate and love, faith and strife, by fault and by yearning; someone who while experiencing war had longed for peace, the kind of peace which only the righteous and the faultless could attain. All people were human beings with the same needs. The Mission was needed to contribute to the peace, and to finding a solution for the problems faced by the indigenous population.

Haussleiter referred to recently published books of possible use to the authorities in the attempt to find a way out of the crisis, including *Die Amtliche Reichstagsdenkschrift*[30] which gave both a short history of the indigenous tribes in South West Africa, and a short description of the reasons behind the insurrection, one of the most decisive of which had been the white businessmen's giving of credit, and their way of collecting the debts owed them. (Article 6 of the Congo Act of the colonial congress of 26 February 1885 had been transgressed. In it, certain fundamental principles, internationally approved of, had been established to protect the indigenous people in the colonies. These principles had never applied when it came to dealing with the peoples of Namibia. In the name of humanity and judiciousness, the indigenous people had to be treated humanely, and also enjoy the protection of the colonial power.)

German colonization, Haussleiter pointed out, had not started as a war of conquest, but rather through a treaty made with indigenous tribes. The Hereros' act of war could therefore be regarded as a deplorable transgression of treaties, and arguably such transgression ought to be punished. The blame was on both sides, however, the white colonizers being equally at fault for what had happened. In the name of the German nation, the task was now to 'rehabilitate those who through our shared fault in our eyes had become guilty enemies'.

It was the duty, and the right, of the Mission to point this out. Above all, the Mission must not remain silent – it must speak out about this in the open.

Haussleiter also referred to author Felix Meyer's 'diagnosis of the disease which led to the rebellion' in an article titled 'Wirtschaft und Recht der Herero'.[31] Meyer had argued that in a number of cases, German colonial politics had acted in opposition to the Hereros' sense of justice. Samuel Maharero had received support as a paramount chieftain even though, according to the Hereros' established order of succession, he had had no right to be the chieftain. In Herero tradition, cattle and grazing were the property of the people and not of separate individuals. Again, no regard had been paid to this important tradition which had shaped the Hereros' way of life. Thus in a number of respects the colonial power had failed to pay due regard to the Hereros' conception of right and wrong. This had occurred both due to ignorance of and indifference to the values of the people. Also, the judicial system of the Hereros, based on tradition, protected for the very existence of the entire people. The German colonizers had, through disregarding the Herero traditions and civilization, wounded them to the core of life.

Haussleiter tried in his articles to address the innumerable queries and issues that had been raised by the colonists, anthropologists, and officers of the German *Schutztruppe* concerning the indigenous population and the colonists' treatment of them, as well as the work of the Mission. He cited some so-called 'experts' who had voiced their opinion about some aspects of colonial politics. One colonist, for instance, had said, in line with 'old Boer tradition': 'Lenient treatment of coloureds is a cruelty against whites.' And an officer of high rank had taken the Ethiopian motto, and reformulated it: 'Africa to the Africans and the Africans to us.' Haussleiter violently criticized such utterances. If the whites in the colony were to have any future, the relationship with the blacks must be built on trust, and on a communion of shared interests; the task ahead was therefore to win and to preserve the Africans' esteem.

Haussleiter demanded that the Africans' human dignity be recognized. This was a minimum demand, and it applied to every aspect of the colony's administration: it must be reflected not only at the workplace and in business, and in the religious and moral sphere, but in the administration's

handling of all social questions and problems. He listed a number of points concerning future African-European relations in the colony:
1   Blacks were needed for industrial development in the colony. If the workers were held in serfdom, the whole colony would be like a penitentiary. The workers needed to take pleasure in their work, and this could only be achieved if they received fair wages, which would also stimulate their purchasing power. Also, their level of education had to be raised, to enable them to share in the colonial tasks as fellow-workers. This, the basis of the community of interests, alone could lead to general prosperity.
2   The administration ought to have as its goal the peaceful coexistence between people of different racial origins and cultural backgrounds. The black people should be allowed to feel 'that their personal rights [were] better protected by the new regime than by their former system of chieftains, that their family life [was being] preserved, and that their children would have a better future through receiving school education'.
3   Just like the colonists, the indigenous people should be allowed to have their own representatives and spokespersons. In order for public security to be just, the administration of justice must be separated from public administration.
4   For the strengthening of moral and religious values, punishment for fraud, brutality, unreliability and fornication ought to disregard skin colour. In other words, equality before the law should apply to all.

Rather than condemn a whole people, one needed, Haussleiter advised, to distinguish between the guilty and the innocent. He urged to put a stop to the mass killings of prisoners of war.

Haussleiter attacked the imperial decrees through which the population had been deprived of all their property and forced into slave labour. He expressed the hope that the German parliament revoke these decrees without delay. Decisions taking away the people's right to own cattle and land were disastrous in their effect, and would most certainly lead to pauperism which in the long run was equally dangerous for all. Instead the authorities should give each family a piece of land as grazing for their cattle, preferably near white-owned farms. The blacks would thus be able to develop into a well-motivated labour force.

In addition to this, a number of larger reserves ought to be placed under the Mission's direct supervision, in which the indigenous population could be re-formed to lead a 'civilized life'.

Haussleiter concluded his series of articles with two quotations from the Bible to back his argument that the Mission had a Christian responsibility to the indigenous population, and therefore that he, as a missionary leader, could not allow himself to be tied down by a one-sided obligation towards the authorities. His concluding remarks to the authorities were: 'May the government in its handling of citizens and inhabitants let itself be guided by the words of the Apostle Paul: "If you want to live in peace with the authorities, then do what is good. If you do what is bad, then tremble in fear – for you will not carry a sword in vain."'

To the indigenous population he gave the following recommendation: 'To the Natives, however, who with broken hearts fear for their lives and who are praying earnestly for peace, the Mission, not only by reason of its vocation, but also in the name of the Christian citizens, must direct the words: "Fear not, for all of us are answerable to God."'

Haussleiter's series of articles are interesting mainly because of the opinions expressed in them, along with the criticism levelled at the colonial power, exhorting it to self-examination. These factors contribute to making Haussleiter's articles an important document in the Church history of Namibia, as they help us understand a vital aspect of the attitude of the missionaries and the Rhenish Mission after the tragic events of the war. Another factor which adds weight to the importance of the document is that it was written in 1906 while the war was still going on. In taking his stand for Christian humanitarian values in times of hatred, Haussleiter demonstrated a manifest degree of moral courage.[32]

Notes

1 Williams, F-N. 1991, 146.
2 Pool, G. 1991, 202.
3 Ibid., 203 ff.
4 Ibid., 245.
5 Ibid., 245 ff.
6 Steer, GL. 1939, 63.
7 Rust, C. 1905, 444-445.
8 Steer, GL, op. cit., 63.
9 Bley, H. 1968, 204.
10 Heywood, A & E Maasdorp. 1995, p xxvii.
11 Goldblatt, I. 1971, 140.
12 Ibid., 143.
13 Bley, H. 1971, 208 ff.
14 Ibid.
15 Ibid., 165.
16 '315. Eintragung: Militärischer Werdegang des Lothar von Trotha'; Von Trotha family archives.
17 Pool, G, op. cit., 243 and 269.
18 Ibid., 273.
19 Gründer, H. 1982, 128.
20 Ibid., note 18.
21 Herz, KH. 1976, 100.
22 Gründer, H, op. cit., note 18.
23 Ibid.
24 Drechsler, H. 1966, 105.
25 Correspondence, of 8 December 1904: Von Trotha to Missionary Kuhlmann; Church Archives, Windhoek.
26 Correspondence, of 7 June 1904: Von Bülow to the Board of the Mission; and of 8 December 1904: Von Bülow to Inspector Haussleiter; Church Archives, Windhoek.
27 11.1-16: 1905; Church Archives, Windhoek.
28 Rohrbach, P. 1907, 28.
29 Haussleiter, G. 1906, 19-30, 108-117, and 172-187.
30 This paper, of 28 November 1904, was an important document in the parliamentary debate on colonial policies, Berlin, 28 November 1904; copy, Church Archives, Windhoek.
31 Meyer, F. 1905.
32 Haussleiter left the service of the Rhenish Mission in 1908 to become Professor of Theology at the University of Halle.

8 German colonization and Mission, 1907-1914

Colonial policy after 1907

The war effort was a terrible financial drain, not only on the German state, but also for the colonizers and the mining companies who had begun extracting the colony's mineral deposits (at this stage, mainly copper and zinc). During the war, the colonizers had to contribute to the maintenance of the German fighting forces. As early as 1905, they sent a delegation to Berlin, not only asking for indemnities for their expenses during the war, but also to present their views on the 'native question' and a future 'native policy'. They demanded that immigrants should have a say in the colony's administration.

Many factors at this stage seemed to point to a lengthy rehabilitation after the financial strains of the war in Namibia; however, this was far from being the case. Instead, a financial boom followed shortly upon the war, which, besides contributing to the financial independence of this German colony from the motherland, yielded vast profits. The main reason for this was the discovery of diamonds outside Lüderitz in 1907. From June 1907 to December that year, 40 000 carats were extracted and were valued at an estimate of 1.1 million Marks. By 1913, the profits had risen to 50 million Marks.[1]

The immigrants, including the Boers who had come from the former Boer Republics, enjoyed good living conditions. Public schools were built, and education for all immigrant children, provided by the authorities, was compulsory. A system for hospital treatment was organized, as well as a banking system subsidized by the state. The number of immigrants increased from about 8 000 in 1907, to more than 14 000 by 1913. In 1914, there were more than 1 000 farms owned by colonizers, the majority of whom were of German origin. Even before the war, the building of railroads had begun, and the total railway network in 1912 amounted to roughly 2 100 kilometres. In 1909, measures were introduced to ensure that the colonizers had political power, by giving those in the outlying administrative districts limited self-government, and appointing an advisory council elected by the colonizers for the central government. The decree which ensured this participation of the colonizers was issued by the chancellor of the Reich on 28 January 1909.

Following the initiative of the Rhenish Mission, a German parish had been established in Windhoek between 1895 and 1896 and was placed under an evangelical *Oberkirchenrat*[2] based in Berlin in 1901. In 1907, the Rhenish Mission negotiated with the *Oberkirchenrat* about sending out a German pastor to all the main locations of the colony. In this way, it hoped to strengthen the level of the colonizers' Christian commitment, without saddling the staff of the local missions with added responsibilities. Maintaining German parish life was considered the mutual task of the colonial authorities and the German Evangelical Church, who put in a joint effort to preserve their conception of German Evangelical Christian culture.[3] There was a strong sentiment of German nationalism among the colonizers, and the German Evangelical Church became an important cultural token for this. In August 1907, foundations were laid for the Christuskirche on a hill in the centre of Windhoek, in a spot which had once been a sacred site of the Herero people. The church was consecrated in 1910, in the presence of the colonial deputy-governor acting as the personal representative of the emperor. On the emperor's birthday in 1912, a statue was uncovered representing the 'German Horseman', to commemorate all those Germans who had lost their lives during the war of 1904-1907.[4] This statue, which in fact still stands today, was raised beside the German fort adjacent to the Christuskirche.

In spite of the financial upswing after the war, the white population were anxious that new upheavals might occur. Their constant fear of renewed insurrections was not lessened by the fact that the number of German soldiers was drastically reduced after the war. In 1913, only 2 000 German soldiers were left in Namibia. That year, an ex-major of the Namibian troops held a lecture on 'The Black Danger' to the Deutsche Kolonialgesellschaft in Berlin, warning that the German government had not taken heed of the lessons it should have learnt from the events of 1904-1907.[5] No-one, in his opinion, was sufficiently aware of the 'unreliable character of the blacks'. They could not be 'civilized' as they were congenitally hostile to 'cultural progress'. The more the Africans were exposed to culture, the more aggressive and dangerous they became. A strong military pressure in the colony was therefore needed to prevent another insurrection. More troops should be sent to the colony to protect the life and property of the colonizers.

Inside the colony, white citizens arrogated the right to themselves to take the law into their own hands, by brutalizing or even killing 'negligent, lazy or insubordinate natives', as many whites referred to the blacks. The indigenous people had adopted a form of resigned passivity, yet occasional strikes did occur, as did instances, individual or collective, of self-defence in the face of grievous encroachments on human rights.[6] Relations between the colonizers and the indigenous population were caught up in a vicious circle, where the black Namibians, who were daily exposed to violence, were prone to lash out in defensive outbursts of resistance and hatred, and where these prompted still more severe methods of repression by the colonizers.

Conditions became so bad that the governor was compelled to take action to restrain the 'indiscriminate killing of Africans'.[7] He made it known that the colonial authorities alone held the law in their hands, and that they would enforce it by police intervention, and provide justice through the courts of justice. This the colonizers viewed as interference and restrictions of their penal rights, as is evident from a letter to the editor of a Lüderitz newspaper in 1912. The writer, who signed it 'A German farmer', deplored the increased police intervention on behalf of his employees. This type of procedure, he claimed, resulted in the loss of a great many precious working hours due to lengthy police interrogation, and to prosecution before the court of justice. He continued that police behaviour led to an increasingly evident lack of respect of the blacks towards their employers. The writer ended with a revealing reflection:

> A good thrashing given at the right moment obviates the necessity to interrogate and take statements from everyone concerned, and is without legal consequences for the employer, and as such, is far more effective with respect to the maintenance of racial differentiation, and will be less harmful to both blacks and whites, than when fear of unpleasant consequences leads the farmer to shy away from executing due punishment against a neglectful labourer.[8]

The colonizers even regarded female blacks as their own property but failed to provide for the children born out of these illicit relationships. At a Rhenish Mission conference in 1914, many reports were delivered of such 'social evils which should be legally prohibited as soon as possible'.[9]

For the advisory council elected by the colonizers, the treatment of blacks became the constant topic of discussion. At a council meeting in 1913, it was pointed out that only in exceptional cases were the authorities notified of incidents of maltreatment of blacks. It was proposed that such cases of maltreatment should lead to the immediate expulsion of the offending colonizer from the colony.[10] Finally, the council unanimously agreed to recommend to the governor that employers who maltreated any of their employees should be deprived of the right to engage black labourers. A report in the press, though applauding this decision for its noble intentions, said it was impracticable in reality.

During his visit to the colony in 1908, the colonial secretary, Bernhard Dernburg, observed that bad labour relations would hardly promote increased productivity in the colony. Though his opinion was taken note of, this did little to change the situation. From the point of view of the colonizers, it was a 'grievous fault for Africans to dare to lead an independent existence [...], independent of toiling for the white man'.[11]

Dernburg's successor, Karl Self, visited the colony in 1912. On the issue of forced labour for the indigenous population, he said that 'the Africans were only awaiting the opportunity to regain their long lost rights in resistance to inhumane oppression'.[12] Following upon Self's visit, the governor appointed 'native commissioners' to exercise 'extensive control and supervising powers in regard to the health, food and maintenance of the native population'[13] and to deliver annual reports to the governor about unfair treatment and sufferings of the blacks. However, their actual power to substantially improve the overall treatment of the indigenous population was severely restricted.

Missionary work, 1907-1915

The regulations which the colonial authorities applied to the indigenous population after the war mostly affected blacks in southern and central Namibia, the so-called 'police zone' reserved for colonizers. Here, whites lived under police protection; and blacks were only admitted as labour for the colonizers. This part of the country was in fact the Rhenish Mission's main sphere of activity (though since 1891 it had two mission stations north of this zone, in the territory of the Ovambo people).

After the war, the Rhenish Mission was, to a greater extent than before, compelled to adapt to the restrictions which were being introduced on the basis of race – the Finnish Missionary Society in the north, by contrast, was able to carry on its activities under relatively undisturbed conditions north of the police zone. The strict rules concerning relations between blacks and whites applied to the missionaries as well. Whites were not allowed to settle near black settlements. Special permission was required for visits to these areas. This made it very difficult for the Rhenish Mission to maintain natural, unbroken contact with its parishes. In addition to this, the authorities began to question the missionaries' rights of possession to land which had been left at their disposal by tribal chieftains before the war. Whenever such land was within a so-called 'white territory', it could be confiscated as crown land.

During the war, the Mission had had to abandon some of its mission stations. The authorities manifested little or no interest in granting permission to put these stations back to use again.[14] The new restrictions on the peoples of Namibia compelled the missionaries more and more to take on the function of travelling evangelists who had no daily contact with their parishes.

In spite of all these difficulties, there was a fairly high increase in the Rhenish Mission's parish membership during the period 1907-1915. The Mission had about 9 000 members before the war. This number virtually doubled within the next few years. By 1914, at the outbreak of World War I, it was reported that the parishes had an estimated 25 000 members.[15]

The question is of course whether the Mission had changed its approach to win all these new members. In his series of articles in the *Allgemeine Missionszeitschrift*,[16] Mission Inspector Haussleiter had specified certain principles to be given priority in work conducted after 1907. He said that the Mission must after the end of the war show respect for the human value of the defeated peoples, as well as restore in them a faith in their future. He had further emphasized the importance of educating black Namibians so that they could have a greater share in shaping the future of the colony.

In spite of all the difficulties introduced through the authorities' restrictions, the Mission scrupulously tried to follow Haussleiter's guidelines to the point. At the Mission's main stations, as well as in surrounding parishes, the Mission therefore intensified its educational activities. These were at a very rudimentary level. Pupils were taught the basic skills of reading, writing, and arithmetics. The best pupils were selected for further training at the mission stations, and trained to work as teachers in the village parishes later on. However, many could not attend school regularly because, like all blacks, they were expected to work for the colonizers from the age of seven onwards. There were frequent clashes between the missionaries and the white farmers who were inclined to regard the Mission's 'useless' instruction as a hindrance to blacks' executing their daily tasks. The Rhenish Mission was, however, encouraged somewhat when the authorities began writing a curriculum, since even they had to concede that an elementary school education held some value when it came to increase the blacks' working performance and usefulness.

On the whole, the indigenous population viewed the Mission's activities favourably; at least here was some hope in an otherwise hopeless situation.[17] The Mission offered hospital treatment so that people living in the outlying villages for the first time had access to medicine and medical treatment. The colonial medical services were nearly exclusively for the benefit of white employers, who were in turn instructed on how to treat the 'natives', especially in the case of epidemics. The missionaries, on the other hand, provided a rudimentary medical service. Also, they remained in touch with blacks, even in areas reserved for whites. The indigenous people trusted them, and 'dared' talk to 'their missionaries', who often provided their only link to the colonists and colonial officials.

With their knowledge of the blacks' harsh living conditions under colonial oppression, the missionaries were often the only ones in a position to plead against the worst cases of mistreatment to some higher authority, and appeal to popular opinion in Germany.

Another important development in the work of the Rhenish Mission between 1907 and the outbreak of World War I was that the Mission had to allow the congregations a certain degree of self-government. Due to the missionaries' restricted freedom of movement, the responsibility for the everyday running of the parishes had to be handed over to blacks. In addition to this, indigenous languages were used in the congregation's life. It can therefore be said that in many ways, the parishes came to be places of refuge from the colonial authorities, as well as from the colonists' endeavour to sunder the blacks' traditional forms of community. The parishes became shelters, protecting the people from the total disintegration of their traditional social life, in addition to which they became places where blacks were trained to manage their own matters of concern.

One example of how the Rhenish Mission fought for the rights of the indigenous population was its taking action against the prohibition of so-called 'mixed marriages'. According to a German law of 1870, children of 'mixed marriages' automatically became German citizens. On 8 January 1900, a law had been passed to recognize such marriages. In connection with the war of 1904-1907, however, a new statute was passed in 1905 in Namibia, prohibiting such marriages. Two years later, such mixed marriages that had been entered into previous to the passing of the law, were annulled. Only in a very few exceptions did the governor grant exemption from the law.

Husbands and wives of different race were submitted to the same restrictions that applied to the indigenous population. The reason for this was growing racism. Views such as 'keep the German blood pure' were unashamedly and publicly expressed.[18] The privileges enjoyed by whites were reserved only for those of a 'pure, European race'. This was not merely a case of prohibiting sexual intercourse between blacks and whites: it was a matter of great importance to the colonists that no children born of mixed parents receive the privileged position that was reserved for their own children.

The new statute, of course, gave rise to many tragedies. The Rhenish Mission had voiced its protests to the governor, even before the law of 1907, decreeing the annulment of mixed marriages, had been passed. The protests of the local missionaries were supported by the Board of the Mission in Germany.[19] The prohibition of mixed marriages would not prevent the birth of children of mixed racial origin even in the future, Haussleiter observed in his series of articles in the *Allgemeine Missionszeitschrift*.[20] If mixed marriages were prohibited, a 'bastard population' would result, and be forced to live without the protection of married parents.

In principle, the Mission did not wish to encourage mixed marriages, but in cases where a white man lived together with a black woman, they should for honour's sake make their relationship legitimate through marriage. If such marriages were not allowed, there was great risk of a class of rootless people developing. Also, prohibition of mixed marriages would prevent the Mission from officiating such marriages. Haussleiter, seeing this question as a problem of conscience, observed that through it, 'citizens were subject to intolerable distress of conscience – and this in the name of Germanism'.[21]

In January 1906, Haussleiter commissioned the local leadership of the Mission to call upon the governor with the request to rescind the legislation of 1905 and 1907 concerning mixed marriages. The request was made on 18 October 1906, but the governor informed the preses of the Mission that he had no intention to change his stand in this issue.[22] To legalize a 'mixed marriage' would be, according to him, 'not only an offence against the maintenance of the purity of the German race and customs, but it would also endanger the white man's position'.[23] The entire issue was a question of guarding the privileged position of the colonists as a 'race'. No-one of mixed race should be considered equal in birth to a white man.

The Mission, however, continued its opposition in this issue. Preses Eich attacked what he referred to as 'social hypocrisy'. To prohibit 'mixed marriages' was to pave the way for illicit relationships between white men and black women in which the men had no obligation towards the women.

The Mission's protests were in vain, however. The consequences of the new law made themselves felt without delay. Now that illicit relationships were practically encouraged, the number of people who fell victim to venereal diseases increased at a catastrophic rate. The medical doctors in the service of the colony attempted to introduce obligatory medical examination for all black unmarried women at their places of work. The Rhenish Mission, indignant at this humiliating treatment of black women, alerted the German press about it. The Women's Association of the German Red Cross took immediate action, and, by rousing public opinion against it, managed to put a stop to this form of treatment. In the future the rule was to apply solely to women who were registered prostitutes.

In 1908, about 500 children were born of mixed parents. Since their fathers did not take care of them, and their mothers often abandoned them, the Rhenish Mission jointly with the Roman Catholic Mission[24] established nurseries especially for these children.

The controversy over the issue of mixed marriages continued for the entire period until the outbreak of World War I. In an article published in July 1913 in the newspaper of the German congregation in Windhoek, Missionary Hasenkamp observed that from a Christian viewpoint, the prohibition was indefensible.[25] It was far removed from Christian ethics, and its sole purpose was to assert the white man's superiority. The law appeared to postulate that such marriages would make the man sink down to his black wife's 'lower cultural level'. According to the debate of the missionary conference of 1913, referred to in the article,[26] it was the married couple's disposition, rather than their skin colour, which determined whether their marriage was Christian or not. The proposal of 'solving' the white man's problem by instituting public, and medically controlled, brothels was also rejected.

In the north, things were totally different with respect to mission. People there lived in relative isolation of the happenings in other parts of the country. In spite of the Ovambos' being divided into seven ethnic groups,[27] there was a strong feeling of belonging among them all.

Only a few Europeans had yet visited this part of the country. A group of businessmen from the Cape Colony established an independent 'republic', Upingtonia, at Grootfontein and Otavi, in 1885-1886 and came in conflict with the Ovambo chieftain Kambone in Ondangwa. The group were after the rich copper deposits in the area. Upingtonia's leader, a coloured businessman by the name of William Jordan, claimed to have bought the land from this chieftain. In 1892, Jordan was killed while on a visit to Ondangwa.

The Germans used this pretext to demand their right to the land; and it was incorporated as a part of the German South West African Company's properties for the extraction of copper. German colonial economic interests had thus shifted closer to the territory of the Ovambos.

During the cattle plague of 1896-1897, a German fort was built at Namutoni; shortly after the turn of the century, another fortification went up at Okaukwejo to hinder the commerce of slaves and the plundering of cattle from the Portuguese colonial territory to the north.

Attempts made to bring about a number of protection treaties with the Ovambo chieftains failed. When Chieftain Nehale, who had attacked Fort Namutoni in 1904, died in April 1908, the German colonial authorities tried again to form treaties with the Ovambos, with the help of German and Finnish missionaries, and did in fact succeed in concluding treaties with five Ovambo chieftains. In practice, however, they were of no or little consequence. The German colonial power lacked the means to establish an effective administration so far up north. In practice, therefore, the Ovambo kingdoms 'continued to function as independent units'.[28]

After 1907, rapid economic growth in the colony gave rise to an urgent demand for fresh labour. With the authorities' support, German employers now turned to Ovamboland to fill their labour needs. However, even in this contact with the German colonial power, the Ovambo chieftains safeguarded their independence. The recruitment of workers was not to be done through coercion, but rather through an agreement between the employers and the respective chieftain. The chieftains, not the workers, signed a contract with the employers, and they received cash as a bounty. Thus the workers were employed by contract for a limited period of time. The Ovambo workers were granted the right to work together for the same employer as well as to have workers' representatives of their own selected by their chieftain.

The German authorities used people from the Finnish Missionary Society to act as interpreters during their labour negotiations with the Ovambo chieftains. In general, however, the Finnish missionaries avoided involvement in colonial politics, while striving to remain loyal and accommodate the authorities' regulations. However, unlike the Rhenish Mission, this Mission was not burdened by nationality, belonging as it did to a nation which had no colonial interests in this part of the world.

Following the christening of 13 people in 1883, the Finnish Mission was increasingly able to overcome the Ovambo chieftains' apprehension of the new faith that was being preached in the country. There never was a mass movement of people wanting to join the Christian congregations, however. At the outbreak of World War I, the Finnish Mission had about 3 000 members in its congregations.

These were calm years for the Mission, during which the foundations of its missionary work and its medical and educational activities were laid, in close contact with the leaders of the Ovambo people. These years thus paved the way for the national Church which came into being after World War I.

The situation was more complicated for the Roman Catholic Mission during its initial years in Namibia under the German colonial administration. In 1879, a group of Catholic missionaries from Angola had tried to establish a base for their activities in Omaruru, which already had a Rhenish mission station. The arrival of the Roman Catholic Mission elicited protests from the local Rhenish missionary. When all else failed, he prevailed upon the local chieftain to drive the stranger missionaries out of the building they, the Rhenish missionaries, had raised, and lock the door.[29] The Roman Catholic missionaries thereupon returned to

Angola. They made other, equally unsuccessful attempts to establish themselves in Ovamboland in 1880, 1884, and 1900.

To the Roman Catholic Mission, it seemed that the Germans were supporting German mission alone, in violation of the agreements of the Berlin Congress of 1884-1885. The chancellor of the German Reich in Berlin was approached about this issue in parliament. He maintained that the colonial authorities were adhering to the agreements stipulated at the colonial congress. However, it was the responsibility of the authorities to take heed of prevailing local conditions. In German South West Africa, for instance, they were required to ensure that 'care [was] taken that the presence of different confessions should not cause disturbance among the natives and, therefore, within certain areas, the confessions should be kept apart'.[30] At about this time, the Roman Catholic Mission was denied entry into the country from the north. In 1896, however, missionaries of the Roman Catholic order of Oblaten des Heiligen Franz von Sales arrived from the south across the Orange River, and reached Windhoek in 1902 via Keetmanshoop. They began their work among the Nama people and people of mixed origin. In 1904, at the outbreak of the German Namibian wars, the authorities asked them to assume responsibility for the care of people unfit for labour, as well as orphaned children. A year later, Governor Leutwein called a missionary conference in Windhoek, with representatives of both confessions. At the conference, the statement made at the Berlin Congress was laid down as a fundamental principle, namely that 'both confessions had the right to carry on mission work among the natives throughout the protectorate, and both confessions were free to hold church services and baptism instruction in the concentration camps along the railway'.[31]

By 1914, the Roman Catholic Mission had baptized about 1 000 people in southern and central Namibia. There were numerous examples of active support for German military operations in 1904-1907 on the part of this Mission; and its missionaries also assumed the function of providing spiritual guidance for the Roman Catholic soldiers among the German troops. The extent of this latter commitment caused great concern to the Rhenish Mission. The fact that the Roman Catholics seemed to possess vast resources also meant that they constituted a major threat to the Rhenish Mission's own position. The Rhenish missionaries feared that the Roman Catholic Church would gain a foothold among the European population, especially since many of the soldiers belonging to this Church intended to stay in the country as colonizers after the end of the war.

There was thus another motive for the Rhenish Mission's continued attempts to win over the colonial authorities to their side in trying to prevent, or at least minimize, Roman Catholic mission in the colony. One Rhenish missionary in Omupando contacted the preses of the Rhenish Mission, Johannes Olpp, in 1915, asking him to explain to the governor that Catholic mission was tantamount to Portuguese infiltration, which in view of the present war situation, threatened German national interests.[32] In a German colony, it was German mission alone that could be relied upon. In the interests of the fatherland, the governor should put a stop to all Roman Catholic missionary activity in the country.

In July 1915, the outcome of the war, with the Germans defeated, put an end to the Rhenish missioners' attempts to mobilize the governor to prevent the establishment of a Roman Catholic Mission. The number of baptized Catholics in the colony was, however, small – a mere 2 000 – and World War I would bring major changes to Namibia.

Notes

1 Baumann, J. (ed.) 1985.
2 Supreme church council.
3 Engel, L. 1976, 58.
4 Mossolow, N. (year of publication unkown), 167-168.
5 This was published in the *Deutsch-Südwestafrikanische Zeitung* in conjunction with the *Swakopmunder Zeitung* on 2 December 1914; Church Archives, Windhoek.
6 Beinart, W. 1981, 204-223; see also Moleah, AT. 1983, 50 ff.
7 Bley, H. 1971, 118.
8 *Lüderitzbuchter Zeitung*, 7 December 1912; Church Archives, Windhoek.
9 Minutes of the missionary conferences, 1844-1925; I.1.1-7; Church Archives, Windhoek.
10 *Evangelisches Gemeindeblatt für Deutsch-Südwestafrika*, IX.1-6: 9 May 1913; Church Archives, Windhoek.
11 Moleah, AT, op. cit., 52.
12 Bley, H.1968, 308.
13 Goldblatt, I. 1971, 184.
14 Gründer, H. 1982, 129.
15 1.5.1-4; Church Archives, Windhoek.
16 Haussleiter, G.1906, 19-30, 108-117, and 172-187; see also Chapter 7.
17 See the Annual Reports of the Rhenish Mission, 1.5.1-4; Church Archives, Windhoek, for more on conflicts between the Mission and white employers.
18 Expressions such as these appear constantly in the *Swakopmunder Zeitung* and the *Deutsch Südwestafrikanische Zeitung* of the time.
19 A number of articles reporting on the work of *Missionsschwestern*, or deaconesses, appear in the Annual/Quarterly Reports of the Rhenish Mission; see 1.5.1-4; Church Archives, Windhoek.
20 Haussleiter, G, op. cit.
21 Ibid.
22 Bley, H, op. cit., 249.
23 Ibid.
24 Established in the colony since 1902.
25 *Evangelisches Gemeindeblatt für Deutsch-Südwestafrika*, IX.1-6: July 1913; Church Archives, Windhoek.
26 See Minutes of the Missionary Conferences, 1844-1925; I.1.1-7 op. cit.; Church Archives, Windhoek.
27 In her Introduction to *Precolonial Communities of Southwestern Africa. A History of Owambo Kingdoms 1600-1920*, F-N Williams, 1991, states

that the term 'ethnic community' is more appropriate a term than 'tribe' for the seven Ovambo groups: these are 'groups of people probably of differing origin, who had come to accept a common identity on the basis of the common values, clan affiliation and the language they share'.
28 Williams, F-N, op. cit., 150.
29 Goldblatt, I, op. cit., 192.
30 Ibid.
31 Ibid.
32 This letter to J Olpp, dated 15 February 1915, appears in the collection of letters titled 'Eingegangene Briefe von Missionaren', or 'Letters from Missionaries 1907-1927', 1.8-1.45; Church Archives, Windhoek.

PART III: Church and Mission under South African Rule, 1915-1966

In South Africa, many groups resisted the idea of becoming involved in World War I. After the defeat of the Boers at the end of the Second Boer War, the country was, in fact, divided. In the war against the English, the Boers had received moral support and had even obtained weapons from Germany. These same Boers now strongly reacted against the notion of entering a war against their 'German friends'. This whole situation caused a revolt among the Boers in 1914.

The Union of South Africa declared war in September 1914, only four years after its own foundation. However, it was not until December that year that they attacked the German colony of South West Africa. Namibia was in fact attacked on two fronts, from Walvis Bay and Lüderitz. The Union's entry into the war was decisive for the colony. The Germans stationed in Namibia could only offer very limited resistance and were forced to capitulate after a few months, in July 1915.

A period of Namibian history under South African military administration was thus initiated. The conditions for capitulation of the German troops and administration were fairly liberal. As far as relations with the indigenous population were concerned, the years under South African military administration were a relief compared with conditions under German colonial rule. There were at least two major reasons for this: with its involvement in World War I, which was still ongoing, the Union of South Africa lacked the necessary resources for running an efficient administration in this recently conquered country. It was thought advisable to offer as much freedom to the various population groups as possible, in order to prevent any uprisings. An exception to this rule, which bore dire consequences for Ovamboland, was preventing Chief Kambone's attempts to overrun those parts of his tribal territories which lay within the Portuguese colony of Angola. For the first time in its history, the entire northern part of the country was incorporated into the holdings of the central colonial administration in Windhoek, in 1917.

Another reason for the more humane treatment of the indigenous peoples was the more liberal attitude of the citizens of English descent of the Union. During the military occupation, most of the officers assigned to administer the affairs of the colony were of English origin. This further nurtured the hopes of the black Namibians for greater freedom enjoyed under 'British rule'.

The Peace Treaty of Versailles in 1919 gave Namibia a new constitutional status – namely, as a League of Nations mandate administered by South Africa. Once Namibia became a mandate administered by the South African Union, a more South African policy could be adopted. The various aspects of this policy can be summarized as follows:

1 The mandated territory was to be administered as an integral part of South Africa, and the administration was increasingly centralized with its base in Windhoek. Windhoek, in turn, was obliged to follow directives from Pretoria. The laws of the South African Union were extended to Namibia. The contacts maintained with the League of Nations would only concern questions pertaining to the black Namibians, and the League would confine itself to offering advice, and loosely monitoring the South African administration of the territory.

2 The overall aim was to make the mandate financially profitable. For this, a larger population of whites was necessary. Immigration of whites

was therefore encouraged, as were investments. The German-speaking population were given the choice of remaining in the territory on condition that they took on English citizenship. These German descendants were granted political influence in the administration, soon after 1918.

3 The South African Union had requested that Namibia should be made into a province of South Africa, and even though this request had not been granted, the South Africans administered the mandated territory as a fifth province. This affected not only the white population but also the Africans.

4 South African racial laws were therefore applied to the mandate as well. This entailed a reversion to strict racial legislation in conformity with the German colonial legislation.

5 An administrator appointed by the government in Pretoria was to be the highest authority with respect to the indigenous population. In the northern parts of the country, a certain degree of freedom was maintained through the application of 'indirect rule'; this meant that the whole of Ovamboland was changed into an Ovambo reserve, with no white colonizers. Only white administrative staff and missionaries were allowed in the region. In the rest of the country, racial discrimination was practised against the black population. Those who were not employed to toil for white farmers were forced to live in reserves, mostly arid areas which were too small to sustain the population and their livestock. We have already discussed the strict rules which applied during the German period concerning blacks inside so-called 'white' areas. The same regulations – often made even more inflexible – were valid under the mandatory administration.

This harsher racial policy gave rise to the spread of discontent and rioting. However, protestations were localized. It was only under the influence of Garveyanism that attempts were made to overreach tribal and ethnic divisions, and bring about a united front against white rule. Among the Herero people, a strong movement aimed at reviving old tribal traditions and religion started in connection with Samuel Maharero's burial at Okahandja in 1923.

This, then, provides the backdrop for the activities of the missionaries. The indirect mode of government which was applied to the Ovambo people promoted the interests of the Finnish Missionary Society. The Finnish, who enjoyed the confidence of the tribal chieftains, were able to work within the confines of a delimited reservation.

The situation for the Rhenish Mission in southern and central Namibia was, however, rather different. During the German colonial period, these missionaries had as Germans often been seen as representatives of colonial rule. Now they belonged to a defeated nation, and were obliged to prove their loyalty to the victorious party by pledging their support to the latter's policy. This applied, among other things, to the South Africans' racial legislation. This put the Rhenish missionaries in a terrible dilemma. Since they had to support the South Africans and their racist policy, they found their own credibility undermined in the eyes of the indigenous population.

In the years between the two world wars, the Rhenish Mission experienced restrictions on and meddling in their work, and a considerable decrease in parish membership.

Added to all this was the political development taking place in Germany. Hitler came to power in 1933, with his particular brand of German nationalism. Many Germans, including the missionaries in Namibia, were stirred by the nationalist ideology of Nazism. Furthermore, the members of the German-speaking population demanded that their countrymen the missionaries should give their wholehearted support to their dreams of re-establishing German colonial rule in Namibia. This section of the German-speaking population actively took part in a German-speaking synod, under the leadership of a Landesprobst, who seemed to be entirely caught up in the doctrines of Nazism.

Several missionaries, alongside their missionary tasks, were also attached as pastors to a German-speaking Lutheran church. Their dual role as missionaries and German pastors deteriorated their relations with both the South African administration and the black Namibians. This dilemma was finally to lead, in the years immediately following World War II, to the birth of a number of independent groupings, parishes and Churches inside the Rhenish Mission, which were gradually to breakaway from their parent mission.

9 Namibia during World War I and the first years of South African occupation, 1914-1920

The war up to the German capitulation

Already before the German colonial period, close contacts had existed between South Africa and Namibia. After the Boer Wars, which lasted from 1899 to 1902, groups of Boers drifted towards German South West Africa. The sympathies that the Boers felt for Germany had been strengthened by the support the German government had given them during the Boer Wars. Furthermore, German colonial policy and the German colonizers' views concerning relations between whites and blacks were entirely in tune with the Boers' views. The Boers considered it their God-given right to view themselves as a 'master race' with respect to the indigenous people.

In 1910, the Union of South Africa was founded and given dominion status which gave the Boers their civil rights back after their defeat in the Boer War. This meant that the tension between the conservative Boers and a more liberal English policy would be omnipresent in the everyday political affairs of the Union. This, then, is the background to the nature of relations between the Union and Namibia before 1914. The Boers with their strong German sympathies opposed the Union's plans to carry out a South African invasion of German South West Africa in 1914.

The first Prime Minister of the Union was a Boer himself. In fact, General Louis Botha had been the supreme commander of the Boer forces in Transvaal during the Boer War. The supreme commander of the Union at the outbreak of World War I, General Beyers, was in fact also a former superior among the Boers during the Boer War. As the Union's leading general, he refused to give his troops the marching order when put in charge of the invasion of German South West Africa. In this he was given the support of several other ex-officers from among the ranks of the Boers. In western Transvaal, and in the Orange Free State, the Boers staged an armed protest against the Union's going to war on the side of England.

When loyalist troops were ordered by the government to curb this wave of opposition and force the troops into obedience, this practically gave rise to the outbreak of a civil war, which Botha could only prevent with the greatest of difficulties.

The German authorities of Namibia gave the Boer insurgents their undivided support. A recruitment office for enlisting Boers in Namibia in support of Germany was opened in Windhoek in September 1914, and a smaller force led by an ex-officer of the Boer Wars invaded the territories held by the Union, south of the Orange River, in 1914. The insurrection as well as the parliamentary debate on the issue delayed the South African invasion of German South West Africa until the end of 1914.[1] At this point the Union was ready with a host of powerful forces, consisting of 50 000 soldiers, 23 000 of whom were Boers, and the rest of whom were English-speaking. Prime Minister Botha held supreme command, with General Jan Christiaan Smuts as his Deputy.

At the outbreak of the war in September 1914, the Germans had occupied Walvis Bay in order to prevent the invasion of an enemy landing force. This town was recaptured by the end of December in 1914, and served as a bridgehead for the inland invasions which the Union carried out from there. A second troop landed in Lüderitz, and pushed its way north-east towards the central regions of the colony.

The Union forces were able to occupy large parts of Namibia during the first half of 1915. The Germans only had 5 000 troops, half of whom were untrained and had been enlisted as reserves. With limited resources, the Germans could merely slow down the invasion. Many German civilians were imprisoned in internment camps inside the Union. Among these were Rhenish missionaries, which prompted the Mission to voice protests against something which they felt went against the basic principles of international law.[2]

The Namibian German army was about to be surrounded when the governor, Theodor Seitz, decided to capitulate. The capitulation was signed at Khorab on 9 July 1915.

The conditions of this capitulation were generally liberal. It was not until the end of the war that the German troops, along with the German staff of functionaries, would be taken back to Germany. Until then, they were allowed to remain in Namibia. The officers were further allowed, upon their word of honour, to keep their weapons, and were entitled to settle down in whichever part of the country they chose to stay in. The reserve troops, most of whom were mobilized farmers, were also permitted, upon their word of honour, to return to their homes. The rest of the soldiers were interned in camps where they were allowed to organize their lives themselves, albeit under supervision.[3]

With the capitulation, German South West Africa formally ceased to exist, and the country was administered by South African military until the Versailles Peace Treaty in 1919.

Military administration and the conditions of missionary work between 1915 and 1920

The conquest of German South West Africa was merely an episode in the total war effort of World War I. In fact, after Namibia, Union troops participated in several battles in Europe as well as in East Africa. One of the effects of this was that the Union lacked the resources to run an efficient administration in Namibia during the war.

In spite of the war, the major part of the Boer population in the Union were strongly sympathetic to the German cause. The Boer Wars had left so many unhealed wounds that this population group would much rather have sided against British colonial rule in their own country than conquer the neighbouring German colony.[4] German sympathies therefore were one of the major reasons for the generously mild terms of the capitulation at Khorab in 1915.

Inside Namibia, the Union lacked the resources to entirely replace the local German colonial staff with a working body composed of their own officers. For this reason, the colony continued being run by German colonial officers under South African supervision for several months after the capitulation; and until further notice, laws and regulations from the German colonial period were still in place.[5] General Beves had been appointed the military governor two days after the capitulation, but was replaced by a civil administrator, a South African of British origin, Sir Hugho Gorges, on 30 October 1915.[6] Martial law nevertheless still remained in force until 1 January 1921.

The country was administered by civilian and military staff until the end of World War I. Few changes were introduced during this period. By practising a liberal policy towards the Germans in Namibia, and through a continued military presence in the country, the Union hoped to prevent any hostilities on the part of the white population in Namibia. The majority of the country's population, however, were blacks who were considered hostile towards any form of colonial administration. These people had just been given the opportunity of observing the defeat of the German colonial power, and were full of expectation regarding the victorious power. Many hoped for greater freedom and a more humane treatment than they had been given under the Germans.

The dilemma the Union found itself in before the final victory of World War I was how to achieve a balance between Namibia's potentially hostile black majority on the one hand, and the defeated, and therefore hostile, German population on the other, who in all likelihood wanted to avenge their defeat and reinstore German colonial rule. In order to protect themselves from one side at least, the occupational power attempted to win over the indigenous population by liberalizing their conditions of life. They justified their occupation of this German colony by making reference to the Germans' cruelties against the blacks. This should be seen in the context of a larger, increasingly more virulent anti-German sentiment which grew as World War I progressed. A so-called 'Blue Book' containing a description of German cruelties in Namibia until the victory of the Union in 1915 was released in 1918. The volume included eye-witness accounts of cruelties against the blacks and recorded by them. The opportunity of bearing witness to cruelties suffered under the German administration before the new rulers further warmed the feelings of the indigenous population towards the Union.[7]

The new legislation on conditions for the indigenous population, then, brought immense relief to the black Namibians. For instance, the age limit for compulsory labour was raised from the age of seven to 14. So-called 'Certificates of Exemption from Labour' were introduced to exempt certain members of the population from compulsory labour, for instance those who could prove their own means of support (who owned at least ten cows or 50 head of small livestock). The 'paternal right of chastisement' which, in practice, had meant the arbitrary maltreatment of 'offending natives' by their white masters, was prohibited. Instead, it was decreed that 'masters and policemen have no power to flog, and any complaints of flogging must be carefully investigated and the offenders prosecuted without respect of person'.[8] Furthermore, cattle owners among the blacks were granted the right to their own land for grazing in so-called 'temporary reserves'. This was especially welcomed by the Herero people with their tradition of cattle rearing. By the end of the South African military period, the Hereros were 'straining every nerve to acquire large and small stock'.[9]

Among the Germans in the territory, there was growing opposition to this South African liberal 'native' policy. One reason for this was that it grew increasingly difficult to recruit indigenous labour. The missionaries were among those who regretted what was generally called the South African 'concessional policy', because this might lead to both an unwillingness to work and an 'insurgent mentality' among the blacks. In 1918, the local leader of the Mission in Namibia, Johannes Olpp, stated that 'British propaganda on the subject of liberating nations from the German yoke immediately awakened in many of [the Africans] a veritable intoxication with freedom. ... the Africans who had been so docile under the German rule, had become unrecognizable.'[10]

In a letter addressed to Olpp, Missionary Hermann Nyhof reported from Warmbad that a German farmer had asked for help to recruit 'a Hottentot family of 40-50 labourers' to work on his farm near Warmbad. According to Nyhof, the new, South African policy regarding the indigenous population made it quite impossible to gratify such a demand. The authorities' plans to establish a reserve for 'the old and feeble' among the Bondelswarts in order to stimulate able-bodied men to work on the farms in Karibib and around Lüderitz were, Nyhof said, impracticable: 'At present, the majority of old *and* young people sit around inside their reservations and thus shall it be, no doubt, as long as the war goes on!'[11]

Signs like this of growing opposition greatly worried the authorities who felt compelled to step up their supervision of the German colonizers. At the beginning of 1918, an attempt to smuggle weapons to German farmers via Angola was discovered. The two Germans responsible were punished in conformity with martial law.[12] However, the lack of labour soon became so acute a problem that the authorities granted the police increased licence to track down those blacks who, in their 'unwillingness to work', had tried to 'hide away'.[13]

The war, however, and the military administration, did not put any obstacles in the way of the furtherance of Christian mission. As we have mentioned, some missionaries had been interned just before the formal capitulation, some in South Africa and others in special camps in Namibia. They were soon released, and allowed to resume their activities. In 1914, the Rhenish Mission had 49 missionaries and approximately 25 000 members in its parishes and 27 mission stations (four of which were in

Ovamboland, though two of them were unstaffed).[14] In the same year, the Roman Catholic Mission, with its 90 missionaries, had a mere 2 000 members, while the Finnish Missionary Society, with roughly 30 missionaries, had 3 000 members.[15]

During the war and the ensuing occupation, the Rhenish Mission was cut off from its headquarters in Germany. Through its connections with the Reformed Church in the Cape Province, it was granted some financial assistance until the end of 1917, after which the South African authorities paid an advance both to the Rhenish Mission and to the Roman Catholic Mission against a security in the Missions' joint properties. This annual advance to the Rhenish Mission amounted to £8 250, or £687.5 per month.[16]

During the war, some serious military complications occurred in Ovamboland, where the Finnish Missionary Society was based, which indirectly led to placing northern Namibia under effective colonial administration: the Germans defeated Portuguese troops in 1915, and then pushed on into Portuguese territory. However, they were unable to follow up this victory owing to the South African invasion of the colony. The Portuguese area that was briefly occupied by the Germans belonged to the Kwanyamas, but when the Germans withdrew to concentrate their forces south and westward, a power vacuum arose here, which prompted the Kwanyama chieftain Mandume to lay claims to this Angolan area as the rightful property of his people. By the end of 1915, the Portuguese drove Mandume back over the old colonial frontier.

It is very possible that Mandume was not aware of the Portuguese alliance with South Africa when he demanded South African military support to drive out the Portuguese. The South African commandant in northern Namibia, Major SM Pritchard, turned down Mandume's request, and instead let his troops re-establish the border which the Germans had transgressed. At the same time, Pritchard gave Chief Mandume 'a stern lecture on how the time had long passed for any native resistance to white rule'.[17] Mandume protested, and was promptly called to Windhoek to present himself to the authorities there. However, as it was against tribal custom for a chief to thus leave his people, Mandume refused to go to Windhoek. This was interpreted as rebellion, and prompted a joint South African-Portuguese expedition of retribution against the Kwanyama people. Thus, on 6 February 1917, more than 100 Kwanyama warriors were killed along with their chieftain, Mandume. This 'marked the first direct intervention in and control of the Ovambo people by a white administrative and ruling power'.[18] The Finnish Missionary Society voiced no protests.

The South African military administration of former German South West Africa came to an end through the armistice in Europe in November 1918. The question concerning the future of the Germans living in their former colony now presented itself with urgency. According to the terms agreed upon at the Germans' capitulation in 1915, German military and administrative staff should be repatriated after the war. In a letter from the secretary of the protectorate, dated 1 April 1919,[19] the South African heads of the administration in Namibia were given orders to carry out the repatriation of all German soldiers and officers without delay. In terms of the Khorab agreement, even German colonizers could be repatriated under this order. This included Germans who:

1   had been found guilty of infringement of the liquor laws;
2   had been guilty of ill-treatment of their black servants;
3   had 'demonstrated bad character for any other reason'; or
4   had, during the period of the occupation, constantly exhibited hostility towards British rule.[20]

The Germans' defeat in World War I brought with it the end of all hopes for Germany to ever turn Namibia into a German colony again. This brought the Rhenish Mission up against the problem of how its missionary work would continue under a government other than its own. Also, it left the Mission to ponder on what was to become of that 'Germanism' which had meant so much to colonial rule and to the German colonizers. In 1918, the Rhenish missionary Gottlieb F Rust of Keetmanshoop put it as follows:

> As we have now been brought under a new authority I know how I shall stand as a Christian in accordance with the commands and the example of Jesus Christ. If now a vow of obedience is demanded of us, I can give in to such a demand with a good conscience in the sense that, as a German citizen, I comply with the regulations of the new government. I hope, however, that it will not be demanded of us to give up our German nationality. If so, I will have to consider leaving this country of my birth, no matter how difficult it might be

for me. To be born a German is a gift of God, and I feel more German now than ever.[21]

In January 1919, the preses of the Mission, Johannes Olpp, asked the missionaries to disregard their nationalities for the sake of 'the eternal kingdom of God'. Missionary Rust objected to this, with reference to the fact that one's nationality was a gift of God. In his reply to Olpp he wrote:

> How will it be when our South West Africa comes under foreign rule and it is perhaps demanded of us that we become British citizens so as to be allowed to remain in the country? I cannot comply with this. As a Christian, I am bound to the book of Romans 13:1; it does not mean, however, that I can give up my nationality. The possibility which now remains is that the Board of the Mission give up its work here, and that it hand over its missionaries to serve another missionary society. This would be difficult to accept. It might be possible for me to preserve my German nationality – my children, however, would be brought up in circumstances which would make them quite as strangers to our own people.[22]

Meanwhile, the South African authorities made investigations in order to decide whether the Rhenish missionaries could remain in the country. The same principles that applied to other Germans in the colony were followed here. Among others, the authorities asked members of the indigenous community to give their opinion on the missionaries and their behaviour during the period of the German occupation.[23]

Four missionaries were ordered to leave the country, among them Heinrich Vedder, later to become one of the Rhenish Mission's most well-known and well-esteemed missionaries. According to a report of a South African official in Tsumeb, Vedder had stowed away documents belonging to the German governor Theodor Seitz, on the Mission's farm in Gaub, in 1915. Vedder had placed these documents in a box which he had buried in the garden. Vedder denied these allegations, but the South African authorities in Tsumeb maintained to have proof of Vedder's doings and said that he was lying. Vedder was further accused of having mistreated the blacks on the Mission's farm. Among other things, he had driven 'all the natives [sic] away from the station as a revenge for the information they had given the magistrate'.[24] Evidence was also presented of the good reputation Vedder enjoyed among German officials, who had often visited him during the occupation. It was therefore 'dangerous to allow [Vedder] to remain in the country'.[25]

The chairman of the Mission, Preses Olpp, was also ordered to leave the country. The reason given for this was his activities in Rehoboth during the war. When World War I had reached Namibia in 1914, the German colonial power had ordered the Rehoboth Basters to take sides with the Germans by supplying them with a company of soldiers, just as they had done during the war of 1904-1907, and as had been agreed upon in the Baster-German treaty. This time, the inhabitants of Rehoboth refused to comply with the Germans' wishes, however. Aware of the fact that this time, Germany was in a position of inferiority, they did not wish to enter the war on the side of the Germans. By keeping out of the war, they hoped they would be able to preserve their identity as a separate group of people, and maintain their relative independence even in a new political situation.

The German authority consequently decided to disarm the Basters and imprison their leaders. On trying to escape, one of these leaders, Petrus Beukes, was shot. As a consequence of this, rebellion broke out. A missionary of the Rhenish Mission who was in the area had supported the Germans' attempts to disarm the Basters. When the rebellion broke out, this Missionary Blecher was forced to flee, and the inhabitants of Rehoboth replaced him with a Reformed pastor. About 20 German soldiers were killed during the insurrection, and the Germans were forced to withdraw. On 8 May 1915, German troops surrounded the fortified camp of the Basters in the Kubis Mountains, approximately 50 kilometres outside the town of Rehoboth. Before the Germans managed to conquer this hold, however, they were forced to withdraw, owing to the South African advance.[26] After the Germans surrendered at Khorab, Missionary Blecher returned, even though the population in Rehoboth had informed the South Africans that he was not welcome.

These events in Rehoboth in April-May 1915 formed the backdrop to the South Africans' decision to banish Preses Olpp. As preses, the latter had given his support to Missionary Blecher, even after the German capitulation in July 1915. In an address written to the congregation in Rehoboth after the capitulation,[27] Olpp had accused the members of the congregation of 'rebellion against the authority', and had taken away their right to receive Communion. The South African authorities claimed that

Olpp had acted in a self-willed manner, and that he ought to have been aware 'that the whole trouble [had arisen] through the Germans and that the Basters were free of guilt'.[28]

The third of the missionaries to be banished was Missionary Hasenkamp. He was ordered to leave the country because he had criticized the occupational forces after the Germans' defeat. In a private letter, which had been read by the South African censors, Hasenkamp had expressed his surprise at the outcome of the war, and at the victorious power's 'monstrous peace conditions'. This prompted his order of expulsion.[29]

Still another missionary, a Roman Catholic who had come to Namibia as an immigrant from Angola during the war, was expelled, for failing to have a residency permit. Apparently, the threat of banishment was sometimes used merely to put the Rhenish Mission down a peg or two, and it was the Rhenish missionaries in Ovamboland who were to suffer the most from this. In this bordering country, with its tensions between the tribal areas in both Namibia and Angola, the presence of German mission was not really welcomed by the South African authorities. Their major concern was to hinder future disturbances of the kind experienced among the Kwanyama people under Chieftain Mandume, in 1917.

At the beginning of October 1919, Missionary Hermann Gehlmann, responsible for the work of the Rhenish Mission in Ovamboland, asked for help from Wilhelm Eich, the preses of the Mission after Olpp's expulsion. He had been called in for a talk with the local South African official. The latter had expressed his great discontentment with the Rhenish Mission, and more specifically, with Gehlmann's activities among the Ovambo people. Gehlmann was accused of having 'said things' and 'acted in opposition to' the interests of the government. He was informed that unless he changed his ways, he would be banished.[30]

Some time later, Gehlmann was able to report to Eich that the local official had instructed him that the Mission was being allowed to continue its work in the area, provided it did not work against the government. The implications of this were that the Mission was expected to support the government by making sure that the people obeyed and submitted to the new rulers without protest, and that they made their 'necessary contribution of work'.[31] Gehlman did, however, not succeed in convincing the South Africans of his loyalty towards them. He was given an order of expulsion. In an urgent request to Eich, Gehlmann asked Eich to try to influence the authorities in Windhoek in his favour. The order of expulsion was retracted, and Gehlmann was allowed to remain in the country; however, he was prohibited from continuing his work as a missionary in Ovamboland. The work of the Rhenish Mission thus ceased in that part of the country.[32]

These developments made the Finnish Missionary Society break its traditional silence, which it had succeeded in keeping through all the events and developments in Namibia. In April 1920, the Board of the Finnish Missionary Society in Helsinki addressed a letter to the resident commissioner in Ondangwa, Major Manning, expressing its concerns for the future of the Mission's work in Ovamboland, and primarily among the Kwanyamas. The Finnish Missionary Society had started to mission among the Kwanyama people, but had handed over the responsibility to the Rhenish Mission in 1891, since the Rhenish Mission worked along 'the same lines as we'. Now that the Rhenish Mission was no longer allowed to remain there, the Board in Helsinki requested that the Finnish Mission be allowed to resume its work among the Kwanyamas. It would be unfortunate if *another* missionary society, with another confession, were allowed to take over the work: 'only trouble would ensue'.[33]

All through the difficulties the Rhenish Mission experienced with the new authority in the country, the Board of the Mission in Germany could only plead with the missionaries to remain calm, and maintain a presence of mind. For German Mission, with its strong national aim, the political changes needed adjusting to, and this was not easy. To ensure the future of the Mission, the local missionaries had to accept whatever happened and to resign themselves to working under 'foreign rule'. The head of the Rhenish Mission in Germany wrote a pastoral letter to the missionaries and congregations in Namibia, dated 3 September 1920; and it read: 'Because of the war your country has come under a new government. We warn you in the name of God to show willing obedience to the new government which now is your authority. This is a duty before Christ! Do not withdraw from what you are commanded and directed to do.'[34]

The Rhenish Mission in Germany thus wished to certify its loyalty to the new authorities of the former German colony. With reference to this, Preses Eich addressed a request to General Smuts, asking that the banished missionaries be allowed to return, and that residence permits be issued to a new group of Rhenish missionaries. In conclusion, Eich assured Smuts 'that the Rhenish missionaries will perform their missionary work with equal loyalty to the new government as to the previous one'.³⁵

In February 1921, Eich's request was granted. This meant that the Rhenish Mission could seriously plan to continue its work which, though interrupted by the war, could now to be resumed under wholly new assumptions. The Mission also cleared its debt owed to the South African government following an advance received by it during the war years. It paid the amount of £20 000 Sterling by selling a number of mission farms.³⁶

World War I ended with the Versailles Peace Treaty on 28 June 1919. As I have mentioned, after the armistice of 1918 began the repatriation of German colonial and military staff, together with a number of 'unwanted persons' of German nationality, in accordance with the terms of the German capitulation at Khorab in 1915. Among the banished was German South West Africa's last governor, Theodor Seitz, who had lived in the country until the making of peace, with few restrictions on his personal freedom of movement. The number of banished missionaries were, as we have seen, exceedingly few. A total of 4 941 Germans were deported, of whom 1 619 were soldiers, 1 226 administrative officials, 873 policemen, and 1 223 'unwanted persons'. In addition to this, 1 433 voluntarily returned to Germany. Approximately 6 700 Germans remained in Namibia under South African rule.

Notes

1. Steer, GL. 1939, 42 ff; see also Goldblatt, I. 1971, 202.
2. Minutes of the Missionary Conferences 1914. In: I.1.22-27: 1906-1937; Church Archives.
3. Bruwer, JJ. 1985, 8.
4. Bertelsmann, W. 1979, 5 ff.
5. See correspondence between Missionary W Peter of Bethanie and Preses J Olpp, dated 4 September 1915, in: 1.8-1.45; Church Archives, Windhoek; also, see the letter from the German mayor of Windhoek, of 3 April 1916, informing the Germans of Windhoek of his resignation; 11.1-16; Church Archives, Windhoek.
6. Goldblatt, I, op. cit., 206 and 298.
7. See His Majesty's Stationary Office. 1918; see also Wellington, JH. 1967, 231.
8. Emmet, T. 1988, 224 ff; see also 11.1-16: 1919-1938; Church Archives, Windhoek.
9. Ibid.
10. Engel, L. 1977, 131 ff.
11. Letter of Nyhof to Olpp, Warmbad, 4 February 1918, in: Letters from Missionaries 1916-1918; 1.8-1.45; Church Archives, Windhoek.
12. ADM/146-C.331: January 1918; National Archives, Windhoek.
13. 11.1-16: 1893-1938; Church Archives, Windhoek.
14. Groves, CP.1958, vol. IV, 22; see also I.1.22-27: 1914; Church Archives, Windhoek.
15. Groves, CP, op. cit., 23.
16. Letter from the Military Magistrate to the Accounting Officer of the Protectorate, of 4 March 1918, in: Correspondence 1915-1920, ADM/ 42, file No. 542; National Archives, Windhoek. For the decision concerning this annual grant, see the letter from the Secretary of the Protectorate to J Olpp, Swakopmund, of 8 December 1917, in: 11.1-16; Church Archives, Windhoek.
17. Extract from the Resident Commissioner's private diary, 6 February 1917; National Archives, Windhoek.
18. Moleah, AT.1983, 21.
19. Circular letter, of 1 April 1919, from the Secretary of the Protectorate to all magistrates, re Repatriation of Enemy Subjects, Windhoek, General File marked 'Matters relating to Missionaries 1919-'; National Archives, Windhoek.
20. Ibid.

21   1.5.1-4: the Rhenish Mission's annual report of 1918; Church Archives, Windhoek; see also Engel, L. 1976, 173.
22   Letter from GF Rust to J Olpp, Keetmanshoop, 28 February 1919. In: General File: 1919-1920, II.I.30b; National Archives, Windhoek.
23   Petrus Swartbooi, Affidavit. In: General File, 1919-1920, II.I.30b; National Archives, Windhoek.
24   Letter from H Gehlmann to W Eich, 27 October 1919: File note (27), 1.8-1.45; Church Archives, Windhoek.
25   Ibid.
26   Engel, L, op. cit., 184.
27   For more on the repatriation of German missionaries, see the General File marked 'Matters relating to Missionaries 1919-'; National Archives, Windhoek.
28   Ibid.
29   Letter from Missionary Hasenkamp to Missionary Wilke, Grootfontein, 19 May 1919, in: General File, 'Matters relating to Missionaries 1919-'; National Archives, Windhoek.
30   Letter from H Gehlmann to W Eich, Tsumeb, 1.8-1.45, 30a; II:I: 7 October 1919; Church Archives, Windhoek.
31   Letter from H Gehlmann to W Eich, 27 October 1919: File Note (27), 1.8-1.45; Church Archives, Windhoek.
32   Letter from H Gehlmann to W Eich, 14 November 1919: File Note (27), 1.8-1.45; Church Archives, Windhoek.
33   Letter from M Torkkanen to H Haahti, Helsinki, 20 April 1920, and from M Torkkanen to the Resident Commissioner, Ondangwa. In: LAND 27009 vol. I. 5905 – vol. II, 27011; see file marked 'Religious General File 1920-'; National Archives, Windhoek.
34   'Hirtenschreiben an die Rheinischen Missionsgemeinden in Südwestafrika'. In: Minutes of the Missionary Conferences 1844-1925: I.1.1-7; Church Archives, Windhoek.
35   Letter from W Eich to JC Smuts, Swakopmund, 4 September 1920, in: 'Behördenschreiben von und an das Gouvernement, 1915-1938', 11.1-16; Church Archives, Windhoek.
36   Groves, CP, op. cit., 23.

10 Namibia as a League of Nations mandate, 1920-1939

Negotiations begin on the mandated territories

The peace after World War I brought with it a great many changes in the colonial division of Africa. As a consequence of its defeat in the war, Germany lost its colonies, and ceased to be a colonial power. The German colonies were not, however, taken over as conquered territories by the winning powers. Instead, a new system of international laws was introduced, whereby they were administered, under the nominal supervision of the League of Nations, as mandate territories by one of the victorious powers, with special consideration given to the interests of the indigenous peoples.

The basis of this new system was a speech by President Woodrow Wilson of the USA to the Washington Congress, on 8 January 1918. Wilson presented 14 points which were to lay the foundation of an agreement of peace with Germany. Concerning the future of the former German colonies, it was stated in point No. 5 that there should be 'a free, openminded, and absolutely impartial adjustment of all colonial claims, based upon a strict observance of the principle that in determining all such questions of sovereignty the interest of the population concerned must have equal weight with the equitable claims of the Government whose title is to be determined'.[1] There was certainly the suggestion that the colonized people would be granted some say in the planning of their own future.

At the end of the war, the victors saw prospects of power ahead for themselves. Annexation of a former enemy's colonies was considered a legitimate form of compensation for losses suffered during war. Therefore, there was some resistance to the 'liberal' view of Wilson's 14 points as concerns the treatment of Germany after its defeat. The European allies of the USA (the 'Central Powers') had borne the main burden of the war before the USA's entry into World War I in 1917. They wanted to bring

Germany to its knees once and for all by imposing the harshest conditions possible. These included tough economic regulations, loss of land, and severe restrictions.

General Jan Smuts of the South African Union played an important part in the Versailles negotiations leading to the peace treaty in 1919. He was one of England's most highly esteemed military men, who had led the Union's troops, first in Namibia, and then in Europe, and also in the East African campaigns against German East Africa. In September 1919, he succeeded the late Louis Botha as the Union's prime minister. Both as the political leader of his own country, and as an influential figure in the peace negotiations, Smuts helped lay the foundations of the League of Nations. In his view, after a devastating war it was important to create the prerequisites for a lasting peace. He therefore attempted to elaborate a compromise as regards the treatment of the former German colonies. These should not automatically be integrated into the winning powers' dominion, but should rather be placed under the trusteeship of the League of Nations and administered as mandate territories by the victorious powers.

Smuts suggested that 'suitable Powers ... be appointed to act as Mandatories of the League in the more backward areas'.[2]

German colonies and areas of interest in Europe and the Middle East would, Smuts suggested, be given the degree of self-determination recommended by President Wilson in his 14 points. Concerning the colonies in Africa and the territories in the Pacific Ocean, however, these ought to be treated differently.

During the negotiations leading up to the Treaty of Versailles, Wilson had recommended a mandatory system which would give the League of Nations all authority and control over the former German colonies. A mandate-administering nation was to be appointed by the League of Nations, the League also having the authority to refuse the former's right to continued administration of the mandate in the case of mismanagement. Smuts proposed that the victors themselves were to apportion the mandated territories between them. His proposal was accepted and inserted into the Treaty of Versailles as Article 119. Furthermore, statutes for the administration of mandates were included in Article XII of the League of Nations' prime document, establishing a mandatory power's obligation to safeguard the mandated territory's wellbeing and development since its inhabitants could not 'stand by themselves under the strenuous conditions of the modern world'. This should be 'a sacred trust of civilisation'.[3]

The mandated territories were divided into three categories. To Category A belonged the so-called 'developed territories' in the ancient Ottoman empire in the Middle East; Category B consisted of former German colonies in East and West Africa, excepting Namibia; while Namibia and the former German-occupied territories in the Pacific Ocean fell under Category C. Because of their geographical proximity to these, the mandates of Category C were to be administered as an integrated part of the mandatory powers South Africa, and Australia and New Zealand respectively.

Originally, the countries which now received the C mandates had demanded that these former German colonies be wholly incorporated into their own territories. The British government had supported this demand saying they deserved compensation for what they had done for the Allied cause.

The League of Nations' authority over the mandatory powers was limited to supervision of the treatment of the indigenous population. For this purpose, the mandatory powers had to submit an annual report on their treatment of the mandate's population to the Mandate Commission of the League of Nations. In contrast to Wilson's proposal, the Commission, charged with looking into these reports, could only give critical feedback and advice, having neither the authority to interfere with the mandatory power's administration, nor the right to discharge any mandatory power from office.[4]

The mandatory power practically had total freedom in its administration of C mandates. It is important to bear this in mind as a background to South Africa's refusal, after 1948, to submit to the United Nation's new regulations concerning mandates. South Africa emphasized the fact that it had been granted the right to administer the affairs of Namibia according to League of Nations principles and that it was not compelled to take another world organization's opinions and demands into consideration.

The German-speaking minority in Namibia under mandatory administration

After peace was made in 1919, it was a matter of great importance for the Union of South Africa to ensure that the development of its newly acquired territory might flourish in accordance with its best financial and political interests. South Africa's prime minister, Smuts, did not feel particularly well disposed towards the indigenous population of Namibia. He maintained that whites should make up a larger percentage of the population to promote the best interests of the country. Extensive white immigration was thus encouraged. In 1920 there were about 7 000 German-speaking inhabitants in Namibia; the rest of the white population, which amounted to roughly 10 000, were largely immigrants from South Africa. The German population still considered themselves to be German citizens.

Smuts' first visit to Namibia in peacetime was made in the latter half of 1920. The Germans awaited his visit with great anticipation – for along with Smuts came the man who was now to assume the responsibility for running the affairs of the country, namely Administrator GR Hofmeyr. The Germans viewed the fact that Hofmeyr spoke German as a favourable sign. However, it was also known that Hofmeyr thought of himself as a Boer.

The Rhenish Mission's report for 1920[5] includes a description of Smuts' visit and mentions that the prime minister demonstrated a 'friendly attitude' towards the missionaries, paying visits to several mission stations accompanied by Hofmeyr. Furthermore, the report goes on to say, on several occasions Smuts expressed sympathy with the Germans in their new political situation. Smuts, who had actively contributed to the German defeat in the war, was considered anti-German. It was now felt that he had been compelled to modify his attitude when faced with political opposition inside the Union, hence his willingness to consider German interests during his first tour of Namibia as the Union's prime minister.

On 14 January 1920, soon after the Treaty of Versailles, Germans in Namibia had founded a 'Landesverband der deutschen Schulvereine', a national association of German school boards, whose overriding purpose was the preservation of German culture and the German language in Namibia.

On Smuts' arrival in Windhoek, the Landesverband submitted a document to him, containing 33 proposals, suggestions, and even demands concerning the future of the German-speaking minority, and expressing hopes that martial law might be abolished immediately, and that the country would be administered as an independent territory, in accordance with the Peace Treaty of Versailles. The document also claimed that since cultural and political conditions in Namibia differed so vastly from those in the Union 'they could not possibly be regulated in detail from the vantage point of South Africa'.[6]

In a speech made to this German delegation on 1 September 1920, Smuts rejected this latter demand for the independent administration of the former German colony. Mandatory rights, as Smuts saw it, should be equated with the right to hold territorial possessions. The League of Nations would, he added, be unable to change this by any means. In other words, the country would be considered as an integral part of the Union and administered accordingly. As far as the German descendants were concerned, this meant that they now had to consider the Union as their highest authority, and that their German citizenship was meaningless. This further meant that prior to their becoming citizens of South Africa, they lacked any form of citizenship whatsoever, a problem which demanded a swift solution.

It would be best for all parties concerned, as Smuts saw it, if the Germans reconciled themselves as soon as possible to the fact that Namibia was now a part of the Union which he, Smuts, aimed to run as a province of this country in accordance with South African policy. It was up to the German population, as a German-speaking minority group, to consider the implications this had for them. Their best option would be to immediately apply for British citizenship, along with a South African nationality.

Smuts nevertheless expressed his understanding of the fact that this might be a difficult decision for them to take, and was prepared to give them due time for consideration. But sooner or later the German-speaking population would have to make up their minds if they wished to remain in the country. Smuts' immediate aim was to appoint a commission charged with finding a solution, in collaboration with the German-speaking citizens, regarding their citizenship status within the mandated territory.[7] (The annual report of the Rhenish Mission commented that no assistance was to be expected from the League of Nations concerning this issue, not even if Germany should become one of its member nations.)

As can be imagined, Smuts' speech came as a heavy blow to the German-speaking community. His policy with regard to Namibia's indigenous population, on the other hand, was received with considerable enthusiasm by the Germans. Much in accordance with their own, prewar legislation, Smuts intended to treat the blacks in Namibia with severity, and rule them with a heavy hand. They were needed as labour, and should therefore be encouraged to be diligent and obedient. While the occupational forces had been 'lenient' towards the black Namibians, the local Germans interpreted this statement as a resumption of the 'native policy' adopted by the Germans before World War I. They experienced great relief at the fact that South Africa in 1920 was 'putting the Africans in their place, forcing them to return to work for the whites, ... restricting their freedom of movement and abolishing their short-lived equality with whites'.[8]

The German-speaking population thus interpreted the South Africans' more liberal racial policy which had been operative during the military administration of 1915-1920 as an effort to appease the indigenous population and thus prevent any possible turbulence during the war, and not as a policy to be adhered to in a civil administration. South Africa's proposed racial policy was in line with the Germans' policy in Namibia after 1907. Since Namibia was to be administered as a part of South Africa, the South African laws of racial discrimination would also be applied in the mandated territory.

Smuts was eager to solve the question of the German descendants' citizenship in Namibia as soon as possible. The Minister of Justice of the Union, Minister De Wet, was assigned to investigate the issue. De Wet's recommendation was automatic citizenship, free from individual application, through a parliamentary legislation in the Union. Individual Germans would have the right to 'decline such citizenship within a certain time'.[9]

At a gathering in Windhoek at the end of 1922, Administrator Hofmeyr presented this proposal to a delegation of German descendants. It was hardly received enthusiastically, however. The Germans subsequently held a meeting of their own at the Hotel Kaiserkrone in Windhoek, where they demanded that a special kind of 'mandatory citizenship' be granted to Namibians of German descent. Residence in the country should be the sole criterion for obtaining this particular citizenship. Furthermore, the demand made during Smuts' visit in 1920 was reiterated concerning internal self-government of Namibia by granting increased powers of execution to the white population. A similar demand which had been proposed to Hofmeyr in 1922, had been revoked by the government of the Union as this would have been tantamount to granting the Germans (a population group of neither South African nationality nor British citizenship) the right to participate in the decision-making process.

But Smuts already had a solution to this problem, unbeknownst to the German-speaking population. In November 1921, he sent a telegram to the South African High Commissioner in London, requesting him to clarify the position of the Union to the League of Nations concerning the German descendants of Namibia: 'Please understand that the Union Government does not admit that Germans of European origin in South West Africa are still German subjects.'[10] Smuts was hoping for a 'declaration by [the] Mandate Commission that [the] position resulting from [the] Peace Treaty is that they have no nationality'. This, according to Smuts, was important so as to hinder 'German intervention for their supposed protection'.[11] At the same time, Smuts was eager to point out that these German descendants were needed for the internal development of the mandate. He therefore hoped that the League of Nations would support De Wet's proposal for a solution resolving the citizenship issue.

In 1922, the League of Nations granted its support for De Wet's proposal, which in turn meant that Smuts had overcome a first major hurdle in carrying out his proposed solution.

In late 1923, Smuts invited representatives of the German government to meet in London for discussions on this question. He managed to prevail upon the German government to recommend to the Germans based inside the mandate to accept a legislation passed by the Union parliament which granted them immediate British citizenship along with a South African nationality. An agreement for this was officially sealed between the Union and the German government in October 1923.[12]

What now remained to be done was to inform the German descendants in Namibia of the outcome of these negotiations. Smuts commanded Hofmeyr to come to Cape Town together with a delegation of German descendants whom he met on 19 September 1924. He gave a brief summary of the agreement, which was 'a final document ... not subject to amendment, and it is not submitted to you for amendment or for alteration in any form. It is a final document, signed by the German government and the Union government.'[13] Smuts informed the delegation that 'On our part ... we are willing to do our best to carry out the letter and the spirit of that document. The German government on their part are going to advise the German nationals in South West to accept this automatic citizenship ...'.[14]

There was nothing much the German delegation could do when faced with this *fait accompli*. At a meeting held two days later they gave Smuts a *de facto* acceptance of the London agreement, pointing out, however, that this agreement still left at least two urgent questions of major importance to them unanswered. The first of these concerned the use of German, both as a language of instruction, and in correspondence with the authorities of the mandate. The second concerned the delicate matter of the Blue Book, on which matter they wrote: 'With particular satisfaction we welcome the assurance ... that there will be no further official reference to the Blue Book on South West Africa.'[15]

In terms of the agreement, German descendants and Germans who had been compelled to leave Namibia after the war were now 'desirable immigrants under the terms of the Union Immigration Laws'. The agreement also contained an item concerning German mission and German ecclesiastical affairs: 'The German Churches and the German Missions have been and will continue to be treated sympathetically by the administration of South West Africa.'[16]

The law concerning the citizenship of German descendants was approved by the Union parliament in 1925. The vast majority of German descendants in Namibia gave up all claims to German citizenship; only 261 chose to remain German citizens. These were allowed to remain in the country as permanent residents, without 'any discrimination of their economic interests'.[17] However, they had no political rights.

As a consequence of this law, the Union could now introduce internal self-government for the white population.[18] In 1925, elections were held in Namibia for a legislative body with 17 seats. Nine of these were taken up by German descendants, who thus formed a majority. The legislative body had no power of influence on laws and statutes pertaining to the indigenous population. The so-called 'welfare' of the black Namibians was a matter for the Union government, in accordance with mandatory regulations. This restriction, however, was of no practical consequence. The gist of the policy of the Union was to subordinate the indigenous population to the interests of the white population in everything.

The attitude towards the black Namibians had hardly changed since post-1907 German colonial rule. After the establishment of a South African mandatory power in Namibia it did not take long before the old order of the German period was restored. To safeguard the interests of the white colonists, special reserves for the blacks were instituted in the

Native Administration Proclamation of 1922. The expropriated territories of the blacks as crown land of the German colonial period were taken over by the South African mandatory administration.[19] One could therefore almost say that in the mandated territory of Namibia, South Africa had acquired a colony of its own which it would administer entirely in the interests of the whites. Not much was left of the mandatory regulation, according to which a League of Nations mandate should be administered for the safeguarding of the development and wellbeing of the indigenous population.

South Africa's racial policy in Namibia, 1920-1939

The defeat of Germany had raised the expectations of the Namibian blacks for better living conditions, so much so that the Hereros who had fled to Botswana and South Africa during Von Trotha's war of extermination openly supported the South African invasion of Namibia in 1914. Their leader, Samuel Maharero, urged his people to go into South African military service. We have also mentioned how the population in Rehoboth with its rebellion had kept the German military busy during the war.

In his study of the development of anti-colonial forces in Namibia, Peter Katjavivi observes: 'Namibians were not therefore naively entertaining hopes of freedom; they worked through physical participation in the Allied effort to contribute to regaining control of their country.'[20]

In 1919, the indigenous population had turned to the governor-general of the Union in Cape Town, Lord Buxton, with a request for greater freedom; they especially stressed the need of being granted the right to own land in their former tribal territories.[21] Leading this initiative was Hosea Kutako, the Herero leader elected as headman by his people in 1915.[22] (The result of the elections had been confirmed by the exiled Samuel Maharero in 1919, asking Kutako to take care of his people.) An answer to this dispatch to the governor-general was never to come. However, soon afterwards, once the administration had firmly established itself in the mandated territory, the laws affecting blacks became extremely harsh.[23]

In the late 1920s, Administrator Hofmeyr appointed a commission to inquire into the treatment of the Namibian blacks; it was to be regarded as a labour question since Hofmeyr had 'received so many complaints from White settlers about the shortage of labour'.[24] The settlers had criticized the Union government for its 'slackness' in its use of black labour.[25]

The commission recommended that the Germans' post-1907 decision, to treat parts of the traditional tribal territories as crown land for colonists, be followed.[26] The commission's recommendations were in line with the whites' demands with regard to recruiting labour by force. Despite the fact that the Germans had recently been the enemy, and that they had lost World War I, the Union was anxious to retain German farmers, and in fact to encourage the settlement of new farmers in the territory. Even those German farmers who had been banished from the country soon after the armistice, in 1918, were encouraged to return. There was now no longer a need to 'depict them as brutal and vicious in their treatment of the blacks'.[27]

Regarding the treatment of the indigenous population, the commission recommended that a strict segregation of the different racial groups be seen to by organizing separate settlement areas for each ethnic group. This implied the removal of large groups of people by force, from areas considered suitable for European settlement, to reserves either set apart during the German colonial period, or now established in outlying areas. The Hereros, for instance, were to be moved east of Gobabis and Waterberg, near the border with Botswana. 'This recommended area was the same dry Kalahari sandveld that the Germans, in their genocide campaign, had forced the Herero into, ... where thousands of Herero men, women and children had perished.'[28]

Kutako protested by taking a delegation to Windhoek and demanding that this decision be changed. Consequently his people were offered land near Epukiro; later, once the South Africans had a stronger foothold in the mandated territory, this was expropriated so that the Hereros were forced to move further east.

Another group who were removed were the Bondelswarts in southern Namibia. Under the leadership of Abraham Morris and Jacobus Christian, they had sided with the South Africans during the war. They were now 'rewarded' with a little inhospitable reserve to the west of Warmbad; when the two leaders protested, they were banished to the Cape Province.[29]

Not only was landhunger the reason for the appropriation of the indigenous population's traditional tribal areas, though: there was 'a deliberate policy to render the Africans landless, and, therefore, cattle-less, and thereby force them into employment for Whites'.[30] Protests had no effect; the mandate was in need of black labour, and this was what determined the policy concerning the blacks. A number of new laws and statutes were introduced, of which only a few will be mentioned here:[31]

1 The **Vagrancy Proclamation Act No. 25/1920** forced the unemployed, and those without a legally registered home abode, to work for whites. Neglect of this led to the penalty of prison or a fine, penalties which could be 'transformed' into forced labour on white men's farms, 'a fruitful source of labour'.

2 The **Masters and Servants Proclamation No. 11/1920** decreed the establishment of pass laws, and the registration of all Africans, in accord with the pattern of German colonial times.

3 **Proclamation No. 33/1922** prohibited blacks from being out on the streets in the towns at night without a written permission of their employer.

4 The **Curfew Regulations Proclamation No. 34/1922** made even clearer the prohibition of so-called 'non-whites' to be in white areas, and forbade all Africans to be on the streets in built-up areas between the hours of 9 pm and 4 am without a special pass.

Furthermore, a number of statutes were introduced to make 'provision for the removal of squatters from crown and Mission land', to 'control [the] movement of all blacks, [and] the branding of black-owned cattle'[32] with branding irons kept by the police, which was done on payment of a special fee. (White farmers kept their own branding irons, and were exempt from the fee.)

After a period of two years' mandatory administration, the Union government commissioned the administration in Windhoek with controlling, managing and seeing to the welfare of the indigenous population, in accordance with the **Native Administration Proclamation No. 11/1922**.

Thus the black Namibians' hopes for better living conditions were shattered soon after the end of World War I. The administration increasingly revealed its intentions of maintaining, and further developing, the regime of oppression built up during the German colonial period. Disappointed expectations soon gave rise to resistance, both active and passive, through strikes, open rebellion, and opposition often inspired by religion.

Christian and syncretistic movements against racialism

Garveyanism

The use of Christian motives, and the setting up of Christian congregations in an effort to preserve the integrity of certain population groups from colonial oppression were already common under Jonker Afrikaner, and became even more apparent under Hendrik Witbooi, who, it will be recalled, referred to himself as having a messianic calling.

Increasing racialism and oppression reminded the black Namibians of the important function of religion and religious community to safeguard their integrity and self-confidence. Christian congregations thus became something of a centre of rebellion against South Africa's legalized racial oppression. Men other than the traditional chieftains now increasingly became leaders in the opposition against the regime.[33]

Katjavivi makes an important observation about the growing revolt against South African dominion: 'In the 1920s, cultural associations developed in the centre and in the south of the country, where German colonial conquest had decimated traditional structures.'[34] As an example of this phenomenon, Katjavivi mentions Garvey's Universal Negro Improvement Association (UNIA). The organization was not a purely socio-cultural movement since through its connection with Garveyanism it had religious roots in Ethiopianism.

The Negro visionary, prophet, and agitator Marcus Garvey[35] influenced the Ethiopianism then existing in South Africa, to develop an increasingly forceful, political 'anti-white' dimension. Garvey formulated a creed of his own for his movement, in affinity with Ethiopianism's dreams and hopes for 'Christian Ethiopia'; it read:

> We believe in one God, Maker of all things, Father of Ethiopia, and in His Holy Laws as it is written in the book Piley,[36] the sincerity of Angel Douglas and the power of the Holy Ghost. Who did Athlyi, Marcus Garvey and colleagues come to save? The downtrodden children of Ethiopia, that they might rise to be a great power among the Nations.[37]

The movement aimed to free the black peoples in the USA and Africa from the oppression of the whites, and reached Namibia in the early 1920s. In 1919, the UNIA had sent a delegation from the USA to the Versailles Peace Conference, demanding that Germany's colonies in Africa be declared independent, and that they be placed under 'the Black peoples' own leadership'.[38] This demand for independence inspired the formation of a local Garveyanist branch in Lüderitz in 1921. The UNIA made similar demands to the League of Nations in 1922, and again in 1928.

During World War I, people of mixed race from both South and West Africa, as well as from the West Indies, had come to live in Lüderitz; some of them had been deported there by the German colonial power in Cameroon, others had come there as sailors on ships which had been seized by the German authorities at the outbreak of the war because they belonged to enemy nations. Fritz Headley and John de Clue were two such 'foreign' men who founded a local branch of the UNIA in Lüderitz in 1921. They began to recruit adherents, and the UNIA soon gained the standing of a national movement, with members from different groups of people and tribes. Included in the UNIA's programme was its welcoming everyone belonging to the black race: tribal links were no hindrance for membership.

The UNIA thus introduced an international dimension to black opposition to white racialism. Blacks all over the world – primarily in the USA and Africa – were exhorted to 'pull together and to unite as one and then they will get their liberty'.[39] The movement hoped that American blacks would soon be able to conquer South Africa and free the whole of its black people. One colonial power had been defeated during World War I; this had kindled the hope that now 'a third external power – especially one perceived as being black – might be able to sweep away the new oppressors'.[40]

Garvey had heard about the harsh living conditions for 'non-whites' in South Africa through a friend in the West Indies, who was married to a coloured South African woman. He set it as his goal to bring about an international brotherhood of blacks to 'permeate the spirit of race, pride and love; to reclaim the fallen, to administer to and assist the needy, ... to assist in the development of independent Negro Nations and communities, [and] to work for better conditions among Negroes everywhere'.[41]

With an ideology inspired by religion, and with its demands to fight for freedom from the cruel methods of the oppressors, Garveyanism reached Namibia when all hopes for better conditions appeared to have faded away with the establishment of the South African dominion. The movement spread throughout the country; after reaching Windhoek it spread to Usakos, Karibib, Okahandja and several other towns further north. Its seal of membership was a ribbon in black and red and green (the same colours later to be used by the liberation party the South West African People's Organization [SWAPO]). The movement soon obtained a form of local leadership, especially among the Herero, Damara, and Nama people. Among the Hereros, Hosea Kutako was restored as the leader of the UNIA, as well as his brother Aaron Mungunda, Travyatt Maharero, a Herero leader in Okahandja, and Clemens Kapuuo, father of the future influential political leader by the same name. By the end of 1922, 'almost all the natives of Windhoek and also of the farms of the districts had joined [UNIA]'.[42]

Yet it was soon evident that the movement was divided. The initiators in Lüderitz who saw themselves as the leaders of the entire organization in Namibia, were in fact 'foreigners', and as such were not accepted by the indigenous population, lacking, as they were perceived to do, any natural ties to the country. Furthermore, they belonged to an entirely different social and economic stratum from the indigenous people. They therefore kept among themselves, and hardly related to any people outside their own circle. This was to become a decisive factor which contributed to lessening the UNIA's importance after an initial period of rapid growth.

The South African authorities, alarmed by the UNIA's success, promptly exploited this tension between the 'foreigners' in Lüderitz and the Namibian blacks. Another factor which played into their hands was the formation of a new organization, with similar goals to those of the UNIA but in opposition to the latter, in Lüderitz during the latter half of 1923. The new organization called itself the South West African National Congress (SWANC), and was modelled after the African National Congress (ANC) in South Africa.

The South African magistrate in Lüderitz took advantage of the competition between these two groups. He reported to his superiors in Windhoek that it would be advantageous nationwide to 'split the membership into different fractions – as has been done here'.[43] He further stated that:

> a purely native Congress can be handled more easily than the UNIA ... with a few Union natives with an ingrained respect for the White

man's authority at the head of the affairs – and if the Congress were taken under the wings of the Government, at its formation, with some unobtrusive, but effectual provisions for Government supervision, it might be a good policy.[44]

This strategy was successful in so far as the UNIA did die out as an organized, united 'anti-white' movement, only to be resurrected in the 1940s as the African Improvement Society – which was not militant but purely cultural in its overriding aims.[45] The decline of Garveyanism, however, was largely due, not to government intervention, but to Marcus Garvey's being sentenced in 1925 for embezzlement of funds in New York, as a result of which he was unable to provide any genuine leadership for his movement.

By mid-1924 the UNIA in Lüderitz had practically ceased to function. Only SWANC still had some adherents and occasionally held meetings. And SWANC was to disappear in 1925.

Despite its short-lived existence, Garveyanism along with the UNIA had succeeded to kindle renewed hope for black Namibians in their opposition to South African racial oppression. Where the UNIA had failed was to achieve unity across tribal barriers. However, the mere existence of the UNIA had caused great anxiety among the white colonizers, who feared a recurrence of the war of 1904-1907. They demanded that the authorities should cut down every tendency towards rebellion of any kind before the rebellious currents should grow too strong.

Uprisings inspired by Garveyanism

Even before Garveyanism with its 'anti-white' propaganda, there were many people in Namibia – including the missionaries – who often felt reminded of how Samuel Maharero and his people had taken the colonial authorities at unawares in 1904, with their sudden attack directed at the German colonial power. They feared that something similar might happen again. The inspector of the Rhenish Mission, Eduard Kriele, in April 1921 observed the phenomenon of a growing 'infatuation with freedom coupled with a spirit of unrepentance' in the blacks which manifested itself, among other things, through an unwillingness to work.[46] At about the same time, the Mission reported that 'natives in Windhoek [were] crying for freedom'.[47] What was especially alarming to them was the fact that Hosea

Kutako and the chieftain in exile, Samuel Maharero, maintained close contact. Samuel's son, Frederick Maharero, was reported to have freely travelled around Namibia speaking openly about seizing the law in his own hands; and this time, he said, there would be no talk of 'sparing German women and children'.[48]

From the mid-1920s, the parishes of the Rhenish Mission among the Hereros became progressively depopulated – a fact which caused lively discussion at missionary conferences, as well as in reports sent to the Board of the Mission in Germany. More and more, there was evidence of 'politicization', with demands for freedom, and a relapse to traditional 'paganism'. All of this, said the missionaries, was an outgrowth of Garveyanism.[49]

In early August 1921, the police in Ovamboland reported that Chief Ipumbu had begun to spread a form of propaganda against the authorities, and that he met regularly with other chieftains and headmen, a 'somewhat peculiar' situation.[50] Many black Namibians made no secret of the fact that they owned weapons; however, there was still no aggression. So even if the situation didn't seem to warrant immediate intervention, vigilance was recommended: 'Ipumbu is the fly in the ointment ... and when you have a large number of natives fairly well armed, who are still independent in a way, it is well to be careful.'[51]

Even individual farmers sent in alarming reports. In mid-March 1922, a German farmer, Carl Schlettwein, was informed by another farmer (a certain Mr B, himself married to a Herero woman, a fact which did not escape comment) that Herero people 'from all over the country' were preparing an armed uprising to seize hold of their rightful territory which, they claimed, 'England had promised them'.[52] The whole affair was said to stem from a 'Kap-Junge' – 'Cape boy' – in Outjo, who gathered 'kaffirs' every evening to attend prayer meetings. Mr B was of the opinion that the instigator, this 'boy' from the Cape, belonged to a revolutionary, 'anti-white' branch of Ethiopianism based in the Cape Province, and that he had been commissioned with the task of organizing an insurrection in Namibia.

Schlettwein reported the said 'outrage' to 'the Highest Quarters' in Namibia – in other words, to Administrator Hofmeyr. He said that the Hereros were trying to get hold of weapons through contacts with the people in Ovamboland. The whole affair should of course, he added, be kept confidential, but the police based in the locality should be keeping an eye on this instigator. Schlettwein offered Hofmeyr the assistance of all the farmers in the area. He was prepared to mobilize 100 to 120 farmers at a moment's notice if he was given access to arms and ammunition.[53]

Hofmeyr answered that he had instructed the authorities in Outjo to investigate matters. However, the magistrate in Outjo had written a letter, at roughly the same time as Schlettwein had written his, to the effect that nothing could be found which could be said to be 'very tangible ... except [the] usual stories of Herero-dwelling and farm-servants' uppish[ness]'.[54] Hofmeyr nevertheless gave the farmers access to 50 rifles and ammunition 'for the rifle club already formed'.[55] The country was by this time alive with rumours about impending uprisings and unrest. The whites felt especially anxious about a retaliation on the part of the Herero people to avenge the cruelties committed by the Germans during 1904-1907.

There were also reports of unrest among the Hottentots, or Namas. In Rehoboth, a police patrol had caught a group of suspect Namas red-handed in the act of 'distributing Garveyanistic propaganda'.[56]

White farmers, as well as other whites, began to make loud demands to the authorities, urging them to prepare themselves for a rapid intervention so that a recurrence of the events of 1904 may be prevented.

In February 1922, the magistrate of Keetmanshoop demanded access to more weapons; some weeks later, the board of the mining company in Tsumeb requested a delivery of at least two machine guns, since a circular, with traces of Garveyanistic propaganda, had been discovered which rallied all Ovambos, Namas, Damaras, Hereros, and San, to form a united front against all whites.

More positive than most of his peers, Missionary Kuhlmann stated at the beginning of 1922: 'If there was a question of an armed rising, we would hardly find it out, for as long as the people talk big, there is no direct danger; but if the hidden spark of hostility continues to smoulder on, there is no saying when it may burst into flames.'[57]

The Bondelswarts insurrection broke out in May 1922. By supporting their cause with Garveyanistic jargon their leaders hoped to gain both outside assistance and support from other indigenous groups within the country. The authorities in Windhoek, aware of this potential danger, reacted very forcefully in their immediate attempts to cut down this uprising. For the very first time in the history of Namibia, there was genuine hope throughout the country of attaining a sense of community beyond tribal limits, and of making 'concerted efforts to transcend the narrow communal divisions of pre-colonial Namibia through innovative ideologies and organisational structures'.[58]

The Bondelswarts uprising, May 1922

On 30 June 1919, the Bondelswarts in southern Namibia sent a deputation to the South African authorities in Windhoek to voice grievances concerning lack of land and work, and about the excessive increase of dog taxes. The spokesman of this delegation, Hendrik Schneuwee, had demanded with reference to his people's dependence on hunting for a living, that the dog tax should be abolished unconditionally. He was told that each family was entitled to own a dog without paying taxes for it. But taxes must be paid for more than one dog.

The question of dog taxes was but one of several underlying causes of the outbreak of the Bondelswarts insurrection in May 1922.[59] Other reasons included land issues, as the Germans under Leutwein had taken possession of a major part of the Bondelswarts' traditional territories in 1906. This had occurred in breach of the terms of the peace treaty that had been sealed after the Bondelswarts revolt of 1903. The Germans' breach of treaty had in fact been one of the reasons which had prompted the Bondelswarts to side with South Africa in 1914-1915. Their leaders at the time were Abraham Morris, the Nama leader Jakob Morenga's henchman, and Chieftain Jacobus Christian – both of whom had been forced into exile during the German period.

After the German capitulation in July 1915, the Bondelswarts had requested permission from the South African authorities for the return of both these exiles. The South Africans had rejected this request in consideration of the prevailing opinion concerning the exiles among the German colonizers. It was felt that the Bondelswarts who during the German colonial period had led several consecutive uprisings were a real menace to law and order in southern Namibia. It was in the South African authorities', as well as the German settlers', best interests to prevent the Bondelswarts from having a dynamic leader, especially in view of the fact that this group had a 'certain degree of communal identity and political organization'.[60] For this reason, the South African authorities appointed no fewer than three consecutive chieftains for the Bondelswarts between 1918 and 1922, without ever giving their people a hearing.

None of the three could be said to have done particularly well in their office, nor did they ever gain much in the way of their people's confidence. William Christian was described by the local magistrate in Warmbad as 'a harmless idiot, incapable of assuming any kind of responsibility whatsoever'.[61] Hendrik Schneuwee was appointed in his place, but was soon dismissed for having embezzled funds. Last in line was Timoteus Beukes who proved to be an obedient servant to the South African magistrates but who seemed to lack any 'desire or particular ability to lead'.[62]

While these three leaders failed to gain the confidence of their own people, the Bondelswarts sought contact with their exiled leaders Morris and Jacobus Christian. In October 1919, the magistrate in Warmbad reported an occurrence of unrest among the Bondelswarts due to their contacts with their countrymen in exile just south of the border; apparently the exiled leaders were being influenced by militant, 'anti-white' currents among groups of Ethiopianists in the Cape Province. The situation was, according to official opinion in Warmbad, serious because Jacobus Christian had crossed the border with an armed group and had behaved in a threatening manner towards a South African police contingent. Christian had been arrested, but had been released again, and been given permission to remain in Namibia.[63]

Further reports of border incidents were to follow. In May 1920, 36 armed men were taken, but many more had managed to cross the Orange River into Namibia. The magistrates in Warmbad maintained that the Bondelswarts' discontent with Hendrik Schneuwee had been occasioned by Jacobus Christian's propaganda for his own cause. They recommended that the authorities in Windhoek see to Christian's, and his group's, removal by force, and deportation to the Cape Province. The magistrates also called for reinforcements, so as to put a stop to the continued infiltration of armed groups. They finally warned that contact had been made between the rebellious among the Bondelswarts, the Hereros in Okahandja, and the Nama people settled around Rehoboth. The influence of Garveyanism, it was feared, was still strong among the rebels.[64]

Around this time, a plan took shape to remove the whole group of Bondelswarts by force to barren areas where they would not be able to earn a living. The plan was to force them to find work on white farms – thus, they would be able to pay their taxes, dog taxes inclusive.

In April 1922, Abraham Morris crossed the border with a group of

15 armed men. The return of this influential man who had succeeded Jakob Morenga, the former leader of rebellion, worried the white colonists. The police were ordered to capture him, but Morris' own people helped him remain in hiding, despite the order that he should be handed over to the police. In response to this refusal the authorities threatened, 'The lead of the government will melt upon you.'[65] Taking this as a direct declaration of war, the Bondelswarts fortified themselves in the desert hills.

This caused such a state of alarm that Administrator Hofmeyr himself led a citizen force of 370 colonists who had been mobilized in all haste, to crush the 'rebellion'. Hofmeyr had in fact not been given the order to attack by the central authorities of the Union. Acting on his own initiative, he also made use of two aeroplanes to bomb the Bondelswarts camps. More than 100 people were killed, among them Abraham Morris. Jacobus Christian was captured, and sentenced to five years' imprisonment.[66]

This whole 'war' effort only lasted a few days. Hofmeyr's method of warfare, especially his use of aeroplanes to bomb camps where women and children lived, made it into both the South African and the international press. The government of the Union appointed a commission of inquiry charged with establishing the reasons for the rebellion, and finding out how it had been counteracted. It was important to learn whether the rebellion had been triggered by movements within the Union, and also to establish what could be done in the future to prevent a repeat of such occurrences.[67]

Led by Major JF Herbst, a former official in Namibia, and major in the South African army, the commission remained in Warmbad for some time in order to interrogate the population there. It was found that the war had been a war of liberation, inspired by Jacobus Christian, who had demanded that the Bondelswarts territories, originally seized by the Germans, be returned to their rightful owners. Together with Abraham Morris, Christian had urged his people to fight so as to once and for all liberate their country 'or else be shot down'.[68]

The commission also maintained that the Bondelswarts had been supported by other groups of people, and that the insurrection could not be seen as an isolated occurrence: it was in fact a direct result of Garveyanism. Even after the rebellion had been crushed, the Herero and Nama leaders had purportedly gathered in October 1922 to assist the Bondelswarts. Furthermore, the commission noted that skirmishes between the police and groups of San people had occurred in Gobabis in the north-east, during which a policeman had been killed by a poisoned arrow.

White colonists now contacted the commission and requested it not to limit its investigation to Bondelswarts. A newspaper column which addressed the commission in the *Landeszeitung* of 12 August 1922 stated that 'no white man's life is safe in Gobabis, Waterberg and Vaalgras'. The blacks were challenging the government, it said.[69] The cause behind all this was, so it was claimed, the American Negro organization led by Marcus Garvey, whose slogan was 'Africa to the Africans'. And the black, red and green bow, the emblem of this movement, was worn by 'almost every second kaffir'.[70] The movement, it was concluded, was dangerous, as it strove to unite formerly rivalling tribes against the Europeans.

There were also rumours that the exiled Herero chieftain, Maharero, had crossed the border from Botswana, and that he and his followers were stirring up leaders of other tribes to prepare for a collective rebellion. It was impossible to confirm any of these rumours, but the commission claimed that there evidently was some co-operation between the Hereros, the Basters and other Rehoboth people, and the Bondelswarts. Apparently for the first time there was unity among the blacks in the country, and this had been born of a mutual feeling of hatred for the South African authorities. Besides, there seemed to be strong forces outside the country fostering feelings of rebellion.[71]

The commission condemned Hofmeyr's warfare; he had used too big a force, and had thus unnecessarily attracted the world's attention to the state of affairs in the mandate. However, Prime Minister Smuts publicly defended Hofmeyr's action, saying there had been reason to crush the rebellion with such force and hinting that the uprising had been due to 'pernicious native propaganda carried out by a certain Marcus Garvey'.[72] A 'native' who had remained loyal to the authorities, and who was not named, had allegedly explained that it was imperative to hit hard against such occurrences so as to avoid more serious trouble, which might be 'impossible to quell'. The official South African attitude towards Hofmeyr was therefore gratitude for his prompt action 'although loss of human life [was] regretted'.[73]

In a private, confidential missive to Smuts,[74] Hofmeyr not only defended himself against the accusations, but also implied that the commission, which was made up of 'British South Africans', tried to arouse suspicions against him as a 'Dutch South African'. South Africa did not need to submit to such 'ultra-Utopian groups' passing verdicts without any knowledge of the circumstances. He, Hofmeyr, had acted towards the 'less privileged race' with a feeling of 'responsibility' unique to a Dutchman. He had been guided in his action by his Christian conscience, his said feeling of responsibility, and his knowledge of the state of things in the country. South Africa had often been much too lenient, something which had allowed the blacks to get out of hand. Hofmeyr pointed out that law and order had reigned during the period of German colonial administration, but that this had changed when the blacks were left without a firm guiding hand, just as had happened in the Union after the Boer War. As a consequence, both the Germans and the Boers in the country were now 'embittered against the natives [sic], owing to want of policy'. In conclusion, Hofmeyr wanted to stress one point, in spite of everything that had been said on the issue: and this was that the rebellion had nothing to do with the increased dog taxation.

The incident made the South Africans more aware of the need to keep an eye out for the emotions and actions of black Namibians. Now more than ever vigilance was called for, especially in the northern part of the country, along the long, unguarded border with Angola. Here, there were no whites, and the authorities had no means of controlling the whole area along the border. The Finnish Missionary Society had already noted an increase in political activity among the Ovambo people, and there were rumours about contacts being made between the Ovambos and other population groups in the country. Also, there were signs that weapons were being smuggled across the border from Angola.[75] What had happened in connection with the Kwanyamas' conflict with South African military in 1917 was still fresh in mind.

The Finnish Missionary Society's request, made in 1920, to be allowed to take over the work of the Rhenish Mission in Ovamboland, was left open for the time being. In Windhoek a wait-and-see attitude was adopted regarding these former German mission stations. Things in northern Namibia first had to be stabilized through a well-ordered administration for the tribal areas. The authorities did not want missionary work to expand among the Ovambo people – not for reasons of principle, but in order to allow the state of things there to be arranged 'in a better way' first.[76]

Besides the Finns, the Roman Catholic Mission was also active in this part of the country, as was the Anglican Mission which had been given permission by the South Africans to establish itself there in 1923. After the Bondelswarts rebellion, the administration in Windhoek took some measures to control missionary activity in Ovamboland. In 1924, the authorities demanded a declaration of loyalty from the missions, especially regarding the following points. The missionaries

1 had to keep within the territories allotted to them by the authorities;
2 were forbidden to enter into special mission contracts, or agreements, with the leaders of the indigenous tribes; and
3 were bound by contract to:
   i) support and promote government policy
   ii) encourage Ovambos to work in the south, and
   iii) teach their members loyalty towards the administration.[77]

This declaration of loyalty roused debate in the Mandate Commission of the League of Nations, since surely this could hazard the missions' religious function.[78]

The Rehoboth rebellion, 1925

One of the aims of the South African administration was to categorically eliminate every form of local self-government among the indigenous groups.[79] Its laws and statutes were intended to limit the freedom of the local population. This gave rise to the Rehoboth rebellion of 1925. In Proclamation 28/1923, it was decreed that regulations concerning the indigenous population also applied to Rehoboth notwithstanding the 'protection and friendship' treaty signed with the Germans in 1885.

Furthermore, it was planned to reduce the Basters' territory in order to make room for more white settlers. The South African administration had forced the Council of Rehoboth to accept these new regulations, without giving them the opportunity to consult their people about the issue. Consequently, Rehoboth declared its council as dissolved and elected a new council, as well as appointing a parliament of its own in April 1924.

On 15 May 1924, the Baster leader Jacobus Beukes declared in a newspaper article that his people were in rebellion against the government.[80] Among other things, the Basters refused to pay their taxes; also, they had sought fellowship with the Hereros settled in the Rehoboth territory.

These developments worried the white population. The council dissolved by the Baster people were still regarded as a legal authority by the South African administration; however, they had lost the confidence of their people. As the South African magistrates in Rehoboth put it, 'the principal old *Raad*members[81] [were] getting tired of a somewhat thankless task and though still anxious to stand by the Administration and the Agreement I think they would be prepared ... to cancel the latter document and even resign in favour of a majority'.[82]

The new council elected by the Rehobothers was declared illegal by the South African authorities in December 1924; at the same time, the South Africans cancelled Rehoboth's traditional right of self-determination. The dissolved council appealed to the League of Nations' Mandate Commission in Geneva, requesting that the Commission should reinstate the independent status of Rehoboth – however, in vain. When, soon following this, there were demonstrations in Rehoboth, the South Africans sent in police reinforcements. In March 1925, 'violence', in the form of strikes and open refusal to pay taxes, erupted. South African troops surrounded Rehoboth, and had the town submit to 'mock attacks' from the air. By 5 April 1925, Rehoboth had given up all resistance. The horrors of the Bondelswarts rebellion were still fresh in everybody's mind: 'The appearance of the much dreaded aeroplanes on the scene at the crucial moment ... distracted the minds of the malcontents from the landforces.'[83] The leaders of the insurrection were sentenced to up to five years' imprisonment with hard labour.

Though the people of Rehoboth continued to send petitions to the League of Nations, the world organization was in no position to intervene. The Basters' conflict with the South African authorities lasted until 1933, when the treaty of 1885 was officially annulled. Instead of their council the Basters were now allowed to elect six representatives to a consultative assembly under the leadership of the local South African magistrate. In 1933, it was stated in Windhoek that the Basters 'were as yet found to be absolutely incapable of managing their own affairs'.[84]

From the Rehoboth example it became clear that the authorities' tactics against uprisings were to demonstrate their military strength to impress upon potential rebels the great power of the state, and thus avert a possible general uprising.

During these uprisings, the Rhenish Mission supported the authorities. Many in the Warmbad and Rehoboth communities were members of the Rhenish congregations. However, the missionaries did not support them since, as they saw it, the people involved in the uprisings behaved like political leaders. According to the Mission, they had thereby failed their Christian faith, which included obedience to the authorities appointed by God. The 'militant anti-white politics', under the influence of the 'false doctrines' of Ethiopianism, were to blame or, worse, the new, 'atheistic Bolshevism'.[85] The Mission maintained that its converts had started to behave 'as if the living Devil governed in their hearts'.[86]

The Mission made common cause with the authorities to re-establish law and order, and thereby induce the people to obedience. Naturally, the stand the Mission took harmed the Namibians' confidence in it. When these oppressed people fought for their freedom and human dignity, they were accused by the white religious leaders of meddling with politics, which the missionaries 'could not condone from a theological standpoint'.[87] Thus, the Mission's influence was reduced, and its membership dwindled. The missionaries were identified with the regime of oppression, and 'it was obvious that the Director of the Mission in Namibia [was] not [making] the slightest effort to see the events from the point of view of those most affected'.[88]

Regarding the living conditions of the members of their congregations, the missionaries shared the whites' general attitude towards blacks. They knew what was best for the indigenous population, which, in actual fact, meant that the whites always first saw to their own interests. The aim was 'to freeze the Africans into permanent under-development'.[89] No armed uprising appeared to be of help against such an attitude. What black Namibians needed was an inner collection of strength from a common identity and shared cultural values; and the emphasis on own identity and cultural values was important also in the context of the Christian congregations.

The beginnings of such a collection of strength appeared at the funeral of the exiled chieftain Samuel Maharero in Okahandja in 1923. This would prove to have consequences for a growing freedom movement.

Samuel Maharero's burial, 1923, and its consequences for the Rhenish Mission

Samuel Maharero died in Serowe, Botswana, on 14 March 1923. He had wished to be allowed to die in his native country, but was never given permission to return from his exile.[90] At his funeral in Okahandja, however, he was welcomed home as a hero of his people. The Hereros' tribal religious traditions were therefore very much alive, despite all the years of Christian influence through the work of the Rhenish Mission. Tribal religiosity and Christian faith were in fact united at the funeral, each given its place of dignity within the tribal tradition. Thus, the beginnings of the syncretistic religiosity which was to become the driving force in the Hereros' struggle for freedom for decades to come, were formed.

After the war of 1904-1907, with its savage massacre of Hereros, and the subsequent suppression of their tribal tradition, there remained only two factors of hope for this people's future. One of these was the community within the framework of the Christian congregation, since with protection from the Mission it was possible to maintain a community there for members of the tribe, where the people could talk in their own tribal language, and, with the permission of the missionaries, elect their own local leader. This uniting factor became one of the reasons for the increase in members of the congregations during the years immediately following 1907.

The other factor was linked to Chieftain Samuel Maharero. Before 1904-1907, he had acted controversially and his loyalty had been questioned by his own people. When the war broke out, however, he was their leader. And though he was defeated he was never taken prisoner, but instead lived in exile, together with whoever had managed to escape Von Trotha's attempt to exterminate the whole tribe.

The Herero people had great expectations of Maharero, even as a chieftain in exile. They maintained contact with him, and followed his directives. One of these was to accept Hosea Kutako as the headman, or vice-chieftain.

The capitulation of the Germans in 1915 raised the Hereros' hopes for positive change. The temporary lenience of the South Africans before 1920 prompted the Herero people, with Hosea Kutako as their spokesman, to request that Samuel Maharero be given permission to return. They had tried to win over their missionaries to support them in this matter, but as

Germans, the missionaries were hardly in a position at this point to use their influence. It is important to note, however, that the missionaries experienced this request as a request for a *political* decision: it was not the Rhenish Mission's policy to mix mission and politics. Furthermore, they viewed Christianity, European culture and colonial, European sovereignty as forming a unity which was necessary for Christian mission. Therefore, they were not willing to contribute to anything which might lead to a strengthening of tribal culture and power.[91]

The request for Maharero's return was rejected. Instead, the South Africans reintroduced restrictive racial laws. This influenced the Hereros' attitude both towards the new authorities and towards the Christian Mission. The missionaries seemed nothing more than stooges of the white regime! The Hereros opposed their demands for authority over their congregations. In an address to Prime Minister Smuts, the Herero people requested that the Rhenish Mission be asked to leave the country. The request was never answered. Behind the request was not the desire on the part of the Hereros to relinquish their Christian faith; it was rather the expression of a view on the African Church inspired by Ethiopianism. In line with tribal politico-religious tradition, the Hereros wished to unite the Christian Church with the traditional tribal power.[92] There was no intention, however, of reviving the old tribal religions. Rather, it was envisioned that traditional religious concepts and Christianity could continue to exist side by side, but under the direction of the people themselves, through their traditional leader.

Disappointed expectations following the introduction of South Africa's racial legislation in 1920 made the Hereros receptive to the influence of the UNIA, especially since one of the latter's leaders was their own leader Hosea Kutako. By 1922, the Hereros 'publicly talked of how they would start a war against the Whites. ... The populace was in an incredible mood, filled with bitterness against the Government, because it had not kept its promises.'[93]

Then, in April 1923, news of Samuel Maharero's death reached Okahandja. The South African authorities granted permission for Maharero to be buried in the heart of Herero country, in Okahandja.[94] As he had been a member of the congregation in Okahandja before going into exile, Maharero's death was announced during public worship in the Okahandja church. His coffin was transported by train from Botswana to Okahandja, which took endless deliberation and many preparations:

only on 23 August 1923 did the funeral procession reach its destination.

In many ways the South African authorities facilitated the task for the Hereros of arranging the funeral for Maharero in accord with the people's wishes. Samuel Maharero was to have a grave side by side with his father's and his grandfather's.

The leading man of the funeral ceremonies was Hosea Kutako. Following a divine church service on 26 August 1923, the funeral was held out in the churchyard, in accordance with tribal tradition. This meant that the Okahandja missionaries would not be performing a Christian burial after having conducted the service inside the church. Thus 'excluded' from the second part of the funeral, they refused to conduct the first. The service was eventually conducted by Missionary Heinrich Vedder.[95]

As we have mentioned, Samuel Maharero's funeral became an important turning point for the tribal community of the Hereros. In connection with it a non-military organization was formed, referred to as *otjiserandu* – which means 'the red ribbon'. Its members, who wear a khaki uniform and a red ribbon, still parade each year on the anniversary of Samuel Maharero's funeral on 26 August. The parade always begins with a divine service in the Okahandja church, followed by tribal ceremonies by the chieftains' graves. *Otjiserandu*, with its red ribbon, is today a Herero organization which gives assistance to the needy in the Herero community.[96]

The funeral also brought a number of traditional religious Herero customs back to life, for example the holy fire and ancestral worship, and circumcision, to mention but a few.

It is important that the proceedings of 26 August 1923 had been sanctioned by the South African authorities. In fact, South African representatives from Windhoek participated. This put the Mission in an awkward position, so much so that it addressed a formal complaint to the authorities.

Relations between the Rhenish Mission and the Hereros were further strained as a result of the funeral. The Mission claimed that the funeral had been a 'reversion to paganism, the direct result of Herero criticism of the divinely ordained political structure and of the white man's power'.[97] The Mission little understood the Christian element of this event. Not only had a service of thanksgiving had been held in the church when Maharero's death had been announced, but the funeral too had been preceded by a divine service, led by a missionary, at the request of Hosea Kutako. This could have been interpreted as an important Christian social function, albeit followed by elements of ancient tribal customs. Instead, the Mission only saw what in its view had been a politicization through a pagan, and therefore reprehensible, public ceremony.

In the light of this missionary attitude, it is not surprising that many Herero members did not wish to maintain any future contact with the Rhenish Mission. As we have said, the Rhenish parishes became quite depopulated towards the mid-1920s, and many were inclined to believe there was no future for the Mission in this area. The missionaries had 'failed to see the political implications of their evaluation of the Marcus Garvey movement and the Hereros' desire for freedom. They [had] also failed to realize that the revival of the Herero religion was directly inspired by the missionaries' own reaction to the Africans' incipient political emancipation.'[98]

The events which took place at Samuel Maharero's funeral were therefore of great importance in the shaping of future events and may be summarized as follows.

1 They represented a form of rebirth for the Hereros' tribal identity and thus resulted in a weakening of African universality which had been formerly proclaimed by Garveyanism.
2 They became an expression of power and renewed self-confidence and thus provided inspiration to strive for political freedom of one's own particular tribe.
3 They represented an attempt to revive some of the tribe's most important religious traditions in conjunction with retained Christian values, with the tribal leader as a collective leading figure.
4 All of the above culminated in a crisis in relations with the Rhenish Mission which clung tenaciously to its particular view of Christian Western civilization and to a pietistic interpretation of Christianity, which makes a distinction between worldly and spiritual rule, according to Romans 13:1.

One may be justified in saying, therefore, that Samuel Maharero's funeral had many, more far-reaching consequences for the future development of Namibia in the country's struggle for independence than Maharero's leadership ever managed to bring about during the chieftain's lifetime and specifically during the war of 1904-1907.

Notes

1 Wellington, JH. 1967, 254.
2 Ibid., 262.
3 See the Peace Treaty of Versailles document.
4 Lejeune, A. 1971, 27; see also Wellington, op. cit., 262 ff. In *Judgment on German Africa*, Steer. GL, writes, 'The Commission's powers are neither compulsory nor advisory ... it gives no orders except that it must be addressed and consulted annually ... In other words, [the Commission] is mild as milk.' (1939: 29)
5 I.1.22-27: 1920; Church Archives, Windhoek.
6 Ibid.; see also Bertelsmann, W. 1979, 11.
7 Hoffmann, H. 1991.
8 Engel, L. 1977, 132.
9 Steer, GL, op. cit., 341; see also Hoffmann, H, op. cit., 92-96. The latter also includes Smuts' speech of 1 September 1920.
10 Smuts to the High Commissioner, London, 17 November 1921; SWA Inhabitants, Nationality of, C 297, National Archives, Windhoek.
11 Ibid.
12 Steer, GL, op. cit., 341; see also Bertelsmann, W, op. cit., Appendix.
13 Steer, GL, op. cit., 340 ff.
14 Ibid.
15 Ibid.
16 Ibid.
17 Constitution for South West Africa, Union Act 42 (1925).
18 Ibid.
19 Innes, D. 1981, 90; see also Goldblatt, I.1971, 227.
20 Katjavivi, P.1988b, 557 ff; concerning the Bondelswarts' support of South Africa during World War I, see Werner, W. 1988, 268.
21 Werner, W, op. cit., 268 ff.
22 Hosea Kutako was born in 1870 in Okahandja where his father was in the service of the Rhenish Mission. During the wars of 1904-1907 he was wounded and held prisoner in Omaruru but managed to escape. After 1907 he was first a teacher in the employ of the Mission but later became a worker in Tsumeb mine. He played an increasingly important role in the liberation struggle. Kutako died at the age of 100 years. For further biographical details on Kutako, see Segal, R. 1962, 38-40.
23 Akweenda, S. 1988a, 515-517.
24 Moleah, AT. 1983, 48 ff.
25 Emmet, T. 1988, 224.
26 Hubrich, HG & H Melber. 1977, 63.

27 Emmet, T, op. cit., 224 ff.
28 Moleah, AT, op. cit., 47.
29 Werner, W, op. cit., 268.
30 Moleah, AT, op. cit., 48.
31 All of the documents to be found in the National Archives, Windhoek.
32 Ibid.
33 Katjavivi, P, op. cit., 557 ff.
34 Ibid.
35 Marcus M Garvey (1887-1940) was born in Jamaica. He founded the UNIA in 1914. In 1916 he moved to the USA where he organized the Back to Africa Movement in 1920. He lost his influence when in 1925 he was convicted of fraud and imprisoned until 1927.
36 The Ethiopian Bible.
37 Sundkler, B. 1948, 58.
38 Pirio, G. 1984, 265.
39 Ibid.
40 Ibid., 266.
41 Katjavivi, P, op. cit., 564.
42 In: ibid.
43 See letter from the Magistrate of Lüderitz to the Administrator in Windhoek: undated; National Archives, Windhoek.
44 Ibid.
45 Katjavivi, P, op. cit., 69.
46 See 'Die Lage der Rheinischen Mission im April 1921. Bericht für die Hauptversammlung von Missionsinspektor E Kriele.' In: file marked 'Preses – Inspector, Correspondence 1888-1932': 1.1-6.; Church Archives, Windhoek.
47 Ibid.
48 Ibid.
49 Minutes of Missionary Conferences, and correspondence between the preses and the headquarters in Wuppertal-Barmen, I.1.1-7 to I.1.43-47 and 5.1-30:1920-1925; Church Archives, Windhoek.
50 Letter, of 6 August 1921, from the Deputy Commissioner, South West African Police, to the Secretary for South West Africa, Windhoek. In: ADM/145:1915-1920, National Archives, Windhoek.
51 Ibid.
52 See correspondence, C Schlettwein to Administrator Hofmeyr, Windhoek, 15 March 1922. In: ADM/145: 1915-1920; National Archives, Windhoek.
53 Ibid.
54 See correspondence, Hofmeyr to Schlettwein, 4 April 1922; see also Hofmeyr's memo, of 29 March 1922, to Outjo's magistrate; ADM/145: 1915-1920; National Archives, Windhoek. The same subject is dealt

with in the correspondence, Secretary to Manning, 5 January 1923, reporting on how a certain 'Orlag' had visited the Mahimbas, asking for weapons from Ovamboland. The report concludes as follows: 'If the Government does not take steps, we shall be compelled to put the kaffirs in their place.'
55 See correspondence, Hofmeyr to Schlettwein, 4 April 1922; ADM/145: 1915-1920, National Archives, Windhoek.
56 Garveyanism at the time was blamed for every sort of popular unrest, so the expression 'distributing Garveyanistic propaganda' is not to be taken literally.
57 Emmet, T, op. cit., 224.
58 Ibid.
59 ADM/125, file No. 3353; National Archives, Windhoek.
60 Emmet, T, op. cit., 236.
61 Ibid.
62 Ibid.
63 ADM/105, file No. 3353; National Archives, Windhoek.
64 Emmet, T, op. cit., 236 ff.
65 Ibid., 241.
66 For more on the Bondelswarts Uprising, see the Report to Hofmeyr; undated (copy not signed). In: ADM/105, file No. 3353; National Archives, Windhoek; see also Vigne, R.1973, 17.
67 Commission of Inquiry, Bondelswarts Uprising, with Recommendations, 21 July 1922; included are also Terms of Reference, 4 August 1922; C300; National Archives, Windhoek.
68 Affidavits to the Commission of Inquiry, Bondelswarts Uprising, 1922-1923; C300; National Archives, Windhoek.
69 *Landeszeitung*, 12 August 1922; C300; National Archives, Windhoek.
70 Ibid.
71 Commission of Inquiry, Bondelswarts Uprising: Affidavits; C300; National Archives, Windhoek.
72 Correspondence, of 22 August 1923, of the Prime Minister to the High Commissioner in London; C300, National Archives, Windhoek.
73 Government Reports on the Administration of South West Africa, 1922; filing cabinet No. XIV; Church Archives, Windhoek.
74 Confidential letter from the Administrator, Windhoek, of 30 August 1922, to Smuts; C300, National Archives, Windhoek.
75 Tötemeyer, G. 1978, 19.
76 Minutes of the Missionary Conferences, I.1.22-27: 1920; Church Archives, Windhoek.
77 First, R. 1963.
78 Ibid.

79 Statistics and Annual/Quarterly Reports, 1.5.1-4: 1931; Church Archives, Windhoek.
80 Article by Jacobus Beukes, in Windhoek's *Allgemeine Zeitung* of 15 May 1924; National Archives, Windhoek.
81 Members of council.
82 Correspondence, Rehoboth magistrate to the Secretary of South West Africa, Rehoboth, 30 October 1925; National Archives, Windhoek.
83 Engel, L.1976, 258.
84 Ibid., 271.
85 Ibid., 272.
86 Ibid.
87 Engel, L. 1977, 140.
88 Ibid., 140.
89 Moleah, AT, op. cit., 53.
90 Pool, G. 1991, 293.
91 Engel, L, op. cit., 131-137.
92 Wienecke, WA. 1962, 85.
93 Engel, L, op. cit., 133.
94 On the burial of Chief Samuel Maharero, see NAW21/15; National Archives, Windhoek.
95 Pool, G, op. cit., gives a detailed description of the funerary proceedings.
96 Katjavivi, P, op. cit., 74 ff.
97 Engel, L, op. cit., 134.
98 Ibid., 136.

11 Mission under South African racial policy, 1920-1939

The Union's racialist legislation in the mandated territory of Namibia

The South Africans applied their legislation of racial segregation in their own country as well as in Namibia. Whites were granted privileges such as internal self-government; they also monopolized the country's natural resources. Black Namibians, on the other hand, were subjected to the same racialist legislation which applied to black South Africans in the Union.

The League of Nations' notion that a mandatory power had a 'sacred trust' was no longer interesting. We have already mentioned all those laws and regulations of the early 1920s, which aimed at achieving increasingly strict control of the indigenous population. In 1922, Administrator Hofmeyr established the Native Reserves Commission, according to whose findings 'the labour question [was] synonymous with the native question'.[1] The system which was introduced in Namibia was the same as that operative in the Union and included:

1 removal by force of blacks away from 'white territories';
2 the disappearance of so-called 'black islands' from within white settlement areas; ·
3 legislation forbidding the leasing of land to blacks in a 'white territory', in order to put an end to what was popularly referred to as 'kaffir farming'; and
4 the establishment of an administrative system aiming at the increased efficiency of the control of 'indigenous reservation areas'.

Ultimately the aim was to undermine the self-sufficiency of the black population groups, and thus to compel them to seek work as labourers for the whites, thereby providing a solution to the problems of supplying black labour to farmers and industries.[2]

The leaders of various tribes and groups protested against these removals to isolated, arid, and practically uncultivable areas. For instance, the Herero leader Hosea Kutako refused to accept the reservation areas which had been allotted to his people, bordering on the desert where so many Hereros had perished during the flight from Von Trotha's genocide campaign during the war of 1904-1907. But all protests were in vain. Kutako now took measures to improve the living conditions in the reservations as much as possible, so that his people would be able to earn their livelihood there without having to seek employment among the whites. However, a number of new restrictions were introduced which limited both autonomous production and the number of cattle they could keep, so that Kutako's attempt at maintaining self-determination was thwarted. It had by now become evident that the power lay entirely in the hands of the South African administration, and that it was a matter of sheer survival to seek work as labourers on the farms or in the mines.[3]

The authorities also strove to limit the blacks' traditional means of taking action. The Native Administration Proclamation No. 11/1922[4] decreed that inside 'native reservation areas', the Union would have the right to wield the highest power of execution, with no consideration for the traditional leadership of the blacks. Control of indigenous labour within the police zone was carried out by a district magistrate who was appointed by the administrator. The densely populated areas in the north were placed under the care of the central administration of Windhoek in 1917, but they were administered differently from the southern and central Namibian areas which lay outside reservations. One might even say that the southern and central regions of the country were made into a white reservation area. Here, the growing white population had ample opportunity to own land and exploit all the natural resources for their own benefit. Blacks were allowed into white areas if their labour was needed. Black Namibians who were employed in the service of the whites were obliged to live in 'locations' at a 'reasonable distance' from white residential areas. This applied equally to larger urban centres and to the countryside.

Northern Namibia was an 'indigenous reservation area' in the purest sense of the term, since no whites were allowed to live there permanently, apart from administrative staff and missionaries. Whites who wished to cross into Ovambo or Kavango reservations needed a special licence. There were no white interests to look after here, and the indigenous people were to go on leading their own traditional tribal life. A commissioner for

- the Ovambos and Kavangos with practically autocratic powers was based in the area along with his staff.

Further laws were introduced which curtailed the black Namibians' rights to self-determination. According to Act No. 38 of 1928, the administrator of Namibia was made the 'Paramount Chief of the Natives'.[5] He was thereby given the right to appoint and revoke chieftains as he saw fit, as well as bring about the forced removal of a tribe or part of it to another part of the country. Also, he had the power to establish the borders of the tribal territories and 'generally to exercise such political power and authority as a Native Chief usually possessed under his own laws, customs and usages'.[6]

In 1928, the post of chief native commissioner was added to the administration of the country: 'Thus, the control of Native matters had clearly become the function of a Division of Native Affairs within the Administration of South West Africa.'[7] This commissioner's duties included, among other things, the recruitment of black labourers. From 1925, the task of recruitment was organized between two recruitment companies, which were financed by the fees paid by white employers for the right of obtaining labour.[8]

The South African mandatory power strove to attain absolute control of Namibia's blacks. There were some isolated attempts at organizing strikes throughout the 1920s and in 1931.[9] When a group of Ovambos under the leadership of Chief Ipumbu revolted against increasing tax pressure in 1932, armed troops were sent in to punish and exile this chief after devastating the principal village of the tribe.[10]

South Africa submitted annual reports on its administration of the indigenous Namibians to the League of Nations' Mandate Commission in Geneva. But although these reports were discussed and queries and opinions presented, the League of Nations had neither the ability nor the authority to actively intervene, being restricted in their function to presenting opinions and quite possibly to protesting. And so, the Mandate Commission 'protested strongly whenever South Africa made more of its laws, including racial legislation such as the Colour Bar Law of 1926, applicable in South West Africa'.[11] However, they 'found it particularly difficult to reconcile the system of Native areas with the spirit of the mandate'.[12]

Divided loyalties within the Rhenish Mission

The Rhenish Mission's divided loyalties between 1920 and 1939 considerably complicated its working conditions. After the German capitulation in 1915, there was tension between Boers and Englishmen within the South African military administration concerning the 'native' issue. The first person in authority after 1915, Sir Hugho Gorges, along with his various office bearers belonged to the English-speaking population of the Union. Their attitude towards the blacks was traditionally more liberal than the Afrikaans-speaking people's. It was during this period, immediately after the German capitulation, that some measures of relief were introduced into the harsh German legislation with respect to the indigenous population in Namibia. As we have seen, in black Namibians this liberalization aroused great hopes of regaining previously lost tribal territories, and of returning to a traditional tribal way of life. Tribal leaders thought they could rely on Gorges for support. They even filed complaints of maltreatment of labourers with the hope of legal intervention on their behalf.[13]

This new, 'liberal' attitude towards the black Namibians led to growing dissatisfaction among the whites who accused the military administration of indulging the blacks. Even the police in Namibia expressed their dissatisfaction, since they witnessed the curtailment of their own powers as a result of Gorges' and his colleagues' policies. The discontented white colonizers generally agreed that Gorges' 'indulgent indigenous policy'[14] undermined the blacks' respect for the white man, which was after all a precondition for effective exploitation of black labour. According to them, the blacks were becoming 'indolent, lazy, inefficient, unreliable and negligent'[15] as a direct result of Gorges' policy.

Just like the other German-speaking whites in Namibia, the Rhenish missionaries were afraid of a recurrence of the war of 1904-1907. The blacks in the country must therefore be taught unquestioning obedience and respect for the powers that be. Far-reaching liberalization might arouse unwarranted hopes and trigger renewed rebellion. In a report addressed to the Board of the Mission in Germany in 1919, Preses Olpp complained that British propaganda of 'liberation from the German yoke' had 'intoxicated' the local tribes,[16] many of whom were now dreaming of freedom and a return to precolonial ways. Olpp claimed he was no longer able to recognize the Africans who had been so obedient towards the German colonial authorities. It was with reference to this report that Engel[17] made the following statement: 'In constant fear of new disturbances among the Africans, which like the uprising of 1904 could destroy their entire life's work, the missionaries anxiously hoped for a strong regime capable of restoring the old order and preserving the Africans from the possible consequences of their destructive lust for freedom.'

There were also strong financial interests involved in the Rhenish Mission's wish to preserve the racialist policy. The Mission had its own farms which were run with the help of black labour. These labourers lived under similar conditions as those who worked elsewhere on white-owned farms. 'Master mentality, terminology and attitudes betraying the owner possession relationship were the same among the European settlers as the farming missionaries: the Black labourers became "my boys" or even "my kaffirs".'[18]

In his report of 1919,[19] Olpp spoke of British anti-German propaganda. It was as a British dominion that the Union had entered the war and defeated the Germans in 1915. The threat against the future of the Mission, a consequence of the liberalization in racial policy, under British/South African officers, seemed to be eliminated after 1920. Since the Boer War, the German-speaking population in Namibia had felt threatened by the English-speaking South Africans – an attitude which did not diminish during World War I. However, when Smuts came to power the Germans felt that here was an officer who sympathized with their position. Expectations grew further when Smuts' successor to the post of prime minister, James Hertzog, visited Namibia in October 1924.[20]

The Rhenish Mission's efforts to demonstrate their loyalty to South Africa and its racial policy were to yield negative consequences for its relations with the indigenous population. The independent groupings who left the Mission's parishes during the 1940s and 1950s gave the Mission's questionable loyalties as one of the main reasons for leaving. The Mission had done little to support the blacks in their struggle against racial oppression. Its inability to stand by the oppressed people was largely due to its own view on the racial issue, and had already manifested itself at Samuel Maharero's burial, where the missionaries reacted against what they viewed as a revival of the traditional heathen Herero beliefs. Against this background, it is fairly obvious that the Rhenish Mission was unable to muster any sympathy for the ideology of Garveyanism, which was after all nothing but dangerous revolutionary propaganda under a quasi-religious cover.

After the funeral, there had been further resumption of traditional religious and social practices among the Hereros. This was seen by the Rhenish missionaries as evidence of a relapse into paganism against which measures involving stricter Church discipline must be taken. Some of these were decided on at a missionary conference in Swakopmund in 1926, at which missionaries noted 'intolerable and unacceptable changes in the attitudes and outlook of the indigenous people as a result of general political bewilderment'.[21]

The issue of Church discipline, which led to no improvements but rather, contributed to a decrease in the number of parish members, grew in importance and became a central issue of the correspondence between the preses and the Board of the Mission based in Germany.

The Mission never even attempted to try to understand the underlying reasons for the black Namibians' striving to attain an identity of their own, and fight the ongoing systematic denigration of their human worth. According to the Mission, blacks were seduced away from its parishes by the lure of worldly gain and advantages; this was leading to moral and religious decay: to a form of 'syncretism' where only Christian faith should stand.

The Mission's unwillingness to understand the needs of a people trapped within the system of racial policy widened the gap between the Mission and the black Namibians. In 1928, Damaras founded the Progressive Association in Windhoek, which aimed to attain greater freedom with respect to the racial legislation, and ultimately, to keep clear of, and aggressively work against, all whites, including the missionaries. In the Association's widely distributed manifesto it was pointed out that the Rhenish Mission was to blame for much of the blacks' social and political distress, as the Mission was clearly striving to 'create an image of blacks as foolish people [who] were obliged to remain so for evermore in order to be held in check'.[22]

The Mission was fast losing the confidence of its remaining black parishioners as well as its credibility as bearer of the message of Christian love and the Christian conception of the infinite worth of all humans, irrespective of the colour of their skin. To black Namibians, the Rhenish Mission was clearly in support of 'the South African racial policy and its status quo'.[23]

When the Mission accused black Christians of being involved in un-Christian activities of rebellious political groupings, and claimed that this was contrary to the teachings of the Christian faith, which preached obedience to the authorities, the blacks felt they

> could ... place no credence in their [the missionaries'] claim to be neutral .... The missionaries used religion to further the onesided White economic and political interests [and] theology was reduced to providing a religious cloak for an unhuman social structure. The Africans ... could not sympathize with the missionaries' preconceived notion of the unity existing between Christianity, White culture and political supremacy, when their own claims and aspirations had no place in this system.[24]

Thus the Rhenish Mission's efforts to remain loyal to South African racial ideology proved detrimental to the furtherance of its activities in Namibia from 1920 onwards.

Meanwhile, there was a strong desire among the Germans who now lived under foreign rule to protect and preserve their German identity. The Union had previously rejected a number of demands by the German population concerning the issue of preservation of Germanism. The unrealistic request to create a specially tailored mandate citizenship for all German descendants had been revoked, along with the demand to make German one of the country's official languages. The Germans were, however, allowed to keep their own German schools provided that English and Afrikaans were taught as well. Furthermore, the authorities agreed that German descendants could correspond with the authorities in German.

It seems, therefore, that the Germans in Namibia were given many privileges, especially considering the fact they had been defeated by the South Africans. One of the reasons was that the German population were needed to ensure the development of the country. They knew Namibia well and were thus able to contribute to making the mandated territory financially profitable for the South Africans. Many of those Germans who had been exiled after the capitulation were allowed to return after a few years and immigration of new groups from Germany was encouraged. In 1920 there were altogether 7 000 German-speaking people living in Namibia, but their numbers grew rapidly.

In fact, the total number of whites in Namibia doubled between 1914 and 1926.[25] Besides the Germans, many South Africans were attracted to the region, especially by the generous conditions they were offered. When the first legislative assembly for whites in Namibia was elected in 1925, the German-speaking population voted as a political national group of their own; as we have said, they even obtained a majority. One of the first steps taken by the new legislative assembly was to demand the immediate revocation of the Blue Book. The reason they gave was the alleged wish to 'establish reconciliation and fellowship between all the groups who were represented in the legislative assembly';[26] questions concerning the truth of the Blue Book's reports on instances of German cruelties against black Namibians were never raised. On 29 July 1926, the legislative assembly unanimously decided to pass a proposition presented by the Deutsche Bund to withdraw the Blue Book as a reliable official document, and seize and destroy all copies. The Rhenish Mission granted its support of this decision, since, as the missionaries saw it, it represented an act of reconciliation.[27] This was a victory for Germanism and its influence on the administration of Namibia.

The Rhenish missionaries, like their compatriots, sent their children to German schools while they themselves became active members of German cultural and social associations. Many mission stations lay within the police zone where strong segregation between whites and blacks was practised. Though the parishes with their churches and schools were often located inside labourers' 'locations' on white farms or near white enterprises, rules, both written and unwritten, for segregation presented an obstacle to natural contact between the missionaries and the members of their parishes.

As Germans, the missionaries also took an active part in the German evangelical parishes. In 1926, all these parishes were united under the denomination of the Deutsche Evangelische Lutherische Synode and led by a Landesprobst.[28] Pastors for the German-speaking parishes were recruited from Germany. However, this proved unpracticable from the start except for larger localities such as Windhoek, Keetmanshoop, Swakopmund, and Omaruru, so that well into the 1960s, 'the spiritual charge of caring for the souls of Germans was largely carried out by missionaries ... of the Rhenish Mission. This even included visits ... to distant farm locations.'[29]

The missionaries thus had a twofold task, and their duties as clergymen sometimes took up more than half of their working time, with the result that they had less and less time to make satisfactory contact with their own mission parishes. The fact that the German language was used in evangelical services, along with racial legislation, meant that it was no longer possible to conduct services for black and white parishioners together. Furthermore, the twofold task of the missionaries meant they were now serving two 'masters': as missionaries, they served under the local and the central Board of the Mission; as pastors of the German-speaking parishes, they obeyed the dictates of these parishes' synods and the Landesprobst.

Their position as pastors of the German-speaking parishes was prestigious since in Germany, missionaries were not entitled to apply for office as regular pastors, and devoted themselves to missionary work alone. In Namibia, on the other hand, they were allowed to serve as regular pastors for their countrymen, besides doing missionary work. Thus the racial issue became an integral part of the way in which the local missionaries viewed their office. It was considered of higher standing to be a pastor for white than a missionary for black parishes: 'The feeling of racial superiority among the missionaries was strengthened by these missionaries' contacts with their white parishes.'[30]

At the same time, gradual ideological changes were manifesting themselves among the German-speaking population in Namibia. These Germans had always harboured 'high German ideals'. They blamed the German defeat in World War I on 'Bolshevik backstabbing' which they claimed had been aimed at those authorities who held high positions inside Germany during the last year of the war. The Imperial period, when Germany had colonies of its own, had been a time of glory when the 'Germanic spirit' had been great, and pure. The subsequent loss of its colonies had been a betrayal of Germanism. In 1923, the main Church of the German-speaking parish in Namibia, the Christuskirche in Windhoek, put up a plaque recording the names of all those Germans who had fallen during the wars fought in the colony.

Thus, it might be said that the parishioners and indeed, the clergymen, were manifesting a new German national pride. Also, Germans in Namibia would sign statements made in Christian colonial circles in their native country, such as: 'The injustice of Versailles must be redressed. ... They have seized our colonies by force, but have as yet been unable to tear them out of our hearts!'[31] And at the first joint synod meeting held in Windhoek in 1926, it was decided that a leaflet should be sent to all the young German immigrants upon their arrival in Namibia, stating the following: 'Beware of the racial dishonour. You have Germanic blood in your veins. ... Remember that you are Christian! Remember that you are white! Remember that you are German!'[32]

With such so-called 'high German' sentiments it is not surprising that the Germans in Namibia easily got carried away by the ideology of Nazism. The Nazi Party began their activities in Namibia as early as 1929. Immediately after Adolf Hitler came to power in Germany in 1933, local Nazi activities were organized with local Party leadership, a local Führer, and a Hitlerjugend,[33] both in Windhoek and in other centres. The swastika was hoisted, and Nazi uniforms were worn at important Party rallies around the country. The Party demanded that all German descendants should swear an oath of allegiance to Hitler and the fatherland.

These new developments caused the authorities great concern in view of the ferment of political activity in Germany. Through the London Agreement, the German government had in 1923 relinquished any right to regard German descendants in Namibia as German citizens. As British citizens of South African nationality, Germans in Namibia were not entitled to dual citizenship. The authorities now took a number of steps to put a stop to, or at least limit, the extent of Nazi influence in the country. In 1934, members of the Hitlerjugend were forbidden to swear an oath of allegiance to Hitler. Efforts were also made to stop the spread of Nazism locally, for example by branding it as a subversive organization.

Back in Germany, the Hitler regime protested against such treatment of Germans in a League of Nations mandate. Nazism in Namibia carried on its activities unperturbed, often under the cover of various other denominations, and less conspicuously. Then, in April 1937, the South African authorities suddenly 'clamped down on political activities that involved disloyalty to the mandatory authority'.[34]

Even many Rhenish missionaries had secretly entertained the hope that Hitler's Germany would claim its former colony, German South West Africa. The missionaries found themselves in a dilemma, firstly in their relations with the South African administration, and secondly with the indigenous population of Namibia. As Germans, they shared the feelings the new German ideology aroused in most German-speaking people in Namibia. In fact, most of the missionaries belonged to a generation who had come to Namibia in the glorious days of German colonialism, and had experienced the Germans' defeat in World War I at first hand. It is necessary to bear this in mind in order to gain a deeper understanding of events that were to affect the Rhenish Mission prior to 1939, during World War II, and after the victory of South Africa's National Party in 1948. These events came to influence relations between the Mission and the black Namibians with their increasingly urgent demands for greater freedom and humane treatment, especially after the World War II.

As Germans, the Rhenish missionaries were soon to come into close contact with the new political movement, especially through their dual position as missionaries and pastors of the German parishes. In the synod, Nazi propaganda was spread openly in accordance with directives from the Deutsche Bund and its leader, a certain Dr Schwiederung who held the title of Führer of all Germans in Namibia.

The rift in the Church in Germany shortly after the Barmen Declaration was proclaimed in 1934[35] made itself felt in Namibia, too. Some pastors declared that their task was to serve all Germans, independent of Party affiliation, but with due observation of the Prussian ideals of 'inner chastisement and discipline'. Others, such as the Landesprobst, a Dr Wackwitz, belonged to the Nazi Party, and began his term in 1933 by forwarding greetings from the bishop of the Reich, Ludvig Müller, the same bishop whom Hitler had appointed as the leader of the Evangelical Church of the Reich. Müller urged the German descendants in Namibia to demonstrate their allegiance in the true German spirit during 'these fateful years in the life of the fatherland'.[36]

When the Christuskirche in Windhoek celebrated its 25th anniversary in October 1935, Landesprobst Wackwitz made sure that the ceremonies were dominated by references to the 'high German ideology of Nazism'. The German consul of Windhoek, Hermann von Oelhafen, the main speaker, paid homage to Nazism and stressed its importance for all German descendants living in Namibia. He ended his presentation with the following words:

> God shall never abandon any German who places his trust in Him. Faith in the future, a united power of the will, and a firm belief in ultimate victory inspires the German native land on its way to renewed greatness. ... one single ardent prayer along with an everlasting hope animates each and every one of German blood

and with one single ardent yearning in the heart: Germany, Germany, Germany![37]

Even the former governor of German South West Africa was one of the ceremonial speakers.

In his presentation, Landesprobst Wackwitz announced that the parish Scout movement had in 1933 joined ranks with the Hitlerjugend. The latter had been prohibited in 1934, however. It was now time for the youth movement to resume its activities in the parish and try to 'find new ways to promote the German spirit'.[38]

It was the German consul who was ultimately responsible for the management of the Nazi Party in the country. After South African authorities had banned Nazi uniforms and manifestations of Nazi activity in Namibia, the consul began to found a number of so-called 'apolitical, German cultural associations' which would further Nazi activities. In December 1935, he announced that all young Germans could expect, as from 1936, to be enlisted for military service in Germany.[39] He further supported Nazi Germany's protest, in 1937, against South Africa's measures against Nazism in Namibia.

Consul Von Oelhafen was invited to speak at a missionary conference held in Windhoek in October 1935, the first missionary conference since the Nazis had come to power in Germany. The Consul's speech was on 'The Importance for the Church and the People of being German and Christian'. Unfortunately, there are no copies of this speech in the Church archives; in the minutes, it was noted that the missionaries thanked him for giving such an in-depth exposition of the Christian responsibility borne by all Germans in the light of the new, positive events taking place in the fatherland.[40]

The formal thanks on behalf of the missionaries were delivered by Heinrich Vedder. This man was the leading, most influential missionary in his day, and would remain so until his death in Okahandja in April 1972. He was reputed for his abilities not only as a missionary, but as a pedagogue, linguist, historian, anthropologist and, after the election of the National Party in South Africa in 1948, a politician, in addition to which he held honorary doctorates in both Germany and South Africa. From his arrival as a missionary in Namibia in 1903, his attitude towards blacks was in the true 'colonial spirit' characterized by a paternalistic benevolence for 'the natives'.

Through his output of scientific works, his great knowledge of tribal languages and tribal history, as well as his personal qualities as a visionary leader, Vedder became a man who was unfailingly listened to in the Mission, as well as among the German-speaking population generally, and even in governmental circles in both Namibia and the Union. Above all, he was, however, a man impregnated with 'high German ideals' even after the defeat of Germany in World War I. In 1937, he became the preses of the Rhenish Mission.[41]

At the anniversary of the battle of Waterberg on 11 August 1929, Vedder led the celebrations of the 25th anniversary 'in memory of those Germans who fell in the Herero war'.[42] It must have struck the Hereros and their leader, Hosea Kutako, as somewhat peculiar that Vedder the missionary was celebrating an anniversary commemorating this battle which had caused the Herero people such nameless suffering! Only a few years earlier, in 1923, Vedder had led the church service in Okahandja held in connection with the burial of Samuel Maharero, the Hereros' leader in the Battle of Waterberg. Now the same Rhenish missionary was leading a celebration on behalf of the victors in that battle, and the oppressors of the Herero people! To mark the end of the celebrations, a poem was presented depicting the Hereros as 'barbarous insurgents'.[43]

Vedder was strongly influenced by Nazism.[44] Thus in 1936 he held the ceremonial speech during the celebration of Hitler's birthday in Windhoek,[45] paying homage to Hitler as the man whom God had appointed to re-establish the power and glory of the German people. He concluded with the following words: 'The Almighty God has performed this miracle. Praise be to God on high!'[46]

Most of the missionaries of the Rhenish Mission sympathized, as Vedder did, with the Nazi cause. Nevertheless, Preses Olpp in 1934 cautioned that missionaries affiliated to the Party should not neglect their missionary work; also, they should exercise discretion in manifesting their political sympathies in consideration of the authorities of the host country: 'With our heart and soul we missionaries are nevertheless entirely on the side of the Third Reich – yes, indeed, we are enthusiastic supporters of the cause. But we must none the less take care to exercise a certain degree of outward restraint.'[47]

Other missionaries, too, warned against excessive political commitment. In some German parishes opposition arose between Nazi sympathizers and others who were more inclined to follow the guidelines set by the Confessional Church in Germany. Missionary Heinrich F Rust in Swakopmund, who was also pastor of Swakopmund's German parish, openly criticized Landesprobst Wackwitz' Nazi leanings. In disregard of Vedder's warnings, he publicly attacked Wackwitz in an article written for the local newspaper, the Swakopmunder Zeitung, in November 1938.[48]

Vedder expressed his concern over the possible consequences this article might have: 'I feel great concern for Rust. What will happen if he refuses to listen to anyone? ... Wackwitz has filed complaints against him with the Board of the Mission in Germany, saying that he "has now had enough". Rust has already withdrawn his membership with the synod. He has also written the Missionary Board a sharp note of criticism aimed at Wackwitz and claims to have done so in self-defence. And now to top it all – this article!'[49]

According to Vedder, a missionary who was merely a 'part-time' worker in a German parish should refrain from criticizing the leader of the German parishes. This was something which only fully employed pastors could allow themselves to do: 'I expect unconditional discipline to reign among the missionaries. ... We have so much important work to do.'[50]

Another missionary who had distanced himself from Nazism was Missionary Pönninghaus. Even in the early 1930s, Pönninghaus manifested great interest in indigenous clerical training and in the development of an indigenous Church.[51] After his return from 'home leave' in Germany in 1933, he attempted by various means to fight the influence of Nazism among his colleagues in spite of the fact that most of them were members of the Nazi Party.[52]

In 1939, the South African authorities urged Landesprobst Wackwitz to leave Namibia. Vedder promptly wrote a letter to Bishop Heckel in Berlin (who was responsible for the work of the national Church conducted among Germans living abroad), expressing his regrets at Wackwitz' departure; Wackwitz had after all 'carried out so much work for the Third Reich'.[53]

On the whole, German nationalism allied to Nazism thus hindered the missionary work by the Rhenish Mission while Nazism was growing in the Mission's native country. The missionaries' adherence to the new German ideology damaged the reputation of the Mission, especially among the indigenous parishes. If things had been otherwise, the 1920s and 1930s might have led to a strengthening of missionary influence through the establishment of tribal or Folkchurches in accordance with work of the Rhenish Mission based in Sumatra. Here, a strong and characteristic Folkchurch grew among the Batak people whose traditional adat-concept provided a unifying force and thus the foundation for the confession of this Church.[54]

The Rhenish Mission in Namibia was, however, working under totally different conditions than its sister mission in Sumatra, especially during the rise of the Third Reich. In Namibia, missionaries faced the dilemma of having to split up their work among the different population groups. Also, reconciling the colonial past with missionary work was not an easy task.

The Finnish Missionary Society starts a Folkchurch

The situation for the Mission in Ovamboland was again completely different. There, the Finnish Missionary Society was able to entirely devote itself to the building of a Church which would serve the purposes of a single people. There were no split loyalties for them.

It was not until after the South African military occupation and the conflict in 1917 with Kwanyama chieftain Mandume that Ovamboland really experienced the consequences of white colonization. Major Pritchard's 'punitive expedition' was a bewildering experience for the people living in this part of Namibia. The futility of resisting this mighty foreign power was convincingly brought home.

Ovamboland was a clearly defined and sheltered missionary territory, which suited the purposes of the Finnish Missionary Society. It was, by Namibian standards, a fairly ideal missionary territory, shielded as it was from the influence of white colonizers and free of intermissionary conflicts due to different creeds. What is more, the Finnish Mission was not burdened by a colonial history in Namibia, belonging, as it did, to a nation with no colonial possessions or aspirations. The Finnish missionary was therefore free to create a climate of mutual understanding between the Mission and the people, which helped to lay the foundations for a Folkchurch among the Ovambos.[55]

There were nevertheless a few hurdles which the Mission had to overcome before it could achieve a major breakthrough. For one, the Ovambo chieftains were suspicious of this new religion preached by the missionaries, which seemed to them to threaten their own position as religious and political leaders of their respective tribes. It was not until January 1883 – after 13 years of missionary presence – that the first baptism of six people was carried out. At the outbreak of World War I, the Mission had a total of 3 000 members in its parishes. By 1920, the number had risen to 7 700, and by 1940, there were approximately 36 000. The real breakthrough involving rapid growth, however, came only in the 1960s.[56]

The Finnish Missionary Society placed great emphasis on 'genuine conversion' before baptizing a non-Christian. There was a strong tendency towards pietistic revivalism within this Mission. This was further made evident by the Mission's strict adherence to a 'two-world doctrine', according to which, mission should refrain from any kind of meddling with the affairs of government. To both the Germans and, later, the South Africans in authority, the Mission took pains to manifest its loyalty and obedience above all else.

However, the Finnish missionaries, too, might be characterized as products of their time, who ultimately represented the ideals of a 'Christian Western civilization'. Thus among them, too, there was some form of institutionalized racism. The Missionary Society clarified its position *vis-à-vis* this issue by referring to Acts 17:26, where Paul in his speech on Areopagus makes claims that God has appointed specific periods of time for the people of the earth and delimited the frontiers within which they should dwell.

In order to guide the local missionaries, especially concerning their relations with the authorities within the missionary territory, the director of the Mission in Helsinki, Natti Tarkanon, sent out a circular letter in 1931, which advised, among others: 'Brothers, you shall in all things preach the Gospel of salvation and refrain from trying to improve society in a Christian spirit, a practice attempted by some American rationalists.'[57]

Concerning the issue of how to relate to the indigenous population, Tarkanon's successor, Martti Vapaavoori, some years later gave the following instructions (he had recently made a tour of inspection of the Ovambo mission stations): 'We are not the masters of the natives, but we must likewise take care to shield ourselves from any false forms of comradeship and should, instead, strive to attain an encounter based on a friendly and unbiased attitude.'[58]

One factor of particular interest here is the Finnish Missionary Board's readiness to include indigenous chieftains in their concept of 'the authorities'. And so it was that freshly arrived missionaries were obliged to pay a courtesy call to the local chieftain. Missionaries who returned to Ovamboland after 'home leave' upon their return paid a visit reporting their presence to the chieftain. All work was conducted in close collaboration with local indigenous authorities. The chieftain was consulted on the erection of schools, hospitals and, of course, mission stations. The Mission not only worked in close collaboration with the local indigenous leaders, but also under their protection.[59]

Missionary work was divided into various sections devoted to supporting and assisting the population as a whole. This strengthened the position of the Mission with respect to the chieftains because it mirrored the Ovambos' own religious outlook, where body and soul were one,[60] each making up a part of the totality.

At the beginning of its work in Namibia, the Finnish Missionary Society was strongly influenced by the Rhenish Mission, especially by its pioneering missionary Carl Hugo Hahn, and the missionary colony which the latter had founded in Otjimbingwe, where practical spheres of activity were part of a missioner's routine, aiming to educate the indigenous population into leading a 'Christian social life'. Among the early missionaries from Finland there were even manual labourers and agricultural experts. The practical aspects of Finnish missionary activity were to be further developed in the future.

The Finnish Mission therefore viewed its task of evangelizing and educating, caring for the sick, and other activities as intertwined from the very start. These principles were strictly followed by Missionary Martin Routanen during the 50 years of his missionary career in Namibia. At the missionary printing shop in Oniipa, a paper was printed from 1901 which apart from biblical accounts also contained practical information on the subjects of agriculture and hygiene. In 1903, Routanen produced a finished translation of the entire New Testament into Oshindonga.[61]

The first Finnish missionary doctor arrived in 1908, and in 1911 a missionary hospital was opened in Onandjokwe, near the principal mission station in Oniipa. In 1913, the Finnish Missionary Society opened a teacher training college for the education of indigenous teachers and parish assistants. Small, simple school buildings were raised around the villages which were also used as church localities.

There was thus an early start in training blacks to take part in missionary work and gradually be invested with greater trust in the carrying out of their duties. This was to become a constant subject of debate at missionary conferences organized by the Missionary Board in Finland. (On these occasions, male and female missionaries came together in a combined Sisters' and Brothers' conference. It might be mentioned in this context that much vital pioneering work, far ahead of its times, had previously been carried out by women missionaries in the field of educating African nurses and teachers.)

In his work, *The Christian Ministry in Africa*, Bengt Sundkler[62] observes that as late as 1925, Namibia did not have a single black pastor. This was not quite true, however. In fact, the Board of the Finnish Missionary Society in 1921 granted permission to local missionaries to start training indigenous pastors. On 27 September 1925, seven Ovambo teachers were ordained as pastors in the main church of the Mission in Oniipa.

The ceremony was held a day after the missionaries made the decision, along with the delegates from various congregations, to organize the first synod of the Ovambo Church. This was the first major step towards establishing an independent indigenous Church. The synod elected a council, which would be responsible for Church affairs, but would nevertheless be liable to report to the Missionary Board in Finland. The missionaries were to constitute the majority in the council, and a presiding missionary elected by the council was to act as its chairman. Furthermore, the council was to name delegates to represent the various parishes as well as the various branches of activity within the Church.[63]

In 1920, the Finnish Missionary Society was given permission to take over the work of the Rhenish Mission in the northern territory which belonged to the Kwanyama people. The Mission built its principal station for work among the Kwanyamas in Engela, just south of the Angolan border.

However, soon afterwards, the Anglican and Roman Catholic Missions were also allowed to take over part of the Rhenish Mission's work in Ovamboland. This caused a great deal of tension between the various Missions, since the latter two had been granted permission to operate in the territory on condition that they 'help the government in its duties and encourage the Africans to enter into migrant work'.[64] In 1926, the same year that the Anglicans and Roman Catholics were granted permission to begin work in Ovamboland, the Finnish Missionary Society spread its field of activities into Kavango territory.[65]

The decision to expand eastwards into the Kavango was taken by the Board of the Mission in Helsinki in 1928, as was the decision to have all operations supervised by a 'deputy presiding missionary' appointed by the Missionary Board.[66]

In 1912, the Finnish Missionary Society finally baptized the first Ovambo chieftains. But already prior to this, a growing sense of fellowship had been fostered between the Mission and the leaders of the Ovambo people.[67] Missionary work resulted in a kind of mutation of the culture, outlook and philosophy of the people.[68] However, the overriding aim of the Mission had always been to ensure that the missionary work, and any changes in the Ovambos' outlook, took place within the overall context of the people's own social and political structure.

The Ovambos' social and political structure, incidentally, was allowed to remain operative even after Ovamboland became a reserve, since it was the objective of the South African authorities to allow no disturbance of the indigenous culture (except in some isolated cases where a South African supreme authority decreed that intervention was justified in order to ensure 'law an order'). The Finnish Mission was for this reason soon considered a 'disturbing element' as far as South African policy *vis-à-vis* this reserve was concerned. Ovamboland was, as envisaged by the authorities, to remain 'the idyll of perfectionist, peaceful and prosperous barbarism'.[69]

The person holding overall responsibility for the Ovambos' reserve after 1915 was Major Carl Hahn, called 'Shongola' after the whip he used for beating people with. This was the grandson of Carl Hugo Hahn, the pioneering missionary of the Rhenish Mission in Namibia.

Major Hahn saw it as his task to protect the Ovambos' traditional lifestyle in order to preserve their integrity. From the early 1920s Hahn sent out reports complaining that 'South African officials have been uneasy over the role and influence of the churches in Ovamboland, particularly as they lead to the breakdown of tribal customs'.[70] Hahn summarized his criticism of the Mission's influence into the following points:

1 It undermined the authority of the chieftains.
2 It disturbed the economy and social life of the people through discouraging polygamy.
3 And it fostered a brand of individualism, the notion of which was alien to the people.

Hahn also said that the competition between the Lutherans, Anglicans, and Roman Catholics was disturbing the unity among the Ovambos. However, most of his criticism was aimed at the Finnish Missionary Society. He expressed his dislike of the 'primitive schools' managed by the Finnish Mission which conducted their activities underneath 'innumerable shady trees'. These kinds of activities were creating a growing group of 'lazy and conceited teachers' who acted as if they were a new brand of folk leaders in the villages.

Another missionary practice frowned upon by Hahn were the Mission's own courts of law 'to settle disputes and even criminal cases'.

Hahn's final verdict after fairly regular complaints from him was, in 1938, the opinion that during its 70 years in Ovamboland 'the [Finnish] Mission had succeeded in breaking up the tribal system and achieved little besides'.[71]

Hahn's criticism was not without effect. In 1932, the authorities through the administration in Windhoek decreed that official control of Churches, mission stations, schools and other missionary institutions would be compulsory. Before, only the local chieftain's permission was required for matters such as the building of a new school. Furthermore, the Mission was obliged to register its schools with the authorities in Windhoek who maintained rights of inspection.[72]

The Finnish Mission duly complied with these restrictions, in line with the Missionary Board's principle of always submitting to the regulations introduced by the authorities. It must therefore have come as a major source of encouragement for the Mission when in 1933 it was given official recognition for its work by the Mandate Commission of the League of Nations.[73]

However, Major Hahn was still not satisfied with the restrictions introduced upon his insistence. He regarded the Mission as a hindrance to the work of the administration in Ovamboland. He pointed out in a report sent to the League of Nations' Mandate Commission in 1937 that the prevailing problems among the Ndonga people, for example, originated from the fact that 'tribal life had been undermined by missionary influence'.[74] The authorities had, he continued, convened a conference in Windhoek to discuss the situation, but had been disappointed by the small number of missionaries who had attended: 'The outcome ... was the decision not to allow the missions to open new stations for a period of three years.'[75]

During these confrontations with the South African authorities, two divergent opinions crystallized concerning relations with the indigenous population: the overriding aim of the Mission was to work within the framework provided by traditional social structure and pay due respect to the existing institutions of leadership; it worked towards Christianization which in turn would provide the stimulus for the growth of an indigenous Folkchurch. Hahn, the South African representative, on the other hand, wished to preserve the status quo through indirect control; this meant above all to avoid any major disruption of the Ovambos' traditional way of life.

In the long run, the missionaries won. Through their systematic building up of relations with the indigenous leadership, they practically had the undivided confidence of the Ovambo people. They were not seen by the latter as representatives of a 'master race' but instead, as friends and benefactors. With loyal endurance they held fast to their own principles, taking care at the same time not to disparage the traditional leadership structure of the people. Hahn's criticism of the Mission, along with his efforts to curtail, or at least to complicate, the furtherance of their work, in the long term achieved the opposite of what he wanted. In fact, the positive attitude of the Ovambo people towards the Mission grew in pace with the criticism which the authorities levelled against the Finns.

The Ovambos' confidence in the Mission was a major step towards the establishment of a Folkchurch. This, it was hoped, would act in close collaboration with both the Mission and the local population. The Church also became a forum for a steadily growing criticism of the racial policy of the authorities, and thus provided an additional source of power for burgeoning opposition.

It can be said that the confidence which developed between the Ovambo people and the Finnish missionaries was due to the missionaries' methodical way of educating black Church leaders and steadily providing them with more and more responsibility. The role which the Ovambo-Kavango Church was to play in the political development during the struggle for freedom leading up to independence in 1990, was established in this early period. By contrast, the vacillation of the Rhenish Mission between divided allegiances gave rise to a confusing formation of sects, and from the onset of the liberation movement following World War II there were doubts as to the role the Rhenish Mission was to play in the liberation struggle.

Other Missions: the Roman Catholics and the Anglicans

The regulation granting freedom of religion which had been established at the Berlin Congress of 1884-1885, also applied to the Roman Catholic Mission in German colonies. The condition made by the authorities in Berlin, however, was that even this Mission should strengthen Germany and the German cultural heritage. We have previously mentioned that the Roman Catholic Mission made a number of attempts to gain a foothold in northern Namibia from bases in Angola. However, they did not succeed. The Mission later decided to set up station in Keetmanshoop, and also established the bishop's residence there. The Roman Catholics' work in Windhoek and surroundings was restricted, in the early 1900s, to the Catholics among German immigrants and the German colonial army, as well as one group of blacks from Bechuanaland.

Only after the war of 1904-1907, and in the face of heavy protest from the Rhenish Mission, did Governor Friedrich von Lindequist give the Roman Catholic Mission an equal degree of freedom in its work in Namibia as granted the evangelical Missions. The Roman Catholic Mission was thus able to establish two mission stations in Ovamboland in 1910.

For all of its work in and around Windhoek and in the north, there was a bishop whose residence was in Windhoek. Up to 1920, membership of the Roman Catholic congregations was not very large – despite enormous contributions of money, and an increase in the Mission's staff.

In 1923, the Roman Catholic Mission, together with the Anglican Mission, signed a declaration of loyalty to the South African authorities. The Mission considered itself to be morally bound by this, and thus it had to support South Africa's racial policy.

Since the Roman Catholic Mission was prosperous, and administered its fortune by running large farms through the orders of the Mission with the help of black labour, it became self-supporting. During World War II this meant it was able to continue its work without any support from outside. In both Keetmanshoop and Windhoek, however, the bishops stuck to their pledge of loyalty to the South African authorities throughout.[76]

A prudent estimate of the Mission's membership in Namibia in 1929 would be around 10 000.

Mission and Apartheid   215

The Anglican Mission came to Namibia following the South African victory in World War I. Anglicans from South Africa moved to Windhoek and other parts of Namibia in order to establish themselves there as businesspeople, farmers, or public officers working in the government service. They needed pastors and churches of their own in the country. At the same time, this made Anglican missionary work among the black Namibians possible.

Anglican missionary activity began in Ovamboland in 1923, in places previously in the Rhenish Mission's care.

It was no problem for the Anglican Mission and Church to sign a declaration of loyalty to the South African authorities. Since the Anglicans were based in South Africa, it was fairly natural for them to remain loyal to that nation. Work in the north gradually increased, but the Anglican congregations remained fairly small. Just before the outbreak of World War II, the number of black members in the Anglican congregations in Ovamboland only amounted to about 2 000. The Mission, however, established a number of schools, in addition to which it devoted itself to providing health care.

Anglican work in Windhoek was only for whites. It would take some time for anyone at the Anglican Mission to take a stand on the racial issue; this was only to happen from the mid-1960s onwards. The contribution of the Anglican pastor Michael Scott after World War II, when he sought to represent the interests of the Hereros, and black Namibians in general, at the United Nations, had nothing to do with the official Anglican Church or Mission in Windhoek. We will have reason to return to this point later on.

Notes

1. Native Administration Proclamation No. 11 (1922); National Archives, Windhoek.
2. Werner, W. 1988, 272.
3. Ibid., 275.
4. Native Administration Proclamation No. 11 (1922) op. cit.
5. Act No. 38 (1928); National Archives, Windhoek.
6. Ibid.
7. Proclamation 15 (1928); National Archives, Windhoek.
8. Moleah, AT. 1983, 61.
9. Katjavivi, P. 1988b, 567.
10. Kiljunen, K. 1981, 145.
11. Tötemeyer, G. 1977, 17.
12. Ibid.
13. Emmet, T, 1988, 229, states: 'Between September 1915 and January 1918 more than 310 cases involving ill-treatment of black servants were brought before the lower courts alone. The more serious cases of murder and assault against white settlers were given prominent attention in the 1918 Blue Book and elsewhere.'
14. Emmet, T, op. cit.
15. Ibid., 224; see also Werner, W, op. cit., 268.
16. See Correspondence: Preses with Wuppertal-Barmen; 1913-1924; II. 5.7; Church Archives, Windhoek.
17. Engel, L. 1977, 132.
18. Hunke, H. 1988, 629.
19. See Circular letters: Preses; 6.1-7: by Olpp, Vedder, Diehl, 1919; Church Archives, Windhoek.
20. Sundermeier, T. 1973, 23.
21. Minutes of Missionary Conferences, 1906-1937; I.1.22-27; Church Archives, Windhoek.
22. Engel, L. 1976, 217.
23. Ibid., 196.
24. Engel, L. 1977, 137.
25. Walker, EA. 1935, 592.
26. See Resolution, of 29 July 1926, by the South West Africa Legislative Assembly to remove and destroy all copies of the Blue Book; 11.1-16; Church Archives, Windhoek.
27. Ibid. The document in the Church Archives, Windhoek, also contains a statement by Preses J Olpp of the Rhenish Mission.
28. Kuntze, L. 1985, 199 ff.

29 Ibid., 200.
30 Sundermeier, T, op. cit., 22.
31 See *Die Evangelische Kolonialhilfe*, Heft 30, 1925, 590.
32 Ibid.; see also Engel, L, op. cit., 307.
33 Hitler Youth Organization.
34 Groves, CP. 1958, vol. IV, 148 ff; see also Reports, League of Nations, Permanent Mandate Commission, 1926-1937; National Archives, Windhoek. It was said that by 1934, approximately 80 per cent of the German-speaking population in Namibia were Nazi sympathizers.
35 See Niemüller, G. 1959, vol II.
36 Circular letter titled 'An die Gemeinden' from Landesprobst Wackwitz, 1.66-74: 1933; Church Archives, Windhoek.
37 See *25 Jahre Christuskirche in Windhoek. Festschrift zum 25jährigen Kirchenjubiläum im Oktober 1935*; National Archives, Windhoek.
38 Ibid.
39 Bertelsmann, W. 1979, 57.
40 Minutes of the Missionary Conferences 1906-1937; I.1.22-27; Church Archives, Windhoek.
41 For background reading on Vedder, see Baumann, J. 1965; see also Moritz, W. 1981. Engel, L, in op. cit., 462, quotes a statement made by Vedder in 1939: 'As long as the white man with intelligence, based on energy and will-power, takes possession of land, it will be impossible for the blacks to chase him away.'
42 Lau, B. 1981.
43 Ibid.; see also Engel, L, op.cit., 312 ff.
44 Vedder, in a letter to J Olpp, undated, wrote: 'In my heart, I am a Nazi of Hitler's type.'; 6.1-7; Church Archives, Windhoek.
45 Engel, L, op. cit., 372.
46 Ibid.
47 Ibid., 38.
48 *Swakopmunder Zeitung*, 12 November 1938.
49 Vedder, Correspondence, 1939-1947. The letter here referred to is dated 14 November 1947 and addressed to 'Lieber Willy!'; II. 9.7-9; Church Archives, Windhoek.
50 Engel, L, op. cit., 409.
51 Pönninghaus, F. 1933, 109 ff.
52 Engel, L, op. cit., 388.
53 Vedder, H. Correspondence, Okahandja 31 December 1938, to Bischof D Heckel; Church Archives, Windhoek.
54 Beyerhaus, P. 1956, 163 ff.
55 Sundermeier, T, op. cit., 287.
56 Tötemeyer, G. 1978, 19 ff.

57 Kjellberg, S. 1972, 10, 25, and 45.
58 Ibid.
59 Auala, L & K Ihamäki. 1988.
60 Ibid.
61 The complete Bible was translated in 1954. See Kjellberg, S, op. cit., Preface.
62 Sundkler, B. 1960, 67.
63 Eirola, M. 1983.
64 Finnish Missionary Society file; National Archives, Windhoek; see also Kjellberg, S, op. cit., 3.
65 Kjellberg, S, op. cit., 3.
66 See Finnish Missionary Society file; National Archives, Windhoek.
67 Auala, L & K Ihamäki, op. cit., 27 ff.
68 Williams, F-N. 1991, 167.
69 Steer, GL. 1939, 85.
70 Ibid., 82.
71 Ibid.; see also Tötemeyer, G, op. cit., 26 ff.
72 Steer, GL, op. cit., 83.
73 Lord Lugard expressed the Commission's gratitude to the Finnish Missionary Society 'for the excellence of its work in the territory'. Quarterly Notes, *Bulletin of the IMC*, No. 38, April 1933.
74 Ibid.
75 League of Nations, Permanent Mandates Commission, 1926-1937: Report for 1937.
76 Hunke, H. 1988, 627 ff; see also Hunke, H. 1980, 80; and Wolf, B. 1985, 68 ff.

PART IV: Church and Mission, and the National Movement of Liberation

Before the war of 1904-1907, the Rhenish Mission in southern and central Namibia had already been identified with European infiltration and colonial power. This had influenced the blacks' view of the Mission since black Namibians were striving to preserve their right to self-determination.

This remained unchanged under the South Africans. It was in the interests of the Rhenish Mission to show its loyalty towards the new rulers of the country. In the years immediately preceding World War II, and during the war years, the Rhenish Mission, being a German mission, was to suffer from the consequences of its pro-Nazi leanings, and of once again belonging to a nation hostile to South Africa. Even the missionaries were restricted in their freedom of movement. Some of them were interned with other German-speaking people who had shown their Nazi sympathies too openly. The South Africans' treatment of the missionaries, however, in no way influenced the blacks' general attitude towards the

Rhenish Mission; the black resistance to racial discrimination, and blacks' demands for an increase of freedom were also directed at the Rhenish Mission.

The black liberation movements before 1939 were separate initiatives of different population groups, although there had been a feeling of national unity, inspired by Garveyanism, in the movement of the early 1920s dealt with earlier. Liberation movements were linked to specific population groups until the end of the 1950s. Usually, the traditional leaders of these population groups took the initiative to form the movements, and so they also became the leaders in the liberation struggle.

In their relations with the Rhenish Mission, the blacks demanded to be freed from the Mission's control over their own congregations; in the late 1940s and all through the 1950s, when these demands were not granted, they worked towards establishing independent black congregations and Churches, tied either to the traditional political leaders of the people or to another Mission.

The missionaries saw these demands for liberation in their congregations as a development towards syncretism, which threatened the existence of the Church and Mission, or else as a politicization of the Church, which needed to be counteracted by a stepping up of Church discipline. The Mission thus determined to strive towards becoming more deeply rooted in its faith; in the process it increasingly isolated itself from the blacks, failing to build up a relationship built on confidence and trust so necessary for its work among the people.

The first changes were to occur through a new generation of missionaries, who were supported by the Board of the Mission in Germany, which was under the influence of new currents in the ecumenical sphere. These changes came at the same time as a change in black leadership in Namibia. This new generation of black leaders, who were often not traditional tribal leaders, were gradually to establish demands for a national unity transcending all tribal boundaries. They knew that such a unity was their only hope of winning the struggle for freedom.

This, then, characterized the liberation movements which were founded in the late 1950s, the South West Africa National Union (SWANU) and the South West African People's Organization (SWAPO). Both these groups in fact were founded by specific population groups: SWANU, by the Hereros, and SWAPO, by the Ovambos. Of the two, SWANU was more bound to its own tribe.

Long before the formation of SWANU, the Hereros had taken liberation initiatives of their own within the framework of their tribal structure, either through politics or through their Church. Thus, they sent a delegation to the League of Nations, and established the Oruuano Church under the leadership of their chieftain, Hosea Kutako. In claiming to be a national liberation movement, SWANU therefore had to wrestle with this tribal burden. In competition with SWAPO, SWANU was seen as a tribal movement and was soon forced to withdraw from the political scene.

In the north, among the Ovambos and Kavangos, there was no tension caused by divided allegiances between the Finnish Missionary Society, its congregations, and the traditional tribal leadership. The Mission worked in a reserve, meaning that the missionaries could live among 'their people'. The work of the Mission was favoured by the fact that the reserve did not allow white settlement. Even after 1948, when apartheid became the official government policy, Ovamboland and Kavango were safe from white intrusion.

In this enormous area, then, the Mission could lay the foundations for a Folkchurch which was to be run by black leaders. These church leaders now also became the leaders of the people, in close contact with SWAPO. This was the basis for that co-operation between the indigenous Church, the Mission, and the national liberation movement which was to become so important for the final phase of the struggle for freedom.

It was also through Ovamboland and the commitment of its Church to the work of the liberation movement that Churches and Missions in the rest of Namibia were drawn into this co-operation. The Rhenish Mission, though with some hesitation at first, made common cause with the national political movement of liberation and the indigenous Church during the last decades of the struggle for freedom.

This section of the book deals with developments leading up to this co-operation and the struggle up to 1965-1966.

12 International and local commitment to the liberation struggle in co-operation with the United Nations after 1945

At the end of World War II, the South African Prime Minister, Jan Smuts, played a leading part in the formation of a new international organization for the maintenance of world peace, the United Nations (UN). As with the formation of the League of Nations following World War I, Smuts attempted to negotiate a special deal for South Africa and its position *vis-à-vis* former German South West Africa. He wanted the UN's approval for South Africa to turn Namibia into a South African province.

Such was the commitment of Smuts that international interest in Namibia rose, not only in the international juridical position of Namibia, but also in the Namibians' struggle for independence and demands for a more humane treatment.

Smuts claimed that the UN could not be expected to take over the League of Nations' responsibility for a mandate. Also, he argued, South Africa as a mandatory power under the League of Nations was not bound to deliver a report to the new organization (the UN) concerning Namibia's public administration. Nor was South Africa under any obligation to answer to the UN's Committee for Mandatory Administration formed at the UN conference of April 1946. In Smuts' view, the UN's Trusteeship Committee lacked the experience that the League of Nations' commission had and there was therefore no reason why South Africa should submit annual reports on the state of affairs in Namibia to this new body.

Between December 1945 and April 1946, when the UN was constituted, Smuts and his government prepared themselves to handle the Namibian question. The proposal to incorporate Namibia into South Africa had been put before the white legislative body in Windhoek, where it had been approved. When it came to collecting signatures from black Namibians, Smuts had to have recourse to another method. The population's consent was to be procured by means of a referendum, which was prepared through a number of consultations between the

South African authorities and Namibia's chieftains. Most of these chieftains had been appointed by South Africa, and were therefore dependent on the goodwill of the South Africans.

During these consultations, all the alternatives for a nationwide referendum for Namibia's 'non-white' population were worked out. The subject of incorporating the country into South Africa as a fifth province was carefully avoided. Instead, maintenance of Namibia's continued link with England was discussed as an issue of utmost importance. 'Namibians were tricked by asking them whether they would like to join the Chinese, the Russians, or the British and they voted British without any idea that they were surrendering the country.'[1]

The outcome of the referendum was that 208 850 voted for the status quo to be maintained, with South Africa as a mandatory power, and as a country within the framework of the British Commonwealth;[2] 33 520 voted against this, while 56 750 abstained. South Africa claimed that, therefore, a majority of black Namibians had voted for incorporation of Namibia into South Africa.

The figures quoted could not carry weight on closer scrutiny, however. In 1975, Gerhardt Tötemyer, then Professor of Political Science at the University of Stellenbosch, was very surprised by the result of the vote, since it was claimed that in the most populated area of Namibia, Ovamboland, 129 760 blacks had voted for incorporation, in spite of the fact that the *total number* of inhabitants in Ovamboland in 1946 was only 170 000. Tötemyer thought there must be some mistake - or else, an attempt to mislead: 'the figure must have included women, who, in terms of tribal custom, had no vote'.[3] Tötemyer's conclusion was that 'the headmen were possibly influenced by officials and ... did not understand what the vote was all about'.[4]

The General Assembly of the UN did not let itself be fooled by this so-called 'referendum', but instead demanded that Namibia as a mandated territory be placed under the supervision of the organization's Trusteeship Committee, which would ensure that South Africa managed the mandate in accordance with the world organization's clearly expressed will that mandated territories developed 'towards bringing about independence'.

South Africa refused to comply with this, however. The South African government insisted that it did not have 'an obligation to place the Territory under the Trusteeship System'.[5] The only concession it could allow itself to make was to 'submit reports on its administration for the information of the UN as a matter of goodwill and not because of any legal acceptance of the claims of the UN'.[6]

What South Africa appeared to aim at in relation to the new international organization, was to legalize its ambitions concerning Namibia. When a mandate had been established under the League of Nations following World War I, this had happened without consulting the indigenous Namibian people, who were most affected by it. South Africa's special treatment of Namibia as a C mandate had naturally also happened without consulting the Namibians.

In 1945-1946, when the UN was constituted, and South Africa had organized a 'referendum' on the question of incorporating Namibia, the Namibian population had for the first time been included in the discussion about the future of their country, albeit under false pretences. This was a turning point in the history of Namibia. The country's position as a mandated territory by constitutional law was no longer merely an international juridical matter between the world organization and South Africa as the mandatory power: it was a matter involving the South Africans, the UN, and the people of Namibia who had been 'consulted' through the so-called 'referendum'. The future of Namibia now became a political issue which concerned Namibia's own people and their wishes. Namibia's people had thus found a forum in the UN for making their voice heard against South Africa.

In addition to this, the internationally recognized fundamental principle named in the UN's basic document - their Charter of Human Rights - supported the Namibians' demands for freedom and for humane treatment; this important document emphasizes the 'fundamental human rights, the dignity and worth of the human person [and] the equal rights of nations, large and small'.[7] It also demands that the UN's member states should show 'due respect for the culture of the peoples concerned, their political, economic, social and educational advancement, their just treatment and their protection against abuses' and assist them in developing self-government and 'in their progressive development of their free political institutions'.[8] Point by point this document and its application to not yet independent peoples and nations was contrary to the South African policy in Namibia.

At the beginning of 1946, the Herero chieftain Hosea Kutako took important steps to enable the Namibian people to make their own voice heard before the UN. In a letter to the UN, Kutako protested against South

Africa's having prepared a referendum of its own for the Namibian people to determine the future of the country. He requested that if a referendum was to be held, it should be supervised by the UN. He further asked that four representatives from Namibia obtain an audience before the UN to report to them the real state of affairs in the country.

All of these applications were hindered by South Africa, which was not willing to issue passports and exit permits to black delegates to the UN. In a telegram to the UN in March 1946, Kutako requested in the name of the Herero people and 'other nations' in Namibia that the country be declared independent and placed under the protection of England and the USA.

Kutako's first attempt to make his voice heard before the UN yielded no substantial results. It was, however, of great consequence for the future. Kutako had proved that South Africa was misrepresenting the Namibians.

Kutako next sought the support of chieftains in Botswana, and leaders in the All-Africa Convention and the African National Congress (ANC) of South Africa for the cause of Namibia; all of whom protested against South Africa's proposal to turn Namibia into another South African province.

Events on the international political arena and developments within the UN now turned the UN into a platform of support of colonized peoples' demands for independence. An important reason for this development was that India, a newly independent nation after its long struggle for independence, had become a member nation of the UN. Opposition within the UN to the incorporation of Namibia into South Africa was soon led by India and its chief delegate, Sir Maharaj Singh. On 14 December 1946, the UN's General Assembly voted on the issue of Namibia's ceasing to be a mandate and instead being transformed into a South African province; 37 member states voted against, and nine abstained. Not a single member state of the UN voted in favour of South Africa's incorporating Namibia.[9]

Still, the greatest obstacle preventing the black leaders in Namibia from gaining international audience was their isolation. They were totally in the hands of the South African authorities who tried to hinder any international contact and prevent them from going abroad by refusing to issue them passports.

For a man like Hosea Kutako, it was a matter of finding ways to break this isolation. One possibility was through contact across the border with the neighbouring country, Botswana. Here, a community of exiled Hereros lived, whose leader was Frederick Maharero, the eldest son of the deceased chieftain Samuel Maharero. On behalf of the Herero people's council, and also 'other people' in Namibia, Hosea Kutako wrote to Frederick Maharero, explaining that South Africa was deceiving everyone with its so-called 'referendum'. The whole country, Kutako maintained - 'the Hereros, the Namas, the Ovambos and the Berg-Damaras'[10] - was on his side in pleading for help from the UN to hinder South Africa's annexation of Namibia. Now he appealed to his fellow-Namibians in exile for help. 'The matter now rests with you. You, who enjoy freedom, are the people who should come here to us.'[11]

A consequence of this letter was the recruitment of an important contact person for Namibians, who for many years to come was to be Kutako's spokesman to the UN. On receiving the letter from Kutako, Frederick Maharero contacted the leading chieftain in Botswana, Tshekedi Khama. The latter introduced Maharero to the Anglican pastor Michael Scott, who was to represent Namibians at the UN and plead their cause from the end of 1946 onwards.

Michael Scott did not know about the Namibians' plight before coming into contact with Frederick Maharero. As an Anglican pastor, however, he had seen the destitution among the poor, the dejected and discriminated, in London's East End, as well as in Calcutta and Johannesburg. His engagement in the struggle for human rights in South Africa, and his fight against racialism finally led to his three-month prison sentence by the South Africans following an incident at a riot against racism. He continued his activities after his release and was blacklisted by the South Africans as an agitator and a dangerous fanatic. At the same time, he won the confidence of the indigenous population. He was therefore well suited for the task with which he was now, through the mediation of Tshekedi Khama, commissioned by Frederick Maharero.[12]

Michael Scott thus became a pioneer when it came to the commitment of churchmen to the Namibian cause. However, his was a personal stand, taken on his own initiative, for which he was criticized both by the Anglican Church and in other established ecclesiastical circles.

In 1946, Scott met with Maharero to discuss the situation in Namibia and Hosea Kutako's demands for help for his own people and also for 'the other people' living in the country. Though Scott assumed the task to act as Namibia's spokesman to the UN, he pointed out time and again that

Namibia's own representatives had to speak for themselves before this international organization.[13]

After this meeting with Maharero, Scott made his way to Namibia to acquaint himself with the situation, and also, to make a personal assessment of local reactions to South Africa's attempts to annex the territory. He met with Hosea Kutako and his council, as well as with one of the Namas' principal leaders, Samuel Witbooi. He understood that all the black leaders of Namibia stood behind Kutako.

Resistance to South Africa's renewed attempts to take over Namibia had created a growing sense of national fellowship. Hosea Kutako, who was at this time 80 years old, was the leader of all opposition against South Africa. In 1946, when Kutako had refused to vote in favour of South Africa's demands for an incorporation of Namibia into the Union, the authorities had responded by no longer recognizing him as a chieftain. In spirit, however, if not in name, he nevertheless remained the leader of the Hereros and increasingly gained ground as a central figure of the growing liberation movement in Namibia, and the 'chief inspirer and leader of the post-war resistance movement which became the source of modern nationalism'.[14]

Convinced that the Namibian people were justified in their resistance to South Africa, Scott returned to Botswana where he and Maharero worked on the draft petition to the UN. The main point of this document was a plea to deny South Africa any further right to the administration of Namibia as a mandate. The country should instead be administered by the UN, be made a British protectorate, or, as a third alternative, be administered and protected by the USA.

As a Namibian emissary, Scott felt he had to return to Namibia to obtain the approval of the Namibian people for this proposal. He therefore returned to Namibia with the draft, and had it approved and signed by the black leaders, on the National Day of the Herero people, 26 August 1947.

The prayer which Hosea Kutako delivered before Scott set off for the UN pays vivid testimony to the extent of his Christian devotion:

> You are the Great God of all the earth and the Heavens. We are so insignificant. In us there are many defects. But the Power is yours to make and to do what we cannot do. You know all about us. For coming down to earth you were despised, and mocked, and brutally treated because of those defects in the men of those days. And for

those men you prayed because they did not understand what they were doing, and that you came only for what was right. Give us the courage to struggle in that way for what is right. O Lord, help us who roam about. Help us who have been placed in Africa and have no dwelling place. O God, all power is yours in Heaven and on earth. Amen.[15]

Kutako's prayer was seen by Scott as an expression of a universal longing of all oppressed African peoples for freedom and self-determination.

Via Scott, therefore, Namibia made its first contact with the UN and was introduced to that organization's Charter of Human Rights, as well as its overriding objective of bringing about a life fit for all human beings in all corners of the earth.

Namibia's cause thus became something of a test for the UN's credibility. Michael Scott's task on behalf of Namibia before the UN 'transformed the South West African issue from a tedious legal wrangle with a minor government into a crusade to save people'.[16] Michael Scott increasingly came to see his appointed task on behalf of the Namibian people as 'symbolical of all the landless and dispossessed people in the world'.[17] For him, it was not so much a political, but a Christian duty which he could not abandon. As we have said, however, he was not given the support of the Christian missionaries, let alone any parishes in Namibia.

This is not the place to give a detailed account of Scott's attempts to fulfil his task. A few main points are important to bear in mind, however. We have mentioned that the South Africans thought of Michael Scott as a troublesome opponent, and did their utmost to complicate the fulfilment of his task. In the end, he was banished from the Union as a *persona non grata*, which prevented him from revisiting Namibia. An increasingly intense propaganda campaign was waged against him, branding him as 'a crank and follower of left-wing causes',[18] an expression which was destined to become chillingly familiar to several other churchmen later devoted to the cause of Namibia's fight for freedom!

On 26 May 1948, the National Party (NP) won the general (white) elections of South Africa, under the leadership of Daniel F Malan. This added a further note of urgency to the Namibian situation. The Party which was well known for its policy of apartheid, won by a narrow margin, mainly through votes from the South African countryside where in accordance with the South African election system[19] the Party was able to harvest more votes than the opposition got from the cities.

The NP adopted a harder line of action towards the UN concerning Namibia than Smuts' government had done. Smuts had, in spite of everything, always been willing to deliver an annual report as a gesture of goodwill. In 1949, the new government of Malan informed the UN's General Assembly that it would no longer send the required reports. The UN had criticized South Africa's administration of Namibia, and the South Africans wanted to make it quite clear to the UN that South Africa's relationship with Namibia had nothing to do with outsiders.

However, the case of Namibia had already imprinted itself on the consciousness of the UN, much owing to Michael Scott's unrelenting work. The General Assembly, not intimidated by the new, aggressive signals from South Africa, appealed instead to the International Court of Justice in the Hague for their opinion on Namibia's position and on the UN's future obligations to the mandated territory, from the perspective of international law.

The International Court of Justice's response, in 1950, included the following main points:

1 even if the League of Nations no longer existed, Namibia was still to be regarded as a mandate;
2 South Africa was bound by duty to account for its administration to the UN;
3 South Africa had no legal obligations to subordinate Namibia to the UN's Trusteeship Committee; and
4 in spite of this, South Africa had no right to change the mandate's internationally recognized political position by incorporating it in the Union without the consent of the UN.

South Africa refused to accept the Court of Justice's ruling. The UN attempted to overcome the problem by appointing an *ad hoc* commission for negotiations with South Africa. This was the first in a number of similar such commissions with varying representative bodies from different member states; also, the International Court of Justice was consulted on several occasions for its advisory opinion on Namibia.

Continued international dealings with the issue of Namibia were, however, of no avail, for South Africa refused to change its policy. As a compromise solution, Malan's government proposed that northern Namibia remain a mandate, and that the central and southern parts of the country be incorporated into South Africa. Such a compromise solution was rejected by the UN.[20]

A positive outcome of these years of negotiations was that, though they did not yield any immediate results, the UN's interest in the cause of Namibia was kept alive. Michael Scott kept up lobbying UN members in the corridors of the UN building.

A breakthrough came in 1951, when the UN invited Namibian leaders to state their case before the General Assembly held that year in Paris. Similar applications for a direct presentation of the Namibian case before the UN had previously been made, but they had fallen through owing to the resistance of primarily England and the USA who had posited that the interests of a whole nation could not be represented by a few traditional tribal leaders, and that therefore these could not been seen as their nation's representatives. On an urgent request from Michael Scott, Hosea Kutako was now invited to come to Paris with several other tribal leaders.

As an expression of the protest of his government, the South African delegate in the commission issuing this invitation left the meeting. In this context it was hardly surprising, therefore, that South Africa refused to issue passports and other travel documents to the Namibian delegation, in spite of the UN's request that South Africa 'facilitate their prompt arrival'.

Michael Scott's secretary, Mary Benson, who was in South Africa at the time, described how she tried to persuade the South African authorities to issue passports.[21] Her address to the Minister of Home Affairs was refused, with the commentary that the government was 'eagerly await[ing] the day when Scott could be declared Prohibited Immigrant'.[22]

Benson also visited Namibia in order to persuade the local authorities to allow the delegation to go to Paris. Previous to this, she had attempted to get support from the South African Christian Council - but in vain. In Windhoek she was met with a wall of resistance from the white population concerning the issue of Michael Scott; the same reaction came from the white Churches and Missions which dismissed Scott as a man lacking knowledge about the state of affairs in the country. His efforts, so Benson was told, were achieving nothing but to put Namibia in disrepute. The fact that Namibians had been invited to appear before the UN was met with scorn: 'What - the natives? Ridiculous!'[23] Being herself an Anglican in the service of an Anglican pastor, Mary Benson now also turned to the Anglican bishop in Windhoek 'in the hope of getting some support for the case, but he was unsympathetic, to say the least'.[24]

In the long run, it was Michael Scott alone who represented the Namibian case to the UN in 1951. He did this in a way which earned him much admiration and the Namibians' gratitude.[25] He was, however, attacked by the South African delegate to the General Assembly, who described Scott's activities as 'a studied insult - maladroit, vindicative and unconstitutional'.[26]

The attempts by South Africa to silence Michael Scott and hinder the UN's commitment to the Namibian cause failed. In 1957, the first Namibian to represent his country's case to the UN was Mburumba Kerina and he was soon to be followed by others.[27] At the same time, internationally, the political climate in Africa was changing, with growing demands for *uhuru* (freedom) for all colonies. In 1959, South Africa was accused of violating the terms of the UN Charter. The UN's Commission for Namibia consequently demanded that the General Assembly, the UN's highest organ, be granted permission to intervene on behalf of Namibia.

In 1960, Ethiopia and Liberia, the only two independent African states to have been members of the League of Nations and to have agreed to give South Africa mandatory power over Namibia, announced their intention of accusing South Africa of maladministration of the mandate. The accusation was to be presented to the International Court of Justice, and the request made that a sentence be given (rather than merely an 'advisory opinion'). The two countries announced their intention during the second conference of independent African states, held in Addis Ababa in June 1960. South Africa was accused of having 'failed to promote to the utmost the material and moral wellbeing and the social progress of the inhabitants' of Namibia'.[28]

South Africa's tough stance, and its attempts to stop the UN debate had the opposite effect, leading to further interest in Namibia and commitment to the country's liberation. The UN increasingly became the organ used by Namibians who sought the UN's help against the NP's harshening of apartheid laws. The physical presence of African nations representing Namibia in the UN 'symbolised that the [Namibian] issue was in its very essence a dispute about the internal political situation, something which South Africa avoided by hiding behind its legalistic manoeuvres about the Territory's international status'.[29]

Then the South African government took its first steps towards incorporating Namibia into South Africa. Through the South West Africa Affairs Amendment Act No. 23 of 1949, all references to Namibia as a mandated territory in the legislation were deleted.[30] The South African parliament withdrew the authority of the legislative assembly in Windhoek over the white population in Namibia. The whites were no longer to have any legislation of their own, but would from now be regarded as a population fully integrated into the Union. This meant that the whites in Namibia had the right to participate in South African elections as well as to elect their own representatives in the South African parliament. Six seats were allocated to Namibia in the South African house of assembly, and two in the senate; and an additional two senators were to be appointed by the governor-general to represent the interests of the black Namibians.

The new legislation meant that black Namibians were now under the rule of South Africa's Minister of Bantu Affairs. As written in the South West Africa Native Administration Act No. 56 of 1954, the administrator in Windhoek was no longer the 'paramount chieftain' of the indigenous tribes. This position went, instead, to the governor-general of the Union.

According to the new legislation, whites and 'non-whites' in Namibia now found themselves in the same position as the corresponding groups in South Africa. The consequence of this for Namibia's black population was that 'the full and final legislation function of the administration and developments of Natives [*sic*] in South West Africa [was now] vested in the Government of South Africa'.[31] In connection with the new legislation, the South African government explained that its policy was one of 'separate development', with special 'homelands' (that is, reserves) for the indigenous tribes and groups of people of Namibia.

The integration into South Africa of Namibia's whites, who were thus given the same voting rights as whites living in South Africa, led to a strengthening of the position of the NP. The policy of apartheid, and the NP's negative attitude towards the UN, were aspects of South African politics which were popular among the whites in Namibia, especially those of German descent: 'Thanks almost entirely to the solid pro-National votes of the three thousand recently refranchised Germans, they gave Malan's Party fifteen as against three United Party seats in 1950.'[32]

The harshening of the apartheid policy led to a strengthening of the opposition among black Namibians. Up to 1958, it was primarily Hosea Kutako and the Herero people's council assembly who had taken the initiative for the liberation movement. Deliberation with leaders of other groups, such as the Namas and the Damaras, became increasingly common. It was Hosea Kutako and his co-operation with Michael Scott which had made it possible to approach the UN.

At the same time, new, more politically oriented, opposition groups were forming. At first, they co-operated with Kutako, but after 1958, they were to become more influential.

Hariretundu Kozonguizi, a Namibian student at Fort Hare, South Africa, where he became an active member of ANC, took the initiative of mobilizing the Namibian youth to form an opposition against the South African government. He primarily addressed himself to the young people who came to South Africa for their studies. Though an active member of Kutako's council, Kozonguizi strove to overcome the tribal conflicts in order to form a united and all-embracing national liberation front in the country. While in South Africa, he established contacts with the Namibians in Cape Town who had founded the Ovambo People's Congress, and whose leader was Andimba H Toivo ya Toivo.

In 1958, Toivo ya Toivo was deported from Cape Town back to his native place in Ovamboland as punishment for his political activities. He was placed under house arrest in Oniipa, but in spite of this he was able to co-operate with Kozonguizi, together with whom he organized the Ovambo People's Organization (OPO), with regional subsections in other parts of the country, and with members coming also from other population groups.

At the same time, the Hereros' council together with Hosea Kutako and his closest man, Clemens Kapuuo, took the initiative of forming a new national organization, the South West Africa National Union (SWANU), in 1959. SWANU's strength and weakness at the same time was that it was primarily Herero, although it aimed to develop into 'an umbrella organization which would bring together the different elements of anti-colonial resistance into a single national organization'.[33]

Tensions soon developed between SWANU and the older, more traditional group around Hosea Kutako. In 1960, they culminated in open conflict about who was to succeed Kutako. The man nominated by Kutako, Clemens Kapuuo, was not considered radical enough for many

SWANU members. The conflict in the end caused Kutako to order all Hereros to leave SWANU - but only a few obeyed his order. The younger generation from various parts of Namibia increasingly made themselves heard.

Behind the formation of this new united front were the acts of violence committed by the South Africans in 1959, when they removed the residents of the Old Location, Windhoek, by force and relocated them to Katutura. In Katutura these people had to live in separate tribal quarters. In view of this, and of Hosea Kutako's deep sense of tribal belonging, the younger members of SWANU maintained that every form of tribal community was a concession to the South African policy of apartheid. Many decided to go into exile, rather than expose themselves to the continued South African acts of violence. Outside, they planned to organize an external opposition movement against South Africa.

Among the exiled was Sam Nujoma, who, together with Andimba H Toivo ya Toivo, was a leader of OPO. Konzonguizi who was in New York at the time, working as Hosea Kutako's special correspondent for the UN, contacted Sam Nujoma and the two of them met in Monrovia in Liberia in April 1960, to negotiate a fusion of SWANU and OPO. Because of opposition from SWAPO's representative to the UN in New York, Mburumba Kerina, and the Herero people's council, these negotiations were to fail. Instead, OPO was transformed into a broader national organization, the South West Africa People's Organization (SWAPO), with Sam Nujoma as president.

SWAPO was divided into two sections - one working in exile, and the other based in Namibia. SWANU was similarly divided, and attempted to live up to its ambition of being an umbrella organization for all Namibians. However, its strong ties with the Herero people changed what was originally its strength into its weakness. It was SWAPO which ultimately became the rallying national organization devoted to the cause of freedom.

Continued acts of violence on the part of the South Africans, along with forceful segregation of the Namibian population into tribal reserves, and steps taken to run Namibia as a *de facto* South African province (notwithstanding the country's international status as a mandate) - all of this brought about a renewed, and growing, national consciousness. This was quite the opposite of what the South African government had originally intended by apartheid policy: instead of weakening the opposition, the practice of splitting up the population into small, isolated tribal units in fact strengthened national consciousness and resistance. All Namibians, regardless of tribal origin, shared the experience of oppression: of severe loss of freedom and human dignity. This united them into a common front against the South African regime.

Close contacts were also maintained between Namibians in exile and those who had stayed behind. SWAPO (and for a short while, SWANU) represented Namibia at the UN. From the beginning, SWAPO built up a network of branch offices based in different countries. Through these, it created a number of vital platforms enabling contacts with governments on both sides of the Iron Curtain. The fact that SWAPO had contacts with East Bloc countries was promptly exploited by South African propaganda agencies who saw an opportunity of branding SWAPO as a 'Communist, atheist terrorist organization'.

It was an important step forward in the Namibians' struggle for liberation that the country was now no longer isolated. The Namibians were able for the first time to make their voices heard internationally and provide an international framework for the liberation movement of Namibia.

This international framework also included the Missions and Churches based in Namibia. The Missions were forced to take sides. Their views on the Namibian question were eagerly expected by an international group of sympathizers to the Namibian cause. The issue of how the Missions reacted to the Namibians' steadily growing freedom movement, and how the Churches, from the 1950s, gradually became indigenous institutions with a growing responsibility for the future of their own people will be the focus of the last two chapters of this book.

Notes

1. Scott, M. 1958, 12.
2. Ibid.
3. Tötemeyer, G. Views expressed in a paper delivered in January 1975 at the summer school of the University of Cape Town; National Archives, Windhoek.
4. Ibid.
5. Serfontein, JHP. 1976, 45.
6. Ibid.
7. See the UN Charter of Human Rights
8. Ibid.
9. UN General Assembly Resolution 65 (I) of 14 December 1946; National Archives, Windhoek.
10. Letter, of 17 June 1946, from N Houcke to S Bingane, Sehitwa, Botswana; National Archives, Windhoek.
11. Ibid.
12. Michael Scott was born in 1907, son of an Anglican priest in England. He moved to South Africa for health reasons and worked there in a leper colony. On his return to England one year later he was ordained in 1932 in the Anglican Church and served as a priest in East End, London, and from 1935 in Calcutta, India. He did his military service in the Royal Air Force in 1939-1943, was discharged for health reasons and again moved to South Africa. There he assisted the bishop of Johannesburg in mission work and witnessed the poverty among the Africans. For more on Michael Scott and his life, see Scott, M, op. cit., as well as De Grunne, D. 1950,109 ff; and Benson, M. 1988, 281 ff.
13. Scott, M, op. cit.
14. Ngavirue, Z. 1972, 243.
15. Scott, M, op. cit., 226.
16. First, R. 1963, 182.
17. Katjavivi, P. 1988b, 563 ff; see also Scott, M, op. cit., 235.
18. Katjavivi, P. 1988a, 38.
19. Seats were allocated according to constituencies, not according to number of voters, so that there was no proportional representation.
20. Regarding the UN's endless negotiations on Namibia during those years, see Serfontein, JHP, op. cit., 45 ff, and Kerina, M. 1958, 8 ff.
21. Benson, M, op. cit., 281 ff.
22. Ibid.
23. Ibid.
24. Ibid.

25 Moleah, AT. 1983, 104.
26 Ibid.
27 Goldblatt, I. 1971, 253 ff.
28 Serfontein, JHP, op. cit., 49 ff.
29 Ibid., 50.
30 Act No. 23 (1949); National Archives, Windhoek.
31 Tötemeyer, G, op. cit., 14.
32 Walker, EA. 1935, 814.
33 Katjavivi, P, op. cit., 43.

13 The Rhenish Mission and growing nationalism among its parishes

The Nama parishes

Western missions often found difficulty in coming to terms with the nationalist movements which arose in Africa after World War II. This was especially true of southern Africa. In the Union of South Africa in 1913, there were approximately 30 independent Churches. Their number increased to 800 by 1946, and to 2 200 by the late 1950s. In his work, *Christianity and the New Africa*,[1] Beetham points out that 'the major factor in the birth of many Independent African Churches was the excess of missionary control and its exercise far too long in the post-1919 world'.

The Africans did not revolt against colonial oppression alone; they wanted to shake off the yoke of Western domination which also burdened them in the Church and in society generally. The Christian faith, which they discovered through the Mission and also through Western cultural tradition, was alien to African faith and philosophy. It was a widespread feeling among the Africans that a 'white Messiah' was being imposed on them, which in turn prompted them to seek 'a Black Messiah ... because people [are] tired and need one to lead them to a new promised land out of the bondage of living for a lifetime in a world the White man has divided, in neither part of which you are really free to be yourself'.[2]

The blacks felt a general urge to reawaken genuine cultural and religious values derived from their own cultural heritage, and blend these with the Christian faith in an attempt to preserve them for the benefit of their own people, and thus also for their people's own Church. The nationalist movement in the Churches was the expression of an overriding wish on the part of the Africans to have to their own history recognized as being of equal worth and substance as the canonical Old Testament story of salvation which had been taught to them for so long by the missionaries.

As far as the missionaries were concerned, who had previously been the unquestioned leaders of their parishes, they now had to adjust to the notion of being considered a major hindrance to the Africans' nationalistic-religious striving. The word of the missionary was no longer law; missionaries were constantly either questioned or rebuffed. Missionaries who dismissed 'nationalism' as 'dangerous alien elements inside the Christian parishes' caused several factions to break away from the Mission and ultimately, to create new Churches.

For many missionaries the first decades after World War II were therefore a period of painful awakening: step by step, they were compelled to give up their former leading positions, rethink their position within these new conditions, and act accordingly.

The Rhenish Mission was confronted with this problem within a year after the war ended. It was difficult for the Mission to perceive how much of what was taking place originated in the nature of its own relations with its parishes during the two World Wars. Old seeds of discontent now blossomed into open 'insurrections' and a demand for respect for the integrity of the indigenous people.

An event taking place soon after 1945 unleashed the first open conflict. There were, as we have previously seen, a great number of Nazi sympathizers among the missionaries. When South Africa entered the war, most of the German-speaking men were interned and kept in camps for the entire duration of the war; all German descendants were disfranchised. In 1942, the local Germans lost their British citizenship and their weapons, radios and cars were confiscated.[3] Six of the Rhenish missionaries were also interned and as a result, all missionary work slowed down. The missionaries generally kept a low profile. As Germans, they were not allowed to move about freely in the country and were forced to live on £10 a month per missionary, the sum of which was paid out as an allowance by the authorities.

When the war was over, Germany lay in ruins. The future of German Mission seemed highly doubtful. It was in this context that the preses of the Rhenish Mission in Namibia, Heinrich Vedder, toyed with the idea of establishing contacts with the Reformed Church in the Cape, and discussing the possibility that it might take over parts if not the entire burden of work previously carried out by the Rhenish Mission. The Reformed Church in the Cape was financially strong, in addition to which it had growing white parishes in Namibia. Informal exchanges to this effect took place between Vedder and Cape Town clergymen in Okahandja in late August 1945.

In a confidential letter of 4 September 1945,[4] Vedder informed his colleagues in the Mission about his Okahandja meetings. Most of the missionaries rejected the proposal that the Reformed Church take over from the Mission, as did the Board of the Mission in Germany.

What it all came down to was in fact a series of confidential preliminary conversations which were not intended for public knowledge or public consideration. Vedder had not consulted his colleagues – nor had he contacted the black parishes for their views on the matter. On 31 October 1945, an article appeared in the South African Afrikaans newspaper *Die Burger* about the Rhenish Mission's offer to the Reformed Church to take over its missionary work in Namibia. It was read by many people in Namibia as well, and gave rise to a great deal of unrest, especially among the Namas in the south.[5]

This marked the beginning of attempts made by the parishes to break away from the Rhenish Mission. That this could happen was inconceivable to most, especially to those older missionaries who had been brought up to adopt a paternalistic and often racialist attitude towards the Africans.[6]

Theo Sundermeier in his work *Wir aber Suchten Gemeinschaft* gives an exhaustive account of separatist movements in Namibian parishes. Relying on archival materials from Windhoek and Wuppertal-Barmen, he made an analysis of the actions of the Mission during these conflicts, and also of the tensions which these movements gave rise to among black Christians in their relations to the Mission, and even among the missionaries themselves in their relations with the Board of their Mission in Wuppertal-Barmen. He points out how the Mission's Board in Germany was yielding to fresh thoughts and theories on missionary theology and missionary strategy, which originated from the Lutheran World Federation (LWF) and the World Council of Churches (WCC). In the light of these new developments it was to be the foremost task of the Mission to ensure the establishment of independent, indigenous Churches as soon as possible. These might later become partners of the older Churches in the worldwide missionary task.

Sundermeier viewed the liberation movements within the black Christians' own cultural context, namely as an attempt on their part to assert their integrity and attain freedom from the twofold menace of South African supremacy and missionary paternalism. With regard to Sundermeier's extensive work, it will not be necessary here to attempt another critical account of these movements in Namibia in this context. Sundermeier's work is extremely comprehensive; it remains for us to eagerly await its translation into English so that it might be more accessible to a wider readership in Namibia.

Here we are mainly concerned with providing some complementary information by trying to account for the process of self-examination which took place among the missionaries as a result of these movements. This process led to a struggle between an older and a younger generation of missionaries, and was exacerbated by attempts to define the exact role of the Mission in the context of South Africa's apartheid policy after 1948.

The beginning of the Namibian freedom movement within the Rhenish Mission's parishes can, as we have mentioned, be traced back to Vedder's decision to contact the Reformed Church – without asking black Christians for their opinion, or even bothering to inform them. The greatest fear harboured among the Nama parishes was the prospect of being forced into a relationship of dependence with the Reformed Church and its racialist attitude. Since 1926, teachers and evangelists belonging to the Nama parishes had held an annual conference of their own, which had, however, provided a kind of forum of contact with the Rhenish Mission.

When this conference took place on 12 February 1946, the abovementioned newspaper article was discussed. Great fear was expressed at the prospect of being made part of the Reformed Church. Also, according to the article, Vedder had labelled the Namas as 'heathen'; this was especially galling in view of the fact that the Namas had hoped to establish their own Nama Church with their own pastors. The very expression, 'heathen', was a denigration and seemed to suggest that the Namas were cultureless or 'undeveloped' people.

It was therefore vital for the Namas to assert themselves now and declare their unwillingness to be 'sold as living slaughter-cattle'.[7] Protests were sent to the Board of the Mission in Germany, demanding to be taken seriously, and to be invited to participate in matters concerning the Nama parishes future existence. Demands were also made for the ordainment of the so-called 'senior evangelists', who had after all performed the functions of pastors during the war when German missionaries had been unable to move about freely.

There was an underlying psychological reason for these demands as well. During the war, the evangelists had served as informers to the authorities who spied on the German missionaries; thus, they had held a kind of supervisory position over the missionaries, their actual superiors in Church hierarchy and training.[8] To make matters worse, while the German missionaries had been restricted in their movements, they stationed a missionary whom the Christian Namas thought of as 'steeped in German farmer mentality' to serve as a leading missionary in Keetmanshoop. In a letter addressed to Vedder in February 1946 the Namas now declared that this pastor was undesirable.

Vedder rejected their demand that he be transferred and made reference to the Mission's rights of authority over its own missionaries. He said he would not tolerate any such 'democratic' principles which he considered alien to the Christian Church.[9] The Nama evangelists interpreted this as yet another manifestation of 'the master-race mentality of the whites and contempt for the views of their parishes'.[10]

Matters were given a further twist by an attempt at mediating between the contending parties. The Mission, refusing to respond to the wishes of the Nama parishes, had caused the Namas to refuse to have anything to do with the Mission at all, and furthermore to express their wish to look after their affairs themselves. It was Missionary Rust who was appointed to mediate, at the end of April 1946. Rust was one of the older generation of missionaries and did not tolerate being contradicted. Apparently disconcerted by this so-called 'rebellion' against the Mission, he declared that all property belonged to the Mission and could not be used by the congregations if they broke away from the Mission.

The breach was thereby accomplished. More than 4 500 members of the Nama congregations left the Rhenish Mission, declaring themselves independent congregations.

In 1901, a branch of the African Methodist Episcopal Church (AMEC) had been established in the Cape Province. AMEC was originally an American Negro Church which had left the white-dominated Methodist Church in the USA. The anti-white attitude of AMEC's Cape section, together with its aim of managing its congregations without the support of whites, suited the independent Nama congregations well. In December 1946, they joined AMEC, thus becoming a new district in the American Church, and submitted to its bishop, who was stationed in the USA.

The conflict led to a breach with the Rhenish Mission, a breach which was motivated by racialism. Ultimately, it had also been caused by the incapacity of the Mission to listen to the views and wishes of the blacks and take them seriously. Any form of criticism against the Mission in the congregations was seen as rebellion which had to be nipped in the bud.

Following the breach, Preses Vedder called an emergency missionary conference in Swakopmund on 6-8 January 1947.[11] The minutes of this conference reveal that the missionaries regarded the Nama congregations' action as an improper attempt by a group of evangelists to show self-assertion *vis-à-vis* the Rhenish missionaries. Of course this could not be tolerated!

The breach was also seen as an attempt by the evangelists to force better conditions of payment. The Mission explained that this was impossible owing to the financial difficulties the Mission had been in ever since the war. Besides, Vedder sharply dismissed the evangelists' request to be ordained. An indigenous clergy surely ought to be introduced gradually, and with utmost vigilance. As a first step, blacks could be made resident assistant pastors, but only under the guidance of the missionaries. In this regard, Vedder suggested that the time was ripe for reopening the Paulinum – the theological seminary of the Rhenish Mission, closed during the war, for the education of black co-workers. He concluded that it was primarily a question of educating people to become evangelists and teachers. The education of pastors, he maintained, belonged to the future: it would be long before the 'locals' would be mature enough to be educated for a position of such great responsibility as that of a pastor.

No attempt at critical self–examination was made during the conference, nor any analysis of the Mission's action. This aspect was attended to by the Board of the Mission in Germany, which was worried by the recent developments. In a letter to Vedder of 23 January 1947 and in a circular letter to all the missionaries, dated 31 March 1947, the Board urged the Rhenish missionaries in Namibia to accept the moral right of the Nama congregations to strive for independence.[12] The missionaries should not criticize, but rather help the congregations in their struggle for greater independence and self-determination.

In another letter, of 23 May 1947, the Board further pointed out the necessity of strengthening the evangelists' position in the near future so as to counter 'the evil movement of defection'.[13]

On 3 July 1947, Vedder retired from his post as preses at the age of 71; he was succeeded by Missionary Hans Karl Diehl. One of the first measures taken by the new preses was to begin an investigation into the training of black clergymen. Another was to call a conference of all of the evangelists and the missionaries so that all 'misunderstandings' could be cleared up 'before our work once again runs the risk of breaking down as happened in Namaland'.[14] Diehl had already noticed some signs of rupture in the Herero congregations.

The Hereros and the Oruuano Church

There were no doctrinal motives behind the Namas' breach with the Rhenish Mission in 1946-1947. The congregations felt they had been passed over and denigrated by the Mission. They therefore strove to break away from the dominance of the missionaries as leaders of the congregations; documents of the negotiations between them and AMEC reveal that they were unaware of the fact that AMEC was a fundamentally different confession from their own. To them, it was of great importance that a black Church had been established in opposition to white dominance in the mother Church. What happened must therefore be seen primarily as the expression of an anti-white and anti-colonial struggle for freedom – a struggle away from the Rhenish Mission with its authoritative manner of treating its congregations.

Similar tendencies could be noticed in the liberation movement occurring around the same time among the congregations in the Herero reserves. In 1946, a prophetic movement for change began – carried forth by a message that independence would be won in the near future, claimed to have been received through divine revelation. It began in November, and has to be seen as a reaction against the referendum organized by South Africa to decide on the future of Namibia. This represented the beginning of the liberation of the Herero congregations from the Rhenish Mission, and eventually led to the formation of the Oruuano Church as the Hereros' Church, in 1949-1950.

The message of the movement was that the Herero people would soon have their country returned to them. First, however, they had to free themselves from the white man's dominion.

Having gained a foothold in Namibia through the Namas, AMEC now attempted to utilize the anti-white sentiment among the Hereros by inviting their congregations to join it. The invitation was refused on the grounds that the Hereros did not wish to belong to an 'American Church' – above all, they did not want to belong to one in connection with the Nama people. However, the invitation gave the Hereros the idea of forming a Church of their own. Samuel Maharero's funeral in Okahandja in 1923 had already sparked, as mentioned, the desire to unite the Christian Church with the traditional tribal power.

At a gathering of Herero chieftains in September 1947, the question of establishing an independent Church was discussed and given a kind of official sanction. This was what prompted Preses Diehl to gather the evangelists of the Mission in an attempt to prevent further dissension among the congregations of the Rhenish Mission. The missionary conference took place at the end of January 1948. In a separate appeal to the evangelists the Board of the Mission in Wuppertal-Barmen urged them to unite. This was dated 8 December 1947, and was translated into all the indigenous languages. It was read out aloud at the opening of the conference, and was then distributed to everyone present. Among other things, it read:

> It is with sorrow that we heard about different movements in your congregations and about the unrest which surely does not come from the Spirit of God. ... Those who destroy [God's] congregations and break down His body do not possess the Spirit of Christ ... . Therefore, we ask you to show vigilance before all voices that speak of desertion, dissension, and division into groups.[15]

The conference took place on 21-22 January 1948.[16] Preses Diehl delivered the opening speech in which he analysed the situation of the Rhenish Mission Church by using the analogy of a house that is attacked by termites. It was a matter, he said, of finding the source of the evil – the termite queen – before it was too late. For this, patience, and love and respect for each other were needed.

Diehl did mention damage done by whites, but he meant the Roman Catholic missionaries, as well as other European inhabitants of the country, with their hostile attitude towards Christianity. He did not mention the Rhenish missionaries and their part in causing the black co-workers to strive for independence and a clergy of their own.

The conference was important in as far as the evangelists openly criticized the Mission, for the first time ever. The crisis in the Nama congregations, they pointed out, had been caused by the lack of friendly relations between the missionaries and the black congregations.

The evangelists further pointed out that they were being treated 'with disdain as minors'. There was no feeling of human dignity, nor was there reciprocal respect. In their work the evangelists were expected to cover large areas, with no means of transportation. They were paid low wages. In addition to this, the discrepancies in their education were enormous, depending on the degree to which the missionaries had committed themselves to seeing to their further education.

Although the evangelists aired their deepest grievances, Preses Diehl and the missionaries did not take them very seriously, responding that the Mission did not have the pecuniary means to 'provide every evangelist with a donkey cart', and that the evangelists ought to show more interest in their work than in their wages! The evangelists were accused of holding on too tightly to their prestige. One positive outcome of the conference, however, was that they were given permission to elect four of their own people to form a council.

Shortly after this conference Diehl sent a circular letter to the missionaries, in which he reported that there was growing unrest and dissension among the Herero congregations.[17] An evangelist in Okahandja had contacted Hosea Kutako about his views on the Herero congregations' demand for greater freedom. In answering, Kutako had referred to the regulations that applied to the reserves, according to which, the population of the reserves should be in charge of matters of their own concern. This surely applied to the Herero congregations in the reserves!

The Herero evangelists now asked for permission from the Mission to negotiate with Hosea Kutako. They wanted clarification about his statement concerning the reserves. The evangelists, who had wanted to meet with Kutako alone, were granted permission by the Mission, but Kutako said he wished to speak about this issue with the missionaries as well. He claimed that he had no wish of establishing a new Church, but only wanted the Hereros and their chieftains to be granted a greater share of responsibility with respect to matters of the congregations' concern. He criticized what he referred to as the Mission's neglect when it came to educating indigenous co-workers, and said that the Mission took its responsibility of providing for widows and orphans, as well as for school education, far too lightly. Referring to this matter, Diehl in another circular letter mentioned the fact that the evangelists had also asked the Mbanderu chieftain, Nikonor Hoveka, for his opinion on the issue, and that he had pledged his loyalty to the Rhenish Mission.[18]

However, there was another reason why, through all these negotiations, the Mission hesitated to sympathize with the black congregations' wish for greater freedom: following the peace of 1945, the Rhenish Mission had made a 'confession of sins' to the South African government for its stand taken during the 1930s and early 1940s. It declared its intention to loyally obey the South African authorities. The promise of fighting any tendency towards nationalism and politicization among the black congregations was also included in this declaration.[19]

The Mission's promise to remain loyal to South Africa in everything complicated matters for the Mission when it came to taking a stand as concerns the new anti-white feelings which were developing in its congregations. Its declaration of loyalty now restricted the Mission in its ability to even to show an understanding for the black Namibians who were striving for more freedom.

Also at about this time, Malan's NP in South Africa was trying to strengthen its poll position before the next elections. One way of going about this was to promise the German descendants in Namibia that they might regain their German citizenship, and thus gain their support for the NP. Many of the Rhenish missionaries were German descendants. So even had the Rhenish Mission been sympathetic towards the cause of national liberation, its pledged loyalty *and* its chance of regaining German citizenship for its missionaries rather diminished its freedom in taking sides in the issue.

However, after World War II there was a breakthrough for taking new initiatives on the international ecumenical front. The LWF was founded in 1947 as a free union of Lutheran Churches. Among other things, the task of its Commission on World Mission (CWM) was to stimulate a transition from working in mission fields to developing indigenous Churches in Africa and Asia. Old and young Churches were to co-operate and carry an equal share of responsibility in fulfilling the worldwide purpose of mission.

In 1948, the World Council of Churches (WCC) was founded, with its ecumenical programme for a common Christian testimony transcending all geographical, ethnographical and confessional barriers. The WCC emphasized the Missions' obligation to see to the establishment of new Churches in all mission fields. This had been an important topic at a meeting of the expanded Committee of the International Missionary Council (IMC) held in Whitby, Canada, on 24 July 1947 – a year before the founding of the WCC in Amsterdam. The summons from Whitby was for a 'Partnership in Obedience'. This meant cancelling the differentiation hitherto made between old and new Churches. All Churches were to be treated as equal and were thus to work on a basis of equality in fulfilling the purpose of mission in the whole world.[20] This was hardly in line with the apartheid ideology, whose entire outlook and philosophy was based on differentiation as its principal foundation.

The problem of the Rhenish Mission in Namibia now was that its missionaries presently found themselves engaged in a whirlpool of events which tended to pull them all at once into a number of directions. They needed to find a way of avoiding head-on conflict with the South African authorities. At the same time they had to wrestle with the problems which had arisen due to liberation movements inside their congregations, along with an increasingly widespread anti-white attitude. On top of all this, a fresh demand came from the Mission's Board in Germany urging them to yield to Whitby's request.

This must have caused a great deal of confusion, especially for the older generation of missionaries in Namibia. The main topic of the missionary conference which was held in Swakopmund on 27-30 September 1948 was consequently how to take position with respect to the Board's demands concerning Whitby. In a letter addressed to Diehl, the Director of the Boards of Missions, Gustav Menzel in Wuppertal-Barmen, had written: 'We can and indeed must act on our own missionary territory in accordance with Whitby's instructions.'[21] Menzel attached great importance to the question of Churches detached from the Mission, and the responsibility held by the latter for the formation of these.[22] Presently, the Mission Board in Germany demanded that all missionaries in Namibia should seriously tackle the task of bringing about a plan of action which would facilitate the establishment of an independent Church in Namibia. In this regard, Menzel said:

> What is a factor of great importance for the future of Africa as a whole is the manner in which the Church chooses to receive the Africans' fully justifiable demands for independence and education. ... The charges which have been levelled against our Rhenish Mission have mainly concerned themselves with the fact that the rules and working methods applied by the Mission have been entirely inappropriate for the needs of the indigenous parishes and Churches.[23]

He added that it was up to the missionaries to find out the reason why congregations were breaking away from the Mission.

At the missionary conference in Swakopmund, Menzel's demands were discussed in great detail. Preses Diehl was of the opinion that conditions in Namibia were so different when it came to the black members of the parishes that it was hardly advisable to uncritically cater to so-called 'outside impulses'. There were three main points to his argument:

1 Due to a widespread decadence of morals the blacks in Namibia were not as educable as Africans in other parts of the continent.
2 Namibian blacks lacked judgment in issues which involved 'a wise discrimination of spiritual values'. For this reason, strict adherence to Whitby's request would be impossible.
3 The issue of delegating increased responsibility to black collaborators must be carefully investigated before there could be any question of granting them the entire responsibility for the Church. (This might just one day place the missionaries in a situation where *they* would be compelled to follow the directives of the black leaders. The day this would happen was bound to come sooner or later, but in the meantime, the Mission must behave responsibly by avoiding any rash imposition of such premature solutions!)[24]

Another speech of vital interest was delivered by Missionary Pönninghaus, who spoke on the subject of 'The Introduction of our Evangelists into the Office of Pastors'. Pönninghaus suggested that evangelists should first serve under the missionaries as some kind of 'assistant pastors'. This would meet the demands of the Board because the auxiliaries would be officially named 'pastors' while being given the title of 'teachers' when they were on duty in the field. In practice, they would of course be subjected to the close supervision of the local missionary in the exercise of every single aspect of their duty. They would not be allowed to wear the gown (the official clergyman's attire among the missionaries), in spite of the fact that the evangelists had already expressed a manifest wish to be attired 'as regular missionaries'.[25]

The discussion then became very animated. The older missionaries led by the former Preses Vedder warned against giving in to the Missionary Board's desire to bring about abrupt changes. They themselves, the

German missionaries who were after all operative in the field, knew better than the Board and were in a position to comment on the 'inherent weaknesses' of the blacks.[26]

The answer which was finally sent to the Board in Germany asked to refrain from having to take any rash decisions because of some statements made in Whitby. It expressed indignation at the accusation that the Rhenish missionaries in Namibia were outdated in the nature of their relations with the black congregations. The situation in Namibia, they claimed, was different and indeed so unique that it was simply impossible for them to allow themselves to accommodate the impulses coming from other parts of Africa. World War II had yanked the people of Namibia out of their isolation, and at present black Namibians were simply overwhelmed by impulses from abroad. For a long time, the country had been threatened by a number of South African 'sects' which spread great confusion amongst the population. Worst of all was the spread of a consuming nationalism which sought by every means to realize its craving for liberation from the white man. Therefore the missionaries thought it advisable to observe great caution. This line of action was in tune with their own views on their black collaborators. These servants of the parishes were liable to nearly every kind of carnal weakness – including weakness of faith. For this reason they could easily fall prey to a number of temptations. Besides, the black Christians did not even know what a Church was. The missionaries nevertheless declared themselves willing to consider a Church constitution that might review some of the demands of their black collaborators.

The missionaries' response, titled 'On the Question of the Realization of the Basic Principles of Toronto upon our South Western Field',[27] was sent to the Board on 9 April 1949. Apart from the view that the Namibian problem was much greater than that of other African countries due to 'flaws in the native [sic] character',[28] the letter suggested that additional difficulties were caused by a confusing partitioning of the country's population into various peoples with weak indigenous leaders who 'were liable to fall prey to temptation of every kind'.[29] How could all these people ever be united into one single unified Church? This was, according to the missionaries, humanly impossible; it was up to God to achieve. In theory, however, the missionaries could envisage the establishment of a federal Church in which various tribal Churches could participate.

In its response, the Board in Germany regretted that the missionaries had avoided the issue of identifying their own responsibility for the breach in the Churches. The Board concluded, 'It often happens that circumstances tend to overwhelm those who are unaware of their own mistakes and shortcomings.'[30]

The outcome of the missionary conference showed that the Hereros would not be able to count on any attempt on the part of the missionaries to empathize with their aspirations for freedom.

However, while the conference went on in Swakopmund, Kutako contacted another churchman, Michael Scott, whose opinion differed substantially from the missionaries'. Whereas the Rhenish Mission was excessively loyal to the powers that be, and appeared unable to understand why the Africans wished to be recognized as a people of equal 'worth' as the whites, Scott identified with the Namibian people in their state of distress, and was prepared to spare no means in fighting the injustices they were suffering under the South African regime.

The reputation of the Mission sunk even lower when its senior member, ex-Preses Heinrich Vedder, who incidentally took pleasure in letting himself be introduced as a father figure to the 'natives', accepted the position of senator in the South African senate, in charge of Native Affairs in Namibia. In his maiden speech addressed to the senate, he commended the apartheid policy of South Africa as an example worthy of being followed.[31]

In mid-1949, the Rhenish Mission in Namibia appointed a committee to begin work on a proposal for a Church constitution.[32] This was due to the announcement that Mission Director Menzel was to visit Namibia in 1950, and had requested to be presented with a finished proposal ready for discussion. The problems associated with a constitution for a united Church composed of six different population groups was intimately connected with the question of apartheid in all its complexity. The question of apartheid was therefore one of the main topics of discussion at the conference held on 23 September to 1 October 1950, at the end of Menzel's tour of inspection. The issue of apartheid was also indirectly referred to in Menzel's inspection report which was submitted at the conference.[33] He informed the missionaries of a 'cheerful message' from the Missionary Board, namely that missionaries should be allowed to choose their citizenship themselves. In other words, they should feel no qualms about opting for South African citizenship, should they wish to do so. At the same time, he was well aware of the fact that this might cause problems for the missionaries in their relations with the indigenous population. But, Menzel argued, the prevailing antagonism between blacks and whites had nothing whatsoever to do with the issue of citizenship.

Missionary Otto Milk delivered a paper on 'The Issue of Apartheid and its Importance for our Work'. He discussed what he thought of as the positive aspects of apartheid as far as the Africans were concerned, and analysed the duties of the Mission in an apartheid society.[34]

Apartheid promoted, according to Milk, 'the natives' separate development in accordance with their distinctive character'.[35] This could only happen if different population groups lived separately from each other. Apartheid, correctly interpreted, should not lead to either oppression or exploitation of blacks. He granted that the term 'apartheid' was an unhappy one which could easily give rise to a number of misconceptions. Another expression, which would more adequately convey the positive intentions underlying this political ideology, might be useful.

However, mission had nothing whatsoever to do with apartheid: racial differentiation and the separate development of various human groupings were in tune with this day and age. It was the duty of the Mission to win heathens over to the kingdom of God in preparation for the ultimate return of Christ, when all things would undergo a total transformation and renewal. Everything to do with race and people seemed to lose its urgency from this eschatological perspective. Considering the present state of affairs, Milk concluded, he could see no reason for the Mission to feel in any way responsible for the apartheid policy, or for it to concern itself with the issue, as it was the same system, and a manifestation of the same authorities, that the Mission had to subordinate itself to until the day of the final revelation of the kingdom of God.

There was disagreement over the question whether or not apartheid, when correctly interpreted, the way Milk suggested, presented an obstacle to the furtherance of missionary work. The Church had a prophetic task when it came to establishing the reign of love, while the task of the state was to assure the maintenance of justice.

It was hardly surprising that during the discussion, Vedder was the foremost supporter and spokesman of apartheid. He maintained that the political ideology of apartheid was nothing new, but had been practised in Namibia for over half a century. He quoted Prime Minister Malan's utterance in praise of the German colonial period and of those conditions which prevailed for blacks under the Germans: 'Our Government in South West Africa has been the depositary of a fine heritage. From the very beginning the German Government carried out that which has unfortunately not yet been attained in South Africa – namely, apartheid.'[36]

Vedder was adamant that apartheid neither curtailed nor trespassed upon the territory of missionary endeavour. He agreed with Milk that the term 'apartheid' had been ill chosen, and that it could indeed give rise to misconceptions. Missionary Pönninghaus then proposed to replace it with 'racial esteem' which, Vedder felt, provided a more accurate rendition of apartheid's ultimate goal: that the blacks should develop in accordance with their own distinctive character – a claim which he corroborated by quoting the Scriptures where it is said that 'God created each and every being according to its distinctive character'.[37]

Another aim of the conference was to discuss the breach of Nama Churches, and report on the activities of AMEC.[38] It was asserted that AMEC was at heart a political movement with a religious cover. There was no reason for the Mission to interfere with what went on within this separatist movement. It all amounted to politics and was as such to be left to the care of the state.

Mission Director Menzel, who chaired the conference, then read out loud some selected parts of his inspection report.[39] Among the Herero people he had observed an alarming growth of neo-paganism, which he referred to as ersatz religion. The lack of confidence which the Hereros manifested towards the missionaries was in Menzel's view linked to the relationship of dependence which had developed between this people and Michael Scott. Allegedly Scott had encouraged the Hereros' dreams of a kingdom of their own extending from Windhoek to Etosha. He had also enticed the Herero people into nurturing hopes for future decisions of major political importance. Menzel condemned the situation which prevailed among the Hereros under the influence of Scott: the danger, according to him, lay in the fact that the reliability of the Rhenish Mission had been fundamentally questioned by the Herero people. The only solution was 'to make this people completely lose confidence in Scott: to see to it, in other words, that their confidence in him was totally shaken'.[40]

The missionary conference of 1950 was revealing as it plainly showed the Mission's attitude towards what was happening among the peoples it was meant to serve. The blacks' reaction to the policy of apartheid was put down to political activity, and had nothing to do with the Mission or the Church. It was in fact the task of the Mission to keep its members away from any form of political activity. Separatist movements such as AMEC's commitment to supporting the Nama congregations that had apostatized, or the Herero people's desire, through the work of Michael Scott, to get an international audience for the critical situation in Namibia, or Hosea Kutako's request for influence in the Herero congregations and his critical view on what the Rhenish Mission had 'neglected to do' – all of this was politics, for which the Mission had no responsibility, and which the missionaries ought to leave to the authorities to deal with.

The expected discussion of the proposal for the new Church constitution never took place during this conference; it was reported that the outline of a constitution was not yet ready and so, the discussion was indefinitely postponed.

When Hosea Kutako met with the evangelists of the Herero congregations at the end of 1948, he stated his wish of arranging a meeting with the local direction of the Mission. This meeting was held on 25 November 1950 in a Herero school at Windhoek. Kutako attended the meeting with the whole of his council. The Mission was represented by Preses Diehl and two other missionaries; furthermore, three newly ordained Herero pastors and a group of Herero evangelists were present. The Hereros had high expectations with respect to the outcome of this conference, hoping it might change the future for their nation and in fact for all Namibians. On the classroom's blackboard they had written EHI RETU! (which means OUR COUNTRY!).

The debate at first primarily dealt with the question of pastors' and evangelists' wages, and the property of the Mission in the Herero parishes.[41] Preses Diehl noted that such matters hardly affected Hosea Kutako and his council, and that they should rather be presented to the synod of the Church. This occasioned Kutako to make a statement of principle regarding the relationship between what the Mission considered to be congregational matters, and that which only applied to the Herero tribal leaders. He declared that according to the Hereros' conception, the Church, as a national Church, could not exist outside the rights of the council of chieftains collaterally with the people's own organ. The synod could not make any decisions about issues concerning the Hereros without consulting the council of chieftains. He called for a closer co-operation between the direction of the Mission and the Herero leaders.

Religion was a matter of concern for the whole of the people, and the chieftain was the leader of the people. It was the task of the Mission, and thus also of the employees of the congregations, to submit to, and serve, the whole of the people.

The same principle had found expression at Chieftain Samuel Maharero's funeral in 1923. It was, however, an unfamiliar way of thinking for the Rhenish Mission in Namibia. For the Mission, it implied a confusion of spiritual and worldly authority, which placed it, the Mission, in a position of dependence on the political currents and worldly attitudes of the African tribes – a state of affairs which was surely dangerous for the continuance of missionary work. The missionaries feared that principles such as the one put forward by Hosea Kutako would lead to syncretistic false doctrines. The Rhenish Mission was not ready to give up its position as the highest authority of the congregations, and co-operate with the Herero tribal leaders.

With regard to the new trends within the Herero congregations, the Mission stressed the importance of countering these by finding ways of deepening the spiritual life of the congregational members, and thereby strengthening the faith of each Christian so as to lead each and every one of them away from the present politicization among the group. The issue of deepening the congregations' spiritual life now became an all-pervading theme in the contacts between the Mission and the indigenous congregations and their leaders. A consequence of this was a growing chasm between the Rhenish Mission and the Hereros. The white missionaries, it soon became apparent, did not want to listen, but only give directives and rule.

This eventually led to conflict: already, AMEC had shown that Church and congregation could survive and grow without submitting themselves to white missionaries. In March 1952, AMEC got a foothold in the Mbanderu congregations whose new chieftain, Stefanus Hoveka, had already become a member of this Methodist Church.[42] A number of meetings between the Rhenish Mission, Hosea Kutako and Stefanus Hoveka resulted from this, but no agreement was reached.[43]

In a letter to the missionaries dated 20 May 1952, Preses Diehl gave a description of the activity of the separatist movements and AMEC among the Herero people.[44] He maintained that the 'apostasy mainly consisted of non-active Christians, and not of the very core of the faithful'.[45] In his view, this 'apostasy' was caused by the topical 'politicoracialist question'. It was therefore of utmost urgency to spiritually cleanse the congregations.

It appears from this letter that Diehl had come to see apartheid not solely as a problem of black versus white, but rather as one concerning the tribal grouping of the people within the Mission's area of work. He had, it seems, begun to realize that this constituted a problem for the Rhenish Mission in its aspiration to bind the six different peoples and tribes together in a future united Church. Perhaps this is what he referred to in his concluding remark when saying that 'a missionary's position has become more difficult than in the past owing to the great number of other whites who have arrived since then'. However, it was the Mission's aspiration 'even in these days, in action and through love, to be and work wholly for the indigenous peoples'.[46]

The policy of apartheid, which became increasingly systematic with its grouping of the population into tribes, had become a challenge for the Rhenish Mission which strove to hasten its work on a Church constitution for an indigenous Church that would consist of several tribes. A first draft of the constitution was submitted to the missionary conference in Swakopmund held from 30 September to 4 October 1952.[47] There it was agreed that what needed to be done was primarily to draft a transitional constitution for the purpose of binding together a Church under the continued guidance of the missionaries. It was also important to emphasize that the Church was to be a united Church: 'our task is to emphasize the people's unity in the Church, and not to undertake a division of this unity'.[48] This was in criticism of apartheid which was threatening the Mission's Church-forming aspirations.

The draft of the new constitution was sent to delegates of the congregations in the four synods of the districts which coincided with the Mission's partitioning of its area of activity. At a subsequent meeting on 30 November 1953, Missionary Kersten summarized the comments on the draft document, which had been submitted by the delegates of the black congregations.[49] On the question of whether now was the time for leaving all responsibility to the indigenous leaders, they had answered: 'We do not as yet have any of these [i.e. any indigenous leaders]'. Kersten added that the people would only gradually come to accept the fact that a feeling of responsibility could develop into an increased independence. According to him, it would be dangerous to enter inter any risky experiments at that point.

Between 1954 and 1955, the chasm between the Rhenish Mission and a great number of Herero congregations widened. One of the first Hereros to have been ordained by the Rhenish Mission in 1949, Reinhard Ruzo, in 1954 declared himself ready to lead a Church of the Hereros' own. With reference to Acts of the Apostles 4:32, he called the Church 'Oruuano', which means 'Communion'. In English the new Church was called the Protestant Unity Church.

The founding of this Church opened renewed talks between the Rhenish Mission and the Herero leaders. A final, decisive talk took place in the Herero school in Windhoek, where Preses Diehl represented the Mission, and Hosea Kutako the Herero people. According to Kutako, the policy of apartheid was the main reason for the Oruuano breach with the Mission. He maintained that it was a direct consequence of the authorities' racialist politics. Apartheid had separated the missionaries from the people and so, had hindered them from the 'practices of the love of Christ'.[50] The separation now was only a logical consequence of this. Oruuano was therefore to be an 'apartheid Church' – existing only for the Hereros and led by the Hereros' own leaders.[51] As a sign of the founding of the Oruuano Church, Kutako received Reinhard Ruzo, and appointed him as the first pastor of the Church. Significantly enough, this happened on 25 August 1955, the day before Herero Day (celebrated as Heroes' Day today).

The further history of this Church, with its tragic partitioning into splinter groups because of personal differences, and tension between different fractions within the Herero people, lies outside the scope of this work.[52]

The Rhenish Mission regarded the Oruuano Church as a new 'heathen sect' which developed as a consequence of nationalist 'confusion and false doctrine'.[53] A number of steps were taken to make its work more difficult. Among other things, hymnals and other texts printed by the Mission were confiscated, and the selling of new books to congregations belonging to this 'apostasy movement' was prohibited.

Two new Churches thus broke away from the Rhenish Mission only a few years after the NP took over government in South Africa. Both Churches were founded as a consequence of the policy of apartheid. The Rhenish Mission at long last began to realize that this policy represented a menace for its aim of forming a unified Church.

New trends within the Mission

Among the younger missionaries there was a growing number who felt that the local direction of the Rhenish Mission was stuck in a paternalistic pattern devaluating the blacks and their leaders, an attitude which in their opinion was irreconcilable with a Christian view of humans. When Nama churches broke away from the Mission, and when the Oruuano Church was founded, they saw these events as proof that the Mission had lost the confidence of the people. Clearly the Mission was at fault. Missionary Wilhelm A Wienecke, for instance, accused his Mission of having adopted the attitude of the white *baas*.[54] 'White missionaries that we are, we share the blame of our white brothers and sisters, who call themselves Christians.'[55]

Soon after the formation of the Oruuano Church, in November 1955, Preses Diehl led a delegation of the Rhenish Mission at the first All-Africa Lutheran Conference in Marangu, Tanganyika (now Tanzania), organized by the LWF's Commission on World Mission.[56] Diehl reported on the Rhenish Mission's work in Namibia and mentioned that there was an 'awakening nationalism especially among the Herero people, [which had] brought a certain revival of the old ancestor worship. It is a new heathenism.'[57] At the same time, he emphasized that the administration was still in the hands of the missionaries.

Among others, the conference took up the question of racialism in the different countries and Churches. An answer had to be found to the question of how to look upon the Africans' nationalistic expectations and their dreams of freedom, and to what extent nationalist trends were a legitimate part of the life of the indigenous Church.

The conference was well attended by African Church leaders. Of 168 participants, 116 were Africans. They deliberated 'the burning issues facing the African Churches today',[58] as well as issues such as improved education for leading clergymen and increased responsibility for Church leadership for Africans. The delegates agreed that it would 'greatly help the propagation of the Christian faith ... if missionaries in their relations with the Africans showed a better example of fighting all kinds of discrimination'.[59]

At the request of the Mission Board in Germany, a missionary conference was held in Okahandja in December 1955, to discuss the relationship between the Mission and the German Church in Namibia.[60]

Several younger missionaries had increasingly found that their twofold responsibility of pastor and missionary was a problem, and in fact saw it as an indirect cause of the subsequent breach between the Mission and the detached Churches: the missionaries were, after all, expected to be loyal both to the German Churches and the synod, and to the African parishes and the Mission.[61]

Eleven missionaries were burdened with the additional task of having to function as pastors in German parishes; as a result, they found themselves in a situation of conflicting loyalties which inhibited their missionary work.[62] Negotiations had begun with the foreign office of the German Evangelical Church concerning the drafting of a new constitution for the German synod in Namibia, which would entail greater independence and thus better prospects for recruiting pastors in Germany. It was therefore decided at the conference to wait and see what these negotiations would amount to, and that the missionaries should in the meantime carry on their duties in the German parishes and thereby 'demonstrate due loyalty to those whom they had been called to serve'.[63]

The future of the Mission with respect to the Herero parishes was also discussed. This matter was closely related to the issue of writing a constitution for a united Church. Many delegates warned that it would be inadvisable to move ahead too rashly: it was better, they felt, to take one step at a time.

With reference to Marangu, blacks should be granted the opportunity of discussing the future of the Church at meetings of their own, with no missionaries present. It was generally agreed that many signs suggested that black collaborators did not yet want total independence. They had clearly seen, through the examples provided by AMEC and the Oruuano Church, what 'neo-paganism' and politicization might lead to.

The conference regretted the prevalent tendency of the Mission Board in Germany 'and others' to insist on laying the blame for such separatist movements on the missionaries alone. After all, by allowing themselves to be seduced by such trends as Whitby, the Mission Board in Wuppertal-Barmen had added fuel to the parishes' demands for independence and freedom from the whites, in spite of the fact that nobody in Germany fully understood local conditions. Though all those present were aware of their urgent responsibility of bringing about the constitution of an independent Church, they would not let themselves be forced by the present crisis into taking unduly rash action. All matters should be conducted 'in a calm and reasonable manner', the ultimate aim being to establish a federal Church where every population group might freely 'develop its distinctive character'.[64]

In response to the demands made by Wuppertal-Barmen, the conference addressed a letter to the Mission Board in Germany saying that the Mission had to protect itself from 'the great danger inherent in [the] situation where syncretism might be seen as the only valid solution to the problem posed by the Gospel and national belonging conjointly'.[65] They declared that the Mission intended to convene a national synod to discuss a new constitution, in 1957.

It appears, then, that the delegates felt they knew better and would not take directives from the Mission Board, let alone allow themselves to be influenced by black people's opinions.

The following year, in response to pressuring by the Mission Board in Germany, Preses Diehl gave a lecture on the subject 'Is an Independent Church a Feasible Option in South West Africa?'[66] He stated that the apostate movement among the Hereros was to be seen as a manifestation of the black people's aspiration to become independent. However, this separatist movement was not aiming solely at constituting a Church; what was really aimed at was a line of nationalist political action. For this reason, the Mission could not tolerate this new Church, let alone recognize it at all in the 'true Christian sense'. A speech by the former Preses Vedder followed Diehl's and expounded the view that it would take decades before any independent Church could be established and that even then, it would have to be under white leadership.

Despite the more 'liberal' views of some of the younger missionaries, many of the Rhenish missionaries in Namibia still shared the apartheid ideology of the NP. They had a tradition of loyalty and obedience to the authorities, and rejected any kind of 'politicization' among the blacks. In the years after the war they adopted a superior know-it-all attitude, both with respect to the indigenous parishes and to the Mission Board in Germany.

Nevertheless, a gradual change of attitude came about owing to the missionaries' concern for the future of missionary work in Namibia, and over the consequences of partitioning. They began to realize that if the apartheid ideology was pursued literally, this might ultimately lead to disunity. Also, it occurred to them that the apartheid ideology was very much to blame for the increased difficulties they as white missionaries were experiencing in trying to establish satisfactory relations with their black parish members.[67] At the same time, many still entertained the notion of white superiority and the right of the white man to be considered a person of authority.

Meanwhile, outside influence increased in the form of criticism against the degradation of human dignity inherent in the apartheid ideology. Such criticism came from Wuppertal-Barmen, but also, and perhaps to a greater extent, from the LWF with its commitment, through the Department of World Mission, to establish Lutheran Churches throughout South Africa and put a stop to, or at least prevent, the bitter consequences of apartheid.

The local Board of the Rhenish Mission was finally giving serious consideration to the idea of founding a federal Church including all tribes and population groups – except the German-speaking whites. There were to be local synods within the larger framework of a nationwide federal Church synod under the unquestioned leadership of the preses of the Mission. The latter, along with the missionaries who worked as his subordinates, should thus be able to prevent any further separatist movements from forming.

The deadline for the decision on the federal Church and its constitution was 1957. Much to the surprise of the Mission, however, the black pastors seemed opposed to the idea of a federal Church. They demanded one single, entirely united Church, with no division into different population groups; and it was to be called the Evangelical Lutheran Church of South West Africa. In a statement made on request of the Missionary Board who asked for an explanation of this name, the black pastors declared: 'We are a Church in a country where we belong to the non-white population. Yet, even if we speak in different languages, we are still united by the faith in one single Lord.'[68]

Despite this reasoning, the Church would still have to grapple with the limitations and restrictions of apartheid. It would have to be registered as an organization under the Ministry for Bantu Affairs. Immediately this became a problem for the parishes in Rehoboth, since the Basters did not wish to align themselves with 'Bantu people'. Belonging to a 'Bantu Church' would definitely constitute a threat and an insult to both their integrity and independence. Furthermore, it was pointed out in Rehoboth that the German Church did not form part of the new Church in spite of the fact that the missionaries also acted as pastors within its parishes.

262   Nationalism among Parishes

A new separatist movement therefore formed in Rehoboth as a direct result of apartheid, since the Basters thought it undesirable to subordinate themselves to a Church Board which presided over a Church, most of whose parish members were black.[69]

The philosophy of being always obedient to the authorities, along with the Mission's defensive position against any 'politicization' of any kind among the indigenous parishes, continued to manifest itself in the Rhenish Mission even after the Church formation in 1957. One notable instance of this was the reaction of the Rhenish Mission to the massacre of the Old Location in December 1959. The black pastors had demanded that the Church synod should formally protest against the authorities' decision to kill peaceful demonstrators who had protested against the forced removal of people from the Old Location to Katutura. Preses Diehl, who held the double function of leader of the Church synod and preses of the Mission, answered that a protest was unwarranted, especially since 'none of those who were killed or wounded in the massacre belonged to their own Church'.[70]

In the missionary homes, apartheid was still practised. Thus, at the missionary conference in Swakopmund on 2-8 October 1960, it was discussed whether blacks should be allowed to be invited to eat in missionary homes or not. Diehl urged missionaries to come to a decision on this issue 'as pastors who have accompanied me on various trips have been treated in a variety of ways at various missionary homes'.[71] Diehl did make special mention of the fine sense of fellowship which seemed to come naturally at all mealtime gatherings among the Finnish missionaries in the territory of the Ovambo Church, but took care to make the following remark: 'In addition to this [sense of mealtime fellowship] the necessary help and training for proper behaviour at the dinner table comes in due course!'[72]

A statement made by Diehl at the 1960 synod not only provides an appropriate tailpiece for this chapter but might also serve as an interesting example of the typical reaction of the missionaries to the birth of the new spirit among the people of Namibia:

> At the present time, politics have taken possession of the nonwhites, and have stirred them up. People no longer take an interest in God's word or His commandments but only occupy themselves with politics; and efforts are being made to involve even the Church

in political activity. But it is our opinion that the Church must keep itself out of the political arena ...[73]

Should this statement be interpreted as an expression of this particular local missionary leader's conception of the Lutheran 'two-world doctrine', or as the manifestation of his (and his colleagues') traditional, negative way of viewing the growing struggle of the black population to attain freedom from oppression? Any definite answer to this question could obviously only be provided by this particular missionary leader alone. Yet with reference to what characterized the attitude of most of the missionaries over so many years it seems that Diehl's statement in fact contains not one but both of these two abovementioned aspects.

Notes

1. Beetham, TA. 1967, 75.
2. Ibid.
3. Emergency regulations 201 (1939); see also *Government Gazette*, South Africa, 1947; National Archives, Windhoek.
4. Vedder to 'Liebe Mitarbeiter!', 4 September 1945: 6.1-7; Church Archives, Windhoek.
5. Sundermeier, T. 1973, 24 ff.
6. Sundermeier, T, op. cit., states that the average age of the missionaries at the time was 65 years.
7. Sundermeier, T, op. cit., 26.
8. Ibid., 31.
9. Ibid.
10. Ibid.
11. See Minutes of the Missionary Coferences 1937-1952: I.1.30; Church Archives, Windhoek.
12. Correspondence with Wuppertal-Barmen, 1947; Church Archives, Windhoek.
13. Ibid.
14. Wienecke, WA. 1955.
15. Letter to the 'Evangelistenkonferenz 1948: die Deputation der Rheinischen Missionsgesellschaft', signed Preses Brendenburg, and Direktor Berner; XIX Church Leadership; Church Archives, Windhoek.
16. Protokoll Evangelistenkonferenz der Rheinischen Missionskirche in Südwestafrika; XIX Church Leadership, Church Archives, Windhoek.
17. Circular letter, of 28 January 1948, from Preses Diehl: 6.1-7; Church Archives, Windhoek.
18. Circular letter, of 14 February 1948, from Preses Diehl: 6.1-7; Church Archives, Windhoek.
19. Engel, L. 1976, 508.
20. Günther, W. 1970, 67-73.
21. Circular letter, of 9 June 1948, from Preses Diehl: 6.1-7; Church Archives, Windhoek.
22. In his circular letter of 9 June 1948, op. cit., Diehl quoted Menzel as saying, 'The question posed to the missionaries is whether things would not have developed differently had we acted in a different way. What we must ask ourselves is whether we have too stubbornly maintained the idea that [the blacks] cannot yet [act responsibly], that we trust them too little ... . Perhaps we have sinned against the Church by sticking too much to maintaining our own leadership.'
23. Minutes of Missionary Conferences 1937-1952: I.1.30; Church Archives,

Nationalism among Parishes   265

   Windhoek.
24 Ibid. See 'Swakopmund Conference, 1948'.
25 Ibid.
26 Ibid.
27 Correspondence between the preses of the Mission and the missionary inspector at the Board of Missions, Wuppertal-Barmen, 1911-1954; Church Archives, Windhoek.
28 Ibid.
29 Ibid.
30 Ibid.
31 Katjavivi, P. 1988a, 85.
32 Circular letter, of 15 July 1949, from Preses Diehl: 6.1-7; Church Archives, Windhoek.
33 Reports of Visitations ('Visitationsberichte'), 1950, Pastor G Menzel, for the year 1950, 8.1-4; Church Archives, Windhoek.
34 Milk's speech appears in: Minutes of Missionary Conferences 1937-1952. Minutes for 1937-1952: I.1.30; Church Archives, Windhoek.
35 Ibid.
36 Ibid.
37 Ibid.
38 See 'Kurzbericht über die Abfallsbewegung im Namaland', 1950. In: Minutes of Missionary Conferences 1937-1952: I.1.30; Church Archives, Windhoek.
39 See 'Visitationsbericht, teilweis gelesen auf der Konferenz in Swakopmund vom 23.9.1950 bis zum 1.10.1950', in: Reports of Visitations ('Visitationsberichte') 8.1-4; Church Archives, Windhoek.
40 Ibid.
41 Minutes of the Meeting with Hosea Kutako, Windhoek 25 November 1950; Church Archives, Windhoek.
42 Circular letter, of 1 April 1952, from Preses Diehl: 6.1-7; Church Archives, Windhoek.
43 Although none of these meetings was minuted, notes suggest that they took place on 29 April, 7 May, and 15 May 1952; Church Archives, Windhoek.
44 Circular letter, of 20 May 1952, from Preses Diehl: 6.1-7; Church Archives, Windhoek.
45 Ibid.
46 Ibid.
47 See Minutes of the Missionary Conferences 1937-1952; Swakopmund 30 September to 4 October 1952: I.1.30; Church Archives, Windhoek.
48 Ibid.
49 Minutes of the board meeting of 30 November 1953: I.1.30; Church Archives, Windhoek.

50 Wienecke, WA, op. cit.
51 For more on the final negotiations of 19 May 1955 with Hosea Kutako, see Wienecke, WA, op. cit.; and Wienecke, WA. 1962.
52 Sundermeier, T, op. cit., 111-178.
53 Wienecke, WA, 1962.
54 An Afrikaans word meaning 'master'.
55 Wienecke, WA, op. cit.; see also Wienecke, WA. 1955.
56 Department of World Mission, Lutheran World Federation. 1956.
57 Ibid.,168 ff.
58 Ibid., 73.
59 Ibid.
60 Minutes of the Extraordinary Missionary Conference in Okahandja, 5-7 December 1955 ('Protokoll der Ausserordentlichen Missionarskonferenz in Okahandja vom 5.12. bis zum 7. 12.1955'); see I.1.30; Church Archives, Windhoek.
61 Correspondence: Preses with Wuppertal-Barmen: 'Das Problem des Doppelamtes in Unserer Kirche und Mission in SWA'. In: I.1.31-37; Church Archives, Windhoek.
62 In 1955, the German-speaking congregations had two full-time pastors in their employ: all the other pastors were missionaries. See *Evangelisches Gemeindeblatt für Deutsch-Südwestafrika*, Windhoek, IX.1-6: 1955; Church Archives, Windhoek.
63 Letter dated 20 January 1956. In: Correspondence: Preses with Wuppertal-Barmen,1953-1963; Church Archives, Windhoek.
64 Minutes of the Extraordinary Missionary Conference in Okahandja, 5-7 December 1955, op. cit.; Church Archives, Windhoek.
65 Letter dated 20 January 1956. In: Correspondence: Preses with Wuppertal-Barmen, 1953-1963; Church Archives, Windhoek.
66 File titled 'Oruuano–Doppelamt, 1955-1956'; Church Archives, Windhoek.
67 At the missionary conference in Okahandja in 1957, the so-called Church Clause in the Natuurlike Staadsgebiede Wysigingswet No. 37 (1957) was discussed. Missionary Milk pointed out that this clause in fact prohibited black Christians from meeting for worship in so-called 'white areas'. In his opinion the government had overstepped its authority in a matter regarding the daily life of the Church. He stated further that the government apparently was not open to any criticism on this matter. See Minutes of the Missionary Conferences 1952-1964: I.1.31-37: Okahandja 1957; Church Archives, Windhoek.
68 Sundermeier, T, op. cit., 212. The Church was constituted at a synod held in Okahandja in 1957: Synodsitzungen; Church Archives, Windhoek.
69 Ibid., 216 ff.
70 See the minutes of the 1960 conference, in: Minutes of the Missionary

Conferences 1952-1964: I.1.31-37; Church Archives, Windhoek.
71 See the minutes of the Swakopmund conference of 2-8 October 1960, in: I.1.31-37 op. cit.; Church Archives, Windhoek.
72 See ibid. for the Report to the Synod, 1960; Church Archives, Windhoek.
73 Ibid.

14 The formation of the Ovambo Church and the liberation movement in Ovamboland, 1939-1966

In 1937, two years before the outbreak of World War II, the Director of the Finnish Missionary Society, Uuno Paunu, paid a visit to Namibia to see for himself how the work carried out by the Finnish Mission in the north was progressing. During his visit, the third group of pastors were ordained.[1] The guidelines for the constitution of an indigenous Church, set at the first synod in 1925, were confirmed. It was envisaged that an independent indigenous Church could be established within ten years. The Mission had more than 34 000 parish members, in addition to which it enjoyed a great deal of goodwill among the chieftains and other leaders of the Ovambo people.

However, after the outbreak of World War II, the Finnish missionaries became increasingly isolated. They were only able to maintain a certain degree of contact with their native country via Sweden, and could thus keep open a vital channel for basic financial transactions. The missionaries who were stationed in Namibia when the war broke out could not, however, be relieved and were therefore compelled to remain there until the war was over. Despite this, the work of the Mission did not suffer any major disturbance due to the war. None of the missionaries was interned, and none of their movements was restricted inside the missionary territory.

In 1942, another ordainment was officiated. These newly ordained pastors, who had received their training at the Rhenish Mission's seminary at Okahandja, included Leonard Auala, who was later to become the first bishop of their Church.

The devastation of World War II largely bypassed the country's north which was one of the few tribal reserves that could live their own lives relatively undisturbed, under the leadership of their own chieftains. Also, there were no white farmers or settlers in this part of the country, nor did the South Africans have financial interests in it. Therefore, apart from a handful of South African officials, the Finnish missionaries were the only whites who inhabited this area. The north therefore continued to live its own life during the years of the war. Also, the harshening racialist policy of the South African government was less noticeable there than in other parts of the country. This might have been one of the reasons why the densely populated Ovamboland voted in favour of incorporation into South Africa in the referendum held in 1946 to decide on the future of Namibia. For them, there was no real reason for pursuing any change.

The missionaries were, as we have previously seen, exposed to a great deal of criticism from the South African administration in Ovamboland. This merely strengthened the position of the Mission with respect to the black population. It was also characteristic of the Finnish Mission that, though they gave the criticism levelled against them due consideration, they nevertheless continued their work in accordance with their own guidelines and principles.

In April 1947, a group of 22 missionaries arrived to relieve the ones who had been stationed in Ovamboland during the war. Now it was possible more systematically to continue working on the plans and develop the work for the establishment of an indigenous Church.

The headquarters for this activity were at Oniipa, together with the main missionary station, the printer's, the teacher training school, and, a few kilometres from there, the Mission's medical centre, the hospital in Onandjokwe. The activities branched out from this centre to districts, or deaneries with local centres for evangelization, school and deacon work.

The apartheid policy introduced by the NP following its victory in the 1948 elections did not appear to rouse much anxiety within the Finnish Missionary Society. Apartheid almost seemed favourable to the missionaries' plans to establish an indigenous Church, since through apartheid, the population in this reserve were protected from outside influence. An inner sense of responsibility and loyalty within the tribe was thereby strengthened – and this encouraged the population to work on a constitution for a national Church of their own. This positive attitude towards apartheid, which was seen as a protection when it came to establishing an indigenous Church, revealed itself in a statement made by the direction of the Mission in Finland in 1950: 'If we want Ovamboland to become independent, we must for the sake of Church education view apartheid in a true and sound sense of the term as being a positive force.'[2]

Only a few years later, however, the first warning signals appeared. On a visit to Namibia in 1952, Mission Director Tuure Vaapavuori explained:

> It is our duty to receive economic support from the government for school and medical work. We ought to show courtesy and gratitude for this, and in every way be modest citizens – we can, however, not always agree with that which our co-operation reveals to us is wrong. Can we, as servants of God, act in accordance with our calling before the government?[3]

On this occasion, the Board in Finland gave special instructions on how the missionaries were to behave towards the authorities. In case of a conflict, they should first await instructions from the Board of the Mission in Finland.

> Every individual missionary should restrain himself from uttering statements about the authorities in the mission field, or from sharing with these authorities his view on the missionary work, and avoid engaging himself in political conflicts. Missionaries shall follow the laws which are in force in the field, obey the authorities' regulations, and be pleasant and generally polite with the people of the administration. ... After having promised this, the missionaries cannot adopt a negative attitude towards apartheid – unless the Direction in Finland asks them to do this.[4]

The fundamental rule about showing obedience and loyalty to the authorities was to be maintained for as long as this did not come to conflict with one's own conscience. The standards for when opposition against the authorities was justified were not to be set by individual missionaries themselves, but by the Board of the Mission in Finland. It was hoped that thereby, conflict could be avoided between individual missionaries and the South African administration.

The consequences of apartheid, however, were to be many when it came to instituting an indigenous Church, and especially when electing leaders for the new Church. Before the establishment of the Church in 1954, the Church and Mission in Ovamboland had participated in the Conference of Churches on Lutheran Foundation in Pretoria, in November 1953. Leonard Auala represented the indigenous Church, while the Mission was represented by the local leader of the Mission, Birger Eriksson. In a letter to the Director of the Mission, Tuure Vaapavuori in Helsinki, Auala expressed his delight and pride at being able to represent his Church at this first conference of unification for the Lutherans of the whole of southern Africa.[5]

When later in the very same year Vaapavuori visited Ovamboland, he declared that everything was ready for constituting an indigenous Church to be registered in accordance with the regulations of South African law.[6] The draft of a Church constitution drawn up by Eriksson and Auala was accepted by the Ovambo-Kavango Church's founding synod, held in Engela from 31 August to 3 September 1954.[7] Assisted by the Director of the Mission and Leonard Auala, Bishop Simajoki ordained 12 new pastors. A few weeks earlier, on 1 August, the first pastor for work in Kavango had been ordained by the visiting Finnish bishop.

The first ordinary synod of the new Church was held at the end of November 1954. One of the foremost points on the agenda was the election of a leader for the Church. It was still to be decided whether to choose a bishop or just a temporary moderator for the post. There was also the question of whether to elect an African pastor or a Finnish missionary as a leader. In a letter to the synod, Bishop Simajoki had expressed his doubts as to whether the time was ripe for electing an African leader for the Church. The local authority of the Mission – the council of the Mission – held a different opinion, however, wishing that from the very beginning the leader of the Church should be an African. If the choice should fall on a missionary, however, he should only be appointed as moderator for a limited period of time.

In the end it was Missionary Birger Eriksson who came to be elected – with Leonard Auala as his closest co-worker in the office of Church secretary. It was decisive for the African synod to consider that only a white person would be respected by the administration of an apartheid society.

The man who argued in favour of a missionary as the first leader of the Church was Leonard Auala. He was of the opinion that a black Church leader would never be able to represent the interests of the Church to the South African authorities. It was not without bitterness that he argued:

> The government listens to missionaries but gives us no regard. That is why we were against the leadership being placed in our black

hands. People with white skin disdain people of black skin, whether the latter be teacher or priest. No matter what you are – you will always be a black – a kaffir. We have observed this disdain and our inner being mourns over this but can do nothing to bring about a change.[8]

The ideology of apartheid thus determined the selection of a first leader for the Ovambo-Kavango Church in 1954.

In Helsinki, the Board of the Mission with its new chairman in the lead, Professor Mikka Juva, emphasized the importance of taking immediate steps to bring the new Church out of its isolation. In 1955, Leonard Auala and Jason Amakutuwe were invited to Helsinki to study theology for four years at the university there. This initiative was stranded by the South African authorities. Only in 1956 were Auala and, this time, Efraim Angula given the opportunity to continue their studies in theology – but then only at the theological seminary in Oskarsberg in South Africa, and for merely one year. In that society of apartheid, a watchful eye was kept on African Church leaders to prevent them from acquiring higher education.

After lengthy negotiations and petitions from the LWF to the South African government, Auala, Amakutuwe and Angula were granted permission to participate in the All-Africa Lutheran Conference in Marangu, Tanganyika, in November 1955 – the same conference which Preses Diehl and his delegation from the Rhenish Mission attended. This was the first international contact between the Ovambo-Kavango Church and worldwide ecumenism. It was the beginning of relations which were to lead to the Church's becoming a member of the LWF in 1961.[9]

In 1958, Birger Eriksson left Namibia to return to Finland. Before leaving his office as Church moderator, he informed the Board of the Mission in Finland of his intention to attempt to convince his colleagues that an African should be elected as the Church leader this time; his reasoning was that 'we from Finland will not do as Church leaders since we come and go. In this manner, there are long, continued interruptions in the leadership of the Church. If an Ovambo gets the office, he will remain in the post the whole time.'[10]

In spite of his attempt to bring about the contrary, the synod again elected a missionary as Church moderator, on 25 June 1958. Missionary Alppo Hukka was in charge of the education of pastors. Auala got one-third of the votes. Once again a majority of voices maintained that the time was not yet ripe for a black man to become the leader of the Church. Both to the missionaries and to the delegates of the Church synod, however, Leonard Auala increasingly appeared as the strongest of the Church's leading figures, and as a man who ought to lead the Church.

The South African authorities, however, viewed the matter differently. This was made evident when Auala was invited as a delegate of his Church to the celebration of the 100 years' anniversary of the Finnish Missionary Society in Helsinki in 1959. The archbishop of Finland had to send Prime Minister Verwoerd a written guarantee that Auala would 'behave himself' during his visit to Finland. In addition to this, Auala was himself made to swear an oath that he would not say anything 'bad about the government' during his sojourn abroad.[11] During this period the South African authorities were particularly careful with respect to Namibia, and allowing Namibians abroad, owing to an increase in the political commitment within the country.

Auala was perfectly aware of the new political climate in his country. Andimba H Toivo ya Toivo from Ovamboland was one of those new national leaders beginning to make their voices heard. Auala had corresponded with Toivo ya Toivo by letter when the latter was still in Cape Town, Auala having visited him there when in South Africa for his studies. As we have mentioned, Toivo ya Toivo was later banished to his home village close to Oniipa, where he was put under house arrest. Here, Auala met with him at regular intervals. In his autobiography, Auala relates that both Alppo Hukka and the Director of the Mission, Olavi Vuorela, were with him during a nightly conversation with Toivo ya Toivo in the latter's home. It is true, Toivo ya Toivo was an Anglican, but first and foremost he was a member of the Ovambo people. This, too, was the reason for his relationship with Auala.[12]

At the synod in November 1960, Auala was elected Church moderator by a great majority.[13] In a conversation in 1977 between Auala, the then exiled leaders of SWAPO, and the director of the Finnish Missionary Society, Alppo Hukka, the view was put forward as to there having been nationalistic, political motives behind the election of Auala as the first indigenous Church leader of the largest Church of Namibia. By supporting the nomination of Auala, the Board of the Finnish Mission and the missionaries wanted to express their protest against the Sharpeville massacre in South Africa in 1960, and also against the massacre at the

Old Location in Windhoek in December 1959.

The year of 1960 also marked the beginning of SWAPO's intensive activity in exile, under the leadership of its president, Sam Nujoma. The latter originated from Ovamboland, which is why he, together with other SWAPO leaders, had a mighty popular support among the Ovambos. The Ovambo people had 'one of their own' as a leader for the liberation movement; and it was now the hope of the congregations also to get one of their own as their Church leader. Auala's personality and good reputation made him the obvious choice for this office.

The synod elections were held a few weeks after the second All-Africa Lutheran Conference in Antsirabé, Madagascar, on 8-18 September 1960. Auala attended as the leader of a delegation from his Church. In view of the occurrences in Sharpeville in March that year, a number of statements were made during the conference on the Church's position *vis-à-vis* racialism, and especially *vis-à-vis* South Africa's apartheid policy. Alexander Tshongwe from South Africa was one of the main speakers, with his lecture on 'The Task of the Church of Christ in Africa today'.[14] Speaking of the missionaries, Tshongwe said, 'Politically the missionary has become a coward to save his skin. ... I know they have hell and have been criticized by their fellow Europeans as "kaffir" brothers – [but] I take my hat off to a missionary who has been chased out of the country rather than sacrifice his conscience on the altar of un-Christian practice.'[15]

The first part of the conference dealt with the subject 'The World We Serve', and the Lutheran Church was urged to actively participate in politics and to 'denounce public evils such as injustice, discrimination, etc. ... even though this prophetic ministry may lead [them] into suffering'. All Christians, independent of racial origin, should be 'included on equal terms in the congregations'.[16] Another part of the conference dealt with the topic 'The Church and Discrimination'. It was stated that everyone was 'under the obligation to remove ... all vestiges of discrimination ... on the basis of race, culture, nation or tribe'; in word and action they were to show that racial discrimination was 'sin and evil'.[17]

A year later, at the conference of the LWF's Commission on World Mission (CWM) in Berlin, it was decided that the CWM 'call attention to the resolution on racial discrimination passed by the All-Africa Lutheran Conference, urging all those associated with CWM earnestly to seek its implementation'.[18]

These impulses from Antsirabé and Berlin, just like the occurrences in South Africa and in Namibia, hastened the debate on where the Church stood in relation to apartheid in Namibia and what stand the Church and Mission should take in relation to SWAPO as a movement of liberation for Namibia. The following instructions, drawn up in connection with Mikka Juva's visit to Ovamboland, in 1961, were an expression of this.[19]

1 Church and Mission should not meddle with politics. Church and Mission are non-political; however, they must be aware of the politics in the country since they form an important part of the lives of the congregational members.
2 It is important to maintain personal contact and a friendly relationship with everyone.
3 One ought never to seek debate but be ready to elucidate problems using the Gospel. Sin is to be found on both sides, but the Church must not take sides in any political programme.
4 Now that SWAPO has an intelligent and purposeful leader, the movement ought to be taken seriously.

In connection with Mikka Juva's visit, three delegates were elected to represent the Church at the LWF's General Assembly in Helsinki in 1963. Leonard Auala, who had ordained 19 more black pastors in 1961, was the leader of the delegation. However, preceding the general assembly of the LWF, and as a continuation of Antsirabé and Berlin, a delegation from the LWF and its headquarters in Geneva visited South Africa and Namibia in May 1962. It was led by the secretary-general of the LWF, Kurt Schmidt-Clausen. Another delegate was the director of the Department of World Service, Bruno Mützelfeldt, and the secretary for Africa of the World Mission section, Ruben Pedersen.

Before departure, the director of the Department of World Mission, Arne Sovik, had prepared the delegation in a number of memoranda.[20] The one to the secretary-general said:

> The Lutheran Churches have never agreed on approaches to the racial problem and have in fact avoided discussion of the matter for fear of breaking open the wounds. The life of the Churches is – I thoroughly believe – in danger if we constantly avoid this important question of Christian ethics. ... It seems to me our approach must be

through personal conversations with Church leaders. Above all we must ask that the South African citizens among missionaries take a positive position in this matter.[21]

In a note to the director of the Department of World Service, Sovik warned that the philosophy of the Rhenish Mission in Windhoek was 'basically apartheid and typical of the old mission attitude that the blacks are incapable of responsibility'.[22] In connection with a meeting with the Council of Churches on Lutheran Foundation (CCLF) which was to prepare for the visit of the delegation, Sovik commented on the report he had been sent as information. He observed that the CCLF had shown great prudence when treating the problem of racialism:

> Can this be permitted to continue indefinitely? Must we not, as one of the important groups working with the Bantu in South Africa and as the dominant confessional group in South West Africa, accept a real responsibility to consider how we as Christians can come to a mutual understanding and a common Christian witness? ... I must say that I do wish that the CCLF would take the risk of disagreement and tension within itself in order to make an attempt to find its way in this very real problem of Christian ethics and indeed of the very existence of the Church.[23]

The Church in Ovamboland experienced the involvement of the LWF as extremely supportive. At their synod in 1963, Auala was elected as the first bishop of the Church. Eelias Gulin, a bishop from Finland, performed the consecration in Oniipa. The Church with its now 140 000 members was the largest in Namibia.

In the meantime, the Board of the Mission in Helsinki accepted the instructions of Mikka Juva to the Church and Mission as concerns the attitude to adopt towards the liberation movement, with one reservation, though: that 'irritating the government' in South Africa ought to be avoided.[24] In connection with the LWF's visit to Namibia, it was decided to make Otjimbingwe a seminary for pastors from both the indigenous Lutheran Churches. As from June 1963, the Paulinum thus became 'a pastoral centre for training of pastors and churchworkers for both Namibian Churches'.[25] This was done in order to counteract the consequences of apartheid by bringing together people from different tribal communities.

The delegation from the LWF was not the only one to visit Namibia in 1962. The UN's Commission for South West Africa visited Ovamboland on 11-12 May 1962, to gather information about the Church's, and primarily Bishop Auala's, view of the South African administration and its consequences for both the country and the Church. This was the first contact between Auala and the UN, and it began with an intensive discussion on the interpretation of the UN Declaration of Human Rights. Auala would later often quote from this document in his confrontations with the South African authorities. He found the Declaration's items corresponded well with a Christian view of humankind.[26]

In that same year, a delegation of quite a different kind visited the headquarters of the Church in Oniipa. It was the Odendaal Commission, instructed by the South African government to draw up a plan for carrying through an apartheid society in Namibia. There are unfortunately no notes of the conversation held between this delegation and Bishop Auala. Many signs indicate, however, that already at this date Auala was viewed as a dangerous opponent of apartheid.

Anxious to silence him, the government offered him the post as leader of the Ovambo people, with generous terms of payment. Auala was not, however, one to allow himself to be bought; he thus 'thanked [them] for the honour of it and answered with a "categorical no"'.[27]

The report of the Odendaal Commission and the realization, after 1964, of its plan were to have enormous consequences for the whole of Namibia.

Both the LWF's delegation and the UN visit in 1962 undoubtedly strengthened the Lutheran Churches' desire to oppose apartheid. As regards the realization of the Odendaal plan, both of the indigenous Lutheran Churches went further in opposing it than did their respective missionaries. Preses Gowaseb in Windhoek and Bishop Auala in Oniipa together protested against the disintegration of the country into tribal unities, the so-called 'homelands': 'Because we consider the whole of South West Africa as the home and fatherland of the different peoples and races of the country, we believe that peace can only be maintained by close collaboration between all inhabitants of this country.'[28]

More and more frequently, protests against the South African policies made themselves heard, especially in northern Namibia, where the majority of the country's indigenous population lived, in addition to which came increased demands of SWAPO for more active resistance.

These developments worried the authorities and the country's white inhabitants.

The Finnish missionaries also anxiously followed this development within the indigenous population towards increased political commitment. On 26 June 1964, one month after Gowaseb and Auala's address of protest, the following statement was made during a missionary conference: 'As Christians we do not accept violence in any form. Our task is to show the right way, which is the Christian way for all, even for agitators in the national movement.'[29] The missionaries also made a summary of the South African racial laws, which they believed would be of help to them when taking a stand in their contacts with 'other races', without breaking the law.

Restraint and political neutrality were thus encouraged. The Board of the Mission in Finland sought a standpoint midway between neutrality and supporting, in a limited way, those who opposed apartheid. In its address to the missionaries written on account of the 'political unrest in the country' following the publication of the Odendaal plan of 1964, the Board of the Mission referred to Galatians, letter 3:28: 'Now we are no longer Jew or Greek, slave or free, man or woman. We are all one united in Jesus Christ.'

This in itself clearly marked a distancing from the South African policy of apartheid. At the same time, however, it was pointed out that the taking of such a stand could entail 'difficulties and suffering' for the missionaries. Therefore, it would be best if they avoided 'meddling with politics' and endeavoured instead to obey the law, since they were nevertheless 'under the protection of the authorities'. In everything they did, however, they ought ultimately to follow the voice of their own conscience, and the word of Paul on the Unity in Christ transcending all barriers separating nations and different peoples.[30]

It was therefore no easy balancing act which was demanded of the missionaries. The Mission's annual report for 1965 expressed some surprise about 'Helsinki's interest in our political stand'.[31] The Mission claimed that the motherland had let itself be influenced by anti-apartheid groups in Finland, with their view of the African liberation movement.

As from 1962, the indigenous direction of the Church under Bishop Auala followed an increasingly consistent line of action in its resistance against apartheid, through a number of statements directed against the South African authorities. Contacts with the LWF and other Churches in

Africa were more and more linked to political liberation movements, thus forming important impulses for open criticism of racial discrimination on the part of the Church. The same applied to contacts established with SWAPO through personal connections between Auala and local SWAPO leaders such as Toivo ya Toivo, as well as through continued contact with the different organs of the UN.

Even in its political involvement, the Church remained something of a national Church: it was supported by the African people and as a Church, it identified itself with the whole Namibian people and their integrity. Under the leadership of Bishop Auala, a strong awareness developed within the Ovambo-Kavango Church about its Christian, socio-political calling to combat the South African apartheid regime and its violent methods. The Church thus increasingly became involved in the struggle for freedom, which came to be carried out with particular intensity after 1966.

As a consequence of SWAPO's deep roots in the Ovambo people, the Lutheran Church in northern Namibia gave its support to this national liberation movement; members and supporters of SWAPO were also members of congregation, just as they were leaders of the Ovambo people's own Lutheran Church. The tribe, Church, and national, political liberation movement coincided.

In addition to this, many of SWAPO's leaders in Namibia and in exile had received their school education in the schools of the Mission and the Church. The majority of the population of Namibia lived in Ovamboland, whose Lutheran Church was the largest in the country. SWAPO, which was both the Ovambos' own liberation movement and responsible for the liberation of the whole country, had a more advantageous point of departure than SWANU, not only in terms of numbers and national support, but also when it came to an agreement between the Church and the liberation movement.

Notes

1 Kjellberg, S. 1972, 26. Previous ordinations took place in 1925 and 1929.
2 Ibid., 50.
3 Ibid., 48 ff.
4 Ibid., 31.
5 Auala, L & K Ihamäki. 1988, 75-76.
6 Ibid., 76-77.
7 History of Namibia 1885-1887, I file XIV; Church Archives, Windhoek.
8 Auala, L & K Ihamäki, op. cit., 78.
9 For Alppo Hukka's statement on the importance of contacts with the LWF, presented to the synod in 1958, see ibid., 87.
10 Letter from Eriksson to Mission Director Vuorela, April 1958. In: Finnish Missionary Society file; National Archives, Windhoek.
11 Auala, L & K Ihamäki, op. cit., 92 ff.
12 Ibid., 97.
13 Auala, L & K Ihamäki, op. cit., 97, relate how Auala and Hukka switched roles: Hukka became the secretary of the Church while Auala was the preses.
14 Department of World Mission, Lutheran World Federation. 1961, 29 ff.
15 Ibid.
16 Ibid.
17 Ibid.
18 Commission on World Mission Minutes, Berlin 1961, paragraph 6e; LWF Archives, Geneva.
19 Kjellberg, S, op. cit., 31-32.
20 Lutheran World Federation (LWF) Delegation, 1962, World Service, LWF, Geneva. File WS/I.2. General Director – Delegation, May 1962, Southern Africa; LWF Archives, Geneva.
21 Letter from A Sovik to K Schmidt-Clausen, 17 March 1962; File WS/I.2.; LWF Archives, Geneva.
22 Letter from A Sovik to B Mützelfeldt, 3 May 1962; File WS/I.2.; LWF Archives, Geneva.
23 Letter from A Sovik to the chairman of the CCLF, PG Pakendorf, March 1962; LWF-WM/V.1: South Africa, General Correspondence, 1962-1966; LWF Archives, Geneva.
24 Kjellberg, S, op. cit., 45.
25 Hunke, H. 1980, 89.
26 For more on how Auala used this Declaration in his discussion with Prime Minister Vorster in Windhoek in August 1971, see Hellberg, C-J. 1979, 117.

27   Auala, L & K Ihamäki, op. cit., 102.
28   Hunke, H, op. cit., 89.
29   Kjellberg, S, op. cit., 33, quotes from the minutes of the missionary conference in Chad, on 26 June 1964.
30   Ibid.
31   See Kjellberg, S, op. cit., for more on the tensions concerning the racial issue between the missionaries and the leaders at the Mission's headquarters in Helsinki, 1964-1965.

Conclusion

An important point of departure for this work of research on the Church history of Namibia was not to limit it to European colonial history. Certainly, Namibia as a country was delimited by the colonial partitioning of Africa in the late 19th century. Different tribes and groups of people lived within the artificial barriers thus formed, all of whom, however, had a history of their own long before European colonization.

In the late 1800s, these indigenous people were quite indifferent to the colonial partitioning of the country. It did not immediately affect their lives. European influence was only to be felt much later, when the foreign colonial power had consolidated its position and began to exploit the colony's natural resources at the expense of the indigenous population. This was only to happen in Namibia after the war of 1904-1907, and primarily concerned the southern and central parts of the country. Until 1917, the densely populated areas in the north were largely unaffected by European colonial rule.

In our research, we have consistently attempted to distinguish between the development taking place in southern and central Namibia, and that taking place in the north. This division largely coincides with the division of the country into two big areas of Lutheran mission. The Rhenish Mission in the southern and central parts of Namibia came to this country via the Cape Colony as a consequence of the Oorlam-Nama invasion of the country, which led to radical changes for Namibia's indigenous population.

Like the missionaries, the Oorlam-Namas also came from the Cape, having fled from the Boers in the northern Cape. As a people of mixed racial origin, they lacked a sense of traditional tribal belonging, and, under the influence of the white population in the Cape Colony, had developed their own socio-political and religious patterns. The original Namas in Great Namaqualand had to give in to the superior military strength of the Oorlam-Namas and for their own survival adapt to the lifestyle of the newcomers. By giving up their nomadic way of life which largely depended on cattle they assimilated into the mercantile social pattern of the Oorlam-Namas. This invasion of Oorlam-Namas, which took place from the beginning of the 19th century, thus was a form of pre-European colonization.

The Oorlam-Namas were largely Christians, and therefore needed missionaries to act as pastors to their own parishes. It was in this function that the first group of Rhenish missionaries were attached to the Oorlam-Namas in 1842. The most successful of the Oorlam-Nama leaders during this period, Jonker Afrikaner, had by the time the Rhenish Mission arrived, established his headquarters at /Ae//gams, close to present-day Windhoek. /Ae//gams was also close to the heartland of the Hereros, whose lives gravitated around Okahandja.

In conformity with the rest of the leaders of the Oorlam-Namas, Afrikaner was not interested in acquiring any kind of geographically delimited colonial territory. Rather, his objective was to control the people he managed to overrun and ultimately exploit them for his own mercantile interests.

The Oorlam-Namas aimed first and foremost at providing the necessary conditions for carrying on an independent way of life in the 'new country', free from an enslaving dependence on the Boers, as well as dependence on other white groups based at the Cape. However, it was impossible for the Oorlam-Namas to free themselves entirely from a dependence on the Cape, as this was where they acquired their basic necessities by selling their cattle. Cattle, in other words, was a vital trading commodity for these people.

The Namas and Hereros, on the other hand, traditionally tended enormous herds of cattle which were the foundation around which their religious and social way of life was organized. To them, cattle was not a mere trading commodity. But the Oorlam-Namas took advantage of their military strength to seize these cattle herds and trade them at the Cape.

The missionaries attached to the Oorlam-Namas, besides fulfilling their religious function, acted as intermediaries, providing fresh market news from Cape Town and forging links between the Oorlam-Namas and the ever-increasing number of white tradesmen who had come to Namibia because of the lively trading activities of the Oorlam-Namas.

The Oorlam-Namas took great care to look after their interests. They did not allow any Europeans to move about freely or conduct any kind of trading activity of their own without prior permission from the Oorlam-Namas. In the long run, this situation became intolerable for the whites. From the 1860s, they began carving out a political and military position for themselves with its centre in Otjimbingwe, and with the tradesman Charles John Andersson as its leader, who was in turn supported by the Rhenish missionaries.

At the same time, a decisive conflict took place between the Oorlam-Namas, led by the Afrikaner family, and the Hereros. In order to secure their own position the Europeans at Otjimbingwe enlisted those Hereros who had lost their tribal connections through loss of cattle, as mercenaries. When the Herero chieftain Maharero moved to Otjimbingwe to escape the supremacy of the Afrikaner group, they made him the paramount chieftain of all Hereros. By so doing, they hoped to strengthen the political and military position of the Hereros in order to counterbalance that of the Oorlam-Namas led by the Afrikaner family. The Europeans in Otjimbingwe therefore acted entirely in their own interests when they offered a certain degree of support to Maharero; the latter would be of use as a 'vassal' and as a means of protection for European interests.

Most of the Europeans in the country at the time were missionaries and merchants, and most had close contacts with Cape Town. To secure their position in Namibia, however, they soon felt they needed the protection of a major European power. Negotiations to this end were thus started with the colonial government in Cape Town and, via Berlin, with the British government in London. This was the opening phase of active overseas colonial interest in Namibia.

The events that took place during Namibia's precolonial history proved to be of great importance for the entire period covered by this investigation:

1   Through the invasion of the Oorlam-Namas, the traditional tribal way of life of the Nama groups gradually disintegrated. These latter were assimilated by the invaders. Within a few decades the Namas and the Oorlam-Namas were practically indistinguishable from one another. The various groups among them were either named after prominent families or after their original locations in the Cape Colony.

Some groups also settled down in delimited territories with an administrative and mercantile centre of their own. This way of life differed considerably from the nomadic life that the traditional Nama groups had led. It was such groups of assimilated Namas who were later to rebel against German and South African colonial power in a variety of contexts, and who asserted their integrity against the dominance of the Rhenish Mission as late as 1946.

The last of the Oorlam-Nama leaders who possessed all the qualities which characterized these people, with their aspirations to found a new mode of existence for themselves independent of European dominance, was Hendrik Witbooi. He deserves a prominent place in the history of Namibia as one who never gave up the struggle for freedom and independence.

2   Until the early 1860s, the Herero tribe, though bound together by a common way of life, a common form of ancestral worship, and a common language, could be subdivided into a number of separate groups, each led by its own chieftain. The paramount chieftainship was only introduced by the Europeans through their election of Maharero as paramount chieftain of all Hereros. The serious problems which arose in connection with this 'office' were aggravated by Maharero's death: through the support of the Rhenish Mission and the German colonial authorities, Samuel Maharero was elected as the next paramount chieftain in spite of the fact that he was unable to fulfil the traditional religious functions of a chieftain as he had adopted the Christian faith. Furthermore, he was not entitled to assume such a position since he was not next in line of succession, as per Herero tradition.

We have seen how the Germans under the leadership of Governor Leutwein resorted to violence and proceeded to silence Samuel Maharero's 'competitors' so as to strengthen his position. Like Maharero before him, Samuel Maharero was kept as a vassal of the colonial power and used to exert control over the Herero people.

Events took an unexpected twist for the Germans when their paramount chieftain suddenly appeared, leading his people into a war of liberation from German colonial domination. In 1907, when this war was over, the Germans moved to the other extreme, by trying to eradicate the Hereros' sense of tribal fellowship and thus to eliminate them as a tribe once and for all. However, the concept of 'paramount chieftain' in the sense of a leading figure uniting the Herero people lived on.

The principal character who held a position of central importance in the course of this development was Hosea Kutako, and the point of departure for this new development, which culminated in a rebirth of the tribal fellowship of the Herero people, was the funeral of Samuel Maharero in Okahandja in 1923. It was as such a paramount chieftain that Kutako was able to oppose South Africa's plan to annex Namibia as a South African province. On several occasions, he was even the spokesman of groups of the population other than his own.

It was in this selfsame position of paramount chieftain that Kutako was in charge of both political and religious functions and thus came into conflict with the Rhenish Mission in the 1950s. The conflict eventually led to the establishment of the Herero people's own Church, the Oruuano Church, also under Kutako's leadership. Kutako relied too much on tribal cohesion, however; and this fact along with his jealously guarded position as leader of all Hereros ultimately became a weakness of SWANU, a Herero liberation movement which originated among the Herero people, but which nevertheless nurtured the ambition of becoming a national liberation movement.

3   It was while all these changes, introduced by invaders from the south and colonizers from abroad, went on that the Rhenish Mission had to carry out its activities in southern and central Namibia. This helps to explain most of the problems faced by the Mission. In addition, as a German mission it was later torn between loyalty to its fatherland and its missionary work. Both under German and under South African colonial rule it was obliged to demonstrate its loyalty to the colonial power. The Mission's nationality, and also its close contacts with the large German-speaking minority in Namibia impelled many of its missionaries to join or at least openly sympathize with the Nazi Party before and during World War II.

The Mission's self-imposed obligation to remain loyal to the colonial power, no matter which, explains its cautious restraint at first and later, its direct opposition to the Namibians' attempts to obtain a greater degree of freedom and demands for more humane treatment. This attitude eventually led to a widespread lack of confidence in the Rhenish Mission, even within its own parishes.

Eventually the pressure exerted by the Board of the Mission in Germany, and the growth of a strong sense of Lutheran fellowship between Churches throughout Africa incited the Rhenish missionaries to give in and begin to work towards the establishment of an indigenous Church. In accordance with the apartheid ideology, which encouraged every population group to 'develop in accordance with its own specific nature', the missionaries made plans for a federal Church which would allow each population group a certain degree of independence within the framework of a Church federation. Much to the Mission's surprise, its black congregations opted for a unified Church instead. Possibly this was a token of protest against the stand the Mission had hitherto taken with respect to apartheid.

4   The situation in Ovamboland was very different. Until quite late, this part of the country maintained no more than a few sporadic contacts with the Oorlam-Namas, the Hereros and even the German colonial power. The Mission there was therefore able to freely carry out its work without any interference from outside bodies which could disturb or break up the prevailing sense of tribal community.

This situation did not change under South African rule even if the South African military defeat of the Kwanyama people meant that this part of the country was now also ruled from the central administration of Windhoek. The territories of the Ovambo-Kavango people were made into reserve areas run by a form of 'indirect-rule administration' with a local South African administrator who 'ruled indirectly' through the agency of the traditional chieftains.

The northern part of Namibia thus remained a sheltered, clearly defined missionary territory. In more ways than one, apartheid thus became a pillar of support for the furtherance of the work carried out by the Finnish Mission whose aim was to establish an African Folkchurch. The Mission and the Church also provided education to the Ovambos, in schools where most of the present-day leaders of the independent Republic of Namibia received their education.

Because there was no single traditional chieftain for the whole of Ovamboland, the Church, conducting activities throughout the region, performed an important function as a co-ordinating institution. This meant that the first indigenous leader of the Church, Bishop Leonard Auala, also became a leading collective figure in the eyes of the entire population. This factor alone was to be of decisive importance for the Church's political influence through SWAPO, the liberation organization with its roots in Ovamboland.

The Church of the Ovambo people, which grew in numbers and support, and which enjoyed the confidence of the population, helped provide the foundations for the close, and personal, co-operation between the liberation movement SWAPO and the Church in this part of Namibia from the late 1950s.

Thus, impulses from northern Namibia gradually came to influence the developments taking place in southern and central Namibia. The co-operation in Ovamboland between the liberation movement and the Church, which during the 1970s came to envelop all the Christian communities within the Council of Churches in Namibia (CCN) is in itself unique to the history of liberation in all of Africa. That period, however, falls outside the scope of this work, one of the aims of which was to offer some necessary background information to an earlier work by this writer, *A Voice of the Voiceless*,[1] which deals with the involvement of the LWF in southern Africa between 1947 and 1977.

Notes

1   Hellberg, C-J. 1979.

Bibliography

Note: a bibliography of the archival material referred to can be found on pp 302-305

Aagard, J. 1977. 'Missionstheologie'. In: *Die Evangelisch-Lutherische Kirche – Vergangenheit und Gegenwart.* Stuttgart: Vilmos Vajta, Evangelisches Verlagswerk.
Akweenda, S. 1988a. 'South Africa's Effective State of Emergency in Namibia'. In: Wood, B (ed.). *Namibia 1884-1984: '100 Years of Foreign Occupation; 100 Years of Struggle'*. Readings on Namibia's History and Society: Papers of the International Conference on Namibia 1884-1984, London 10-13 September 1984. London: Namibia Support Committee, in co-operation with the United Nations Institute for Namibia, Lusaka.
Akweenda, S. 1988. 'The Wounds of Martial Law: Namibia in Military Occupation of the Union Forces 1915-1920 and Beyond'. In: Wood, B (ed.). *Namibia 1884-1984: '100 Years of Foreign Occupation; 100 Years of Struggle'*. Readings on Namibia's History and Society: Papers of the International Conference on Namibia 1884-1984, London 10-13 September 1984. London: Namibia Support Committee, in co-operation with the United Nations Institute for Namibia, Lusaka.
Alexander, J. 1838. *An Expedition of Discovery into the Interior of Africa through the Hitherto Undescribed Countries of the Great Namaquas, Boschmans, and Hill Damas.* London: Henry Colbourn.
Alexander, N. 1983. 'The Namibian War of Anti-Colonial Resistance 1904-1907'. *Namibia Review Publications*, No.1.
Andersson, CJ. 1989. 'Trade and Politics in Central Namibia 1860-1864. Diaries and Correspondence'. In: Lau, B (ed.). *Charles John Andersson's Papers*, vol. 2. Windhoek: Archives Service Division of the Department of National Education of SWA/Namibia.
Auala, L & K Ihamäki. 1988. *Messlatte und Bischofsstab. Ein Leben für Namibia.* Erlangen: Verlag der Vereinigten Evangelischen Mission.
Baumann, J. 1965. *Mission und Ökumene in Südwestafrika dargestellt am*

Bibliography

Lebenswerk von Hermann Heinrich Vedder. Leiden/Köln: Ökumenische Studien, vol. VII.

Baumann, J. 1985. 'Die Missionare – Europa kommt nach Afrika'. In: Baumann, J (ed.). *1884-1984: Vom Schutzgebiet bis Namibia.* Windhoek: Interessengemeinschaft deutschsprachiger Südwester.

Beetham, TA. 1967. *Christianity and the New Africa.* London: Praeger Library of African Affairs.

Beinart, W. 1981. '"Jamani." Cape Workers in German South West Africa 1904-1912. Patterns of Migrancy and the Closing of Options on the Southern African Labour Market.' In: Wood, B (ed.). *Namibia 1884-1984: '100 Years of Foreign Occupation; 100 Years of Struggle'.* Readings on Namibia's History and Society: Papers of the International Conference on Namibia 1884-1984, London 10-13 September 1984. London: Namibia Support Committee, in co-operation with the United Nations Institute for Namibia, Lusaka.

Benson, M. 1988. 'Notes on Research and Personal Experiences Relating to Namibia, the United Nations and Britain's Role'. In: Wood, B (ed.). *Namibia 1884-1984: '100 Years of Foreign Occupation; 100 Years of Struggle'.* Readings on Namibia's History and Society: Papers of the International Conference on Namibia 1884-1984, London 10-13 September 1984. London: Namibia Support Committee, in co-operation with the United Nations Institute for Namibia, Lusaka.

Bertelsmann, W. 1979. *Die Deutsche Sprachgruppe Südwestafrikas in Politik und Recht.* Windhoek: Interessengemeinschaft deutschsprachiger Südwester.

Beyerhaus, P. *1956 Die Selbständigkeit der Jungen Kirchen als Missionarisches Problem.* Wuppertal-Barmen: Verlag der Rheinischen Missionsgesellschaft.

Bley, H. 1968. *Kolonialherrschaft und Sozialstruktur in Deutsch Südwestafrika 1894-1914.* Hamburg: Leibniz-Verlag.

Bley, H. 1971. *South West Africa under German Rule.* London: Heinemann.

Bley, H & R Tetzlaff. 1978. *Afrika und Bonn. Versäumnisse und Zwänger Deutscher Afrikapolitik.* Reinbek bei Hamburg: Rowohlt Taschenbuch Verlag.

Bridgman, J & DE Clarke. 1965. *German Africa. A Select Annotated Bibliography.* Hoover Institution Bibliographical Series XIX. Stanford, CA: Stanford University.

Brincker, H. 1857. *Unsere Ovambomission so wie die Landleute, Religion, Sitten, Gebräuche, Sprache.* Wuppertal-Barmen: Verlag der Rheinischen Missionsgesellschaft.

Broadbent, S. 1857. *The Missionary Martyr in Namaqualand.* London: publisher unknown.

Bruwer, JJ. 1985. *AUS 1915-1919. Errichtung, Bestehen und Schliessung des Kriegsgefangenenlagers bei Aus*. Windhoek: Rat für Nationale Denkmäler, Staatsmuseum.

Büttner, CG. 1885. *Kolonialpolitik und Christentum, betrachtet mit Hinblick auf die Deutschen Unternehmungen in Südwestafrika*. Heidelberg: Universitätpresse.

Davidson, B. 1991. *Afrika i det Tjugonde Seklet*. Uppsala: Nordisk Afrikainstitutet.

De Grunne, D. 1950. 'Les Hereros et Michael Scott'. *Le Bulletin des Missions*, No. 2.

De Vries, L. 1971. 'The Influence of German Colonialism on the Missionary Activities of the Rhenish Mission Society in the Former German South West Africa 1880-1914/1918'. Doctoral thesis. Brussels.

De Vries, L. 1978. *Mission and Colonialism in Namibia*. Braamfontein: Ravan Press.

Dedering, T. 1989. 'Southern Namibia 1810 to 1840'. Mimeographed Master's thesis. University of Cape Town.

Department of Church Co-operation, Lutheran World Federation. 1977. *All-Africa Lutheran Consultation, Gaborone, Botswana, 7-16 February 1977*. Geneva: Lutheran World Federation.

Department of World Mission, Lutheran World Federation. 1956. *Marangu – a Record of the All-Africa Lutheran Conference, Marangu, Tangayika, November 12-22, 1955*. Geneva: Lutheran World Federation.

Department of World Mission, Lutheran World Federation. 1961. *Antsirabé, A Record of the Second All-Africa Lutheran Conference, Antsirabé, Madagascar, September 8-18, 1960*. Geneva: Lutheran World Federation.

Department of World Mission, Lutheran World Federation. 1966. *Addis Ababa. A Record of the Third All-Africa Lutheran Conference, Addis Ababa, Ethiopia, October 12-21, 1965*. Geneva: Lutheran World Federation.

Dönhoff, M. 1989. *Der Südafrikanische Teufelskreis. Reportagen und Analysen aus drei Jahrzehnten*. München: Deutscher Taschenbuchverlag.

Drechsler, H. 1966. *Let Us Die Fighting! The Struggle of the Herero and Nama against German Imperialism (1884-1915)*. London: Zed Press.

Du Plessis, A. 1950. *Quo Vadis Südwest?* Windhoek: Du Plessis, A.

Duchrow, U. (ed.) 1977. *Lutheran Churches – Salt or Mirror of Society? Case Studies on the Theory and Practice of the Two Kingdoms Doctrine*. Geneva: Lutheran World Federation, Department of Studies.

Eichholz, K. 1977. 'The Dispute between Black and White Lutherans in Namibia after the Open Letter of 1971'. In: Duchrow, U. (ed.) 1977. *Lutheran Churches – Salt or Mirror of Society? Case Studies on the Theory and Practice of the Two Kingdoms Doctrine*. Geneva: Lutheran World Federation, Department of Studies.

Eirola, M. 1983. *Namibiana in Finland. Guide to the Finnish Archival Sources*

Concerning Namibia before 1938. Helsinki: Juentsuuo University.
Emmet, T. 1988. 'Popular Resistance in Namibia, 1920-5'. In: Wood, B. (ed.) *Namibia 1884-1984: '100 Years of Foreign Occupation; 100 Years of Struggle'*. Readings on Namibia's History and Society: Papers of the International Conference on Namibia 1884-1984, London 10-13 September 1984. London: Namibia Support Committee, in co-operation with the United Nations Institute for Namibia, Lusaka.
Engel, L. 1976. *Kolonialismus und Nationalismus im Deutschen Protestantismus in Namibia 1907 bis 1945. Beiträge zur Geschichte der Deutschen Evangelischen Mission und Kirche im Ehemaligen Kolonial- und Mandatgebiet Südwestafrika*. Bern: Theologische Fakultät.
Engel, L. 1977. 'The Mission and Political Awakening of the Namibians after the First World War'. In: Duchrow, U. (ed.) 1977. *Lutheran Churches – Salt or Mirror of Society? Case Studies on the Theory and Practice of the Two Kingdoms Doctrine*. Geneva: Lutheran World Federation, Department of Studies.
Evangelischer Gemeinderat zu Windhoek. 1935. *Christuskirche. 25 Jahre Christuskirche in Windhoek. Festschrift zum 25jährigen Kirchenjubiläum im Oktober 1935*. Windhoek: Evangelischer Gemeinderat zu Windhoek.
Fabri, F. 1884. *Bedarf Deutschland der Kolonien? Eine Politisch-Ökonomische Betrachtung*, 3. Ausgabe. Gotha: FA Perhes Verlag.
First, R. 1963. *South West Africa*. Harmondsworth: Penguin Books.
Fischer, E. 1971. *Die Rehobother Bastards und das Bastardierungsproblem beim Menschen*. Anthropologische und Ethnographische Studien am Rehobother Bastardvolk in Deutsch-Südwest-Afrika. Graz: Akademische Druck- und Verlagsanstalt.
Freislich, R. 1964. 'Last Tribal War – History of the Bondelswarts Uprising in South West Africa 1922'. Mimeographed paper. University of Cape Town.
Goldblatt, I. 1971. *History of South West Africa from the Beginning of the Nineteenth Century*. Cape Town: Juta.
Gottschalk, K & C Saunders (eds.). 1981. *Africa Seminar. Collected Papers*, vol. 2. Cape Town: University of Cape Town.
Government Printer of South Africa. 1960. *Report of the Commission of Enquiry into the Occurrences in the Windhoek Location on the Night of the 10th to the 11th December, 1959, and into the Direct Causes which Led to these Occurrences*. Pretoria: Government Printer.
Green, RH, M-J Kiljunen & K Kiljunen (eds.). 1981. *Namibia. The Last Colony*. London: Longman.
Groth, S (ed.). 1972. 'Kirchliches Handeln oder Politische Aktion? Modell Südwestafrika'. In: *Dokumentationsreihe der Vereinigten Evangelischen Mission*, No.2.

Groves, CP. 1958. *The Planting of Christianity in Africa*, vol. II-IV. London: Lutterworth Press.

Gründer, H. 1982. *Christliche Mission und Deutscher Imperialismus: eine Politische Geschichte ihrer Beziehungen während der Deutschen Kolonialzeit (1884-1914) unter Besonderer Berücksichtigung Afrikas und Chinas.* Paderborn: Schöningh.

Gunther, J. 1955. *Inside Africa.* London: Hamish Hamilton.

Günther, W. 1970. *Von Edinburgh nach Mexico City. Die Ekklesiologischen Bemühungen der Weltmissionskonferenz (1910-1963).* Stuttgart: Evangelischer Missionsverlag.

Hamutenya, H. 1988. 'One Century of Imperialist Occupation and Anti-Colonial Resistance: an Historical Flackback'. In: Wood, B. (ed.) *Namibia 1884-1984: '100 Years of Foreign Occupation; 100 Years of Struggle'*. Readings on Namibia's History and Society: Papers of the International Conference on Namibia 1884-1984, London 10-13 September 1984. London: Namibia Support Committee, in co-operation with the United Nations Institute for Namibia, Lusaka.

Haussleiter, G. 1906. 'Zur Eingeborenenfrage in Deutsch-Südwestafrika'. *Allgemeine Missionszeitschrift,* No. 1, 2.

Hellberg, C-J. 1965. *Missions on a Colonial Frontier West of Lake Victoria. Evangelical Missions in North-West Tanganyika to 1932.* Lund: Studia Missionalia Upsaliensia VI, Gleerups Publisher.

Hellberg, C-J. 1973. *Namibia.* Stockholm: Verbum.

Hellberg, C-J. 1977. *The Prophetic Role of the Church as Experienced in Namibia. Papers in Honour of Barbro Johansson.* Uppsala: The Scandinavian Institute for African Studies/The Swedish Institute of Missionary Research.

Hellberg, C-J. 1978. 'Namibia – Recent Developments'. In: Programme to Combat Racism (PCR) Information Reports and Background Papers, 1. Geneva: WCC/PCR.

Hellberg, C-J. 1979. *A Voice of the Voiceless. The Involvement of the Lutheran World Federation in Southern Africa 1947-1977.* Lund: Studia Missionalia Upsaliensia XXXIV, Verbum Publisher.

Herz, K. 1976. *Two Kingdoms and One World.* Minneapolis, MN: Augsburg Publishing House.

Heywood, A & E Maasdorp (translators). 1995. *The Hendrik Witbooi Papers*, 2nd enlarged ed. Windhoek: National Archives of Namibia.

His Majesty's Stationary Office. 1918. *Report on the Natives of South West Africa and their Treatment by Germany.* London: His Majesty's Stationary Office.

Hoffmann, H. 1991. *Deutsch Südwestafrika wird Mandatsland. Südwester Geschichte, 1914-1925.* Okahandja: Selbstverlag.

Holmberg, Å. 1991. *Historiskt Sampsel mellan Religion och Politik i Sydafrika.* Stockholm: Tro och Politik.

Hubrich, HG & H Melber. 1977. *Namibia – Geschichte und Gegenwart. Zur Frage der Dekolonisation einer Siedlerkolonie.* Bonn: Isa Verlag.

Hunke, H. 1980. *Namibia. The Strength of the Powerless.* Rome: International Documentation and Communication Center.

Hunke, H. 1988. 'The Role of European Missionaries in Namibia'. In: Wood, B. (ed.) *Namibia 1884-1984: '100 Years of Foreign Occupation; 100 Years of Struggle'*. Readings on Namibia's History and Society: Papers of the International Conference on Namibia 1884-1984, London 10-13 September 1984. London: Namibia Support Committee, in co-operation with the United Nations Institute for Namibia, Lusaka.

Hunke, H & J Ellis. 1978. *Torture – a Cancer in our Society.* London: Catholic Institute for International Relations in co-operation with British Council of Churches.

Innes, D. 'South African Capital and Namibia'. In: Green, RH, M-L Kiljunen & K Kiljunen (eds.). 1981. *Namibia. The Last Colony.* London: Longman.

International Institute of Human Rights. 1976. 'Namibia and Human Rights, Past and Future'. *Human Rights Journal, International and Comparative Law,* vol. IX, March 1976.

Irle, J. 1906. *Die Herero. Ein Beitrag zur Landes-, Volkes- und Missionskunde.* Gütersloh: Rheinische Mission.

Jacob, EG (ed.). 1935. *Kolonialpolitisches Quellenheft. Die Deutsche Kolonialfrage, 1918-1935.* Bamberg: CC Büchner Verlag.

Katjavivi, P. 1986. 'The Rise of Nationalism in Namibia and its International Dimensions'. Mimeographed Doctoral thesis. Oxford: St Anthony's College.

Katjavivi, P. 1988a. *A History of Resistance in Namibia.* Paris: UNESCO Press.

Katjavivi, P. 1988b. 'The Development of Anti-Colonial Forces in Namibia'. In: Wood, B. (ed.) *Namibia 1884-1984: '100 Years of Foreign Occupation; 100 Years of Struggle'*. Readings on Namibia's History and Society: Papers of the International Conference on Namibia 1884-1984, London 10-13 September 1984. London: Namibia Support Committee, in co-operation with the United Nations Institute for Namibia, Lusaka.

Katjavivi, P & P Frostin (eds.). 1989. *Church and Liberation of Namibia.* London: James Currey.

Kerina, M. 1958. 'South West Africa and the United Nations'. In: *Africa South,* October-December 1958.

Kiljunen, K. 1981. 'National Resistance and the Liberation Struggle.' In: Green, RH, M-L Kiljunen & K Kiljunen (eds.). 1981. *Namibia. The Last Colony.* London: Longman.

Kjellberg, S. 1972. 'Finsk Mission och Apartheid i Namibia. En Översikt av

Finska Missionssällskapets Inställning till Rassegregation i Sydvästafrika'. *Institutet för Ekumenik och Socialetik vid Åbo Akademi*, Nr. 10.

Kremkau, K. (ed.) 1974. *EKD und Kirchen im Südlichen Afrika. Das Problem der Kirchlichen Einheit im Rassenkonflikt*. Bielefeld: Epd-Dokumentation Band 12, herausgegeben von Hans-Wolfgang Hessler.

Kuntze, L. 1985. 'Die Deutsche Evangelisch-Lutherische Kirche — ihre Entwicklung, ihre Probleme, ihre Hoffnungen'. In: Baumann, J (ed.). 1985. *1884-1984 Vom Schutzgebiet bis Namibia*. Windhoek: Interessengemeinschaft deutschsprachiger Südwester.

Lau, B. 1987. *Namibia in Jonker Afrikaner's Time*. Windhoek: Windhoek Archives Publication Series No. 8.

Lau, B. 1981. 'Thank God! The Germans Came: Vedder and Namibian Historiography.' In: Gottschalk, K & C Sauders (eds.). 1981. *Africa Seminar. Collected Papers*, vol. 2. Cape Town: University of Cape Town.

Lau, B. 1982. 'The Emergence of Kommando Politics in Namaland, Southern Namibia 1800-1870'. Master's thesis. University of Cape Town.

Lau, B (ed.). 1984a. *Carl Hugo Hahn. Tagebücher 1837-1860. Part I: 1837-1845; Part II: 1846-1851. A Missionary in Nama- and Damaraland*. Windhoek: Archives Source Publications Series, Archives Services Division.

Lau, B. 1984b. 'Pre-Colonial Namibia Historiography: What is to be done?' Paper presented at the Conference on Research Priorities in Namibia, Institute of Commonwealth Studies, London, held on 23-25 July 1984.

Lau, B. 1987. *Namibia in Jonker Afrikaner's Time*. Windhoek: Windhoek Archives Publication Series No. 8.

Lau, B (ed.). 1989. *Charles John Andersson's Papers*, vol. 2. Windhoek: Archives Service Division of the Department of National Education of SWA/Namibia.

Lawrie, G. 1964. 'New Light on South West Africa. Some Extracts from and Comments on the Odendaal Report'. In: *African Studies*, vol. 23, No. 3-4. University of Witwatersrand: University Press.

League of Nations. 1919-1946 Annual Reports. *Report by the Government of the Union of South Africa. Government Reports of the Administration of South West Africa*. Geneva: League of Nations Publications.

Lejeune, A. 1971. *The Case for South West Africa*. London: Tom Stacey Ltd.

Leutwein, T. 1908. *11 Jahre in Deutsch-Südwestafrika*, 3. Auflage. Berlin: ES Mittler.

Loth, H. 1963. *Die Christliche Mission in Südwestafrika. Zur Destruktiven Rolle der Rheinischen Missionsgesellschaft beim Prozess der Staatsbildung in Südwestafrika (1942-1893)*. Berlin:Akademie-Verlag.

Lüderitz, CA (ed.). 1945. *Die Erschliessung von Deutsch-Südwestafrika durch Adolf Lüderitz. Akten, Briefe und Denkschriften.* Odenburg: G Stalling Verlag.

Lutheran World Federation. 1952. *The Proceedings of the Second Assembly of the Lutheran World Federation, Hannover, Germany, July 15 – August 3, 1952.* Geneva: Lutheran World Federation.

Lutheran World Federation. 1958. *The Proceedings of the Third Assembly of the Lutheran World Federation, Minneapolis, Minnesota, USA, August 15-25, 1957.* Geneva: Lutheran World Federation.

Mbuende, K. 1986. 'Namibia, the Broken Shield. Anatomy of Imperialism and Revolution'. Doctoral thesis. Malmö: University of Lund.

Mbuende, K. 1989. 'Church and Class Struggle in Namibia'. In: Katjavivi, P & P Frostin (eds.). 1989. *Church and Liberation in Namibia.* London: James Currey.

Menzel, G. 1978. *Die Rheinische Mission. Aus 150 Jahren Missionsgeschichte.* Wuppertal: Verlag der Vereinigten Mission.

Metzges, J. 1959. *Otjimbingwe aus Alten Tagen einer Rheinischen Missionsstation im Hereroland, 1849-1890.* Windhoek: SWA Wissenschaftliche Gesellschaft.

Meyer, F. 1905. *Wirtschaft und Recht der Herero.* Berlin: Springer.

Milly, J, N Kautja, M Oliphant, K Shipingana & D Ridgway. 1990. *An Investigation of the Shooting at the Old Location on 10 December 1959.* Windhoek: University of Namibia, Publication Series 'Discourse'.

Moleah, AT. 1983. *Namibia – the Struggle for Liberation.* Wilmington: Disa Press.

Moorsom, R & WG Clarence-Smith. 1975. 'Underdevelopment and Class Formation in Ovamboland, 1844-1915'. *Journal of African History,* vol. 16, No. 3.

Moritz, E (ed.). 1917. 'Aus den Ältesten Reiseberichten über Deutsch-Südwestafrika'. *Mitteilungen aus den Deutschen Schutzgebieten I-II, 1915-1916.*

Moritz, W. 1981. 'Dr. Heinrich Vedder. Vom Ravensberger Seidenweber zum Berühmten Afrika-Missionar'. *Aus Alten Tagen in Südwest,* 2. Auflage, Heft 8.

Moritz, W. 1988. 'Erlebnisse im Hereroaufstand, 1904'. *Aus Alten Tagen in Südwest,* 3. Auflage, Heft 3.

Morris, J. 1974. 'The Black Workers in Namibia'. In: *The Role of Foreign Firms in Namibia. Studies on External Investment and Black Workers' Conditions in Namibia (South West Africa).* Uppsala: Africa Publications Trust.

Mossolow, N. (year of publication unknown). *Windhoek Damals/This was Old Windhoek.* Windhoek: N Mossolow.

Müller-Hill, B. 1988. *Murderous Science. Elimination by Scientific Selection of Jews, Gypsies and Others, Germany 1933-1945.* Oxford: publisher unknown.

Ngavirue, Z. 1972. 'Political Parties and Interest Groups in South West Africa: a Study of Plural Societies.' Unpublished D Phil thesis. Oxford: St Anthony's College.

Niemüller, G. 1959. *Die Erste Bekenntnissynode der Deutschen Evangelischen Kirche in Barmen,* vol. II. Göttingen: Texte-Dokumente-Berichte.

Oliver, R & J Fage. 1962. *A Short History of Africa.* Harmondsworth: Penguin African Library.

Olpp, J. 1884. *Angra Pequena und Gross-Namaland.* Elbersfeld: Wuppertal-Barmen: Missionsverlag.

Pirio, G. 1984. 'The Role of Garveyanism in the Making of Namibian Nationalism'. In: Wood, B. (ed.) *Namibia 1884-1984: '100 Years of Foreign Occupation; 100 Years of Struggle'*. Readings on Namibia's History and Society: Papers of the International Conference on Namibia 1884-1984, London 10-13 September 1984. London: Namibia Support Committee, in co-operation with the United Nations Institute for Namibia, Lusaka.

Pönninghaus, F. 1933. Der Mangel an Eingeborenen Pastoren in Südwestafrika und sein Grund'. *Rheinische Missionsberichte,* 1933, 109 ff.

Pool, G. 1991. *Samuel Maharero.* Windhoek: Gamsberg Macmillan Publishers.

Rohrbach, P. 1907. *Deutsche Kolonialwirtschaft in Südwestafrika.* Berlin: publisher unknown.

Rust, C. 1905. *Krieg und Frieden im Hererolande.* Publisher and place of publication unknown.

Saunders, C. 1982. 'Towards the Decolonisation of Namibian History. Notes on Some Recent Work in English'. *The Namibian Review,* No. 25, January – March 1983.

Schmidt, WR. 1965. *Mission, Kirche und Reich Gottes bei Friedrich Fabri.* Wuppertal-Barmen: Verlag der Rheinischen Mission.

Schultze, EA. 1932. *Das Eingeborenenrecht.* Berlin: publisher unknown.

Scott, M. 1958. *A Time to Speak.* London: Faber & Faber.

Segal, R. 1962. *African Profiles.* Harmondsworth: Penguin African Library.

Serfontein, JHP. 1976. *Namibia?* Pretoria: Fokus Suid Publishers.

Shejutaamba, N. 1990. 'Church and State in Namibia 1806-1989'. Mimeographed Master's thesis. St Paul, MN: Theological Seminary.

Smuts, D. 1985. 'Notstandgesetze. Wirkung und Folgen'. In: Baumann, J (ed.). 1985. *1885-1984. Vom Schutzgebiet bis Namibia.* Windhoek: Interessengemeinschaft deutschsprachiger Südwester.

Soggot, D. 1986. *Namibia – the Violent Heritage.* London: Rex Collins.

Steer, GL. 1939. *Judgment on German Africa.* London: Hodder & Stoughton.

Stuebel, H. 1953. 'Die Entwicklung des Nationalsozialismus in Südwestafrika'. *Vierteljahrshefte für Zeitgeschichte*, No.1, 1953.

Sundermeier, T. 1973. *Wir aber Suchten Gemeinschaft. Kirchenwerdung und Kirchentrennung in Südwestafrika.* Erlangen: Luther-Verlag Witten, Verlag der Evangelischen Mission.

Sundkler, B. 1948. *Bantu Prophets in South Africa.* London: Lutterworth Library.

Sundkler, B. 1960. *The Christian Ministry in Africa.* Uppsala: Swedish Institute of Missionary Research.

Sundkler, B. 1965. *The World of Mission, Stockholm 1963.* Grand Rapids, MI: Lutterworth Press, WMB Eerdman's Publishing Company.

SWAPO. 1978a. *Information on Namibian Prisoners.* London: SWAPO Department of Information and Publicity, Lusaka.

SWAPO. 1978b. *Information on SWAPO. A Historical Profile.* London: SWAPO Department of Information and Publicity, Lusaka.

Taylor, JV. 1957. *Christianity and Politics in Africa.* Harmondsworth: Penguin Books.

Toivo ya Toivo, AH. 1969. *Statement to the Court during the 1967-8 Terrorism Trial in Pretoria: Trial and Sentencing of Namibians in South Africa.* New York, NY: United Nations.

Tötemeyer, G. 1977. *South West Africa/Namibia. Facts, Attitudes, Assessment and Prospects.* Randburg: Fokus Suid Publishers.

Tötemeyer, G. 1978. *Namibia Old and New: Traditional and Modern Leaders in Ovamboland.* New York, NY: St Martin's Press.

Troup, F. 1950. *In Face of Fear. Michael Scott's Challenge to South Africa.* London: Faber & Faber.

Tshongwa, A. 1961. 'The Task of the Church of Christ in Africa Today'. In: Department of World Mission, Lutheran World Federation. 1961. *Antsirabé, A Record of the Second All-Africa Lutheran Conference, Antsirabé, Madagascar, September 8-18, 1960.* Geneva: Lutheran World Federation.

United Nations. 1974. *A Trust Betrayed: Namibia.* New York, NY: United Nations Publication.

Vedder, H. 1929. 'Maharero und Seine Zeit im Lichte der Dokumente Seines Nachlasses'. *Journal, South West Africa Society*, V.

Vedder, H. 1966. *South West Africa in Early Times.* New York, NY: Barnes & Noble.

Vigne, R. 1973. *A Dwelling Place of our Own. The Story of the Namibian Nation.* London: International Defence and Aid Fund.

Von François, C. 1899. *Deutsch Südwestafrika. Geschichte der Kolonisation bis zum Ausbruch des Krieges mit Witbooi, April 1893.* Berlin: Reimer.

Von François, H (ed.). 1895. *Nama und Damara, Deutsch Südwest-Afrika.*

Magdeburg: E Baensch Verlag.
Von Rohden, L. 1888. *Geschichte der Rheinischen Missionsgesellschaft*. Barmen: Missionsverlag.
Walker, EA. 1935. *A History Of Southern Africa*, 2nd ed. Cape Town: Maskew Miller.
Wehler, HU. 1976. *Bismarck und der Imperialismus*, 3rd ed. München: Deutscher Taschenbuchverlag.
Wehler, HU. 1991. *Det Tyska Kejsarriket 1871-1918*. Stockholm: publisher unknown.
Wellington, JH. 1967. *South West Africa and its Human Issues*. London: Oxford University Press.
Werner, W. 1988. 'Struggles in the Namibian Countryside 1915-1950: some Preliminary Notes'. In: Wood, B (ed.). *Namibia 1884-1984: '100 Years of Foreign Occupation; 100 Years of Struggle'*. Readings on Namibia's History and Society: Papers of the International Conference on Namibia 1884-1984, London 10-13 September 1984. London: Namibia Support Committee, in co-operation with the United Nations Institute for Namibia, Lusaka.
Wienecke, WA. 1955. *Geschichte der Selbständigkeitbewegung der Herero*. Unpublished manuscript. Windhoek: Church Archives.
Wienecke, WA. 1962. 'Die Gemeinschaft der Ahnen und die Gemeinde Jesus Christi bei den Herero'. Mimeographed Master's thesis. Hamburg: Missionsakademie.
Williams, F-N. 1991. *Precolonial Communities of Southwestern Africa. A History of Owambo Kingdoms 1600-1920*. Windhoek: National Archives of Namibia, No.16.
Winter, C. 1977. *Namibia. The Story of a Bishop in Exile*. London: Lutterworth Press.
Winter, C. 1981. *The Breaking Process*. Suffolk: Namibia Institute.
Witbooi, H. 1982. *Afrika den Afrikanern! Aufzeichnungen eines Nama-Häuptlings aus der Zeit der Deutschen Eroberung Südwestafrikas 1884 bis 1894*. Ed. by Reinhard, W. Berlin: Verlag JH Dietz.
Wolf, B. 1985. 'Wir sind noch Unterwegs. Die Katholische Kirche in Namibia'. In: Baumann, J (ed.). 1985. *1884-1984. Vom Schutzgebiet bis Namibia*. Windhoek: Interessengemeinschaft deutschsprachiger Südwester.
Wood, B (ed.). 1984. *Namibia 1884-1984: '100 Years of Foreign Occupation; 100 Years of Struggle'*. Readings on Namibia's History and Society: Papers of the International Conference on Namibia 1884-1984, London 10-13 September 1984. London: Namibia Support Committee, in co-operation with the United Nations Institute for Namibia, Lusaka.
World Council of Churches. 1988. *The Way to Namibian Independence. UN Resolution 435*. Geneva: Programme to Combat Racism.

Archival Records

National Archives (NA) of Namibia

General file marked 'Matters relating to Missionaries 1919- ':
Repatriation of German Missionaries 1919-1920.
Confidential Letters re Repatriation of Enemy Subjects 1919-1920.
Other Matters Related to Missionaries 1921- .
II.I.30b. General file 1919-1920, containing letters, memos, affidavits, etc.
ADM/42: Correspondence 1915-1920, 1924-1939.
    File No. 550/2: Protestant Ministers (German) Conferences.
    File No. 542: Grants to Rhenish and Roman Catholic Missions.
    Letter from the Magistrate, Lüderitz, to the Administrator, Windhoek; undated.
    Correspondence, Rehoboth Magistrate to the Secretary of South West Afica, Rehoboth, 30 October 1925.
ADM/105: Native Unrest.
    File No. 3353: Hottentots-Bondelswarts and Others – including a number of letters marked 'Confidential', 1917- .
    File No. C297: SWA Inhabitants, Natinality of: 17 November 1921.
    File No. C300: Commission of Inquiry, Bondelswarts Uprising, 1922-1923.

LAND 27009, vol. 2 – 27011, vol. 1.5905: Religious General 1920-
ADM/145: Correspondence 1915-1924. Native Unrest, Kaokoveld, etc.
ADM/146-C331: Correspondence 1918. Illegeal Traffic in Arms and Ammunition.
NAW 21/15: Burial of Chief Samuel Maharero.
L.563-571: German Evangelical Lutheran Church 1930- .
    Letter from N Houcke to S Bingane, Sehitwa, Botswana: 17 June 1946.
Finnish Missionary Society file.
File containing acts and laws: Native Administration Proclamation No. 11 (1922).
    Constitution for South West Africa, Union Act 42 (1925).
    Proclamation No. 15 (1928).
    Act No. 38 (1928).
    Emergency regulations 201 (1939).
    Government Gazette of South Africa: 1947.
    Act No. 23 (1949).
    Odendaal Report of 1964. *Report of the Commission of Inquiry into South West Africa Affairs 1962-1963*, R.P. No. 12 (1964).
File containing newspaper excerpts: *Allgemeine Zeitung*, of 15 May 1924: declaration of rebellion by Baster leader Jacobus Beukes.

Die Evangelische Kolonialhilfe, vol. 30, 1925.
25 Jahre Christuskirche in Windhoek. Festschrift zum 25jährigen Kirchenjubiläum im Oktober 1935.
Other: Private diary of the Resident Commissioner: extract, 6 February 1917.
Reports, League of Nations, Permanent Mandatd Commission, 1926-1937.
UN General Assembly Resolution 65(I) of 14 December 1946.
Tötemeyer, G. 1975. Unpublished paper delivered in January 1975 at the summer school of the Unicersity of Cape Town.

Church Archives (CA): Evangelical Lutheran Church in Namibia (ELCRN)

Missionary Conferences – Church Synods:
I.1.1-7: Minutes of the Missionary Conferences 1844-1925.
I.1.8-11: Supplements to the Minutes 1860-1899.
I.1.12: Losses during the Wars of 1904-1907.
I.1.22-27: Minutes of the Missionary Conferences 1906-1937.
I.1.30: Minutes of the Missionary Conferences 1937-1952.
I.1.31-37: Minutes of the Missionary Conferences 1952-1964.
    File titled 'Oruuano – Doppelamt, 1955-1956'.
I.1.40: Supplements to the Conference Minutes 1901-1905.
I.1.43-47: Missionary Conferences 1911-1923.
Internal Administration ('Innere Verwaltung'):
1.1-6: Preses – Inspector: Correspondence 1888-1932.
1.8-1.45: Letters from Missionaries 1907-1927.
1.1.48: Lists of Inhabitants 1909-1914.
1.5.1-4: Statistics and Annual/Quarterly Reports 1906-1964.
1.46-55: Letters from Preses to Missionaries 1909-1920.
1.56-65: Letters from Preses to Missionaries continued 1921-1927.
1.66-74: Other Correspondence.
XIX Church Leadership: 'Evangelistenkonferenz 1948'.
    Minutes of meeting with Hosea Kutako ('Referat: Besprechung mit Hosea Kutako'), 25 November 1950, and notes of subsequent meetings with Kutako.
Correspondence: Preses:
2.1-4.7: Preses – Inspector: copies of correspondence 1911-1954.
Correspondence: Preses with Wuppertal-Barmen:
5.1.-30: listed under correpondents' names 1880-1936.
    Correpsondence with Wuppertal-Barmen, 1911-1954.
    Correspondence: Preses with Wuppertal-Barmen, 1953-1963.
II.5.7: 'Briefe u.a. an den Direktor, 1913-1924'.

II.9.7-9: Vedder, Correspondence, 1938.
Vedder, Correspondence, 1939-1947.
Circular letters: Preses:
6.1-7: by Olpp, Vedder, Diehl, 1911-1964.
Reports of Visitations:
8.1-4: for the years 1909, 1913, 1940, 1950, and 1957.
Correspondence with the government ('Behördenschreiben von und an das Gouvernement'):
11.1-16: 1893-1938.
Correspondence, other: Correspondence: VonTrotha – Missionary Kuhlmann, 8 December 1904.
Correspondence: Von Bülow to the Board of the Mission, 7 June 1904.
Correspondence: Con Bülow to Inspector Haussleiter, 8 December 1904.
Government Reports on the Administration of South West Africa: Filing cabinet No. XIV: for the year 1922.
I file XIV: History of Namibia 1885-1887.
File containing newspaper excerpts: *Reichtagsdenkschrift*, Berlin, 28 November 1904.
IX.1-6: *Evangelisches Gemeindeblatt für Deutsch-Südwestafrika.*
IX.1.7-13: *Deutsch-Südwestafrikanische Zeitung* and *Swakopmunder Zeitung* of 2 December 1914: copy of the lecture on 'The Black Danger' by German ex-major to the Deutsche Kolonialgesellschaft, in 1913.
Lüderitzbuchter Zeitung of 7 December 1912: article by 'A German farmer' on the consequences of increased police intervention on behalf of black employees.
Swakopmunder Zeitung of 12 November 1938.
Other: Reichskolonialamt: 'Akten betr. der Pfarrers Dr Büttner', vol. II, file 1469, December 1885.
Reichskolonialamt: 'Akten betr. der Kämpfe zwischen den Nama und Herero', vol. III, file 2130, 17 November 1890.
Quarterly Notes, *Bulletin of the International Missionary Council* (IMC).
From the Von Trotha family archives: *Militärischer Werdegang des Lothar von Trotha.*

Lutheran World Federation (LWF) Archives, Geneva

Agenda and Minutes:
Commission on World Mission, 1948-1966.
Commission on World Mission, Executive Committee, 1960-1966.
Commission on World Mission, Committee on Southern Africa, 1953-1966.
Committee of Lutheran Missions/SA, 1948-1965.

Committee of Churches on Lutheran Foundation, 1960-1965.
Correspondence Files:
Department of World Mission, General Correspondence; Reading Files; South African Correspondence; Reports on Staff Visits, 1949-1966.
Commission on World Service:
WS/I.2: General Director – Delegation, May – December 1962, Southern Africa.
WS/v.1: South Africa, General Correspondence, 1962-1966.

Index

A

Addis Ababa 231
/Ae//gams 30, 31, 32, 34, 48, 49, 50, 51, 57, 58, 283. See also Windhoek
African Improvement Society 174
African Methodist Episcopal Church (AMEC) 242, 244, 253, 255, 259
African National Congress (ANC) 173, 225
Afrikaner 33
/Ae//gams 31
Afrikaner, Christian 56
Afrikaner, Jager 25, 48
Afrikaner, Jan Jonker 57, 58, 61, 62, 63, 66, 71, 84, 91, 93
Afrikaner, Jonker 26, 29, 30, 32, 33, 35, 36, 49, 53, 54, 56, 67, 88, 93, 97, 283
/Ae//gams 49, 50, 283
alliance with Tjamuaha and Kahitjene 32, 33, 49, 52
Andersson, Charles John 56
clashes with the Hereros 29, 30, 32, 34, 55, 66, 284
expedition to Ovambo territories 52, 56, 70
leading the Oorlam-Namas to Namibia 35
preaching to the Hereros 47
relations with the Rhenish missionaries 34, 49, 50, 51, 52, 55, 69, 70, 171
road to Walvis Bay 31
trade with the Cape 33, 36
Alexander, Captain James 29
All-Africa Convention 225
All-Africa Lutheran Conference, Antsirabé

Auala, Leonard 274
Tshongwe, Alexander 274
All-Africa Lutheran Conference, Marangu 258
Amakutuwe, Jason 272
Angula, Efraim 272
Auala, Leonard 272
Amakutuwe, Jason 272
AMEC. See African Methodist Episcopal Church
ANC. See African National Congress
Andersson, Charles John 52, 61, 70, 284
alliance with Maharero and the Hereros 53, 56, 95
and Jonker Afrikaner 56
and the Rhenish Mission 55, 69
contact with Ovamboland 58, 70
Anglican Mission 181
arrival in Namibia 215
in Windhoek 215
Ovamboland 210, 215
loyalty to the South African government 215
South African racial policy 214
Angola 55, 58, 70, 84
border with Namibia 5, 181
Roman Catholic Mission 137, 155, 214
trade with 7
Angra Pequena 22, 82, 84. See also Lüderitz
Angula, Efraim 272
Antsirabé 275. See also All-African Lutheran Conference, Antsirabé
Apartheid 233. See also Racialism
Auala, Leonard 277, 278
Baster supremacy 262
Church, the 275

Finnish Missionary Society 269, 278
Folkchurch, the 287
German Namibians (white vote) 232
homelands 277
indigenous churches 257, 270, 271, 272, 274, 279
Katutura 234
Ministry of Bantu Affairs 261
Mission 241, 248, 251, 252, 254, 256, 260, 261
missionaries 262
National Party 228
Odendaal Commission 277
opposition of Lutheran Church 277
Oruuano Church, the 257
Ovambo-Kavango Church 272
Paulinum 276
Rhenish Mission 276
  the federal church 286
San people 10
separate development 234, 262
UN, the 231
unified church, a 257
Vedder, Heinrich 251, 252, 253
Archbell, John 29
Auala, Leonard 268, 271, 272, 273, 274, 275, 276, 277
  anniversary of the Finnish Missionary Society 273
  becoming bishop 276
  Declaration of Human Rights 277
  first African leader of the church 273
  first contact with the UN 277
  homelands 277, 278
  Odendaal Commission 277
  resistance to apartheid 278
  South African government 277
  SWAPO 279, 287
  Toivo ya Toivo, Andimba H 273, 279
  UN Commission for South West Africa 277
  Verwoerd, Prime Minister 273
Australia 162

B

Basters 66, 85

apartheid 261, 262
  German treaty of 1885 110, 154
  Maharero, Samuel 110, 111
  military assistance of 111
  military resistance to Germans 154, 155
  supremacy 262
  under South African rule 180, 182, 183
Bechuanaland. See also Botswana
  Herero escape 117
  Morenga, Jakob 115
Benson, Mary 230
  Scott, Rev Michael 230
Bergdamaras. See also Damara people
Berlin 40, 62, 64, 65, 75, 79, 82, 83, 84, 85, 88, 93, 98, 104, 108, 112, 113, 114, 128, 129, 206
  colonial congress, 1906 121
  Commission on World Mission (CWM) 274
  CWM 275
  general staff 113, 115
  parliament in 116
Berlin Congress of 1884-1885 138
  division of Africa 6, 77, 79, 80, 84, 86, 97
  freedom of religion 214
Berlin III 43. See also Evangelische Missionsgesellschaft für Deutsch-Ostafrika -
  Bethanie 48, 83
  Cornelius of 115
  Missionary Schmelen, Johan Heinrich 29, 48
Beukes, Jacobus 182
Beukes, Petrus 154
Beves, General 148
Beyers, General 146
Blecher, Missionary 154
Blue Book 149, 167, 200
Board of the (Rhenish) Mission 62, 119, 134, 153, 156, 175, 196, 198, 201, 206, 211, 220, 240, 241, 243, 245, 248, 249, 250, 251, 270, 272, 276, 278, 286. See also Wuppertal-Barmen

Board of the Finnish Missionary Society 210, 273. *See also* Finnish Missionary Society
Boer War 111, 142, 146, 147, 148, 181, 197
Boers 18, 25, 54
  clashes with the Oorlam-Namas 18, 25, 282, 283
  Germans during WWI, and the 142, 147
  Great Trek, the 23
  Hofmeyr, Administrator GR 163
  immigrants to Namibia 24, 63, 128, 146, 181
  influence of the British administration 23, 24, 146
  Union invasion of German South West Africa 146, 147
  Union military, in 196
  white supremacy 146
Bondelswarts 150, 169, 177. *See also* Nama people
  Knudsen, Hans Christian 48
  Morenga, Jakob 112
  Schneuwee, Hendrik 177
  under South African rule 177
  uprising 1903 111
  uprising, May 1922 177
    Christian, Jakobus 177
    Morris, Abraham 177
Botha, General Louis 146, 161
Botswana 115, 168, 169, 180, 185, 186, 225, 226, 227. *See also* Bechuanaland
Brincker, Missionary 92, 93
British Cape Colony
  harbour sites in Namibia 24
Burial, 1923, of Maharero, Samuel 144, 185
  Rhenish Mission, the 197
  Vedder, Heinrich 187, 205
Bushmen. *See also* San people
Büttner, Missionary 64, 87, 88, 89, 90, 91
Buxton, Lord 168

C

Caô, Diego 22

Cape Colony 47, 50, 54, 64, 89
  British administration 23, 24, 67
  Dutch, the 23, 24, 63
  escape of Morenga, Jakob 112, 115
  Ethiopian Church 119
  missionaries from the 29
  Oorlam-Namas, the 3, 282, 284
  Rhenish Mission, the 282
  trade with 6, 35, 64, 97
  traders from 2, 136
Cape Cross 22
Cape Town 18, 24, 29, 35, 47, 49, 50, 61, 62, 63, 64, 65, 67, 70, 82, 83, 84, 85, 86, 89, 91, 94, 96, 97, 166, 168, 233, 239, 273, 283, 284
Caprivi 12
Caprivians 12
Cattle plague 12, 56, 104, 105, 106, 109, 110, 136
CCLF. *See* Council of Churches on Lutheran Foundation
Charter of Human Rights, UN 228. *See also* United Nations
Christian,
  Jacobus 169, 177, 178, 179
Christian Western civilization 39, 66, 112, 188, 208
Christuskirche 201, 203, 217. *See also* German Evangelical Church
Coetze, Jakob 22
Commission on World Mission (CWM) 247, 274
Committee of the International Missionary Council (IMC) 247
Conference of 1870. *See also* Peace Conference of 1870
Conference of Churches on Lutheran Foundation, 195
  Auala, Leonard 270
  Eriksson, Birger 270
Cornelius of Bethanie. *See* Bethanie
Council of Churches on Lutheran Foundation (CCLF) 276
CWM. *See* Commission on World Mission (CWM)

D

Damara people. *See also* Bergdamaras 12
Darwinism and pan-Germanism 80
de Clue, John 172
De Wet, Minister of Justice of the Union 165
Department of World Service 275, 276
Dernburg, Bernhard 131
Deutsche Kolonialgesellschaft 129. *See also* German Colonial Association
Deutsche Kolonialgesellschaft für Südwestafrika
  Lüderitz, Adolf 87
Deutscher Kolonialverein
  Fürst zu Hohenlohe-Langenburg, Hermann 79
Diamonds 123, 128
Dias Bartolomeu 22
Diehl, Hans Karl
  Missionary 90
  Preses 243, 245, 246, 248, 249, 254, 255, 256, 257, 258, 260, 262, 272

E

East Africa 40
  origin of the Nama People 16
  Union troops in 148
Ebner, Johann Leonard 25
Eich, Preses Wilhelm 135, 155, 156
  return of banished Rhenish missionaries 157
Engela. *See also* Finnish Missionary Society
  Ovambo-Kavango Church synod, the 271
Eriksson, Birger 271, 272
Ethiopianism 171, 175, 184, 186
  Athlyi 171
  Cape Province 178
  Douglas, Angel 171
  Piley 171
Europe 23, 40, 43, 78
  Union troops in WWI 148

Europeans 4, 19, 43, 47, 48, 52, 54, 55, 57, 59, 98, 103, 104, 136
  appeal to colonial powers 5, 53, 61, 62, 64, 284
  explorers 55, 69
  Herero chieftainship 14
  precolonial contacts 33, 34, 35, 36, 37, 283
Evangelical Church of the Reich
  Müller, Ludvig 203
Evangelical Lutheran Church of South West Africa 261
Evangelische Missionsgesellschaft für Deutsch-Ostafrika
  Peters, Carl 40
Explorers 18, 36
  Andersson, Charles John 70

F

Fabri, Friedrich 42, 65, 82, 86. *See also* Christian Western civilization
  demand for overseas protection 62, 64, 65, 66, 67
  German Colonial Association, the 41
  Rhenish Mission, the 40, 41
Finnish Missionary Society 71, 76, 144, 151, 210. *See also* Board of the Finnish Missionary Society
  colonialism 152
  criticism from Hahn, Major Carl 212
  education 209, 212, 213
  Engela 210
  establishment in Ovamboland 110
  Folkchurch 207, 271, 287
    and Apartheid 269
  German colonialism 132, 137
  hospital 209
  Kavango 210
  Major Manning 156
  membership 151
  Ovambo pastors 268
  Ovambo-Kavango Church 213, 221
  Ovamboland 208, 211
  printing shop 209
  Rhenish Mission's influence 209
Fish River
  Namas living near the 16

Index

Folkchurch 76, 207
  critism from Hahn, Major Carl 213
  Ovambo Church 207
  Ovambo People 207, 213, 287
  Rhenish Mission, the 207
  Sumatra, Sister mission in 207
  SWAPO 221
Fort Namutoni. *See* Namutoni

G

Galton, Francis 55
  contact with Ovamboland 70
Games 30
Garvey, Marcus 171
Garveyanism 144, 171, 175, 176
  Ethiopianism 171
  Garvey, Marcus 174, 180
  Lüderitz 172
  UNIA 171
  uprising inspired by 174, 176, 178
  West Indies, in the 172
Gehlmann, Missionary Hermann 155
German Colonial Association 86. *See also* Deutsche Kolonialgesellschaft
German colonization 18, 19, 20, 59, 82, 83, 87, 88, 93, 123
  appeal by the Rhenish Mission 53
  Mission, and 87
  threat of Witbooi, Hendrik 88, 89, 91
German East Africa 81, 112, 161. *See also* Evangelische Missionsgesellschaft für Deutsch-Ostafrika
German empire 44, 74, 77
  rise of 77
German Evangelical Church
  Christuskirche 129
  constitution of the German synod 259
German military 91, 94, 96, 102, 110
  Leutwein, Theodor 111
  Maharero, Samuel 109, 110, 111
  Morenga, Jakob 112
  Roman Catholic Mission, the 138
  under South African occupation 147, 152
German Namibian Wars. *See also* Namibian wars of 1904-1907 98, 138
German South West Africa 79, 81, 86, 98, 138, 146, 147, 148, 152, 157, 202, 204, 222. *See also* Deutsche Kolonialgesellschaft
German South West African Company 136
Germanism
  Fabri, Friedrich 42
  missionary congress, Berlin, 1886 40
  under South African rule 199, 200, 201
Gibeon 30, 88, 89, 91, 94, 101, 109
Gobabis 169, 180
  Nikodemus 100, 101
Gochas
  Namas living at 16
Gorges, Sir Hugho 148, 196
Göring, Heinrich Ernst 91, 93, 94
  protection treaty with Maharero 90, 94
  Rhenish Mission, and the 89, 91
Gowaseb, Preses 277, 278
Great Namaqualand 282. *See also* Namaqualand
Gulin, Eelias 276

H

Hahn, Carl Hugo 32, 33, 34, 49, 50, 51, 57, 58, 61, 64
  Afrikaner, Jonker 47, 49, 50, 69
  influence on the Finnish Missionary Society 209
  Ovamboland 70
Hahn, Major Carl
  Ovamboland 211
  criticism of Finnish Missionary Society 212, 213
  opposition to Mission 212, 213
Hasenkamp, Missionary
  eviction by South Africans 155
  mixed marriages 135
Haussleiter, Gottlob 119, 120, 121, 122, 123, 124, 125, 126, 132, 134, 135

Headley, Fritz 172
Helsinki 156
 Centenary celebrations
  Auala's invitation 273
  Tarkanon, Natti 208
  Vapaavoori, Martti 208, 271
Herbst, Major JF 179
Herero people 91, 94
 Christuskirche 129
 contact with the Oorlam-Namas
  55, 56, 57, 85, 91, 93
 culture and history 13, 285
 election of chieftain after Maharero's
  death 95, 100
 election of Hosea Kutako 168
 escape to the Omaheke region 122
 Garveyanism 175, 176
 Herero Day 227
 Maharero in exile 185
 Maharero, Samuel's
  burial 144, 286
 Namibian Wars of 1904-1907
  109, 112, 113, 120
 Oruuano Church 244, 257
 relations with the Rhenish Mission
  49, 69, 70, 95, 105, 106, 117,
  120, 175, 186, 253, 254, 255,
  257, 259
 SWANU 220, 233
 under South African rule 169
 under Union of South Africa occupation 149
 Von Trotha 114, 116
 wars with the Namas 32, 34, 35,
  65, 66, 284
Hereroland 4, 15, 30, 54, 62, 100
Hertzog, Prime Minister James 197
Hitler, Adolf 145, 202
 Vedder, Heinrich 205
Hoachanas 30, 36
 Namas living near 16
Hofmeyr, Administrator GR 163, 166,
  168, 176, 180
 Bondelswarts uprising 179
 citizenship of Germans in Namibia
  165
 Native Reserves Commission 193
 Paramount Chief of the Natives
  195

Hoornkrantz 93
Hop, Hendrik 22
Hottentot 176. *See also* Nama people
Hoveka, Nikanor 246
Hoveka, Stefanus 255
Hukka, Alppo 272, 273
Hunters and explorers 6, 18, 36

I

IMC. *See* International Missionary Council
India 22, 225
International Court of Justice 229, 231
International Missionary Council 247
Ipumbu, Chief 175, 195
Irle, Rev 14, 17

J

Johannesburg 226
Jordan, William 136
Juva, Mikka 272, 275, 276

K

Kahimemua 15
 attack on Germans 101
 execution 102
Kahitjene
 Afrikaner, Jonker 32, 49, 69
Kalahari Desert 7, 169
Kambazembi 15
Kambone, Chief 136
Kaokolanders 13
Kaokoveld 14
 Namas in Kaokoveld 16
Kapuuo, Clemens
 Kutako, Hosea 173
 SWANU 233
Kavango people 76, 287
 culture and history 12
Keetmanshoop 22, 30, 101, 111,
  138, 152, 200, 214, 242
 Namas living near 16
Kerina, Mburumba
 SWAPO 234

312 Index

Kerina, Mburumba *continued*
  UN, the 231
Kersten, Missionary 256
Khama, Tshekedi 226
Khoikhoi. *See also* Nama people
Khoisan. *See also* San people
Khorab 147, 148, 152, 154, 157
Klein Windhoek. *See also* /Ae//gams 30
Kleinschmidt, Hans Heinrich 32, 49
Knudsen, Hans Christian 32
  Bondelswarts, the 48
  Rhenish Mission,
    the 48, 49, 50, 51
Kozonguizi, Hariretundu 233
Kubis Mountains 154
Kuhlmann, Missionary 176
Kunene River 55
Kutako, Hosea 168, 169, 285, 286
  All-Africa Convention 225
  efforts to approach UN 224, 225
  forced removals 194, 234
  Kapuuo, Clemens 233
  Konzonguizi, Hariretundu 233, 234
  leader of liberation movement 233
  Maharero, Samuel 175, 185
    burial of 187
  Native Reserves Commission,
    the 246
  Orruuano Church, the 257
  referendum of 1945-1946 227
  request for USA and UK protection
    in 1946 225
  Rhenish Mission, the 254, 255
  Scott, Rev Michael 226, 251
    prayer 227
  South Africa blocks invitation to
    UN 230
  SWANU 221, 233
  UNIA 173, 186
Kwanyamas
  Finnish Mission, the 156, 210
  Mandume, Chief 151, 155, 207
  South African-Portuguese retribution 151, 181, 207

L

Landesprobst 145, 200, 201, 203,
204, 206
Landesverband der deutschen Schulvereine 163
League of Nations
  Basters, the 183
  creation of the UN
    and Smuts, Jan Christian 222
  Ethiopia and Liberia 231
  mandate 143, 160, 162, 168
  Mandate Commission of 143
  Nazi Germany 202
  Oruuano Church, the 221
  sacred trust and South Africa 193
  Smuts, Jan Christian 161, 164
    citizenship of German
    Namibians 164, 166
  South African stance post
    WWII 162, 195, 224
  UNIA 172
  Wilson, President of the USA 161
Leutwein, Theodor 98, 99, 100, 112, 177, 285
  agreement with
    Witbooi 100, 101, 109
  Morenga, Jakob 112
  Namibian wars of 1904-1907
    war 111, 112, 122
  Rhenish Mission, the 100, 138
  Von Trotha, and 113
  war against Witbooi, Hendrik 100
  Witbooi, Hendrik 115, 119
Liberation movements 220, 240
  Church, and the 279
  Garveyanism 220
  Rhenish Mission, and the 248
Liberation struggle
  Rhenish Mission 213
  traditional leaders 220
  UN, the 222
London 62, 65, 68, 82, 84, 85, 166, 202, 226
London Missionary Society (LMS) 25, 29, 51
  paving way 26
Lüderitz 7, 128, 130, 142, 150
  Angra Pequena 22
  arrival of the Germans 1
  arrival of the Union troops 147
  Garveyanism 172, 173

Index   313

Lüderitz, Adolf   82, 86
  role in German colonization of
    Namibia   82, 83, 84
Lutheran
  Church   145, 261, 274, 275, 276,
    277, 279
  LWF   247, 261
Lutheran World Federation (LWF)   247,
  258, 261, 274, 277, 278, 288
  Auala, Leonard   272, 275, 276
  Mützelfeldt, Bruno   275
  Pederson, Ruben   275
  Schmidt-Clausen, Kurt   275
LWF. See Lutheran World Federation

M

Maharero   284
  alliance with the Europeans   52,
    53, 61, 62, 63, 71, 85, 90,
    91, 94
  conflict with Afrikaner, Jan
    Jonker   66
  death of   95, 96
  letter from Witbooi   94
  negotiations with German
    colonizers   66, 85, 89, 90, 94
  paramount chieftainship   95, 285
  quarrel with Witbooi at Osana   88,
    90
  treaty with Witbooi, Hendrik   89
  war with the Namas   91
Maharero, Frederick   175, 226, 227
  Scott, Rev Michael   226
Maharero, Samuel   14, 52, 56, 95, 103
  alcohol dependence   105
  alliance with Europeans   56, 57,
    58, 285
  Basters, the   110, 111
  cattle plague   105
  death of   186
  defeat   114
  escape to Omaheke   113
  execution of Nikodemus   102
  exile   168, 180, 185
  fight for land   101, 102, 106
  funeral   184, 185, 187, 188,
    197, 205, 245, 255, 286
  Kutako, Hosea   168, 175
  negotiations with German

  colonizers   113
Ovambo people, the   110, 111
paramount
  chieftainship   52, 58, 100, 124,
    285
South Africans, the   168, 185
wars of 1904-1907   109, 110,
  111, 112, 185
Waterberg   112, 113
Witbooi, Hendrik   111
Maharero, Travyatt   173
Malan, Daniel F   228, 232
Namibian Germans   247, 252
UN, the   229, 230
Manasse   90
Mandate Commission of the League of
  Nations   162, 166, 182, 183,
  195, 212
Mandatories of the League of Nations
  161
Mandatory administration   144, 162,
  168, 170, 222
Mandume, Chief   155, 207
  Pritchard, Major   151
  southern Angola   151
Manning, Major   156
Marangu   259, 272. See also All-Africa
  Lutheran Conference, Marangu
Mbanderus   15. See also Herero people
Menzel, Gustav   248, 251, 252, 253
Middle East   161, 162
Milk, Missionary Otto   252, 253
Mining   9, 84, 86
  copper   128
  Walvis Bay Mining Comany   56
Minor Namaqualand   6. See also
  Namaqualand
Mission hospital   133
Mission printing press   209, 269
Missionaries   2, 3, 4, 5, 5-18, 20,
  25, 26, 29, 31, 33, 36, 40, 43,
  46, 47, 48, 49, 50, 74, 75, 81,
  84, 85, 87, 88, 89, 92, 95, 98,
  99, 103, 104, 105, 109, 110,
  111, 118, 119, 120, 126, 132,
  133, 136, 137, 138, 144, 145,

Missionaries *continued*
150, 153, 155, 156, 157, 163, 174, 175, 182, 184, 185, 186, 187, 188, 194, 196, 197, 198, 199, 200, 201, 202, 203, 204, 205, 207, 208, 209, 210, 212, 213, 219, 220, 228, 238, 239, 240, 241, 242, 243, 244, 248, 249, 250, 251, 253, 255, 257, 258, 259, 260, 261, 262, 268, 269, 270, 273, 274, 278, 283, 284, 286
mixed marriages 134
Missionary conference of 1906 43
Missionary conference of 1913 136
Missionary conference of 1926 198
Missionary conference of 1935 204
Missionary conference of 1947, emergency 243
Missionary conference of 1948 245, 248
Missionary conference of 1950 253
Missionary conference of 1952 256
Missionary conference of 1955 258
Missionary conference of 1960 262
Mixed marriages 134, 135
Morenga, Jakob
  Morris Abraham 177, 179
  Morris and Cornelius of Bethanie 115
  Namibian wars of 1904-1907 112, 115
  Witbooi, Hendrik 115
Morris, Abraham 115, 169, 177, 178, 179
Müller, Ludvig 203
Mungunda, Aaron 173
Mützelfeldt, Bruno 275

N

Nama Church 241, 253, 258
Nama parishes 238, 241, 242
Nama people
  Afrikaners 5
  culture and history 15, 16
  invasion by the Oorlam-Namas 2, 20, 25, 28, 29, 31
  liberation movement 173
  Oorlam-Namas 10
  Roman Catholic Mission 138
  wars with the Hereros 244
Nama-Damara region 3
Namaqualand
  Great 6, 7, 282
  Minor 6
Namib Desert 6, 21, 22
Namibia 18, 22, 24, 25
  boundaries 3
  culture and history 1
  literature on 1, 2
  mandated territory, as a 143, 160, 193, 224
  name, the 22
  Oorlam-Nama invasion, the 25, 26
Namibian nationalism 257
  Nama parishes 241
  Oruuano Church, the 244
Namibian wars of 1904-1907 98, 138, 154, 168, 174, 185, 188, 194, 196, 214, 219, 282
Namutoni 5, 110, 112, 136
National Movement of Liberation 219
National Party (NP) 203, 204, 229, 232, 247, 257, 260, 269
  apartheid 228
Native Administration Proclamation of 1922 168
Native Reserves Commission 193
Naukluft Mountains
  Witbooi's camp 100
Nautilus 84
Nazi Party 202, 203, 204, 206, 286
Nazism 80, 145, 202
  Pönninghaus, Missionary 206
Nazism in Namibia
  Hitlerjugend, the 202
  local Führer, the 202
  uniforms 202
  Vedder, Heinrich 205
  Von Oelhafen, Herman 203, 204
  Wackwitz, Dr 203
Ndonga people 212

Nehale, Chief 112, 136
New Zealand 162
Nikodemus 95
  attack on the Germans 101
  direct line of descent 95
  execution 102
  Maharero, Samuel 15, 100
NP. *See* National Party
Nujoma, Sam
  OPO 234
  SWAPO 274

O

Oasib, Chief 30, 33, 35
Odendaal Commission 277
Okahandja 33, 34, 35, 52, 55, 56, 58, 61, 62, 66, 90, 91, 95
  Auala, Leonard 268
  Maharero, Samuel's burial 144 184, 186, 205, 245, 286
  Namibian wars of 1904-1907 109, 111
  Nikademus' trial 102
  Rhenish Mission, the 69, 71, 95, 103, 258
  treaty between Maharero and the Germans 90
Okaukwejo 136
Olpp, Missionary Johannes 139, 150
  on colonialism 150
  Preses 196, 197, 205
  eviction by the South Africans 154, 155
  on nationality 153
  Witbooi's baptism 88
Omaheke 113
Omaheke region 114
Omaruru 137, 200
  Namibian wars of 1904-1907 111
Omupando 139
Onandjokwe
  mission hospital 209, 269
Ondangwa 70, 136
  Major Manning 156
  Namibian wars of 1904-1907 111
Oniipa

Toivo ya Toivo, Andimba H 233, 273
Oorlam-Namas 28, 46, 61, 64, 88.
  See also Nama people
  Afrikaner family, the 25
  arrival from the south 3, 4, 19, 28, 29, 282
  clashes with boers 19, 63
  frontier raiders, as 19, 24, 28
  invasion of the
    Nama 29, 30, 31, 35, 36, 46
  invasion of the Namas 9, 29, 284
  Namibian wars of 1904-1907 111, 120
  Rhenish Mission,
    the 43, 46, 69, 106
  war with the Hereros 20, 30, 32, 34, 65, 66, 91
  Witbooi, Hendrik 97
  Witboois, the 88, 89
OPO. *See* Ovambo People's Organization
Orange Free State 146
Orange River 6, 8, 18, 19, 22, 23, 24, 25, 26, 29, 31, 35, 36, 54, 112, 138, 147, 178
Oruuano Church, the 244, 257, 259
  liberation movement, the 221, 244, 286
  Rhenish Mission, the 258
  Ruzo, Reinhard 257
Osana
  quarrel between Maharero and Witbooi 90
Otavi 24, 136
Otjikango 51
Otjimbingwe 56, 94
  Andersson, Charles John 56, 57, 58, 70, 284
  attacks by Oorlam-Namas 91
  Göring, Heinrich Ernst 87
  mission work and Hereros 91
  mission work and the
    Hereros 51, 52, 53, 69, 71
  moving of German headquarters 93
  Paulinum 276
  Rhenish Mission, the 61, 70, 71, 92, 209
Ovambo Church 210, 262, 268

Ovambo people 5, 7, 11, 12, 63, 76, 181
  culture and history 11, 136
  Finnish Mission Society, the 71, 137, 144, 181, 211, 213, 268
  German colonization, during 110, 111, 136
  labour force for the colony 137
  Major Pritchard 152
  Missionary Gehlmann 155
  Missionary Hahn's visit 67, 70
  Rhenish Mission, the 131
  SWAPO 279
  trade with Angola 70
Ovambo People's Congress
  Toivo ya Toivo, Andimba H 233
Ovambo People's Organization (OPO)
  Toivo ya Toivo, Andimba H 233
Ovambo-Kavango Church 213, 272
  Auala, Leonard 279
Ovokuruvehi 10. See also San people

P

Pacific Ocean, German possessions in 79, 161, 162
Palgrave, William Coates 63, 64, 65
  agreements with Maharero 63, 65, 85, 89
Paramount chieftainship 52, 56, 58, 90, 91, 95, 96, 100, 106, 124, 284, 285
  Maharero, Samuel 109, 285
Paulinum 243, 276
Paunu, Uuno 268
Pax Germana 4
Peace Treaty of Versailles
  administration of South West Africa 143
  Smuts, Jan Christian 164
Peace Treaty of Vienna 18
Pedersen, Ruben 275
Peters, Carl 40
Pönninghaus, Missionary 249
  apartheid 253
  opposition to Nazism 206
Portugal 8

Precolonial history 1, 2, 4, 5, 284
  Oorlam-Namas 25
Pretoria 143, 144, 270
Pritchard, Major SM 151, 207
Progressive Association 198
Prussia
  treaty with Maharero 90

Q

R

Racial policy of the South Africans 165, 168, 169, 186
  Colour Bar Law of 1926 195
  Curfew Regulations Proclamation No. 34/1922 170
  Finnish Missionary Society, the 278
  Masters and Servants Proclamation No. 11/1920 170
  Native Administration Proclamation No. 11/1922 170, 194
  Proclamation No. 33/1922 170
  Rhenish Mission, the 186, 193, 197, 198, 201, 220, 240, 241, 242, 252, 253, 256, 257
  South West Africa Native Administration Act No. 56/1954 232
  Vagrancy Proclamation Act No. 25/1922 170
Racialism 39, 40
  Darwinism 80
Racialism, opposition to 171, 226, 261
  Bondelswarts uprising, 1922 177
  Garveyanism 171, 172, 174, 178, 197
  Progressive Association 174, 198
  Rehoboth rebellion 182
Referendum of 1945-1946 222, 223, 244, 269
  Kutako, Hosea 225, 226
  UN, the 223, 224
Reformed Church, Cape Province 151, 239, 240, 241
Rehoboth 39, 89, 91, 110, 154, 168, 176, 178, 183, 261
  Maharero 85, 89

Namibian wars of 1904-1907   111
Rehoboth rebellion   154, 182, 183
  Beukes, Jakobus   182
  Proclamation No. 28/1923   182
Rhenish Mission   41, 44, 46, 49, 52,
    55, 57, 69, 71, 74, 75, 145, 150.
    See also Wuppertal-Barmen and
    Board of the Rhenish Mission
  Andersson, Charles John   56, 57,
    58, 69, 110
  apartheid   256, 257, 258
  association with the Commissioner
    of the Reich   87, 89, 90
  education   133
  establishment in southern Namibia
    7, 26, 48, 49, 69, 106, 282
  Fabri, Friedrich   40, 41
  Finnish Missionary Society, the   71,
    181
  German colonialism   133, 137, 219
  German parishes   129
  Namibian wars of 1904-1907
    117, 118, 119
  Governor Leutwein, Theodor   98,
    122
  Haussleiter's criticisms   121, 126
  indigenous Church   251, 261
  influence of Garveyanism   174, 175
  Maharero   95
  Maharero, Samuel   96, 105, 186
  Maharero, Samuel's
    burial   185, 187
  mixed marriages   134, 135
  Namibian wars of 1904-1907
    109, 116, 119, 120
  nationalism   258
  Okahandja   69, 71, 95
  Oorlam-Namas   88
  Oruuano Church, the   257
  Paulinum   243
  racialism   132, 276
  role in German colonialism   20, 61,
    62, 64, 66, 67, 82, 84, 85, 87,
    92, 93, 106, 131, 132, 154
  Roman Catholic Mission   138, 139
  Scott, Rev Michael   253
  traditional authority   255
  under mandatory administration
    145, 152, 163, 183, 186
  under South African rule   151,
    153, 196, 219, 238, 239, 241,
    242, 244, 246, 247, 248, 251,
    255
  Von François, Curt   93, 99, 100,
    103, 105
  Witbooi, Hendrik   88, 89, 96
Rhenish missionaries   49, 64
  Afrikaner, Jonker   32, 50, 51,
    55, 68
  apartheid   145
  diplomatic roles   101
  Finnish Missionary Society, the   110
  German colonialism   67, 85, 105
  internment in World War I   147
  military actions   58
  Namibian wars of 1904-1907   106
  pioneers of Great Namaqualand   51
  Roman Catholic Mission,
    the   137, 138
  South African occupation   153,
    155, 156
Rohrbach, Paul   121
Roman Catholic Mission   138, 139
  Angola, from   137
  apartheid   214
  attempts to establish itself from the
    north   138
  colonialism   138
  Keetmanshoop   214
  membership   151
  mixed marriages   135
  Ovamboland   181, 214
  under South African occupation
    151
  WW II   214
Routanen, Missionary Martin   209
  translation of the New Testament
    into Oshindonga   209
Rust, Missionary Gottlieb F   152,
    153, 242
Rust, Missionary Heinrich F
  opposition to Nazism   206
Ruzo, Reinhard   257

S

San people See also Bushmen and
    Khoisan and Ovokuruvehi
  culture and history   10
  apartheid   180

Schlettwein, Carl 175, 176
Schmelen, Missionary Johan Heinrich 26, 29, 32, 48
Schmidt-Clausen, Kurt 275
Schneuwee, Hendrik 177, 178
Scott, Rev Michael 253, 254
   Anglican Church, the 226
   Benson, Mary 230
   Kutako, Hosea 227, 230, 233, 251
   Maharero, Frederick 226
   opponent of South Africa 228
   UN, the 215, 227, 228, 229, 230, 231
Self, Karl 131
Separate development 252. *See also* Apartheid
Serowe 185
Shikenga, Chief 70
Singh, Sir Maharaj 225
Slavery 23, 63, 106, 115, 121, 125, 278
Smuts, Jan Christian 11, 147, 156, 186
   citizenship of Namibian Germans 164, 166
   League of Nations 161
   racialism 163
   referendum of 1945-1946 222
   UN Committee for Mandatory Administration, the 222
   UN, the 222
   Versailles 161
   visits Namibia 163
South Africa 51, 71, 142, 229
   mandatory power 143, 162, 167, 193, 195, 222, 223, 224, 231
   NP, the 228, 229, 231, 232, 247, 257, 260
   Peace Treaty of Versailles, the 161
South African Christian Council 230
South African rule 142, 287
   administration just after WW I 143, 150, 151, 152, 157, 164, 182, 185, 196
   apartheid laws 143, 144, 165
   citizenship of German descendants 164, 166, 202, 251
   eviction of Rhenish missionaries 153, 154, 155, 206
   German rule of law 148
   International Court of Justice, 1950 229
   International Court of Justice, 1960 231
   mandatory administration 162, 164, 168, 195
   Mandume, Chief 151
   military administration 148
   Namibia as a South African province 144, 164, 222, 225, 227, 230, 232
   Namibians under the Minister of Bantu Affairs 232
   Nazism 202, 204, 239
   occupation during WWI 146, 150
   racial
      policy 168, 186, 193, 195, 228
      and Finnish Mission 271, 278
      and the Rhenish Mission 197, 199, 247, 251
      Roman Catholic and Anglican Missions 214
   referendum of 1945-1946 222, 224, 244, 269
   separate development 232
   WW II, after 224
South West Africa 121, 123, 142, 153, 166, 167, 173, 195, 202, 204, 222, 232, 253, 260, 276, 277
South West Africa National Union (SWANU) 220, 233
   Herero people 234, 286
   Kapuuo, Clemens 233
   Kutako, Hosea 233, 234
   UN, the 235
South West Africa People's Organization (SWAPO)
   Auala, Leonard 234, 273, 279
   Church and Mission, the 275
   Garveyanism 173
   Kerina, Mburumba 234
   Nujoma, Sam 234, 274, 275
   Ovambo people 220, 279, 287, 288
   Toivo ya Toivo, Andimba 279
   UN, the 235

South West African National Congress (SWANC) 173
Sovik, Arne 275, 276
Sundermeier, Theo 240
Swakopmund 7, 120, 198, 200, 206, 243, 248, 249, 251, 256, 262
    Witbooi attack on Germans 97
SWANC. See South West African National Congress (SWANC)
SWANU. See South West Africa National Union (SWANU)
SWAPO. See South West Africa People's Organization (SWAPO)
Sweden 268
Syncretism 198, 220, 260

T

Tarkanon, Natti 208
Tilly 82
Tjamuaha 33
    Afrikaner, Jonker 32, 35, 36, 49, 52, 56
    line of succession 95
Tjetjo 15
Toivo ya Toivo, Andimba H
    Auala, Leonard 273, 279
    Oniipa 233, 273
    OPO 233, 234
    Ovambo People's Congress 233
Tötemeyer, Gerhard 223
Transvaal 23, 146
Treaty of Versailles 143, 161, 163, 164
Trittelvitz, Walter 43
Tsaobis
    German military post 94
Tshongwe, Alexander 274
Tsumeb 24, 153, 176

U

UN. See United Nations
Union of South Africa 142
    founding of 146
    occupation of Namibia 143

UNIA. See Universal Negro Improvement Association
United Nations (UN)
    Auala, Leonard 277
    Commission for South West Africa 277
    Committee for Mandatory Administration 222
    Declaration of Human Rights 277
    India 225
    International Court of Justice, 1950 229
    Kerina, Mburumba 231
    Kutako,
        Hosea 224, 226, 230, 233
    NP, and the 229
    referendum 1945-1946 223, 224
    Scott, Rev Michael 226, 228, 229, 230, 231
    Smuts, Jan Christian 222
    South African National Party 232
    South African rule 224
    South Africa's violation of the UN Charter 231
    SWANU 234
    SWAPO 234, 235
United Nations Trusteeship Committee 222, 223, 229
Universal Negro Improvement Association (UNIA) 171, 172, 173, 186
Upingtonia 136
USA, the
    AMEC 242
    American Congress 160
    Berlin congress, 1884-1885, at the 79
    Namibia, a USA protectorate 225, 227
    President Wilson, Woodrow 160
    resistance to Namibian representation at the UN 230
    UNIA 171, 172
Usakos 173

V

Van Wyk, Hermanus
    Rehoboth Basters 110, 111
Vapaavoori, Martti
    Ovamboland, in 208

Vedder, Heinrich 23, 52, 53, 204
  Anniversary of Waterberg, 25th 205
  as Preses 242
  establishment of the indigenous church 243, 249, 260
  'high German ideals' 205
  contacts with the Reformed Church 239
  criticism of Missionary Rust's anti-Nazism 206
  ethnographical studies 4, 12, 13, 14, 16, 25
  eviction by the South Africans 153
  German colonization 4, 5
  Maharero, Samuel's burial 187
  member of the South African Senate 251
  Nazism 205, 206
  supporter of apartheid 252, 253
Viehe, Missionary 90, 101, 105
Vogelsang, Heinrich 82, 83, 85
Von Bismarck, Chancellor Otto 77, 81
Von Bülow, Chancellor 116, 117, 119
Von Caprivi, Leo 96
Von François, Curt
  arrival in Namibia 92
  establishment of military posts 93
  Landeshauptmann 93, 95, 96
  leading the Rhenish Mission 93
  Witbooi, Hendrik 96, 97, 98
Von Lindequist, Governor Friedrich 214
Von Oelhafen, Hermann 203, 204
Von Schlieffen, General 115
Von Trotha, Lothar 112, 113, 114, 115, 116, 118, 120
Vuorela, Olavi 273

W

Wackwitz, Dr
  eviction by the South Africans 206
  Nazism 203, 204, 206
Walvis Bay 7, 22, 61, 62, 64, 66, 82
  Afrikaner, Jonker's road 31
  annexation by the Cape Colony 24, 64, 67, 84
  arrival of first German troops 92
  German occupation at the beginning of WW I 147
  South African invasion 142
Warmbad 26, 48, 49, 150, 169, 178, 179, 183
  LMS, the 29
Wars 109, 145
  Boer Wars 146, 147, 148
  German Namibian wars. See below Namibian wars of 1904-1907
  Herero and Oorlam-Nama wars, the 57
  Namibian wars of 1904-1907 98, 138, 154, 214, 219, 282
  World War I 142, 143, 146, 147, 148, 149, 150, 151, 152, 154, 155, 157, 168, 174, 185, 188, 194, 196, 208, 215, 222, 224
  Treaty of Versailles 157
  World War II 145, 203, 213, 214, 222, 247, 268, 286
Waterberg 15, 112, 169, 180
  Battle of 113, 115, 119, 122, 205
WCC. See World Council of Churches
Wesleyan missionaries 26, 29, 51
  Afrikaner, Jonker 49, 51
Whitby 247, 248, 250, 259
White Nossob River 15
Wienecke, Missionary Wilhelm A 258
Wiker, Hans Johan 23
Wilson, President Woodrow 160, 161
Windhoek 7, 30, 31, 66, 96, 103, 143, 147
  geography 7
  German parish, first 104
  headquarters of the mandated territory 143
  Katutura 234, 262
  Maharero 94
  Namibian wars of 1904-1907 111, 112
  new colonial capital 93, 94
  Old Location 234, 262, 274
Witbooi, Hendrik 53, 85, 285
  agreement with Leutwein, Theodore 111
  attack on the Germans 91, 97

baptism 88
death of 115
establishment of Christianity 171
inspired leadership 88, 89, 97, 119
Leutwein, Theodor 115
Morenga, Jakob 115
Namibian wars of 1904-1907 109, 111, 115
quarrel at Osana 90
relations with the British 97
relations with the German colonialists 88, 89, 91, 94, 96
treaty with Maharero 89, 90, 94, 96
Von François, Curt 96, 97, 98
war with the Hereros 93

Witbooi, Samuel
Scott, Rev Michael 227

Women's Association of the German Red Cross 135

Woodhouse, Sir Philip 61

World Council of Churches (WCC) 240, 247

World War I (WW I) 4, 142, 143, 148, 152, 160, 163, 165, 167, 169, 170, 172, 197, 201, 203, 205, 208, 222, 224
arrival of the Anglican Mission 215
Blue Book 149, 167, 200
deportation of people of mixed race to Namibia UNIA 172
first years of South African occupation 146, 148, 165, 169, 170, 197
General Beyers 146
German defeat 201, 203
Peace Treaty of Versailles 160

World War II (WW II) 4, 145, 215, 219, 268
Rhenish Mission and Nazism, the 286
Rhenish Mission, the 203
Roman Catholic Mission, the 214
UN, the 222

Wuppertal-Barmen 41, 65, 71, 119, 240, 245, 248, 259, 260, 261

WWI. *See* World War I

WWII. *See* World War II

Studia Missionalia Upsaliensia

Editors: I-XXVII Bengt Sundkler XXVIII- Carl F Hallencreutz

I	Peter Beyerhaus, *Die Selbständigkeit der jungen Kirchen als missionarisches Problem.* 1956.
II	Bengt Sundkler, *The Christian Ministry in Africa.* 1960.
III	Henry Weman, *African Music and the Church in Africa.* 1960.
IV	Tore Furberg, *Kyrka och Mission i Sverige 1868-1901.* 1962.
V	Eric J Sharpe, *Not to Destroy but to Fulfil: the Contribution of JN Farquhar to Protestant Missionary Thought before 1914.* 1965.
VI	Carl-Johan Hellberg, *Mission on a Colonial Frontier West of Lake Victoria.* 1965.
VII	Carl F Hallencreutz, *Kraemer Towards Tambaram. A Study in Hendrik Kraemer's Missionary Approach.* 1966.
VIII	Johannes Aagaard, *Mission, Konfession, Kirche. Die Problematik ihrer Integration im 19. Jahrhundert in Deutschland. I, II.* 1967.
IX	Gustav Bernander, *Lutheran Wartime Assistance to Tanzanian Churches 1940-1945.* 1968.
X	Sigfred Estborn, *Johannes Sandegren och hans Insats i Indiens Kristenhet.* 1968.
XI	Peter Beyerhaus and Carl F Hallencreutz (eds), *The Church Crossing Frontiers. Essays on the Nature of Mission. In Honour of Bengt Sundkler.* 1969.
XII	Sigvart von Sicard, *The Lutheran Church on the Cost of Tanzania 1887-1914 with Special Reference to the Evangelical Lutheran Church in Tanzania Synod of Uzaramo-Uluguru.* 1970.
XIII	David Lagergren, *Mission and State in the Congo. A Study of the Relations between Protestant Missions and the Congo Independent State Authorities with Special Reference to the Equator District, 1885-1903.* 1970.
XIV	Sigbert Axelson, *Culture Confrontation in the Lower Congo from the Old Congo Kingdom to the Congo Independent State with Special Reference to Swedish Missionaries in the 1880's and 1890's.* 1970.
XV	Per Oesterbye, *The Church in Israel. A Report on the Work and Position of the Christian Churches in Israel with Special Reference to the Protestant Churches and Communities.* 1970.
XVI	Marja-Lisa Swantz, *Ritual and Symbol in transitional Zaramo Society with Special Reference to Women.* 1970.
XVII	Stiv Jakobsson, *Am I not a Man and Brother?* 1972.
XVII	Jonas Jonson, *Lutheran Missions in a Time of Revolution. The China Experience 1944-1951.* 1972.
XIX	Tord Harlin, *Spirit and Truth. Religious Attitudes and Life Involvement of 2200 African Students.* 1973.

XX	Carl F Hallencreutz, Johannes Aagaard and Nils E Bloch-Hoell (eds), *Mission from the North, Nordic Missionary Council 50 Years.* 1974.
XXI	Josiah Kibira, *Church, Clan and the World.* 1974.
XXII	Axel Ivar Berglund, *Zulu Thought-Patterns and Symbolism.* 1975.
XXIII	Ingemar Bergmark, *Kyrka och Sjöfolk. En Studie i Svenska Kyrkans Sjömansvård 1911-1933.* 1974.
XXIV	Håkan Eilert, *Boundlessness. Studies in Karl Ludvig Reichelt's Missionary Thinking with Special Reference to the Buddhist-Christian Encounter.* 1974.
XXV	Sven Arne Flodell, *Tierra Nueva. Svensk Grupputvandring till Latinamerika. Integration och Församlingsbildning.* 1974.
XXVI	Håkan Zetterquist, *Stad och Stift. Stiftsbildning och Församlingsdelningar i Stockholm 1940-1956. Ett Bidrag till Stadens Missiologi.* 1974.
XXVII	Olav Saeveraas, *On Church-Mission Relations in Ethiopia 1944-1969 with Special Reference to the Evangelical Church Mekane Yesus and Lutheran Missions.* 1974.
XXVIII	Ingvar Kalm, *Mission in Linköpings Stift. Biträdets-Missionssällskapets Verksamhet 1841-1875.* 1977.
XXIX	Bengt Sundkler, *Zulu Zion and some Swazi Zionists.* 1976.
XXX	Herman Schlyter, *Der China-Missionar Karl Gützlaff und seine Heimatsbasis. Studien über das Interesse des Abendlandes an der Mission des China-Pioniers Karl Gützlaff und über seinen Einsatz als Missionserwecker.* 1976.
XXXI	Carl F Hallencreutz, *Dialogue and Community, Ecumenical Issues in Interreligious Relationships.* 1977.
XXXII	Gustav Arén, *Evangelical Pioneers in Ethiopia.* 1978.
XXXIII	Timothy Yates, *Venn and Victorian Bishops Abroad.* 1978.
XXXIV	Carl-Johan Hellberg, *A Voice of the Voiceless. The Involvement of the Lutheran World Federation in Southern Africa 1947-1977.* 1979.
XXXV	Johan Hultvall, *Mission och Revolution i Centralasien.* 1981.
XXXVI	Emmet E Eklund, *Peter Fjellstedt - missionary Mentor of Augustana.* 1984.
XXXVII	Johan Lundmark, *Det splittrade Gudsfoket och Missionsuppdraget. En Studie i Relationen mellan Kyrkan och Judendomen.* 1983.
XXXVIII	Manfred Lundgren, *Proclaiming Christ to His World. The Experience of Radio Voice of the Gospel 1957-1977.* 1984.
XXXIX	*"Daring in Order to Know", Studies of Bengt Sundkler's Contribution as Africanist and Missionary Scholar.* Ed. by Carl F Hallencreutz et al. 1984.
XL	Hugo Söderström, *God Gave Growth. The History of the Evangelical-Lutheran Church in Zimbabwe.* 1985.
XLI	Per Erik Gustafsson, *Tiden och Tecknen. Israelmission och Palestinabild i det Tidiga Missionsförbundet.* 1984.
XLII	Sigfrid Deminger, *Evangeliet på indiska Villkor. Stanley Jones och den Indiska Renässansen 1918-1930.* 1985.
XLIII	Agnes Chepkwony, *The Role of Non-Governmental Oganisations in Development.* 1987.
XLIV	Johnny Bakke, *Christian Ministry. Patterns and Functions within the Ethiopian Evangelical Church Mekane Yesu.* 1987.
XLV	Åsa Dalmalm, *L'Eglise à l'Epreuve de la Tradition. La Communauté*

Evangélique du Zaïre et le Kindoki. 1986.
XLVI Aasulv Lande, *Meji Protestantism in History and Historiography.* 1988.
XLVII Tord Fornberg, *Jewish-Christian Dialogue and Biblical Exegesis.* 1988.
XLVIII Johan S Pobee, *Church and State in Ghana.* 1989.
XLIX Anders S Hovemyr, *In Search of the Karen King: a Study in Karen Identity with Special Reference to 19th Century Karen Evangelisations.* 1989.
L Carl F Hallencreutz (ed.), *Pehr Högströms Förrättningar och övriga Bidrag till Samisk Kyrkohistoria.* 1990.
LI Karl-Johan Lundström, *The Lotuho and the Verona Fathers. A Case Study of Communication in Development.* 1990.
LII Lissi Rasmussen, *Religion and Property in Northern Nigeria.* 1990.
LIII John Hultvall, *Mission och Vision i Orienten. SMFs Mission i Transkaukasien-Persien 1882-1921.* 1991.
LIV Alf Helgesson, *Church, State and People in Mozambique. An Historical Study with Special Emphasis on Methodist Developments in Inhambane Region.* 1994.
LV José Marin Conzales, *Peuples indigenes, Mission religieuses et Colonialisme interne dans l'Amazonie Peruvienne.* 1992.
LVI António Barbosa da Silva, *Is there a new Imbalance in Jewish-Christian Relations?* 1992.
LVII Kajsa Ahlstrand, *Fundamental Openness. An Enquiry into Raimundo Panikkar's Theological Vision and its Presuppositions.* 1993.
LVIII Eskil Forslund, *The Word of God in Ethiopian Tongues. Rhetorical Features in the Preaching of the Ethiopian Evangelical Church Mekane Yesus.* 1993.
LIX Joel Yrlid, *Mission och Kommunikation. Den Kristna Missionens och Transportnätets Utveckling i Belgiska Kongo/Zaïre 1878-1991.* 1994.
LX Olaus Brännström, *Peter Fjellstedt. Mångsidig men Entydig Kyrkoman.* 1994.
LXI Tord Fornberg, *The Bible in a World of many Faiths.* 1995.
LXII Josef Nsumbu PN. *Culte et Société. Le Culte Chrétien comme Réflexion critique d'une Société moderne Africaine: Cas du Chant dans la Communauté Evangeliqué du Zaïre.* 1995.
LXIII Carl-Johan Hellberg, *Mission, Colonialism and Liberation: the Lutheran Church in Namibia 1840-1966.* 1997.
LXIV Göran Gunnar, *När Tiden tar slut. Motivförskjutningar i frikyrklig apokalyptisk Tolkning av det Judiska Folket och Staten Israel.* 1996.
LXV Gurli Hansson: *Mwana Ndi Mai, towards an Understanding of Preparation for Motherhood and Child Care in the Transitional Mberengwa District, Zimbabwe.* 1996
LXVI Øyvind M Eide, *Revolution and Religion in Ethiopia. A Study of Church and Politics with Special Reference to the Ethiopian Evangelical Church Mekane Yesus, 1974-1985.* 1996.